INTERNATIONAL FORENSIC SCIENCE
AND INVESTIGATION SERIES

# FIREARMS, THE LAW, AND FORENSIC BALLISTICS

## Second Edition

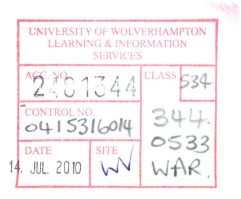
## Tom Warlow

# CRC PRESS

Boca Raton   London   New York   Washington, D.C.

## Library of Congress Cataloging-in-Publication Data

Warlow, T. A. (Tom A.)
    Firearms, the law and forensic ballistics / T.A. Warlow. — 2nd ed.
       p. cm. — (International Forensic Science and Investigation series)
    Includes bibliographical references and index.
    ISBN 0-415-31601-4 (alk. paper)
      1. Firearms—Law and legislation—England. 2. Firearms—Law and legislation—Wales.
3. Forensic ballistics.  I. Title.

KD3492.W37 2004
344.4205′33--dc22
                                                 2004053698

**Visit the CRC Press Web site at www.crcpress.com**

# Acknowledgments

This updated and expanded second edition of my book is dedicated to the pioneering workers Colonel Calvin H. Goddard (1892–1955) and his colleagues C.E. Waite, Philip O. Gravelle, and John H. Fisher, who established the Bureau of Forensic Ballistics in New York City in April, 1925 to provide firearms identification services throughout the United States, and to Dr J.H. Mathews and his milestone publication *Firearms Identification* (Springfield, IL: Charles C Thomas, 1962). Some aspects of their work and that of others are contained in Chapter 3, Marks and Microscopy: The Emergence of a New Science.

The *Oxford English Dictionary* defines the expression 'forensic' as pertaining to or used in a court of law, and in relation to the detection of crime. The expression 'ballistics' is defined as the science of the motion of projectiles; especially that part of the subject connected with firearms. 'Exterior and interior ballistics' are defined as dealing respectively with motion after and during the period when a projectile is subject to propulsive force or guidance. Strictly speaking, a good deal of their work was related to the microscopic comparison of marks left upon cartridge cases with test firings obtained from suspect firearms. However, most of these same marks are imparted during the firing process. The expression 'forensic ballistics' forms part of the title of this book, as a good deal of it explains how such marks are produced during the process of interior ballistics, the flight of projectiles and the consequences of their impact upon human tissue and other objects.

Finally, I must give due recognition to the outstanding and continuing contributions to the science made by members of the Association of Firearm and Tool Mark Examiners (AFTE). I can but urge membership of this organisation to all practitioners and students of this fascinating subject.

**Tom Warlow**

# Foreword

I worked with Tom as a member of the Firearms Consultative Committee for 5 years. Turning the pages of his book was a riveting experience for me. It rekindled the interest of bygone days; the Parliamentary debates, amending the law on firearms, and Tom sitting in the Minister's Advisers' box on the floor of the House of Commons, and subsequently on the red leather of the House of Lords. We all looked to him for guidance on the complex issues involved.

Away from Westminster, at the Huntingdon Laboratory, some of us were able to see the operation of the 'Outstanding Crimes File System'. Over the years this system has been a powerful source of crime intelligence for the police and for the authorities in accurately predicting the most likely make of weapon used in a criminal incident and then, in turn, linking its use with other serious offences, such as acts of murder, terrorism and armed robbery, in widely scattered parts of the realm.

Tom has been a proficient user of firearms of all types, whether this involved their use on the firing range, the field or upon the hill, and many a deer must have been thankful for death by a good, clean killing shot. His lifelong fascination with old firearms ensured that on many occasions in his youth he might be found walking up game on a rough shoot or out on the marshes after duck or curlew with an old muzzle-loading shotgun.

However, the nature of his employment also caused him to witness the darker side of the misuse of firearms or shotguns. He might be called out in the middle of the night to journey across country to attend the as-yet-undisturbed scene of a serious shooting incident in one of the northern industrial cities such as Manchester or Newcastle, or to a hill farm in South Wales, an opulent residence in Essex or a pub in Devon. There he would assist the police investigative team in untangling the often confusing effects remaining at the scene, so as to determine the likely previous course of events. This initial task would be followed by assisting the Home Office pathologist in the interpretation of the injuries and recovered missiles during the subsequent postmortem examinations, and by then arranging for the necessary collection and transfer of crucial exhibits to the laboratory for examination. All of these tasks would constitute the necessary preliminary to him eventually acting as an expert witness at the subsequent court hearing. Despite such experiences, and much else, he always attempted to speak up and act in the best interests of responsible sportsmen and target shooters. He provided technical support to the Home Office and to the Firearms Consultative Committee. He never shrank from speaking out against those who by their irresponsible conduct so endangered the interests of the vast majority of decent sportsmen.

Tom so obviously revelled in his work and his desire to share his knowledge. The charm and simplicity of his style reflects his obvious pleasure in writing about his life's work.

I am more than honoured that he should have asked me to add this Foreword to a subject so near to my heart.

**The Lord Kimball**

I was delighted to be asked by Tom Warlow to pen a few words in introduction of his new work.

I first met Tom some 4 years ago when I was appointed Chairman of the Firearms Consultative Committee. Interesting times were just around the corner, and although none of the FCC had any idea of what was to happen in the near future at that state, a great deal of work was being undertaken by the Committee. Tom—from my day one—stood out amongst the members of the FCC as a solid and forthright expert not only in the field of forensic ballistics, but also as a lifelong shooting and countryside enthusiast. His knowledge of weapons, their history, evolution and use is very wide indeed, to say the least.

Then in March 1996, the most awful tragedy at Dunblane took place, and immediately the FCC was thrown to the forefront of a highly emotional and political matter. The rest of course is history, and the 1997 Firearms (Amendment) Acts put a complete stop to the private ownership of handguns. Tom's help and advice to me throughout those unhappy days was superb, and I simply do not know how he has found time to pen this excellent book!

**The Earl of Shrewsbury and Waterford**

# Preface

From my youth to middle age I have been fascinated by firearms and their application. Over the years I have tried, and in some instances mastered, just about every type of firearm and shooting discipline. Even today I am still filled with awe by the accuracy of a fine rifle and its ability to deliver a compact package containing so much destructive force to a distant target. My own rifle, which I use for target shooting and deer stalking, frequently produces subminute of angle groups at one hundred yards. (Somewhat less than one inch in measurement between the centres of the most distant bullet strikes in the group.) When one considers that such feats are achieved with what is in reality a heat engine of Victorian design, the results seem even more remarkable.

One day many years ago I decided to extend my interest further by accepting an offer of employment from the Home Office at the National Firearms Laboratory of the Forensic Science Service at a laboratory location in the centre of Nottingham. This unit was later moved to a new and expanded site at Huntingdon, Cambridgeshire, where it dealt with firearms cases received from 41 of the 43 police forces in England and Wales. The subsequent restructuring of the Home Office Forensic Science Service also resulted in the integration of the London Metropolitan Police forensic laboratory. As a result, I was moved, along with two of my colleagues, to the London firearms section, where I continued to work for the final two years of my service until my retirement in February 2000. The restructuring also involved the creation of the Northern Firearms Unit of the service, situated in Manchester, where the remainder of the old Huntingdon firearms reporting staff were relocated. Both units have been subject to expansion in both staff and facilities, including the acquisition at both sites of Ibis integrated ballistics identification systems from Forensic Technology.

In order to consider oneself to be an expert witness in such a specialised field it is necessary to try to understand all aspects of the subject, rather than to lock on to one small discipline. I have decided therefore to start this book with a short chapter on the development of arms and ammunition from the fourteenth century to the present day in order that a balanced understanding of firearms and ammunition can be acquired. I hope that this chapter will also be of general interest to all those who have a genuine interest in firearms, as although wide-reaching, it is set out in a relatively condensed form, which will not be found elsewhere. This is followed by a chapter concerned with firearms law around the world, with particular emphasis upon the situation in the United Kingdom, followed by a chapter on the origins and the development of the new science, the controversies, the pioneers in the new field and the quack purveyors of pseudoscience. The chapter concerning the mechanisms of various firearms, although not comprehensive, should be a useful guide for any forensic examination. The three chapters concerning internal, external and terminal (wound) ballistics, followed by the one on the role of the ballistics expert at the scene of crime investigation, should then provide the basic foundation for the other aspects of the work of a forensic firearms examiner to build upon.

Along with my working colleagues I have dealt with and experienced a great many things over the years. It now seems appropriate that I should try to set down on paper some of the positive products of this experience, which I hope will prove to be of use to others wishing to take up a similar profession, to some already in this field and, finally, to those fellow souls who share a similar interest in all matters relating to firearms.

**Tom Warlow**

# The Author

Tom Warlow has over 40 years experience in using and handling firearms and is a member of the statutory Firearms Consultative Committee which advises the UK Government on firearms and firearms legislation as well as providing an annual report to Parliament. He was a casework reporting officer for over 20 years in the national Firearms Unit in the UK and has a keen interest in gun sports.

# Table of Contents

# The Beginnings

1

From the earliest days of prehistory, man has used his ingenuity to devise weapons capable of killing at a distance. All of the early primitive weapons utilized his muscular power to achieve this end. The stone or spear could be released instantly so as to be thrown a short distance. The bow stored this energy inside a tensioned structure to allow its instantaneous release. However, to achieve greater range and power it was necessary to devise a completely new energy source. Crude chemical mixtures resembling gunpowder are known to have been used in fireworks over 1000 years ago in China and India. However, in Europe it is generally accepted that Roger Bacon was the first person to mention and record the formulation of true gunpowder, an intimate mixture of saltpetre, sulphur and charcoal, in the year 1242. However, there is evidence that the Arabs invented black powder. It is said that at about 1300 they had developed the first real gun made from a bamboo tube reinforced with iron. This primitive gun used a charge of black powder to discharge an arrow. As Bacon was able to read Arabic, it is possible that his knowledge came from Arabic sources. Initially the ingredients for making gunpowder were ground up together by hand with a mortar and pestle. Later on, crushing devices using wooden stamps inside stone bowls were used for this process, followed by further mechanisation. The first water-powered powder mill was erected near Nuremberg in Germany around the year 1435. The regular manufacture of gunpowder commenced about 1412 in England, and the Government powder works at Waltham Abbey dates back to the year 1561.

Saltpetre was originally extracted from compost piles and animal waste. Deposits found in India provided a source of this essential ingredient for many years. During the 1850s, large deposits of sodium nitrate were mined in Chile. Although this "Chile Saltpetre" was deliquescent, and powder made from it was not as potent as those using the potassium salt, it could be used to produce blasting powder for use in quarries. The potassium salt for making gunpowder for small arms was obtained by reacting the sodium salt with potassium chloride, of which there was a plentiful supply. Although the composition for gunpowder has remained the same over the last 250 years, its formulation and the production processes involved were subject to change over earlier years in order to improve its performance so as to increase its burning rate and energy yield, and to generate higher missile velocities (Table 1.1).

The process of powder manufacture normally ends up after the 'corning' and granulation processes, with the powder being graded into fine, dense granular form, which in relatively recent times has included a glazing process achieved by tumbling it in a drum with powdered graphite. The size of the grains affects the rate of burning, as this is a surface phenomenon, and thus the finest grain powders have the fastest burning rates. By way of an example, the designations F, FF and FFF, or No. 6, No. 4, and No. 2, employed by Curtis & Harvey's Limited, indicate coarse, medium and fine grain powders, respectively. It follows that coarse grain powders would be better suited for use in pistols, and that the coarser granulations would be better suited for use in long-barrelled, large-bore rifles and shotguns. Very coarse grain powders such as 'Col. Hawker's Duck Powder' or 'Capt. Latour's Punt Powder' would be used in massive wildfowling punt guns of bore sizes up to 2 in (51 mm). The density of the powder grains (1.6–2.0 g/cm³), is a function of the manufacturing process, and this too will affect burning rate, with the densest powders, for a given grain size, possessing the longest burning times. Leonardo da Vinci (1452–1519) asked himself questions concerning internal ballistics that are still relevant today. "*What shape of powder ignites the quicker? What difference does it make if ignition takes place at one end or the other or the middle of the powder charge, and what if with the same weight of powder the grains are long or short, round or cubic?*" He also explained correctly the cause of the noise caused by the discharge of a gun.

The modern manufacturing of black powder involves placing the sulphur and charcoal in a rotating hollow drum, referred to as a 'ball mill', along with heavy steel balls to pulverise the contents. In the interests of safety, the saltpetre is crushed separately by heavy steel rollers. Several hundred pounds

**Table 1.1   The Changing Formulation for Gunpowder from the Thirteenth Century (%)**

|            | Saltpetre | Charcoal | Sulphur |
|------------|-----------|----------|---------|
| About 1250 | 41.2      | 29.4     | 29.4    |
| 1350       | 66.6      | 22.2     | 11.1    |
| 1550       | 50.0      | 33.3     | 16.6    |
| 1650       | 66.6      | 16.6     | 16.6    |
| 1750       | 75.0      | 12.5     | 12.5    |
| 1751 to date | 75.0    | 15.0     | 10.0    |

of the mixture of the three finely ground ingredients are then continuously turned over by devices called 'plows', then ground and mixed by two rotating iron wheels weighing 10 to 12 tons each for several hours, with water being added periodically during the process to ensure the mixture remains moist. The resulting mixture is then put through wooden rollers in order to break up the larger lumps, before being formed into cakes under a pressure of 210–280 kg/cm$^2$ (3000–4000 psi). The cake is broken down by coarse-toothed rollers into manageable pieces ready for the 'corning mill', where rollers of various sizes reduce the material to the various granulations desired. The powder grains are then 'glazed' by tumbling them for several hours in wooden cylinders with finely powdered graphite. The forces involved round off the corners of the grains, and at the same time, forced-air circulation ensures that the powder is brought to the correct moisture content. The powder is then graded using a series of sieves, and the different granulations packaged separately in kegs.

The manufacture of black powder is a lengthy and exacting process that can also be relatively hazardous due to the possible formation of dust and its low ignition temperature of about 320°C (600°F), and it is not unknown for explosions to occur in powder plants. Sulphur, which serves as both a fuel and a binding agent in black powder, is also responsible for lowering its ignition temperature. As a result, some firms have chosen to discontinue their manufacture of black powder. Upon ignition, most of the decomposition products are solids. As a consequence, one gram of black powder liberates 280 cm$^3$ of gas, when measured at 0°C and one atmosphere pressure, compared to about one litre of gas liberated upon the ignition of the same amount of nitrocellulose powder. The foul-smelling solids are composed of approximately 56% $K_2CO_3$, 25% $K_2S$, 16% $K_2SO_4$, 5% KCNS and traces of $KNO_3$, $K_2S_2O_3$, $(NH_4)_2CO_3$, S and C. The unique properties of black powder, especially for the production of civilian and military pyrotechnic devices and certain cartridge loadings, ensure that its manufacture will continue somewhere in the world to meet these needs and those of enthusiasts who choose to shoot original or reproduction muzzle-loading arms.

However, the choice of the type of wood used to produce the charcoal affects the performance of the powder, as can the nature of the manufacturing process, as it is essential to produce a truly intimate assembly of the three ingredients. There is a small muzzle-loading mortar in the Gun Barrel Proof House in Birmingham designed to test the performance of batches of black powder since the mid-nineteenth century. The distance to which a measured charge of powder is able to project a ball of standard weight has been used as a measurement of quality since that date. Proof Masters have assured me that their tests conducted with the various brands of black powder currently available, have never been able to match the test results shown in their earlier records. The tighter regulations associated with the manufacture, storage and shipping of black powder have, in recent years, resulted in the development of less hazardous substitute propellants for use by shooters of muzzle-loading and black-powder weapons. These new propellants and the forensic implications associated with them are covered in Chapter 9 of this book.

The manufacturers claim that these new black powder substitutes produce similar ballistic performance when used by enthusiasts with muzzle-loading guns and black-powder cartridge arms. The first successful commercial product was introduced by the Hogdon Powder Company of Shawnee Mission, Kansas, under the name 'Pyrodex'. When used as instructed on an equal-volume basis to conventional black powder, this results in a reduction in the charge weight of about 20%. Transportation and storage regulations are less onerous due to its much higher ignition temperature of about 400°C (750°F), and the special licensing requirements in the UK are avoided. It is marketed in the granulations 'P' for use in pistols, 'RS' for rifles and shotguns, and 'CTG' for use in cartridges, which roughly equates to the black powder granulations FFF, FF and F. Although thought by some to be a nitrocellulose-based substitute, Pyrodex is a modified black powder formulation (Table 1.2).

Further alternative black powder propellants have been launched under the names 'Black Canyon Powder' from Las Vegas, Nevada, 'Black Mag Powder' by Arco of Hollywood, Florida, and 'Clean Shot Powder' from Clean Shot Technologies, Whitewater, Colorado. These three powders are all based upon potassium nitrate and ascorbic acid (vitamin C) and are thus similar to an earlier substitute powder called 'Golden Powder' which was not a commercial success. Around the end of 1999, the Goex Company facility at Doyline, Louisiana, launched a new substitute powder under the name 'Clear Shot', not to be confused with 'Clean Shot' previously mentioned. This powder also uses potassium nitrate as an oxidizer, but does not contain ascorbic acid or any of the organic constituents associated with Pyrodex.

The earliest firearms produced in Europe during the fourteenth century were cannons and hand cannons; simple tubes closed at one end except for

**Table 1.2   The Formulation of Pyrodex**

| | |
|---|---|
| Potassium nitrate | 45 parts |
| Charcoal | 9 parts |
| Sulphur | 6 parts |
| Potassium perchlorate | 19 parts |
| Sodium benzoate | 11 parts |
| Dicyandiamide (1-cyanoguanidine) | 6 parts |
| Dextrin | 4 parts |
| Wax/graphite | <1 part |

a small touch-hole drilled into the breech end of the bore. The designs of both of these weapons necessitated the manual application of fire to the touch-hole in order to fire them. The next century saw the development of serpentine (match-lock) weaponry which allowed the mechanical lowering of a smouldering nitrated cord or fuse into a pan of powder adjacent to the touch-hole. The sixteenth century saw the development of wheel-lock arms that utilised a serrated iron wheel which was caused to rotate by clockwork against a piece of iron pyrites to produce a shower of sparks directed towards the flash pan. These weapons were extremely expensive to produce and, as a result, saw limited use only amongst those people able to afford their extremely high cost. The first reference to the wheel-lock system is contained in a working drawing of such a device in Leonardo da Vinci's *Codex Atlanticus,* which is believed to have been published in 1580.

The flint-lock ignition system which followed, however, could be made at a price which allowed its universal implementation, causing it to be the preferred system for a period of 200 years extending into the first quarter of the nineteenth century. In this system a flash pan was attached to the side of the breech alongside the touchhole leading to the main powder charge. A hinged cover, the 'frizzen', for the flash pan protected the priming powder charge and also served as a striking surface for the piece of knapped flint held in the jaws of the hammer. When the trigger was pulled, the mainspring brought the hammer down with sufficient force for the flint to strike sparks upon its glancing impact with the frizzen, at the same time causing it to be flung open so that the priming charge was exposed to the shower of sparks. The flash from the priming charge was communicated through the touch-hole to the main charge, which fired after a very short interval (Figure 1.1). The first lock using this ignition system was seen in Spain around 1630 and was referred to as the Miquelet-lock. A similar system was seen in Holland around this same period, and was referred to as the Snaphaunce-lock. The final definitive flint-lock system was subject to considerable improvement over the 200 year period of its use. The finest examples of super-fast locks were seen on sporting arms manufactured by makers such as Manton in England. The main drawbacks with the flint-lock system were the slight delay between the primary ignition and the firing of the main charge, misfire due to the use of poor quality flints, and the susceptibility of the priming charge to the ingress of water during bad weather. The very best black flint used in the knapping (from the Dutch word *knappen* to crack) of the most reliable gunflints came from an area around Brandon in Suffolk. An ancient Neolithic flint mining area to the north of the town called 'Grime's Graves', because of its appearance, is now owned by the National Trust, who have uncovered some of the 'graves' to reveal mine shafts sunk downwards approximately 4000 years ago through

**Figure 1.1**  The firing of a flint-lock musket. The flash of the priming charge in the pan, which immediately precedes the firing of the main charge, provides the illumination for this picture.

the sandy heathland into the chalk layers below which hold several layers of flint nodules before reaching the most sought-after seam of fault-free, smooth, silky black flint known as the 'floorstone'. Galleries leading off from the bottoms of the shafts follow a chalk layer containing the thick seam of black flint floorstone, which was dug out using pieces of red deer antlers as picks; hundreds of discarded antler picks have been recovered from the galleries. The workings were studied by Sydney Barber Josiah Skertchly, who had previously studied under T.H. Huxley and Charles Darwin. He describes them in his publication of 1879 with the resounding title *On the Manufacture of Gunflints; The Methods of Excavation for Flint; The Age of Palaeolithic Man; and the Connexion between Neolithic Art and the Gun-Flint Trade.* Before dying in 1926 at Molendinar, Queensland, Australia, where he spent the last 30 years of his life, he took an interest in the Queensland Museum in Fortitude Valley and presented it with a valuable collection of flint artefacts from the Brandon district including Grime's Graves, Mildenhall, Snake Wood and other areas in which, in more recent years, I have shot deer and game.

The highly skilled and precise knapping process used for the making of gunflints involves the use of a knapping hammer, often made from a reshaped old file attached to a hickory handle and a small anvil to support the flint as it is struck. The primitive tools and weapons made in earlier times were knapped by the application of precisely aimed blows using a piece of deer's antler upon a suitable flake broken from a flint nodule. Many of the older houses in the area are constructed from precisely knapped black flint blocks instead of the more usual fired clay bricks. When first experimenting with flintlock arms as a young man, I was still able to send postal orders for freshly knapped gunflints to a certain Herbert Edwards, care of the 'Flintknappers Arms' public house in the centre of Brandon. During the flintlock period vast quantities of gunflints were hand-knapped to the desired shape and size in this area to supply domestic needs and to serve orders and contracts received from Africa, South America and other countries; one order received at Brandon from the Turkish Government in the mid-nineteenth century just prior to the Crimean War was for 11,000,000 carbine flints, while another in 1935 from the Abyssinian Army called for 35,000 to 40,000 mixed flints each week for use in the defence of their country against the Fascist invasion of Mussolini's forces. During this same period gunflints were being exported as far as Bangkok and China. During the 1950s five employees at Herbert Edwards works were knapping 40,000 gunflints a week, most of which were for the African market. The African market shrank as restrictions upon the type of firearms allowed for general use there were relaxed to the point where, in 1963, Edwards' exports to Lagos, Nigeria, fell to 50,000 gunflints in the first three months of the year. During the 1980s his son-in-law James English and one part-time knapper were producing between 70,000 and 75,000 gunflints each year, a great part of which was destined for use by hobbyist flintlock shooters in the US.

## 1.1  Blow-Pipes, Air and Gas Guns

One of the earliest forms of barrelled weapons was of course the blow-pipe, which is a primitive form of smooth-bore air gun. The first recorded report of a mechanical air weapon attributed to Lobsinger was in 1560, and Henry IV (1589–1610) had one made for him by Martin Bourgeois of Lisieux, Normandy, capable of firing many projectiles from a single charging of its reservoir. Otto von Guericke of Madgesburg invented an air pump for charging such weapons in 1602.

An Austrian air rifle corps was issued with 1799 pattern Giardoni 12.8 mm (.499 in) calibre pneumatic air rifles, which they used with good effect upon Bonaparte's army during the Battle of Wagram. The psychological effects of these rifles, which killed at a distance without noise flash or smoke, had a profound effect upon the French troops. One account of an incident, which took place during a retreat, describes how an orderly sergeant standing next to General Martier suddenly leapt up high into the air then fell upon the ground. When his clothing was removed, a wound caused by an air rifle ball was found, and an Austrian rifle corps man was seen getting away from the scene of the incident. All captured soldiers from the air rifle corps who fell into French hands after this incident were treated as assassins instead of soldiers and were summarily executed by hanging. It required two men operating a hand pump mounted upon a cart to charge the reservoirs of these rifles using 2000 pump-strokes to achieve a pressure of approximately 33 atmospheres. Although this would allow the firing of up to 40 shots, the reservoirs were usually recharged after the firing of 20 shots.

An air rifle was carried during the Lewis and Clark expedition to explore the American Northwest in 1804–1805. The Indians, who were familiar with conventional firearms, were astonished by its lack of flash and noise when they witnessed it being fired. Powerful pneumatic air guns and air canes were made in considerable quantities during this period in calibres between 4.5 and 12.8 mm (.177 in and .50 in), and their manufacture continued in England up to the outbreak of World War I. A number of the earlier weapons had false flint-lock mechanisms upon them to disguise their true nature, as there was still a measure of suspicion concerning the intents of people owning such near-silent weapons.

In 1873 Giffard was granted a patent for the use of carbonic acid as a propellant system for use in firearms. Carbon dioxide gas conveniently liquefies at about 36 atmospheres pressure (540 psi), making it capable of storage in simple metal reservoirs. Weapons made from about 1899 were in 6 and 8 mm calibre and were capable of firing 150 shots from a 9 in reservoir. An exchange system was set up, similar to that used today for soda water syphons, where spent cylinders could be handed in as part exchange for recharged cylinders.

In 1833 work was undertaken in the US on large-calibre air guns designed to fire dynamite charges. The USS Vesuvius used such weapons in the Spanish American War of 1898 during the destruction of Santiago Harbour. Tests conducted on Mefford dynamite air guns in New York Harbour involved these weapons firing shells up to distances of 1900 m (2100 yd). Steam engines were used to charge up the reservoirs of these guns, which ranged in bore sizes between 100 and 380 mm (4 and 15 in). The 455 kg (1000 lb) 15 in missile was discharged at a velocity of 190 m/s (625 ft/s). The 136 kg (300 lb) 8 in shell had a muzzle velocity of 320 m/s (1049 ft/s) and, when fired at 30° elevation, had a maximum range of 4570 m (5000 yd). Although direct hits by dynamite charges of this weight were undoubtedly very effective, difficulties were experienced at the time with long-range accuracy when firing such weapons from the heaving decks of ships. In addition the steam engines used to compress the air to power these weapons were not convenient to operate or sufficiently mobile for use in general warfare. Gunpowder provided the means of supplying great amounts of energy on demand from a compact and portable source.

## 1.2  Percussion Ignition

The Reverend Alexander John Forsyth, a Scottish clergyman took out a patent dated 11 April 1807 which described the application of detonating sensitive chemical mixtures to allow their use in the exploding of gunpowder in firearms. He conducted experiments in the Tower of London with a view to applying the system to existing arms. In his patent he describes the use of sensitive explosive materials such as potassium chlorate and mercury fulminate.

> I do make use of one of the compounds of combustible matter, such as sulphur or sulphur and charcoal, with an oxymuriatic salt; for example, the salt formed of dephlogisticated marine acid and potash, or of fulminating metallic compounds, such as fulminate of mercury or of common gunpowder, mixed in due quantity with any of the aforementioned substances, or with an oxymuriatic salt as aforesaid.

During the beginning of the nineteenth century percussion-sensitive explosive mixtures were used to develop a range of new firing systems based upon the percussion system. This material was used as priming pellets, in paper cap rolls, inside copper tubes, or within copper caps which were placed upon a nipple screwed into the touch-hole at the breech end of the gun barrel. These percussion systems were superseded during the second half of the nineteenth century by breech-loading arms utilising self-contained cartridges containing powder, cap and bullet in one convenient package (cartridge). Self-contained cartridges of needle-fire, pin-fire, rim-fire and centre-fire design were then used with true breech-loading arms. The era of muzzle-loading arms was ended.

The Prussian needle-fire system adopted by their armed forces in 1842 proved to be extremely effective in the Danish War of 1864 and further conflicts in 1866 and 1870, as their men could reload their weapons without the need to stand up, as was common practice with long-barrelled, muzzle-loading arms. The French adopted a similar system for their Chassepot service rifle, before it was subsequently converted to fire the 11 mm Gras centre-fire cartridge. The needle-fire cartridge utilised a nitrated paper cartridge which could be pierced through its base by a long needle-shaped firing pin to fire the sensitive priming patch fixed on the other side of the powder charge to a wad underneath the bullet. The long needle striker was prone to corrosion and occasional breakage, and there were constant problems of gas leakage at the breech with this system, which eventually led to its demise. In addition, the superior weatherproofing afforded by metallic ammunition was a great additional bonus.

The Frenchman Lefaucheux produced a gun and cartridge based upon the pin-fire system in 1836. The cartridge had a pin projecting from the side of its base. In this system the hammer struck the projecting pin, pushing it into the cartridge interior to strike an internal percussion cap. Again, problems associated with gas leakages at high pressures reduced this system mainly to relatively low-intensity loadings. It was, however, a successful system used for a long period both for sporting shotguns and revolvers. Cartridges for these weapons were still produced in quantity, particularly in France, well into the twentieth century. A close inspection of some of the old hammer shotguns received in criminal casework submissions has occasionally revealed them to be centre-fire conversions of pin-fire guns.

## 1.3   Modern Rim-Fire and Centre-Fire Cartridges

The final victors were, of course, the rim-fire system for low-intensity loadings, and the centre-fire system for all other loadings. After an earlier rim-fire patent by Roberts in 1831, the Frenchman Flobert introduced the BB-cap rim-fire cartridge in 1845, which was soon followed by a range of more powerful .22 in cartridges based upon this system, which are still mass-produced today. Smith and Wesson introduced their first revolver, the Model 1, Number 1 based upon the Rollin White patent in 1857 and chambered for the .22 rim-fire Short cartridge, still so popular today. The rim-fire system was used in a range of larger calibre loadings, which were popular particularly in the US in repeating arms. The .56 in-56 rim-fire cartridge used in the Spencer repeating carbine during the American Civil War by the Union Army is said to have given them a critical edge over the Confederate forces at Gettysburg, due to the greater firepower afforded by its use. The Henry lever-action rifle manufactured between 1860 and 1866, prior to the firm being reorganised by the Winchester Repeating Arms Co., was chambered for a .44 in cartridge using a flat-nosed bullet. The .56 in-50 Spencer loading of 1864, which was used in a repeating carbine the following year, was quite a powerful loading, using a 350 grain (22.7 g) bullet which was said to be capable of penetrating 305 mm (1 ft) of pine at a distance of 46 m (50 yd). Large-calibre rim-fire loadings such as .32

in, .38 in and the .41 in cartridge used in Derringer pistols saw considerable use in the US well into the twentieth century.

In 1861 a centre-fire cartridge similar to that devised by Pottet and little different from the modern shotgun cartridge was introduced for use in shotguns. The British gunmaker Daw exhibited centre-fire guns and cartridges at the International Exhibition of 1862. The Boxer metallic cartridge primer was introduced by Colonel Boxer in England in 1867 and was used to replace the pasteboard Pottet-type priming system cartridges used in 1853 pattern .577 in British service muzzle-loading rifles which had been converted to breech-loading centre-fire operation in 1866 using the American Snider system (Figure 1.2).

The Boxer primer utilising a single separate internal anvil, first introduced in 1867, is the most popular priming system used today. The system was taken up in the US and was popular because it allowed convenient reloadability of the spent cartridge case, which was very important in the US during this early period in the use of breech-loading arms. Curiously, the British and their Continental counterparts rejected it in favour of the American Berdan system introduced in 1866, as for many years the reloading of metallic cartridges was neither popular nor encouraged by the cartridge manufacturers. In this system a central anvil was formed inside the cartridge case, thus allowing the primer to consist of a simple cup containing the priming material and a paper or foil cover. The two flash-holes positioned on each side of the integral anvil made removal of the spent primer difficult for would-be reloaders, who preferred the simplicity of the single central flash-hole of its Boxer counterpart, which allowed a punch to be passed through it to dislodge the spent primer. In some respects, however, if reloadability is not an issue, the elimination of the composite primer as used in the

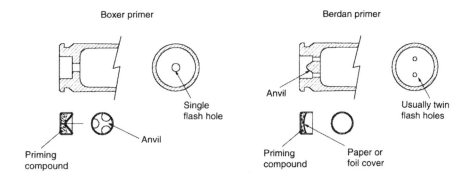

**Figure 1.2**  Rim-fire and centre-fire (Boxer and Berdan) cartridge priming system.

Boxer system removes one critical variable in the manufacturing operation. It is of interest to note in recent years, that the less sensitive lead-free priming formulation used in CCI Blazer ammunition was initially marketed using a single offset flash-hole variant of the Berdan system, in an attempt at reducing the possibility of a misfire. In recent years European shooters have taken up the practice of cartridge reloading to such an extent that domestic cartridge manufacturers have had to respond to the market demand for reloadable Boxer primed ammunition (Figure 1.3 and Figure 1.4).

## 1.4  Smokeless Powders and Modern Arms

Schonberg discovered nitrated cellulose (guncotton) in 1845 and demonstrated its use as a smokeless propellant for use in small arms at the Woolwich Arsenal in England the following year. Attempts then followed to regulate its burning rate to suit particular applications. Nitroglycerine was discovered in 1846 in Turin by Sobrero, but was a hazardous explosive material completely unsuitable on its own for use as a propellant.

In 1866 Colonel Schultze produced a shotgun powder made from nitrated wood cellulose mixed with barium or potassium nitrate and formed a company to produce it two years later. In 1882 Reid introduced E.C. shotgun powder. Both of these powders were unsuitable for use in military rifles. A method of treating nitrocellulose was devised which allowed its use as an ingredient for military arms. This involved its incorporation with suitable solvents which destroyed its fibrous nature and which, upon evaporation, left a compact material devoid of pores and capable of burning only from its exterior, layer by layer towards its centre. The gelatinised material, before complete evaporation of its solvent, could be rolled or pressed into sheets, cords or other desirable shapes, that were retained after the drying process was completed. The first smokeless military rifle powder was invented by the

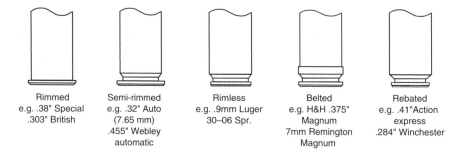

| Rimmed | Semi-rimmed | Rimless | Belted | Rebated |
|--------|-------------|---------|--------|---------|
| e.g. .38" Special | e.g. .32" Auto | e.g. .9mm Luger | e.g. H&H .375" | e.g. .41"Action |
| .303" British | (7.65 mm) | 30–06 Spr. | Magnum | express |
| | .455" Webley | | 7mm Remington | .284" Winchester |
| | automatic | | Magnum | |

**Figure 1.3**  Cartridge case head designs.

# The .22 rimfire cartridge

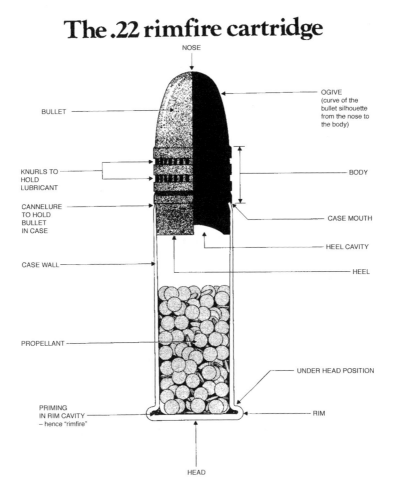

**Figure 1.4** The .22 cartridge.

French chemist Vieille in 1884 for the then new 8 mm Lebel rifle. After taming the explosive nature of nitroglycerine with Kieselguhr in 1867 to produce dynamite, Alfred Nobel later went on to develop gelatinised 'blasting gelatine'. In 1886 he used equal proportions of nitroglycerine and nitrocellulose, to produce a material that could be rolled and cut up into granules of the desired shapes and sizes. This powder was patented in 1888 as 'Ballistite', although the addition of camphor used to moderate its burning rate was subsequently discontinued due to its tendency to be lost by evaporation during storage, thus causing changes to the ballistic properties of the powder.

The British developed 'Cordite', named after its appearance resembling lengths of cord or spaghetti, in order to obtain a military propellant that would retain constant chemical and ballistic properties. It was composed of nitroglycerine and guncotton gelatinised with the solvent acetone. It also contained a small amount of mineral jelly to reduce metallic fouling in the barrels of rifled arms, although it was later found to act also as a beneficial cooling agent that helped maintain uniformity of stability of the propellant under varied climatic conditions. However, it was soon shown to be a relatively hot burning and thus erosive propellant, and as a result its nitroglycerine content was reduced from the 58% level of its Mark I formulation, down to 30% in its 'Cordite M.D.' (Modified Cordite). Although this improved matters, its erosive properties were still greater than those of, for example, American I.M.R. or Dupont No. 16 powder which did not contain nitroglycerine; large quantities of this powder were imported for the loading of British Service ammunition and referred to as propellant 'N.C.Z.' Over the years many other single and double base powders were introduced by manufacturers to meet the needs of both the military and the civilian markets.

Smokeless powders based upon nitrocellulose or nitrocellulose and nitroglycerine (single base and double base propellants) were then used in place of black powder. This allowed the generation of higher missile velocities and less fouling of the barrel bores. In 1886 the French 8 mm Lebel bolt-action rifle utilised a high-velocity jacketed bullet loading. By the end of the century self-loading pistols, rifles and machine guns were perfected utilising recoil or gas operated systems (Figure 1.5). The modern centre-fire shotgun cartridge was developed during the 1860s and was initially used with hammer guns and later with hammerless guns. Smith and Wesson produced the modern revolver based upon the Rollin White patent in 1857. Lever-action and pump-action rifles and shotguns were developed and became popular in the US. Recoil and gas operating systems for self-loading and automatic weaponry were also developed for use with the new high-velocity smokeless powder loadings. The choke boring of shotgun barrels similar to that patented by Roper in the US and Pape in England in 1866 after earlier beginnings going back to 1781 became commonplace around 1874, and fluidised compression steels replaced the ornate but less robust Damascus system of barrel manufacture (Figure 1.6). In reality the basic designs of modern weaponry were completed around the turn of the century while Queen Victoria still sat upon the throne of England.

The basic weapon designs were developed further during the twentieth century mainly with modern methods of cheap mass-production in mind. Alternative materials have been introduced over the years, such as stainless steels, light alloys and plastics. However many of the original weapons of earlier manufacture, constructed from durable materials, have withstood the

**Figure 1.5** The Borchardt recoil-operated self-loading pistol of 1893 was chambered for a 7.65 mm cartridge employing a charge of nitrocellulose powder and a jacketed bullet. Shown here in its case with attachable shoulder stock.

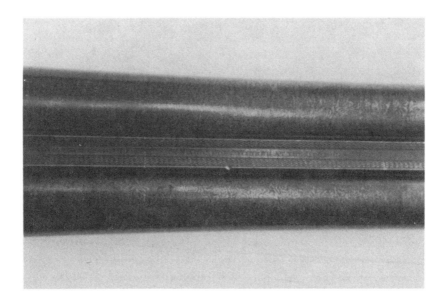

**Figure 1.6** A pair of shotgun barrels exhibiting the beautiful decorative pattern of the Damascus process used in their manufacture which was in general use before the introduction of fluidized compression steels in the latter part of the nineteenth century.

passage of time and still exist in operable condition today. Many of these are, of course, chambered for cartridges which are still popular and so remain viable weapons for use in crime. It is for these reasons that many of these 'antique' firearms are so often encountered in criminal casework.

Firearms can initially be broken down into two groups—handguns (Figure 1.7 and Figure 1.8) and longarms. These groups can in turn be subdivided into two further categories—rifled arms and smooth-bored guns. Smooth-bored guns are used predominantly with cartridges containing loadings of multiple small-sized lead pellets; most of these arms will be regarded as shotguns, although their legal classification in the various countries will often depend upon dimensional considerations. Rifled arms are generally designed to fire a single missile, usually referred to as a bullet. The internal bores of these weapons are engraved with a spiral pattern of grooves, referred to as the rifling. The rifling engraves its form upon the exterior of the bullet during its passage through the bore, which in turn imparts a rotational spin upon the bullet about its longitudinal axis. This high degree of rotational spin acts like a gyroscope to stabilise the bullet in flight by ensuring that its nose remains pointed in the initial direction

**Figure 1.7**  Powerful five-shot 38-bore (.50 in/12.7 mm) Adams double-action muzzle-loading percussion revolver of the mid-nineteenth century and the famous Mauser 10-shot self-loading recoil operated pistol of 1896 represent the dramatic pace of arms developments over the latter half of this century. The Mauser pistol loadings generated advertised muzzle velocities of 1410 ft/s (430 m/s).

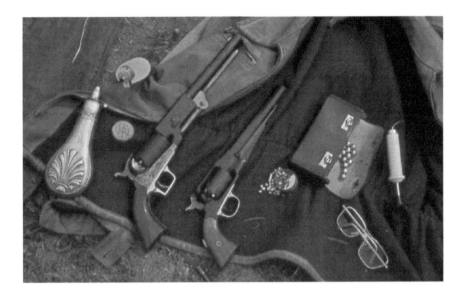

**Figure 1.8** Modern Italian-manufactured muzzle-loading percussion revolvers used on a firing range by black powder enthusiasts. 1847 Colt Walker and 1861 Remington Army reproductions with powder flasks, percussion caps, .454 inch diameter cast lead balls, and lubricant grease.

of departure from the muzzle end of the gun barrel; this mechanism is the reason for the high intrinsic degree of accuracy of this class of weaponry.

In general however, handguns, although rifled, are intended for use at short ranges, and rifled longarms (rifles and carbines) are intended for use at longer ranges and can be made to fire more powerful loadings. Shotguns have no use for such stabilising influences, as such weapons are not intended to be precision arms and the effects of rifling can disturb the shot patterns. The individual pellets in the shot charge begin to separate from each other shortly after their departure from the muzzle end of the gun barrel to assume divergent flight paths. To simplify matters, one can assume that the pattern of shot is circular in form as it flies away from the gun, and that the diameter of its spread increases with the range of firing. There are always exceptions to any rule, and the now discarded Holland & Holland 'Paradox' guns are just such an example. They were large bore guns that were chambered for shotgun cartridges, deemed equally suitable for use with both shot and bulleted cartridges. To increase the accuracy of single slug loadings, their barrels were bored smooth, with the exception of the last few inches at the muzzle, which was rifled. The users of so called 'long range pistols' on the ranges at Bisley, indulge in competitive shooting at ranges of up to 1000 yards (914 m), using long-barrelled, generally single-shot, stockless guns, chambered for standard or modified powerful centre-fire rifle cartridges. I can recall meeting some of the members of the club on the Bisley range some years ago as a visiting member of the Firearms Consultative Committee. After demonstrating the use of one of the guns, I was invited to fire three shots at a standard rifle target set up at 300 m (328 yd). The owner informed me that the 'pistol' in question was chambered for the .375 inch Holland & Holland Magnum cartridge, necked down to .30 inch and fire-formed so as to allow the loading of an even heavier charge of powder. The long eye-relief telescope sight was set at 24× magnification, which as a consequence reduced the exit pupil diameter to less than 2 mm, which made target acquisition somewhat difficult. Sandy Ewing, the then Chief Executive of the NRA, produced the printout of the results from the piezoelectric target marker that indicated, to my surprise, that I had shot one 'bull's-eye' and two 'inners'. However, even more impressive were its recoil, the extent of its brilliant muzzle flash, and the magnitude of its muzzle blast.

## Further Reading

Arnold, R. 1955. *The Shooter's Handbook*. London: Nicholas Kaye.

Boothroyd, G. 1970. *The Handgun,* London: Cassell.

*The Encyclopaedia Britannica.* 1999.

Forrest, A.J. 1983. *Masters of Flint,* Lavenham: Terrence Dalton.

Greener, W.W. 1910. *The Gun and its Development,* New York: Bonanza.

Haag, L.C. 2001. Black powder substitutes: their physical and chemical properties and performance. *AFTE Journal,* **33** (4) 313–325.

Pollard, Major J. 1923. *Shot-Guns,* London: Sir Isaac Pittman.

Roads, C. 1978. *The Gun,* London: British Broadcasting Corporation, Purnell.

Russell, M.S. 2000. *The Chemistry of Fireworks.* Cambridge: The Royal Society of Chemistry.

Smith, W.H.B. 1957. *Gas Air and Spring Guns of the World,* Harrisburg, PA: Military Service Publishing Co.

Wesley, L. 1965. *Air Guns and Air Pistols,* London: Cassell.

Winnant, L. 1970. *Early Percussion Firearms,* London: Hamlyn.

*Textbook of Small Arms.* 1929. London: The War Office. HMSO.

# Firearms Legislation and the Definition of a Firearm

# 2

## 2.1   History of Weapons Legislation in Britain

Over the years the authorities in England perceived a need for appropriate legislation to control the ownership and use of firearms from as far back as the sixteenth century. The Firearms Act 1968 is currently regarded as the Principal Act; this in turn has been added to and amended a great deal by subsequent legislation designed to tighten up controls further.

1.  1508 – Henry VII. Act forbidding the use of guns or crossbows without Royal Letters Patent.
2.  1515 – Henry VIII. 'An Acte Avoidyng Shoting in Crossebowes and Gonnes.' Only persons with property to the value of 300 Marks allowed to own crossbows or guns.
3.  1542 – Henry VIII. First issue of hunting licences, subject to property value of £100. Recognised the use of firearms by criminals; 'nowe of late the saide evill disposed persons have used and yet doe daylie use to ride and go on the Kings high Wayes and elsewhere having with them Crossbowes and lyttle handguns ready furnished with Quarrel, Gunpowder, fyer and touche, to the great perill and fear of the Kings most loving subjects.'
4.  1549 – Edward VI. An act forbidding the shooting of birdshot.
5.  1824 – Vagrancy Act. Power to arrest any person armed with a gun, pistol etc. with intent to commit a felonious act.

6. 1828 and 1844 – Night Poaching Acts, 1831 Game Act, 1862 Poaching Prevention Act. These acts recognised the use of firearms in the taking of game.
7. 1870 – Gun Licence Act. Specific control on the sale of firearms.
8. 1903 – Pistols Act. First act to regulate the sale and use of pistols.
9. 1920 – Firearms Act. First effective act to regulate the sale and use of firearms and ammunition in general.
10. 1937 – Firearms Act. Introduced the controls on pistols and rifles.
11. 1968 – Firearms Act. Based upon the 1937 Act but also introduced shotgun certificates.
12. 1969 – Firearms (Dangerous Air Weapons) Rules. This placed power limits upon air weapons which were not subject to firearms certificate control.
13. 1982 – Firearms Act. Deals with imitation firearms capable of being converted to allow the discharge of a missile.
14. 1987 – Crossbows Act. Restricted sale to adults.
15. 1988 – Firearms (Amendment) Act. Introduced new classes of prohibited weapons, redefined shotguns, introduced the official deactivation of firearms, disallowed down-conversions of certain weaponry. New stricter form of shotgun certificate introduced along with the need to notify transfers of shotguns.
16. 1992 – Firearms (Amendment) Act. Allows the extension of the lives of shotgun and firearms certificates.
17. 1992 – Firearms (Amendment) Regulations. Transfer of EC Weapons Directive into domestic legislation. Effective 1 January 1993 in setting minimum standards of control common to all members of the European Community, but at the same time allowing individual Member States the right to apply more rigorous controls as they see fit. Special use of the powers of derogation included to lessen the effects of the EC Directive, which included disguised firearms and loadings incorporating expanding projectiles.
18. 1993 – Firearms (Dangerous Air Weapons) (Amendment) Rules. Modification of Dangerous Air Weapons Rules to take into account effects of EC Weapons Directive in respect of disguised air weapons.
19. 1994 – Firearms (Amendment) Act. Creates new offence for the use of firearms or imitation firearms to cause fear of violence.
20. Firearms (Amendment) Act. Placed ban on ownership of most handguns.
21. 2003 – Anti-Social Behaviour Act. Ban on marketing of all air cartridge weapons; currently owned weapons subject to certificate control or destruction without compensation.

## 2.2  Legislation and Gun Control

It is imperative that the expert witness should fully understand domestic firearms legislation in order to be able to prepare written statements for use by a court or to give evidence directly to the Court. The expert will always be expected to give reasoned evidence on matters relating to the classification of weapons and ammunition, and this must be done in a competent manner during cross-examination, when his opinion can be subjected to vigorous challenge. I have acted as a technical advisor on firearms matters to the Home Office as part of my job for many years, although the major part of my duties has been concerned with criminal casework submissions to the laboratory and visits to the scenes of shooting incidents to assist the Police investigative teams. I have assisted with the drafting of new firearms legislation, and have acted to advise the Ministers dealing with Parliamentary Bills in the House of Commons during their Committee and Debate stages, and also to be on hand to advise their counterparts during the passage of Bills through the House of Lords.

Sitting in a cramped box next to the Speaker's Chair in the House after many hours of debate during an all-night session is not the most comfortable of conditions to consider the finer points of firearms legislation. After a Member of Parliament has vigorously made his point during a heated debate, perhaps assisted in his endeavours by waving some marginal firearm object above his head which has suddenly been produced from a paper sack positioned on the floor between his feet, one only has the briefest of moments to identify the object from a distance, and then write the Minister a scribbled, but hopefully legible briefing note identifying the object, its application and its appropriate classification in law, or the proposed legislation along with supportive stated case references, and for this note to be then hurriedly passed down to the Minister before he gets back on his feet in response. One is also under the additional pressure of knowing that when the subsequent written transcript appears in Hansard afterwards it will be duly scrutinised by interested parties at leisure in the hope of spotting some technical error which in turn can be used to help form an embarrassing question or justify a subsequent demand for a satisfactory explanation from the Minister.

In 1992 I was sent to represent UK interests when serving on a panel of technical representatives from the various European Community Member States at a meeting in Brussels intended to resolve perceived problems associated with the introduction of a common European Weapons Directive. My brief was to help resolve perceived difficulties if such a directive were absorbed into our own domestic legislation. The draft of the European Weapons Directive had unfortunately already been agreed within the central 'Schengen Group' of countries; the Directive, in a suitably modified form, was subsequently incorporated into our own domestic legislation in 1992. It is at times like this when one has to assimilate the sometimes puzzling vagaries and ramifications which are the inevitable outcome of simultaneous translation. At one stage in the proceedings I recall a particular period of misunderstanding when a critical term contained in the translation provided from the French original draft came out as 'magazine'; it was some time before I became aware that they were in fact referring to a revolver cylinder. At a later stage when dealing with the proposals to ban pistol ammunition incorporating expanding bullets, which the UK was resisting on behalf of the interests of sportsmen and target shooters as well as the fact that the proposed legislation would be unenforceable, that my French counterpart leaned across the table and in an accusatory manner reminded me (through the headphone translator) that it was we British who were the culprits responsible for first introducing these diabolical 'Dum Dum' ammunition loadings in India during the period of the Raj. The technical representatives meeting did eventually turn out quite well from our point of view, with a fair measure of accord being accomplished in areas which, for some time, seemed beyond hope. I recall that immediately after initially point-ing out some of the less than useful parts of the original draft, the Commission's representative pronounced on the constant problems associated with the UK predilection for constantly being out of step with the rest of the Community in almost all matters. I responded by going around the table asking four rep-resentatives in turn their understanding of this previously agreed but poten-tially contentious first section, and it came as no surprise to me to receive four quite different responses. At this stage I was able to speak on the matter in detail, after which genuine discussion followed. I knew things were going well when the Italian Chairman (it was this nation which held the Presidency at the time) started disagreeing with each intrusion from the Commission's repre-sentative and proceeded to give anecdotal accounts to support what I had last said, and the Dutch representative commented that after signing up to the draft they were amazed upon first speaking to target shooters that the proposed prohibited ammunition was in general use in their country. Finally, the French representative began agreeing with me, which then ensured a downhill aspect to the rest of the meeting, although it was necessary for the UK to apply derogation in respect of certain sections to lessen the effects of the Directive which were beyond further negotiation at the ensuing meeting of Ministers.

The *Shorter Oxford English Dictionary* (1993 edition) defines a firearm as—'A portable weapon from which a missile is propelled by means of an explosive charge; a rifle, gun, pistol, etc.' This does not of course cover all weaponry capable of discharging a missile, and most certainly does not cover arms employing compressed air or gas as a propellant system. In the UK a legal definition of a firearm is provided in Section 57 of The Firearms Act 1968 (often referred to as the Principal Act):

In this Act, the expression 'firearm' means a lethal barrelled weapon of any description from which any shot, bullet or other missile can be discharged and includes

a. any prohibited weapon, whether it is such a lethal weapon as aforesaid or not; and
b. any component part of such a lethal or prohibited weapon; and
c. any accessory to any such weapon designed or adapted to diminish the noise or flash caused by firing the weapon;

and so much of Section 1 of this Act as excludes any description of firearm from the category of firearms to which that section applies shall be construed as also excluding component parts of, and accessories to, firearms of that description.

This form of wording clearly allows any weapon utilising a barrel to discharge a missile possessing lethal potential to be regarded as a 'firearm'. A barrel can be regarded as the tubular part (of a gun) from which the shot or bullet is discharged. Lethal means causing or capable of causing death. In the previous case of *Moore vs. Gooderham,* Queens Bench Division, 21 October 1960, it was ruled that even a low-powered air pistol able to discharge a pellet or pointed dart which, if fired from a close range, was capable of inflicting a lethal injury if the missile were to strike a vulnerable unprotected part of the body, would fulfil the definition of a 'firearm'. My own casework experience and those of working colleagues over the years have included a number of tragic incidents in which people had sustained serious or fatal injuries from pellets discharged from air weapons. Examples follow.

- Death of an adult male caused by a shot to the temple by a .22 in calibre pellet fired from an air rifle. 147 m/s, 10 J (velocity 482 ft/s; energy 7.4 ft·lb).
- Death of an adult male caused by a shot to the abdomen by a .22 in pellet fired from an air rifle. 182 m/s, 15 J (velocity 596 ft/s; energy 11.07 ft·lb).
- Death of an adult male caused by a .22 in pellet to the chest fired from an air rifle. 173 m/s, 14 J (velocity 567 ft/s; energy 10.42 ft·lb).
- Death of an 11-year-old girl caused by a .22 in pellet fired at the head from an air rifle. 160.6 m/s, 11.7 J (velocity 527 ft/s; energy 8.62 ft·lb).
- Death of a 10-year-old boy by a .22 in pellet to the head from an air rifle. 162.5 m/s, 11.6 J (velocity 533 ft/s; energy 8.57 ft·lb).

- Child killed by a .22 in pellet fired at the eye. 98.8 m/s, 6.4 J (velocity 324 ft/s; energy 4.1 ft·lb). (Reported by Metropolitan Police Laboratory.)
- Girl killed by a .177 in pellet fired at chest. 143.2 m/s, 6.4 J (velocity 470 ft/s; energy 4.7 ft·lb). (Reported by Metropolitan Police Laboratory.)

It follows therefore that even relatively low-powered air weapons or other barrelled weapons can be 'firearms' for the purposes of English law. In addition, component parts of such lethal barrelled weapons along with accessories such as silencers and flash eliminators may also be regarded as 'firearms' in respect of certain sections of the Act, and in Section 1 or Section 5 weaponry authorisation by way of firearm certificate or in some instances a prohibited weapons authority as well. Prohibited weapons (Section 5 automatic or burst-fire arms or weapons designed to discharge noxious materials such as CS irritant agent and electrical stun guns) are also considered to be 'firearms' together with their component parts even if these are for prohibited weapons which do not possess barrels.

It is an offence under Section 1 of the 1968 Act for a person to possess, purchase or acquire firearms or ammunition unless so authorised by a firearm certificate. Section 1(3) provides exemption from Section 1 control for shotguns, i.e., smooth-bored guns of 24 in minimum barrel length and for air weapons of a type not declared by the Secretary of State under Section 53 of the Act to be specially dangerous. The Firearms (Dangerous Air Weapons) Rules 1969 sets out kinetic energy limits for missiles discharged from such air weapons of 16.3 J (12 ft·lb) for rifles and 8.1 J (6 ft·lb) in respect of pistols. Air weapons of greater power are subject to firearm certificate procedure. Similarly, under Section 1(3)(a) shotguns of barrel length less than 24 in are also deemed to be subject to Section 1 control. In addition, the act of shortening the barrel or barrels of a shotgun below 24 in is an additional offence under Section 4 of the same Act, unless this is being done by a gunsmith as part of a process of repair such as resleeving the barrels (Figure 2.1). This Section also makes it an offence for a person to convert an imitation firearm in order to allow it to discharge a missile possessing lethal properties. Section 1(4) of the Act provides exemption from certificate control of shotgun cartridges, provided that they contain at least five pellets which are not greater than 9.1 mm (.36 in) in diameter, ammunition for air weapons and blank cartridges not more than 25.4 mm (1 in) in diameter measured immediately in front of the rim or cannelure of the base of the cartridge.

Section 5 of the Principal Act is in effect an extension of Section 1. It applies to a category of arms referred to as 'prohibited weapons', the acqui-

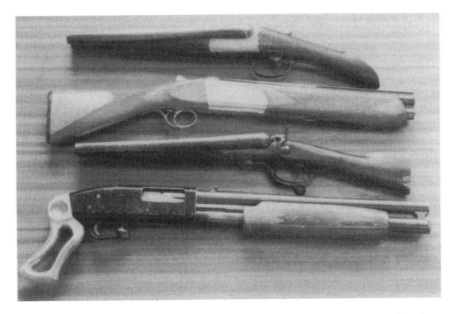

**Figure 2.1**    Sawn-off shotguns received at the laboratory in casework submissions. Derived from: double-barrelled side-by-side English pattern gun, double-barrelled over-and-under gun of the type commonly used in clay pigeon shooting, Jones action double-barrelled side-by-side hammer gun manufactured in the 1860–1870 period and an American Mossberg pump-action gun.

sition or possession of which requires additional authorisation from the Secretary of State at the Home Office in England and Wales or the Secretary of State for Scotland where appropriate. This Section was amended by the Firearms (Amendment) Act 1988 and the Firearms Acts (Amendment) Regulations 1992 to cover the following weapons and ammunition (Figure 2.3 through Figure 2.6):

- Automatic and burst-fire weaponry (machine guns, submachine guns and assault rifles)
- Mortars and rocket launchers intended for the launching of stabilised missiles, other than devices intended for line-throwing, pyrotechnic or signalling purposes
- Any cartridge loaded with a bullet designed to explode on or immediately before impact, any ammunition containing a noxious substance and, if capable of being used with a firearm of any description, any grenade, bomb (or other like missile), or rocket or shell designed to explode as aforesaid
- Any weapon designed or adapted for the discharge of any noxious liquid, gas or other 'thing', (in the case of *Flack vs. Baldry*, House of

Lords, 25 February 1988, it was ruled that electrical stun guns were included in this category)

- Any ammunition containing or designed or adapted, to contain noxious substances
- Self-loading or pump-action rifles other than those chambered for .22 in rim-fire ammunition
- Any self-loading or pump-action smooth-bore gun, other than those chambered for .22 in rim-fire cartridges, which has a barrel less than 24 in length or (excluding any detachable, folding, retractable or other movable butt-stock) is less than 40 in in length overall
- Any smooth-bore revolver gun which is not chambered for 9 mm rim-fire cartridges (e.g., the Dragon or Striker 12-bore guns)
- Any firearm which is disguised as another object
- Explosive military missiles and their launchers, which includes any rocket or ammunition which consists of or incorporates a missile designed to explode on or immediately before impact and any missiles for such loadings (e.g., grenade launchers, anti-tank missiles and guided rockets or bombs)
- Any military incendiary ammunition and any missiles for such ammunition (*note:* this is not meant to refer to simple tracer loadings)
- Any military armour piercing ammunition or the missiles for such loadings
- Any pistol ammunition loaded with a bullet which is designed to expand in a predictable manner when entering tissue, and the missiles for such loadings (i.e., soft-point and hollow-point loadings)

The UK chose to interpret this particular European Community Directive as only applying to ammunition of a chambering used exclusively with pistols and further allowed target shooters and sportsmen to possess the few remaining pistol-only loadings left on a suitably worded firearm certificate by applying special powers of derogation.

Further implications of the Firearms (Amendment) Act 1988 caused certain smoothbore guns to be raised from Section 2 (shotgun certificate control) to the more restrictive control of Section 1 of the same Act.

1. If the bore size exceeded 50.8 mm (2 in)
2. If the magazine of a repeating firearm was detachable or if it was capable of holding more than two cartridges, (e.g., bolt-action or lever-action guns)
3. If the self-loading or pump-action .22 in smooth-bore gun had a detachable magazine or was capable of holding more than two cartridges

4.  Smooth-bore revolver shotguns chambered for 9 mm rim-fire cartridges, or of muzzle-loading design (modern reproduction percussion arms)

Sometimes guns or devices of a type never intended for use as weapons can be regarded as 'firearms'. A Verey signalling pistol was ruled to constitute a 'firearm' in the case *Read vs. Donovan*, Kings Bench Division, 12 December 1947, as it was held that such items had been used on occasions as weapons during warfare. A similar ruling was provided in respect of a pen-type flare launcher in the case of *Regina vs. Singh*, Court of Appeal, Criminal Division, 22 May 1989. These two cases indicate that it is at times possible to regard items not designed for use as weapons as being 'firearms' for the purposes of English law.

The two cases, *Cafferata vs. Wilson*, Kings Bench Division, 20 October 1936, and *Regina vs. Freeman*, Court of Appeal, Criminal Division, 17 February 1970, both related to starting pistols which were designed to fire blank cartridges. In each case it was established that the blockages contained in their barrels, which were intended to prevent their use with bulleted cartridges, could be drilled out using simple tooling; on this basis they were both ruled to be 'firearms'. This principle of easy convertibility of imitation firearms (Figure 2.12) was later incorporated in the Firearms Act 1982.

Section 58(2) of the Principal Act allows the exemption from certificate control for antique firearms which are sold, transferred, purchased, acquired or possessed as curiosities or ornaments. An actual definition of an antique firearm is not however provided, thus resulting in a mixture of court rulings, which were coloured by perception, the condition of the weapon and the circumstances of possession. However, in the case *Bennett vs. Brown*, High Court of Justice, Queens Bench Division, 1 April 1980, it was ruled that two old weapons—an 8 mm Mauser rifle and a 7.65 mm Mauser self-loading pistol which had been converted to fire .22 in rim-fire cartridges, were both weapons which could have been used in World War I. It was further ruled that any weapon capable of having been used in twentieth century warfare should not be eligible for the exemption from certificate control offered for antique arms (Figure 2.2). The passage of time however, is likely to put considerable strain on the relevance of this decision. Modern reproductions of antique arms are also ineligible for exemption from control. (*Regina vs. Howells*, Court of Appeal, 18 February 1977, ruled that a .31 in Colt percussion revolver of modern manufacture should not be regarded as an antique firearm.) The statutory Firearms Consultative Committee, of which I was a member at that time, set down a list of obsolete calibres. Any genuine old weapon chambered for one of the listed cartridges can now be considered for the exemption from certificate procedure provided in Section 58 of the

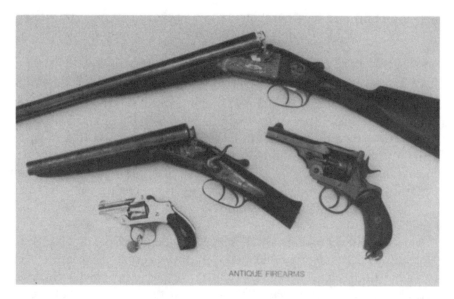

**Figure 2.2**    In other circumstances some might consider these nineteenth century arms to constitute antique firearms. Greener shotgun, Webley Mark 1.455
in revolver, Bland hammer shotgun and late model .32 in Smith and Wesson
hammerless 'Lemonsqueezer'.

Principal Act, along with their muzzle-loading counterparts. The listing was
later expanded by the addition of other obsolete cartridge loadings, including
those for old shotguns chambered for obsolete cartridge loadings. The proposed additions appeared in the *Tenth Annual Report of the Firearms Consultative Committee* published on 9 December 1999. The complete updated
listing was then included in the Home Office publication *Firearms Law:
Guidance to the Police, 2002*.

A sound moderator (silencer) for a firearm normally requires a separate
certificate entry, in the same way as an additional firearm. However a weapon
fitted with a non-removable integral silencer was ruled not to be subject to
similar control in the case of *Broome vs. Walter,* High Court of Justice, Queens
Bench Divisional Court, 25 May 1989. Flash eliminators would be treated in
the same way, unless they also allow the launching of explosive rifle grenades,
as this would then place the entire rifle in the prohibited category if fitted.

Section 5(1)(a) of the Principal Act, as amended, refers to prohibited
weapons capable of automatic or burst fire. In the case of *Regina vs. Clarke,*
Court of Appeal, Criminal Division, 19 December 1985, it was ruled that the
component parts of such weaponry should also be subject to Section 5
control. In the case of *R v Pannell* at the Court of Appeal, Criminal Division,
on 27 July 1982, it was held that a self-loading version of the 9 mm 'Sterling'
submachine gun was subject to Section 5(1)(a) of the Firearms Act 1968, on

**Figure 2.3** Shotguns of the type prohibited under the Firearms (Amendment Act) 1988. The Israeli "Dragon" 12-shot revolver gun, the Italian Franchi "SPAS 12" eight-shot pump-action/self-loader, and the Korean manufactured "USAS 12" self-loading gun available with detachable 10-shot box or 20-shot drum magazine (also available in full-automatic capability). All guns depicted are chambered for 12 bore ammunition.

the basis that limiting the rearward movement of its trigger would allow full automatic fire. Similarly, in the case of *R v Law*, heard at the Court of Appeal, Criminal Division, on 1 February 1999, a self-loading open-bolt variant of an Ingram MAC-10 based submachine gun, previously marketed in the UK as a 'target pistol', was also ruled to be subject to control as a 'prohibited weapon', under Section 5(1)(a) of the Firearms Act 1968, as amended by the 1988 legislation. This decision overturned a ruling to the contrary, given at a lower court in the case of *R v Savage,* on the same type of weapon. Tests proved that bursts of automatic fire could be produced by restricting the rearward movement of the trigger during firing, by the simple expedient of interposing the middle finger behind it. Although the Defence had argued that it was not the intention of the maker that the weapon should produce such an effect, the ruling was simply given that, 'if the weapon is capable of burst fire, then it is caught by the words of the section.'

**Figure 2.4**    Centre-fire self-loading rifles were also banned by the 1988 legislation. Weapon shown is the semi-automatic Chinese P .56 Kalashnikov rifle, with a handkerchief tied to its front sight, which Michael Ryan threw from the top floor window of a school after the end of the Hungerford Massacre before committing suicide with his Beretta pistol.

Section 7 of the Firearms (Amendment) Act 1988 indicates the retrospective nature of this legislation relating to the newly prohibited weapons, and further disallows the conversion of rifled arms possessing barrels less than 24 in long into shotgun or air weapons.

Section 8 of this same Amendment Act sets out standards to which firearms can be deactivated to allow them to be possessed without the need for a certificate (Figure 2.7). This includes the inspection and marking of such deactivated arms by the Gun Barrel Proof Houses to confirm that this work has been done to the necessary standards. The year 1996 witnessed the massacre of 16 small children and a woman teacher of a school in Dunblane, Scotland, by a man using a legally registered Browning 9 mm self-loading pistol and a large number of special 20-shot magazines pre-loaded with a mixture of standard ammunition and cartridges loaded with expanding pattern bullets. Lord Cullen was chosen to head what, in Scotland, is referred to as a fatal accident inquiry and, at the same time, was given a wide brief to allow him to make recommendations in respect of any changes thought necessary to British firearms legislation. The Dunblane massacre was followed soon afterwards upon the same year by the slaughter of 35 people at

**Figure 2.5** Semi-automatic variants of sub-machine guns were also caught by the 1988 legislation. Typified by the Israeli UZl range—standard arm with mini and micro variants.

**Figure 2.6** Burst-fire arms such as this Beretta Model 93R 9 mm pistol were also classified as prohibited weapons by the 1988 legislation. Weapon shown with attachable shoulder stock and 20-round magazine is designed to allow either one shot to be fired each time the trigger is pressed or a burst of three rounds at a very high cyclic rate.

**Figure 2.7**   Details of Sten Gun deactivated to approved standards. Shown here is ring of weld material inside the body, and a thin shim from the original bolt rigidly welded to the cartridge case ejection port, as seen from open magazine well.

a tourist site in Port Arthur, Tasmania, by a deranged man armed with self-loading rifles.

Lord Cullen's report, entitled 'The Public Inquiry into the Shootings at Dunblane Primary School on 13 March 1996' was published by the Secretary of State for Scotland in October 1996 (The Stationery Office, Cm 3386). The publication was released on 16 October along with a Government White Paper representing 'Government Response' (The Stationery Office, Cm 3392). On the same day the Home Secretary announced the Government's intention to ban the private ownership of all centre-fire handguns and to impose severe restrictions upon the ownership and storage of .22 in rim-fire handguns used for formal target shooting. In addition, all cartridge loadings employing expanding pattern missiles were to be placed in the prohibited category, along with the expanding pattern bullets used in the hand loading of such ammunition. At that time hollow-point and soft-point loadings were used for shooting vermin to ensure more certain kills and thus avoid needless suffering. Deer shooting legislation throughout Britain demanded the use of similar expanding bullet loadings for the shooting of deer, for the same humanitarian reasons. The provision of such loadings for the legal shooting of vermin or deer were to be enabled by the issue of suitably worded firearms certificates in lieu of prohibited weapons (Section 5 arms and ammunition) authorities. Parliamentary time was then set aside to allow the speedy intro-duction of the new legislation that the leaders of all political parties had agreed to support. However, it soon became apparent that the then Shadow Government, the Socialist Party, along with the Scottish Nationalists, wanted the ban to extend so as to include .22 in rim-fire handguns. This resulted in the passing of two new Firearms (Amendment) Acts in quick succession. The first Bill being introduced by the then incumbent Conservative Government, in February, and the second by the Socialist Government in November of the same year after being voted into office.

When drafting the Bill for the Firearms (Amendment) Act 1997 it was necessary to define the class of weapon in mind, as past experience had shown that advocacy allowed the expressions 'pistol' or 'handgun' to be distorted almost beyond belief. A decision was soon reached to dispense with these terms and to adopt the approach used in the American legislation and within the recently introduced European Weapons Directive. This is to be found in Section 5(1)(aba) added to the Principal Act (Figure 2.8):

> any firearm which either has a barrel less than 30 centimetres in length or is less than 60 centimetres in length overall, other than an air weapon, a small-calibre pistol, a muzzle-loading gun or a firearm designed as signalling apparatus.

For the purposes of the above and for the changes introduced by the 1988 Amendment Act, Section 1(8) insists that any detachable, retractable or other

**Figure 2.8**    Author's .22 inch and .45 inch pistols, just prior to the Government's compulsory buy-in scheme introduced after the passing of the 1997 handgun legislation.

**Figure 2.9**    Zinc alloy imitation firearm resembling Colt .45 inch Model 1911-A1 self-loading pistol.

movable butt-stock shall be disregarded when measuring the length of any firearm (Figure 2.9). In the above sub-section the exemption allowed for air weapons only refers to those not sufficiently powerful so as to be deemed subject to the Firearms (Dangerous Air Weapons) Rules 1969, as amended in 1993. It was also necessary to introduce a definition for muzzle-loading guns to safeguard the exemption from abuse from certain members of the gun trade. These safeguards were similar to those built into the 1988 legislation, as prior to the passing of this legislation all manner of smooth-bore military firearms, including RPG anti-tank rocket launchers were being sold by some dealers as 'sporting shotguns'.

It was then necessary to modify sections of the 1988 legislation to remove the terms 'rifle' and 'carbine', and to modify other expressions to fit in with the newly introduced exemptions, to cater for certain pest control and humane killing of animals requirements, and to cover the starting pistols used in athletic meetings. Section 5(1A)(f) of the Principal Act had also to be replaced to cover all expanding ammunition and expanding pattern bullets used in the assembly of such loadings:

> any ammunition which incorporates a missile designed or adapted to expand on impact.

Once again, a provision was offered so that rifle owners involved in deer shooting or pest control could have a special variation written into their firearm certificates to cover the acquisition and purchase of expanding ammunition or bullets for those reloading their ammunition, in lieu of a Section 5 authority. By way of a concession to serious target shooters, the definition of air guns was amended to cover those arms using carbon dioxide gas as a propellant, thus avoiding the need for Section 5 control and hence inclusion into the prohibited category. A similar concession was made out in respect of shooters of muzzle-loading pistols, as these had little track record of use in crime.

Section 7 of the new Act was introduced by way of a response to the Parliamentary plea to preserve so-called 'heritage arms'. It allowed the continued ownership of certain handguns using rules and a vetting panel that considered their relative merit on the basis of their age, rarity or unusual provenance. This Section 7 allowed continued or limited ownership of handguns under two categories. The continued ownership of certain pistols at the owner's residence, subject to agreed conditions of security and without the provision of ammunition, was offered for those manufactured prior to 1 January 1919, and not chambered for use with cartridges contained in a proscribed calibre listing that included popular cartridges such as the 9 mm Luger. The second category of limited access ownership was offered for other handguns at specified secure heritage sites, where they could be displayed for viewing by interested students, and fired on rare occasions for demonstration purposes only.

The Firearms (Amendment)(No. 2) Act 1997 extended the ban to cover .22 inch rim-fire pistols and air pistols which were already subject to the Firearms (Dangerous Air Weapons) Rules 1969, as amended in 1993.

The Australian Government gave advance notification of severe changes in their own domestic firearms legislation within 10 days of their Port Arthur Incident, with the additional intention of applying them uniformly throughout the various States, which at that time applied very different measures of firearms control. A declaration was made that the civilian ownership of automatic and semi-automatic longarms posed an unacceptable degree of risk to the public, and that their use should be restricted to the military, the police and to professional hunters contracted to exterminate certain large feral animals. This prohibited Category D class of weapons includes self-loading centre-fire rifles designed or adapted for military purposes as well as nonmilitary, centre-fire self-loading rifles, self-loading or pump-action shotguns with magazine capacities of more than five rounds, and self-loading rim-fire rifles with magazine capacities greater than 10 rounds. All handguns, including air pistols, are placed in special restricted Category H.

The massacre of 14 women on 6 December 1989 at Montreal's Ecole Polytechnique by a man armed with a Ruger Mini 14 self-loading 5.56 mm rifle caused the Canadian Government to embark upon a course of phased legislative change concerning the registration, manufacture and importation of certain weapons, and the placing of certain types into the prohibited category. Compact, concealable handguns of .25 in (6.35 mm) or .32 in (7.65 mm) calibre possessing barrels less than 105 mm (4.14 in) in length cease to be regarded as viable 'target pistols'. A range of weapons described as assault pistols, shotguns or rifles (typified by the AK-47, AR-15, Mini-14 and FN/FAL rifles, the SPAS 15 shotgun and the Intratech TEC-9 pistol) are placed in this prohibited category (Figure 2.10). Additional restrictions are placed upon

**Figure 2.10**    Self-loading (semi-automatic) arms, sometimes mistakenly referred to as "assault weaponry." High fire-power arms of this type, along with their semi-automatic Kalashnikov counterpart, were picked up by legislative changes in the UK, the US, Canada and Australia after the high profile incidents described in Chapter 2. Seen above: US 'Ruger Mini-14' 5.56 mm carbine, Austrian 'Steyr AUG' 5.56 mm rifle, US 'Colt AR-15 Commando' 5.56 mm carbine, US 'Calico' 9 mm carbine with 50-round helical magazine, Israeli 'Mini Uzi' 9 mm carbine and US 'MAC-10' 9 mm carbine.

crossbows, replica firearms and the power of air weapons. The new prohibited category legislation does not however, have the same degree of retrospective status as that applied in Britain in the post-Hungerford 1988 legislation, in that existing owners of such registered prohibited arms are allowed the choice of their continued ownership for the remainder of their lives, but will not be allowed to transfer them.

It is interesting to note how much of the new or proposed firearms legislation around the world has now moved in the same direction as that which the British Government has taken. In the past, civilian target shooting using weapons similar to those used by the military was encouraged. It was seen to be a means of producing competent riflemen who would be of good service to their country in the event of any future conflict. It now seems that, with changes in social attitudes, the increase in drug-related crime and high-profile incidents of mass-murder, the consequences of the continued posses-sion of current-generation high-firepower weaponry is perceived by the authorities to demand an unacceptably high price to be paid in respect of public safety.

A contrary move has however taken place in a number of States in America, despite several additional high profile shooting incidents and Pres-ident Clinton's previous anti-gun stance. This has resulted in first Texas, and then a number of other States issuing permits authorising the concealed carry of handguns to members of the public for purposes of self-defence.

The origin of this trend goes back to 16 October 1991 when a pick-up truck driven by a George J. Hennard crashed through the front of Luby's Restaurant in Killeen, Texas. At first the diners went to his aid thinking that he had suffered a heart attack. However, Hennard then got out of the vehicle and began firing upon them causing the deaths of 22 and injuring others. He then killed himself after being wounded by police officers who later attended the scene.

Among the victims were Al and Ursula Gratia; their daughter Suzanne, who was dining with them, escaped injury. She later testified before the Texas State Legislature that she had left her own handgun in the car parked outside in order to comply with the then existing regulations. She then went on to say that she could have saved many lives if she had taken it with her into the restaurant, as she would have had several clear shots at Hennard. She gave similar evidence before hearings in other States as a witness supporting the American National Rifle Association's campaign to promote the concealed carry of handguns by adults without previous criminal convictions. During the November 1996 elections she was elected to the State House of Repre-sentatives.

## 2.3  Firearms and Crime

The type of weapon most frequently used in crime will be partially determined by the local firearms legislation in the country in question. In the UK for example, rifled arms have been subject to a far more stringent level of control than shotguns for a considerable number of years, and as a consequence smooth-bored guns, usually in the form of sawn-off shotguns, are a most popular weapon for use by criminals if only on account of their easy availability. Rifles feature infrequently in criminal casework in mainland Britain, even in their shortened form. Unlicensed service pistols and revolvers from past military endeavours are frequently encountered along with old revolvers manufactured around the turn of the nineteenth century and handguns acquired from the burglary of gunsmiths shops and from the homes of licensed target shooters; in a small but regrettable number of instances the owners of licensed weapons are also involved in serious offences.

In addition to the weapons from the above sources we also see revolvers used in crime which were manufactured during the second half of the nineteenth century; these revolvers are usually chambered for cartridge loadings which are still available today such as .22 in, .32 in, .320 in, .38 in, .380 in, .450 in and .455 in. In some instances, cartridges are also adapted to allow their use with some of these older weapons or the chambers are drilled out to allow the chambering of a more modern cartridge. As previously stated, old hammer shotguns, often in sawn-off form, frequently appear in criminal casework. The victim of a charge of shot fired from one of these 120-year-old Damascus-barrelled guns receives just the same injury as if the offence had been committed with a weapon of more recent manufacture. Despite the stated perils of using nitrocellulose propellant cartridges in old Damascus-barrelled guns of this period, I have never seen one burst when used in the commission of an offence of armed robbery or murder. Apart from encountering some old shotguns which had been converted from the pin-fire cartridge to the modern centre-fire system, I have dealt with one offence which involved the firing of modern 12-bore cartridges in a Lancaster shotgun of the type originally designed to fire a base-fire cartridge introduced in 1852. As this system was later replaced by the 'modern' cartridge system around 1862, the original owner had at some time in the past had it modified so as to allow its use with this new type of ammunition, which is of course dimensionally identical to modern shotgun ammunition.

During the late 1970s there followed a significant upturn in casework involving handguns, and this trend has continued in step with the dramatic increase in drug-related crime. This was caused by drug dealers and others associated with, or involved in, the trafficking of such materials choosing to go about their business constantly armed with a handgun. Such concealable weaponry in many instances replaced the more usual sawn-off shotgun previously taken out on isolated occasions for some specific task. The main increase was in the use of 9 mm self-loading pistols, although modern revolvers, including those chambered for magnum cartridge loadings, also featured significantly. Many of the incidents being dealt with from Northern cities enduring serious drug-related crime involved relatively young persons. A pattern of offences similar to that witnessed in the US developed, involving drive-by shootings and individual hits followed by consequent retaliation shootings. The relaxations in border controls which were a consequence of the progressive move towards European union also introduced a fear of an increase in the illegal import of firearms and ammunition, including weaponry from former members of the Communist Bloc.

However, during the early 1990s a significant number of handguns seized by the police, often in drug-related investigations, were found upon their subsequent examination at the laboratory to have originated from deactivated arms which had been freely exchanged under the provisions of Section 8 of the Firearms (Amendment) Act, 1988. Disturbing numbers of reactivated pistols and automatic weapons in the form of compact submachine guns and assault rifles were also encountered, particularly from the Northern cities previously referred to. The bulk of these automatic weapons had originated from legal importations of surplus military automatic arms by dealers possessing the necessary Home Office 'Prohibited Weapons' authority. The weapons, often of East European or Chinese origin, had been deactivated and inspected by the two official Proof House authorities, and subsequently passed on for sale to the general public. They had then been reactivated and their automatic-fire capability had been restored (Figure 2.11). In some instances the submachine guns involved proved to have been, at some previous time, variants of the newly prohibited self-loading rifles or carbines which had been marketed as 'target pistols' by a few dealers in an attempt to circumvent the provisions of the Firearms (Amendment) Act 1988 (Figure 2.12). In the past, automatic weaponry was only really encountered in mainland UK in casework involving terrorist activity. The emergence of this new class of military automatic weaponry in crime other than terrorism was regarded as a disturbing escalation in criminal activity. Although initially these weapons were reactivated by crude techniques often employing lengths of unrifled tubing of suitable bore as replacement barrels, there followed a steady upturn in the standard of reactivation as skills were learned by a few individuals having access to more sophisticated machining and welding equipment. Replacement rifled barrels machined from rifled barrel blanks became commonplace. Significant numbers of these arms had been reactivated by a common pattern of machining operations which clearly indicated

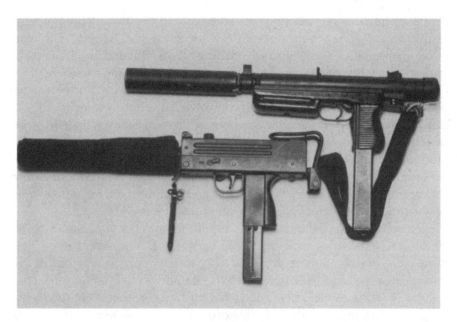

**Figure 2.11**    Reactivated arms. Czech CZ25 9 mm submachine gun with silencer and Ingram MAC-10 9 mm submachine gun with silencer.

**Figure 2.12**    Post Firearms (Amendment) Act 1988 5.56 millimetre self-loading AR-18 design based carbine fitted with 90-round drum magazine, marketed as a "target pistol." The screw used for providing additional security for attaching the shoulder stock to its body was not supplied, and the title "Pistol" was inscribed upon its side, in an attempt to circumvent the ban on self-loading centre-fire rifles and carbines.

the involvement of particular operators. Most of the items of this nature were recovered during police drug raids.

A review of the deactivation standards had already been authorised to deal with certain difficulties encountered by the two Proof Masters of the Gun Barrel Proof Houses in their day-to-day activities with members of the Gun Trade. The casework developments caused this review to be speeded up and reconsideration made as to its scope. In this respect I was assisted by the two Proof Masters, and in the latter stages with suggestions made by the Gun Trade Association in drafting the new standards which were introduced by the Home Office Minister David Maclean on 1 October 1995, with the simultaneous release of the uprated and greatly expanded deactivation standards, printed in a loose-leaf binder to form a living document which could be altered or added to in the future as the need arose. The standards of deactivation for all types of arms were upgraded or simplified, while those in respect of portable automatic weaponry and arms based upon these designs, (sub-machine guns, assault rifles and self-loading centre-fire rifles and carbines), were set to a far stricter standard. It was accepted, however, that even these standards would not afford complete proof against dedicated individuals using sophisticated machining facilities, although it would make the task involved far more onerous and thus less attractive. One of the effects of the tightened UK legislation has been the criminal restoration of officially deactivated firearms, the conversion of blank-firing handguns to allow their use with bulleted ammunition, and the conversion of air weapons. In past years a modest number of converted spring-powered, barrel-cocking .22 in (5.6 mm) air rifles and pistols were received at the laboratory I worked in. The most common method of adaptation would involve the reduction in length of the mainspring to reduce its power, drilling out the exposed breech end of the barrel to allow the chambering of a .22 in rim-fire bulleted cartridge, and the fitting of a firing pin of suitable shape in the air-transfer port at the end of the compression chamber. However, in recent years converted air cartridge pistols and revolvers have become commonplace in a spate of drug-related incidents in the UK. The Brocock-type air cartridge weapons utilise a rechargeable patent air cartridge closely resembling a conventional centre-fire cartridge. The air guns that use them are made to a similar design to that used for conventional centre-fire weapons. The air reservoirs of the cartridges are charged with compressed air from a hand pump or diver's compressed air bottle, followed by the insertion of an air gun pellet in a recess in the cartridge nose. The forcible impact of the gun's firing pin upon the base of the cartridge opens up a valve that allows the escape of the compressed air behind the pellet.

The modification to the revolver air cartridge guns usually involves drilling out the brass air cartridge body, or the provision of a turned steel chamber sleeve, so as to allow the firing of .22 in rim-fire ammunition or 8 mm blank cartridges. In the case of the conversion to centre-fire blank cartridge use, an air gun pellet or other missile of suitable bore size is inserted into the cup-shaped recess in the frangible plastic cartridge closure. I have recently encountered .22 in air cartridge revolvers adapted to fire .22 in centre-fire 'Hornet' cartridges, by simply fitting lengths of metal tubing of suitable bore diameter into the cylinder chambers. Self-loading design air cartridge pistols use a smaller size rimless air cartridge, which is dimensionally similar to the 9 mm PA blank cartridge. Here the only adaptation, apart from perhaps the reshaping of the flat firing pin, is to insert a .22 in missile in the cup-shaped recess in the plastic closure wad in the end of the cartridge. The Firearms Consultative Committee have discussed this relatively recent trend, and the Government have now banned the marketing of this type of air weapon. A further effect of the tightened legislation in recent years has been an upturn in the number of converted blank pistols and revolvers used in drug-related crime. Most of these guns were originally made with hard blockages contained inside the soft die-cast alloy barrels and cylinders to prevent their use with bulleted ammunition. Guns chambered for 8 mm K, 9 mm PA and .380 in/9 mm blank cartridges feature the most, the first two being self-loading pistols. In most instances the original blocked alloy barrels are replaced in whole or in part with plain unrifled steel tubing of appropriate length, chambered for use with adapted blank cartridges or common commercial bulleted ammunition. It is not uncommon for some of these successful conversions to involve the use of the relatively powerful 9 mm Luger cartridge.

The degree of control on the possession and transfer of firearms varies a great deal from one country to another. In the US regulations vary from state to state, particularly in respect of handguns and how they can be transported. The many opponents of gun control argue that in the end it is only the law abiding citizens who are likely to obey the law, and that in effect more stringent controls restrict the otherwise legitimate pursuits of decent people and at the same time do nothing to constrain the actions of determined criminals. In the US the Second Amendment is seen to define a true democracy in terms of the right of the citizens to keep and bear arms, rather than to apply to the authorities for the necessary authority, which in turn is likely to be reluctantly granted as a special concession or privilege. It is often argued also that the widespread possession of firearms by members of the public can act as a deterrent to crime against the person. The authorities, on the other hand, will argue that free access to firearms will inevitably result in their increased criminal use, particularly in respect of domestic crime and accidents involving young persons in the home. I will leave it to others to argue the merits of their particular causes elsewhere; however it is interesting to look at the following statistics contained in a Canadian report published in 1995. In order to consider the great differences in population of the countries involved, rates are expressed in terms of suicides and homicides involving the use of firearms per 100,000 head of population. The most recent figures were used in compiling these statistics in 1995; in some instances they represent the average values over several years (Table 2.1). The homicide figures involving firearms for France and for Switzerland above include attempted murders.

The UK, with a population of 51.4 million, recorded eight accidental deaths caused by firearms in 1992. Firearm ownership is estimated at 1.7 million legally held firearms, of which 1.32 million were shotguns. A firearm certificate, issued by the Chief Officer of Police of the location in which the applicant resides, was required in respect of handguns, rifles, bulleted ammunition, large-magazine-capacity pump-action or self-loading shotguns, and conventional shotguns of barrel length less than 60.96 cm (24 in). Good reasons must be tendered for every acquisition in advance before the certificate is varied to authorise each transfer or purchase. Such good reasons will include membership of a recognised shooting club with a range safety certificate allowing the particular type of firearm and calibre involved. Authorisation for use of a rifle for sporting purposes must initially involve the applicant having written permission from the landowner of the suitable ground; in some instances the police will carry out a land inspection to ensure that it is safe for the purposes envisaged. All firearms and ammunition must be kept under secure conditions of storage; in some instances the police or their crime prevention officers will request sight of the storage facilities and may insist upon changes being made. Authorisations for use of a handgun for sporting purposes are relatively rare and will need to be supported by good reason for the carrying of this type of weapon. An application for a firearm for self-defence is not recognised as constituting good reason except

**Table 2.1  Incidence of Homicide and Suicide Involving Firearms vs. Gun Ownership in Different Countries**

| Country | Suicides | Homicides | Firearms Ownership |
|---------|----------|-----------|--------------------|
| Canada | 3.6 | 0.67 | 24138 |
| Australia | 2.5 | 0.36 | 19444 |
| New Zealand | 2.5 | 0.49 | 29412 |
| Japan | 0.14 | 0.06 | 414 |
| Switzerland | 5.8 | 1.4 | 42857 |
| UK | 0.4 | 0.14 | 3307 |
| France | 4.9 | 2.32 | 22.6% of households |
| US | 7.1 | 6.4 | 85385 |

in very special cases. Paragraph 6.8 (h) of the Home Office publication *Firearms Law: Guidance to the Police*, states:

> Applications for the grant of a firearms certificate for the applicant's protection or that of his premises should be refused on the grounds that firearms are not regarded as an acceptable form of protection in this country. This principle should be maintained even in the case of applications from representatives of banks and firms who desire to protect valuables or large quantities of money.

This contrasts sharply with the situation in the US where most handguns and many firearms are purchased for home security or self-defence. A certificate will not be issued to persons of known intemperate habits or of an irresponsible nature. Convictions for drunk driving, drug offences, domestic violence or similar incidents will constitute good reason for the revocation of a certificate. Persons who have previously been sentenced to serve a period of imprisonment or other form of detention in excess of three months shall constitute 'prohibited persons' in respect of the possession of any firearm or ammunition for a period of five years. Persons having been sentenced to periods of imprisonment in excess of three years are 'prohibited persons' for the rest of their lives.

The certificate controls the amount of ammunition which can be purchased or possessed at any one time and includes the recording of any such transfer in the firearm certificate. Transfers of firearms must be notified within a short time period to the police authorities involved. A firearm or shotgun certificate has a life of five years and must be renewed before the end of this period by way of a formal application, otherwise the firearms must be disposed of to persons possessing the necessary authority.

Canada, with a population of 25.15 million, recorded 63 fatal accidents with firearms. Private ownership of firearms is approximately 7 million. Australia, with a population of 18 million, recorded an annual rate of 18 accidents with firearms at the time of the report. Private ownership of firearms is approximately 3.5 million.

New Zealand, having a population of 3.4 million, recorded four accidental firearm deaths in 1993 against an average of 6.2 between 1988 and 1993. Private ownership of firearms is approximately 1 million.

Japan, having a population of 125 million, recorded 57 fatal accidents involving firearms in 1993. Japan has the most restrictive firearms controls in the world. In 1991, 517,675 licensed firearms were held, of which 474,252 were rifles or shotguns.

Switzerland, with a population of 7 million, recorded 84 firearms injuries in 1993. Firearms ownership is estimated to be somewhere between 3 million and 12 million; 60 per cent of which are military weapons.

France, having a population of 57 million, has no data available at national level on firearm accidents. In 1989, it was estimated that 22.6 per cent of all households possessed firearms of some kind.

The US, with a population of 260 million, recorded 1441 fatal accidents involving firearms in 1991. It has been estimated that there are 222 million firearms in the possession of its citizens at the beginning of 1994, of which 76 million were handguns.

Official Home Office statistics for the criminal use of firearms in England and Wales for the period 1985 to 1994 give some insight into shifts in the rates of use of different firearms in serious crime. These figures are for England and Wales and relate initially to homicides and secondly to attempted murders which have involved the use of firearms. Table 2.2 shows the figures for attempted murders and also includes other serious acts such as wounding and endangering life.

**Table 2.2   Home Office Statistics for the Criminal Use of Firearms in England and Wales**

| Year | Shotguns | S/O Shotguns | Pistols | Rifles | Air |
|------|----------|--------------|---------|--------|-----|
| 1985 h | 22 | 7 | 8 | 6 | 1 |
| w | 125 | 32 | 57 | 1 | 99 |
| 1986 h | 31 | 6 | 10 | 0 | 0 |
| w | 134 | 45 | 40 | 9 | 87 |
| 1987 h | 33 | 10 | 10 | 15 | 0 |
| w | 201 | 40 | 58 | 39 | 124 |
| 1988 h | 19 | 8 | 7 | 0 | 1 |
| w | 200 | 70 | 65 | 7 | 125 |
| 1989 h | 19 | 7 | 13 | 2 | 3 |
| w | 216 | 41 | 81 | 8 | 146 |
| 1990 h | 25 | 8 | 22 | 1 | 1 |
| w | 173 | 65 | 114 | 9 | 191 |
| 1991 h | 25 | 7 | 19 | 2 | 2 |
| w | 200 | 70 | 199 | 20 | 192 |
| 1992 h | 20 | 5 | 28 | 3 | 0 |
| w | 182 | 69 | 193 | 15 | 207 |
| 1993 h | 29 | 10 | 35 | 0 | 0 |
| w | 192 | 95 | 270 | 13 | 200 |
| 1994 h | 22 | 14 | 25 | 5 | 0 |
| w | 203 | 64 | 267 | 14 | 207 |

Note: *h* = homicide, *w* = wounding

The statistics are interesting in that they confirm the relatively low incidence of rifles used in serious offences apart from the 'blip' caused by the
pick-up of figures from the Hungerford incident, which involved the use of
a semi-automatic Kalashnikov rifle, which in turn created the political mood
for additional restrictive legislation. The figures for 1989 onwards show a
continuing upward trend in the use of handguns; many of these crimes are
drug-related. The relative figures for woundings versus weapons type should
be treated with caution as they do include reported injuries involving the use
of air weapons, where the nature of the injury can vary greatly with the power
of the weapon involved. However, it is true to say that a significant number
of people receive serious injuries as a result of air weapon misuse, and the
statistics indicate an average close to one fatal air weapon wounding each
year. As a matter of technical interest however, I can only recall one fatal
incident over the years I have been working in this field, where an air weapon
of a type which would be declared especially dangerous was involved.

## 2.4   The Firearms Consultative Committee

The Firearms Consultative Committee is a statutory body set up under Section 22 of the Firearms (Amendment) Act 1988. Members appointed to the
Committee are chosen from those who appear to the Home Secretary to have
the knowledge and experience of the possession, use (in particular for sport
or competition) or keeping of, or transactions in firearms; or weapon technology; or the administration or enforcement of the provisions of the Firearms Acts. The Committee shall consist of a chairman and not less than 12
other members appointed by the Secretary of State.

Under Section 22(8) of the 1988 Act the Committee initially existed for
a period of five years from 1 February 1989. The life of the Committee was
extended for a further three years until 31 January 1997. Lord Shrewsbury
assumed the Chairmanship from Lord Kimball from 1 August 1994 and was
appointed until 31 January 1997. Members of the Committee are appointed
for a period of two years, which may be renewed. There have been a number
of changes to the compliment of the Committee since its inception.

The function of the Committee is to keep under review the working of
the provisions of the Principal Act of 1968 and all subsequent firearms
legislation and to make to the Secretary of State such recommendations as
the Committee may from time to time think necessary for the improvement
of the working of those provisions. It may make proposals for amending
those provisions as it thinks fit and advise the Secretary of State on any other
matter relating to those provisions which he may refer to the Committee.

The Committee shall in each year make a report on its activities to the Secretary of State who shall lay copies of the report before Parliament.

The Committee membership has included up to this date the Head of F8 Division of the Home Office along with supportive secretariat staff, two chief constables representing police firearm interests in England and Wales and in Scotland, the Chief Crown Prosecutor for the South East Area of the Crown Prosecution Service, the Head of the Police Division of the Scottish Office and a member of the firearms reporting staff of the Huntingdon Forensic Science Service Laboratory; in this latter respect it has been my privilege to serve the Committee for 9 years. Other members have included the Keeper of Exhibits and Firearms at the Imperial War Museum, The Proof Master of the Worshipful Company of Gunmakers of the City of London, a Scottish Advocate and Queens Counsel, the Chairman or Firearms Officer of the British Association for Shooting and Conservation, the Chairman of the Gun Trade Association, the Chief Executive of the National Rifle Association, a Barrister and Tutor in Law who was also coauthor of a book on firearms law, the President of the Clay Pigeon Shooters Association, City councillors for the two main political parties who also have firearms-related backgrounds and interests, well-known international sporting shooters, gun and rifle makers or managers of sporting shoots. Most of these members will also be regular shooters whose interests will cover all imaginable forms of sporting and target shooting interests. Members of the Committee are however expected to serve as individuals upon the Committee despite any other declared interests or positions.

The Committee holds meetings throughout the year at the Home Office building in Queen Anne's Gate London, and at other locations of interest which include Bisley and at least one suitably historic venue in Scotland. A work programme is drawn up and released to the press each year. The Committee considers each topic in turn at the meetings, and also listens to the presentations of the conclusions of the work of subcommittees on special interest topics drawn up from the membership but often also including co-opted external representatives. Consideration is also given to written submissions from committee members, outside interest groups and some individuals, which have been submitted to the Secretariat over the year; these inputs can in turn create an extension to the previously published work programme. At the end of each working year the membership is given time to consider or advise upon the need for change in the draft report of events drawn by the Secretariat from the various meetings which have taken place over the year. A small drafting group is then drawn from the membership to consider these issues and to agree upon a final draft for publication which truly represents the consensus viewpoint of the Committee and which will also indicate if there had been any differences in opinions voiced at the meetings on some issues. The chairman then presents the final publication to the Home Secretary which is published in mid-July for distribution to Parliament and to the public through Her Majesty's Stationery Office outlets. The Secretary of State then gives consideration to the various proposals contained in the report. Acceptable proposals which do not require primary legislation for their implementation may be put into effect very quickly; others requiring changes in the law have to await the arrival of the necessary Parliamentary time. In some instances where there is seen to be the need for rapid implementation to deal with some pressing matter changes can be carried out mid-term once the solution has been identified by the Committee. Of course, it is true to say that not all of the suggestions made by the Committee will be approved. In some instances this may result in the particular topic being revisited in the following work programme in the hope of finding some other course of action, although inevitably there will be some topics left unresolved. In 2004 the Government wound up the activities of the Firearms Consultative Committee.

## 2.5   The European Weapons Directive

The Council Directive of 18 June 1991 of the Council of the European Communities relating to the uniform control of the acquisition and possession of weapons within the Member States provides minimum common standards of firearm control. Individual Member States at present have the right to apply more stringent domestic standards to suit their own particular needs. Four classes of firearms are recognised. The movement of these firearms within the Member States is subject to a sliding scale of control.

### 2.5.1   Category A — Prohibited Firearms

1. Explosive military missiles and launchers
2. Automatic firearms (this includes burst-fire arms)
3. Firearms disguised as other objects
4. Ammunition with penetrating, explosive or incendiary projectiles, and the projectiles for such ammunition
5. Pistol and revolver ammunition with expanding projectiles and the projectiles for such ammunition, except in the case of weapons for hunting or for target shooting, for persons entitled to use them

### 2.5.2   Category B — Firearms Subject to Authorisation

1. Semi-automatic or repeating short firearms
2. Single-shot centre-fire short firearms

3. Single-shot rim-fire short firearms of less than 28 cm length
4. Semi-automatic long firearms where the magazine and chamber together are capable of holding more than three cartridges
5. Semi-automatic long firearms of less than three-shot capacity, with removable magazines or which can be adapted using simple tooling to hold more than three cartridges
6. Repeating and semi-automatic long smooth-bore firearms not exceeding 60 cm in length
7. Semi-automatic firearms for civilian use which resemble automatic weaponry

### 2.5.3   Category C — Firearms Subject to Declaration

1. Repeating long firearms other than those listed in category B, point 6
2. Long single-shot rifled firearms
3. Semi-automatic long firearms other than those in category B, points 4 to 7
4. Short single-shot rim-fire firearms of not less than 28 cm length

### 2.5.4   Category D — Other Firearms

#### 2.5.4.1   *Single-Shot, Long Smooth-Bore Firearms*

The expression single-shot can refer to multibarrelled guns, such as double-barrelled shotguns. It does not refer to single-barrelled repeating magazine arms.

1. A short firearm is one with a barrel not exceeding 30 cm or whose overall length does not exceed 60 cm.
2. A long firearm means any firearm other than a short firearm.
3. Automatic means capable of discharging more than one round each time the trigger is pulled.
4. Semi-automatic arms reload automatically each time a round is fired by pulling the trigger.
5. Repeating arms are manually operated magazine fed weapons.

## 2.6   Legislation in the US

Firearms legislation varies between different countries, and in the US some aspects of its interpretation may vary between states and cities, particularly in respect of handguns and how they can be carried. The National Firearms Act contains a definition of certain firearms which are subject to special control through the Bureau of Alcohol Tobacco and Firearms and the imposition of a Federal transfer tax. These include:

1. Shotguns possessing barrels less than 18 in long
2. Weapons made from a shotgun, if such weapons as modified have overall lengths of less than 26 in, or barrels less than 18 in long
3. Rifles having barrels less than 16 in long
4. Weapons made from rifles which are less than 26 in long, or which have barrels less than 16 in long
5. Any other weapon, as defined in category D, (5): a machine gun; a muffler or silencer; destructive devices. An exemption is offered for antique firearms, other than machine guns or destructive devices, for which, although designed as a weapon, if the Secretary or his delegate finds by reason of the date of its manufacture, value, design and other characteristics, it is primarily a collector's item and is not likely to be used as a weapon.

At the time of beginning to write this book some radical changes were made in the American legislation under the Clinton administration relating to so-called 'assault weapons', making it unlawful for a person to manufacture, transfer, or possess a semiautomatic assault weapon. The term 'assault weapon' goes back to the German weapons development which took place during World War II. The title *Sturmgewehr* was used in respect of a selective-fire rifle designed to fire a 7.92×33 mm Kurz cartridge which was intermediate in power between conventional pistol and rifle ammunition (Figure 2.13). The rifle was relatively cheap to manufacture and was more control-

**Figure 2.13**   World War II German Sturmgewer Stg .44 assault rifle, chambered for the intermediate power 7.92 mm Kurz cartridge, gave Kalashnikov the inspiration during combat he experienced on the Eastern Front, to design the AK47 and AKM assault rifles, chambered for a cartridge of similar power, the M.43 7.62x 39 mm.

lable when fired in the automatic mode due to the lower recoil of the cartridge compared with standard 7.92×57 mm rifle ammunition. In this respect the term, which is loosely used in the US legislation, is something of a misnomer and has since taken on sinister and emotive connotations.

The American assault weapons legislation differs markedly from the British Firearms (Amendment) Act 1988, which targeted a similar class of weaponry, in that it is not retrospective. It can only be applied, therefore, to weapons and magazines manufactured from 1 October 1993. So-called assault weapons possessed prior to this date may be retained and transferred in a normal manner. The term 'semi-automatic assault weapon' means the following:

1.  Any of the firearms, or copies or duplicates of the firearms in any calibre, known as
    a.  Norinco, Mitchell, and Poly Technologies Avtomat Kalashnikova (all models)
    b.  Action Arms Israeli Military Industries UZI and Galil
    c.  Beretta Ar70 (SC-70)
    d.  Colt AR-15
    e.  Fabrique National FN/FAL, FN/LAR and FNC
    f.  SWD M-10, M-11, M-11/9 and M-12
    g.  Steyr AUG
    h.  INTRATEC TEC-9, TEC-DC9 and TEC-22
    i.  revolving cylinder shotguns, such as (or similar to) The Street Sweeper and Striker 12
2.  A semi-automatic rifle that has an ability to accept a detachable magazine and has at least two of the following:
    a.  a folding or telescoping stock
    b.  a pistol grip that protrudes conspicuously beneath the action of the weapon
    c.  a bayonet mount
    d.  a flash suppressor or threaded barrel designed to accommodate a flash suppressor
    e.  a grenade launcher
3.  A semi-automatic pistol that has an ability to accept a detachable magazine and has at least two of the following:
    a.  an ammunition magazine that attaches to the pistol outside of the pistol grip
    b.  a threaded barrel capable of accepting a barrel extender, flash suppressor, forward handgrip or silencer
    c.  a shroud that is attached to, or partially encircles the barrel and that permits the shooter to hold the firearm with the non-trigger hand without being burned

      d. a manufactured weight of 50 oz or more when the pistol is un-
         loaded
      e. a semi-automatic version of an automatic firearm
4. A semi-automatic shotgun that has at least two of the following:
      a. a folding or telescoping stock
      b. a pistol grip that protrudes conspicuously beneath the action of
         the weapon
      c. a fixed magazine capacity in excess of 5 rounds
      d. an ability to accept a detachable magazine

The new legislation also contains a ban on the possession or transfer of large capacity magazines or other ammunition feeding devices. The term 'large capacity ammunition feeding device' is provided. It means a magazine, belt, drum, feed strip or similar device manufactured after the date of enactment of the Violent Crime Control and Law Enforcement Act of 1994 that has a capacity of, or that can be readily restored or converted to accept, more than 10 rounds of ammunition; but it does not include an attached tubular device designed to accept, and capable of operating only with .22 calibre rimfire ammunition.

Additionally, large capacity ammunition feeding devices manufactured after the date of the enactment of this sentence shall be identified by a serial number that clearly shows that the device was manufactured or imported after the effective date of this subsection, and such other information as the Secretary may by regulation prescribe.

It is unlikely that this legislation will be upheld with universal enthusiasm by all parties in a country such as the US, and it is common knowledge that a considerable quantity of large capacity magazines were manufactured just prior to the commencement date, presumably to service future sales transactions. However, it is interesting to note the number of very similar elements contained in the UK, the European Community and the US firearms legislation. These of course relate to an apparent officially held antipathy towards the ownership of high firepower weaponry by civilian target shooters or hunters. In turn this appears to have been reflected in the similarity in response towards high-profile incidents in which apparently deranged persons have used such weaponry in mass-shootings. In the UK, the Hungerford incident, which involved the use of a semi-automatic Chinese manufactured Kalashnikov rifle (Figure 2.4), invoked a rapid legislative response in the form of the Firearms (Amendment) Act 1988. In previous times target shooting, using weaponry similar to that employed by the Military, was encouraged, as it was seen to be a means of producing competent riflemen who would be of good service to their country in the event of any future conflict. In some respects this seems to have been changed to refer only to previous generation weaponry.

## Further Reading

A Review of Firearm Statistics and Regulations in Selected Countries. 1995. Research Statistics and Evaluation Directorate, Department of Justice, Canada.

Anti-Social Behaviour Act 2003. The Stationery Office.

Arms and Ammunition. *The Firearms (Amendment) Act 1997. (Transitional Provisions and Savings) Regulations 1997.*

Arms and Ammunition. *The Firearms Acts (Amendment) Regulations 1992.* HMSO.

Arms and Ammunition. *The Firearms (Amendment) Rules 1992.* HMSO.

Arms and Ammunition. *The Firearms (Dangerous Air Weapons) (Amendment) Rules 1993.* HMSO.

Arms and Ammunition. *The Firearms (Dangerous Air Weapons) Rules 1969.* HMSO.

Arms and Ammunition. *The Firearms (Dangerous Air Weapons) (Scotland) Amendment Rules 1993.* HMSO.

Arms and Ammunition. *The Firearms (Dangerous Air Weapons) (Scotland) Rules 1969.* HMSO.

Arms and Ammunition. *The Firearms (Museums) Order 1997.* The Stationery Office Limited.

Arms and Ammunition. *The Firearms Rules 1989.* HMSO.

Bisley. The National Shooting Centre. (1994) The National Rifle Association – Bisley Camp.

Consumer Protection. *The Novelties (Safety) Regulations 1980.* HMSO.

*Crossbows Act 1987.* HMSO.

*Firearms Act 1968.* HMSO.

*Firearms Act 1982.* HMSO.

*Firearms (Amendment) Act 1988.* HMSO.

*Firearms (Amendment) Act 1992.* HMSO.

*Firearms (Amendment) Act 1994.* HMSO.

*Firearms (Amendment) Act 1997 : The Law on Guns of Historic Interest.* The Home Departments.

*Firearms (Amendment) Act 1997.* The Stationery Office Limited.

*Firearms (Amendment) (No. 2) Act 1997.* The Stationery Office Limited.

The Firearms Consultative Committee, *Third Annual Report.* 1992. HMSO.

*Firearms Law: Guidance to the Police.* 1989. HMSO.

*Firearms Law: Specifications for the Adaptation of Shot Gun Magazines and the Deactivation of Firearms.* 1995 Revision. HMSO.

*Guidance Notes No. 2. Captive-Bolt Stunning of Livestock. 2nd Edition.* 1998. The Humane Slaughter Association.

*Guidance Notes No. 3. Humane Killing of Livestock Using Firearms.* 1999. The Humane Slaughter Association.

Guidelines on the Design, Construction or Adaptation of Imitation Fire-arms. *The Firearms Act 1982.* HMSO.

Murray K. 2003. Identifications based on firing pin channel impressions. *AFTE Journal,* **35** (3).

Possession of Handguns. (1996). House of Commons Home Affairs Committee. Fifth Report Volume 1. HMSO.

The Public Inquiry into the Shootings at Dunblane Primary School on 13 March 1996—The Government Response. The Scottish Office. Cm 3392. The Stationery Office.

The Public Inquiry into the Shootings at Dunblane Primary School on 13 March 1996. The Scottish Office. Cm 3386. The Stationery Office.

Warlow, T. 1994. 'La Derettiva Europea e il Regno Unito', presentation at the Decimo Convegno Nazionale di Studio Sulla Disciplina delle Armi, Brescia Chamber of Commerce, Italy.

Warlow, T.A. 1996. Recent trends in the criminal use of firearms, *Science and Justice,* **36** (1), 55–58.

Warlow, T.A. 1997. Legislative Responses To The Criminal Use Of Firearms. *Contact* 25,3-8. Information Services—The Forensic Science Service.

# Marks and Microscopy: The Emergence of a New Science

# 3

## 3.1 The Pioneers

The association of a missile with the particular weapon from which it was discharged is not in itself a new science. Roman legions used to impose their emblems upon the cast lead missiles used by their slingers. About the same period in which firearms were first introduced, English archers were in the habit of putting distinctive marks upon their arrows. Most nineteenth century hunters in America used to cast their own bullets, either for use with their muzzle-loading arms or for reloading metallic ammunition. Juries in the courts of the period were able to examine a recovered bullet and compare it themselves directly with the particular pattern of mould used by the suspect in the making of his ammunition.

On 2 May 1862 General 'Stonewall' Jackson received an injury to his left arm and right hand when returning to his own lines. Dr. Hunter McGuire recovered a .675 in spherical ball from the hand during treatment which also involved the amputation of the left arm; despite the good doctor's efforts the General subsequently died. Investigations conducted at the time came to the conclusion that the General had been accidentally shot by his own side by a bullet fired from a Confederate smooth-bore musket, as the Union Army had abandoned the use of such obsolete weaponry the previous year.

The death of the Union General Sedgewick was subjected to similar scrutiny. In this instance, the long .451 in bullet recovered had clearly been fired from an English muzzle-loading percussion Whitworth rifle which was bored with a distinctive hexagonal form of rifling. The Whitworth rifle was noted for its great potential accuracy. It was later claimed that the shot had been fired by a Sergeant Grace of the Fourth Georgia Infantry from a distance of 800 yd.

In June 1900 an article appeared in *The Buffalo Medical Journal* written by Albert Llewellyn Hall expressing the results of his findings over the years of his medical practice concerning firearm-related injuries and techniques which could be used in the identification of the crime bullets.

In 1907, staff of the Frankfurt Arsenal were asked to conduct examinations on fired cartridge cases and bullets against a number of .30 in rifles which were suspected of having been used by soldiers who had rioted in Brownsville, Texas. From their observations of the operational markings left upon the spent cartridge cases they were able to place 33 of them into four groups which in turn could be attributed to four of the suspect weapons. They were unable however, to form any firm conclusions with the remaining six cartridge cases or the bullets. During this period the investigators had, in effect, acquired the basic skills of a science which would be subject to considerable development in the following years. Unfortunately their work received little publicity and was effectively buried by the then incumbent Chief of Ordnance.

From about 1912 onwards, a Professor Balthazard working independently at the University of Paris, learned the fundamental principles of what would later become the forensic examination of fired cartridge cases and bullets. The Professor took a series of photographs around the circumferences of both the crime bullet and a test-fired bullet from the suspect weapon. The process of examination was of course laborious, especially when one considers the equipment and materials used at the time. Additional difficulties were encouraged with badly damaged bullets. Other experimenters around this same period used more direct techniques such as rolling the bullet along a piece of soft lead, or a sheet of carbon paper held on top of a piece of plain white paper to get an impression of the bore features left upon the exterior of the bullet. Again, difficulties were encountered even with this simple technique if the bullets exhibited impact deformation.

## 3.2   Experts and Charlatans — The American Experience

Meanwhile, in the US this was the Golden Age for quack ballisticians who travelled from court to court ever eager to offer their services, for the right price, to anyone sufficiently gullible or corrupt to pay their fees. Articulate in speech and able to perform impressively in public, in some other life these people would have made passable snake oil salesmen or lapsed preachers. At that time there was a general ignorance concerning firearms matters within the judiciary which was only matched by a childlike willingness to believe in the claimed expertise of these charlatans. It would be reassuring, but incorrect, to say that such creatures do not exist even today, both in the UK and US.

The famous murder trial of Charlie Stielow in 1915 in New York was one in which the so-called 'expert' evidence secured a conviction. The jury brought in a guilty verdict based on the dubious evidence of the ballistics expert. As this would normally invoke death by the electric chair, Stielow was pressed by his counsel to confess (at last) to the murder in a deal struck in exchange for a reduction in sentence to 20 years' imprisonment. The verdict was upheld despite a number of appeals on behalf of Stielow. On 4 December 1916 the State Governor, uneasy about the verdicts, ordered a Syracuse lawyer George H. Bond to investigate the matter further with the assistance of a Mr. Waite from the Attorney General's office. Subsequent investigations, which included the results of firing tests conducted with Stielow's revolver and the assistance of properly qualified people, finally resulted in a pardon from the Governor. The real differences between the test-fired bullets from Stielow's revolver and the recovered murder bullets were glaringly obvious, as was the falsehood of some of the previous 'expert evidence'.

After the satisfactory conclusion of the case Waite travelled about the country to a number of firearm manufacturers in order to accumulate as much information as was possible concerning firearm manufacturing methods and standards. Over this period he managed to accumulate a mass of data on both firearms and ammunition. At a later stage three of his associates went on to use the information contained in this data bank. Major Calvin Goddard, a doctor and former member of staff of the Ordnance Corps who also possessed an outstanding knowledge of firearms, was assisted by Philip O. Gravelle, a trained microscopist, and John E. Fisher, an experienced person in machining methods. They went on to work in a small laboratory in New York, firing and testing weapons and ammunition. In April 1925 they purchased one of the newly introduced comparison microscopes which they put to good service. This instrument now offered the direct and simultaneous comparison of bullets and cartridge cases.

Waite was involved with the production of two articles which appeared in the *Saturday Evening Post* in Philadelphia in June of the same year entitled 'Fingerprinting Bullets'. Major Goddard also became a prodigious writer of technical articles on the same subject, operating from a private organisation called the 'Bureau of Forensic Ballistics'. Gradually police departments and the courts became aware of the value of the new and very real expertise which was on hand, and he gave evidence on many occasions to courts throughout the East. One notable case concerned the St. Valentine's Day Massacre on 14 February 1929.

Goddard visited 13 countries in Western Europe, spending time in their medico-legal institutes and crime laboratories. Goddard became the head of the 'Scientific Criminal Investigation Laboratory' which opened in April 1930 and which was associated with Northwestern University in Illinois. The curriculum of the FBI National Police Academy, which was established by the Federal Bureau of Investigation in 1935, included lectures on firearms identification. During the early 1930s the true science of firearms identification was established.

## 3.3   Court Battles — The English Experience

Back in England Robert Churchill ran the firm of gunsmiths of the same name at various addresses in London, which included 32 Orange Street, Leicester Square. About the same period a Major Gerald Burrard lived at Willow Lodge, Hungerford, Berkshire, a sleepy English country town which was later to become the scene of a massacre involving a Kalashnikov rifle, which in turn precipitated the restrictive firearms legislation of 1988. Robert Churchill teamed up with Sir Bernard Spilsbury, a Home Office pathologist, and they gave evidence together to the courts on firearms cases over a 50-year period. In 1927, Churchill visited Major Goddard at the Bureau of Forensic Ballistics in New York. On his return he arranged for the firm Watsons to build him a comparison microscope for his own use. Churchill was a colourful character who did not see eye to eye with this other expert; it would be fair comment to say that the feelings were mutual, and that they were freely expressed in public on a number of occasions. Churchill came to be identified as the Home Office firearms expert of the period, operating as a forensic double act in criminal investigations and when giving expert evidence to the courts with his pathologist friend Sir Bernard Spilsbury. He jealously guarded this standing against all comers who might usurp his position, and in particular—Burrard. The two were archrivals. Churchill saw himself and his cosy relationship with Spilsbury, in a secure position as both 'top dog' and the establishment's preferred expert. Burrard, with his media connections and outlets questioned both Churchill's commercial judgement and also the integrity of his evidence given to the courts. He hounded him continuously and, in the trial of George Kitchin, called in a gaggle of experts to help 'expose' him; one of these experts, Greener, was also very much a commercial rival.

To understand some measure of the antipathy involved one only has to look at the saga concerning the sporting use of short-barrelled guns which Churchill had begun to market around 1924. Churchill advocated the use of these short, light, fast-handling shotguns fitted with 25 in barrels. In his book

*How to Shoot*, which he published in conjunction with another expert of the period, Pollard, he abandoned the principle of shooters attempting to estimate the correct forward lead on moving targets and to replace it with an instinctive style of shooting, where one swings the gun through the bird from behind—'stroking it from the sky' as if one had rapidly drawn a line on a sheet of paper with a pencil through a picture of a pheasant. Burrard, who wrote technical articles in the shooting publications *The Field* and *The Shooting Times,* reviewed these guns very unfavourably, although at the time they had a number of advocates. Pollard, the shooting editor of yet another publication *Country Life,* supported Churchill. Not content with this, Churchill produced a booklet entitled *Myself and 'The Field'* in which he reproduced all correspondence, previously published or unpublished, as well as 48 octavo pages in which he indicted *The Field's* expert and called upon him in capital letters to withdraw his previous statements. The argument went on for some time after this unabated. These same temperaments were to be revealed both in their court appearances and also in their published works. The published accounts of their casework both contain photographic evidence to support the accounts of their work, some of which were taken with the aid of comparison microscopes. The work covered by Major Burrard is detailed and well set out and has long been regarded as the standard reference book on the subject when used in conjunction with his other three books concerning guns, cartridges and weapons testing.

In the trial of George Kitchen, a farmer charged with the murder of his son James on a farm in a Lincolnshire fen in 1931, the weapon involved was a cheap double-barrelled hammer shotgun which the Defence claimed had been caused to discharge by accident: it fell to the ground after being propped up against a wall and was left with both its hammers cocked, as there were geese about. It was suggested that the farm dog, subsequently referred to as 'the silent witness', had knocked the gun over. The evidence of Churchill's pathologist friend Spilsbury was that the shot had been fired from a range of between 1 and 3 yd, or possibly less, and that the apparent line of fire was markedly downwards in the body, forming an angle of 55° with a line drawn horizontally through the point of entrance. He concluded that this could only be explained if the deceased had been standing erect when the shot was fired by another person positioned a short distance away from him. The evidence provided by Churchill after examining the gun was that the trigger pull necessary to fire the left barrel, the one fired in the incident, was 7 lb, which was about 2 lb heavier than would generally be considered normal for a sporting gun. He concluded that it would be impossible for the wound to have been self-inflicted, and that he did not believe that the death had been caused by accident.

However, Burrard found a defect in the lock for the left barrel of the gun, which was confirmed by Dr. Wilson, a firearms expert and an officer in the Royal Artillery, Territorial Army, William Mansfield, a director of the gunmakers Holland and Holland, and H.L. Greener of the Birmingham gunmakers of the same name. At the trial, the evidence of Sir Bernard Spilsbury became less certain. He stated that how James Kitchen had died remained a matter of pure speculation, adding 'there is nothing exact'. When replying to a question put to him by the judge—'It is pure speculation as to how this man died?'—he responded—'Put that way, my Lord, it is'.

After some consultation with prosecuting Counsel, the Judge instructed the jury that they could not convict the accused of the murder in the light of this evidence. To the great consternation of the experts for the Defence the case was dismissed, thus denying them the opportunity to give their evidence, which would cause great doubts to be expressed concerning the reliability of the expert previously favoured by the Home Office. During subsequent Parliamentary enquiries Burrard appeared to accuse Churchill of having tampered with the gun during a second examination so as to restore it in part to a good condition by filing some material from the protruding tail of a faulty sear. In view of the accusations the Home Office had to make a full enquiry.

The findings of this enquiry were that the allegations made against Churchill were unfounded. However, the media coverage of the results of the enquiry was not up to the standard Churchill would have appreciated. He felt that if the result had gone the other way they would have been reported in sensational terms. Mud sticks, and a subsequent article published in the *New Statesman and Nation* was headed 'The Menace of the Expert'.

There were further differences of opinion between Burrard and Churchill in the courts over the years which are recounted, as they individually recall them, in their books—*The Other Mr. Churchill* (Hastings 1963) and *The Identification of Firearms and Forensic Ballistics* (Burrard 1934). One curious aspect of the Kitchen murder trial is to be found in Burrard's authoritative and informative publication, which gives some insight into the emotions this case had effectively brought to a head.

> I was so impressed by the mistakes made by the Prosecution in this case that I bought the gun in question and sealed it in a case in front of witnesses directly it was handed over to me and before it had been in any custody other than that of the Prosecution and Home Office. This sealed gun case is still in my bank.

At a previous trial concerned with the murder of Gutteridge, an English country police officer in 1928, unfavourable comments were made that the methods used to associate a suspect revolver with the crime were effectively the same as those employed in the disputed murder trial of two former Italian radicals Sacco and Vanzetti held in Massachusetts, US in 1927. The subsequent execution of these two men had caused disturbances and criticisms around the world because it was widely held that politics had intruded in the way of justice. Examination today of photographs furnished by Goddard for Hatcher's book on the subject of test-fired cartridge cases produced from the .32 in Colt pistol found on Sacco compared with a crime cartridge case appear to leave little doubt as to its association with the incident. However, many criticisms have been levelled at the conduct of the police investigation. Eminent philosophers from all over the world made pleas for mercy on their behalf. Sacco and Vanzetti were both executed by electrocution on 22 August 1927. George Bernard Shaw was one of the most vociferous protestors and continuously repeated his total disbelief in the new science in subsequent years. Shaw held great sway during this period as a man of great intellect whose opinion would have been respected by many even though he was dealing with a subject in which the great man was clearly out of his depth. His opinions at the time were a very real threat to the emergent science. Since the court ruling in 1923 in the case of *Frye vs. US*, involving the acceptance of tool-marks evidence, that scientific testimony should be allowed if it 'gained general acceptance in the particular field in which it belongs', the US Courts and practically all of the individual States have allowed the admissibility of expert evidence given by competent witnesses. However, in 1993 the US Supreme Court in the case of *Daubert vs. Merrell Dow Pharmaceuticals* dismissed this general acceptability standard and insisted that the 'Federal Rules of Evidence' should control the admissibility of expert evidence. Rule 702 states that an expert can give evidence only if the body of knowledge is regarded as a proper subject for testimony and the witness is shown to be suitably qualified. Rules 401 and 404 state that such evidence must be shown to be relevant so that its admissibility can be decided by the trial judge. The effect of the Daubert decision, which effectively establishes the trial judges as 'gatekeepers' in these matters, also set down four (not necessarily all inclusive) criteria for the acceptability of expert evidence:

1. Testability of scientific principle
2. Known or potential error rate
3. Peer review and publication
4. General acceptance in a particular scientific community

Many scientific papers have been published over the years concerning the identification of the particular firearm or tool involved in leaving individual markings upon bullets and cartridge cases, as well as the association of other tool-marks that might be left on an object or at the scene of a crime. Papers are subjected to peer review prior to their publication, declared and undeclared tests of the competence and the reliability of laboratory practitioners are published, and a number of new papers have been published recently, particularly in the *Journal of the Association of Firearm and Tool Mark Examiners* (AFTE), which are intended to meet 'The Daubert Challenge'.

## Further Reading

Bonfanti, M.S. and Kinder, J.De. 1999. The influence of manufacturing processes on the identification of bullets and cartridge cases — a review of the literature. *Science & Justice* **39** (1), 3–10.

Burrard, Major Sir G. 1934. *The Identification of Firearms and Forensic Ballistics*, London: Herbert Jenkins.

*Daubert v Merrell Dow Pharmaceuticals Inc.* 113 S. CT. 2786 (1993).

Federal Rules of Evidence.

*Frye v United States.* 293 F, 1013 (D.C. Civ. 1923).

Goddard. Col. C.H. 1953. A history of firearms identification to 1930. *AFTE Journal* **31** (3), 225–265.

Grzybowski, R.A. and Murdock, J.E. 1998. Firearms and toolmark identification—meeting the Daubert challenge. *AFTE Journal* **30** (1), 3–14.

Gunther, J.D. 1935. *The Identification of Firearms,* New York: John Wiley.

Hamby, J.E. 1999. The history of firearm and toolmark identification. *AFTE Journal* **31** (3), 266–284.

Hastings, M. 1963. *The Other Mr. Churchill,* London: Harrap.

Hatcher, J.S. 1935. *Textbook of Firearms Investigation, Identification and Evidence,* Plantersville SC: Small-Arms Technical Publishing Co.

Hatcher, J.S. and Weller, J.A.C. 1957. *Firearms Investigation, Identification and Evidence,* Harrisburg PA: Stackpole.

Matthews, J.H. 1962. *Firearms Identification,* Springfield, IL: Charles C. Thomas.

Matthews, Dr. and Howe, W.J. 1963. *Firearms Identification* (first printed in the *American Rifleman*). *AFTE Journal* **31** (3) 1999, 285–290.

Miller, J. and McLean, M. 1998. Criteria for identification of toolmarks. *AFTE Journal* **30** (3), 15–61.

Smith, S. and Glaister, J. 1931. *Recent Advances in Forensic Medicine,* London: J.A. Churchill.

# Manufacture, Mechanisms and Design Aspects of Firearms

# 4

## 4.1 Hinged Barrel Designs

All breech-loading arms allow access to the chamber for the direct manual loading or unloading of a cartridge into the chamber or for the user to check the safe condition of the gun. In the case of shotguns of conventional (English) design and for some rifles made to a similar pattern this is easily done. This is normally achieved by the downward hinging of the barrel after first pushing the breech-opening lever or some similar fitment to one side. This constitutes the most user-friendly system of operation, in that it is extremely simple and takes only a few seconds. With most sporting shotguns of conventional English pattern it also automatically reapplies the safety catch. It has the added advantage, especially during periods between beats when someone is shotgun shooting or if there is an obstacle to cross, such as a ditch or gate, that the gun can instantly be made safe and at the same time the visible open breech of the weapon clearly signifies to others that it is in a safe condition. This is one of the major drawbacks with American-style repeating shotguns, whether of pump-action or self-loading design, and one of the reasons why weapons of this type are frowned upon or not tolerated at most formal game shoots in the UK.

## 4.2  Hammer Shotguns

Older examples of these weapons have external hammers which must be manually cocked or uncocked. Many cheap, single-barrelled guns will reduce this effect by merely having the hammer spur exposed above the action; such weapons are sometimes referred to as being 'semi-hammerless' guns. The very oldest hammer guns have a 'half-cock' position for the hammer to be set by the user when the weapon is not about to be fired. This type of lock design is a leftover from the muzzle-loading period. The locks on the majority of hammer guns allow the hammer to be rested at a safety stop or rebound position (Figure 4.1) or at the fully cocked position ready for immediate firing (Figure 4.2). On firing, the hammer falls to strike the firing pin and is then drawn back a short distance to the rebound position, where a deep notch (bent) cut in the lower part of the hammer securely retains the nose of the sear to ensure the hammer cannot come into contact with the firing pin again. This is also the rest position for the hammer when the loaded gun is being carried, the idea being that the hammer will not move forward, in circumstances where it has been inadvertently knocked or drawn back close to the cocked position and then released to cause discharge as a result of the hammer spur being snagged in clothing or some other object.

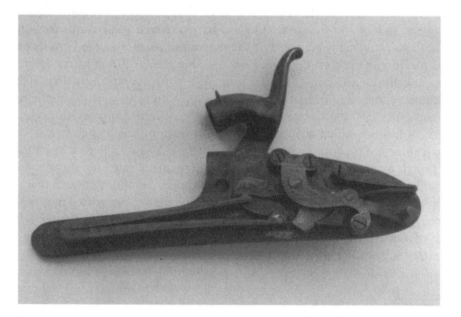

**Figure 4.1**  Hammer shotgun lock showing sear engaged in deeply cut bent (notch) of the safety rebound position. Wear on this bent or that for the full-cock position can result in an increased tendency for accidental discharge.

**Figure 4.2** Hammer pulled fully back to the full-cock position with sear engaged in the normal bent ready for firing.

Unfortunately, many of these cheap guns have been made from inferior materials, or certain vital components are of insufficient hardness or have been poorly case-hardened. In use, wear on the sear and the bent eventually causes the trigger pulls to change from their original settings and to allow for excessive movement to be created in the rebound safety system. Hammer guns in this mechanically unsound condition are prone to accidental discharge if the back of the uncocked hammer is struck in some mishap, or if the hammer is prematurely released as it is being manually uncocked in order to render the weapon safe; many accidental discharges have taken place over the years with weapons of this type in such unsound condition. Inevitably in some of these instances injury or loss of life has occurred.

## 4.3 Accidental Discharge

During any forensic examination of a firearm which has been used in a shooting incident where injury or loss of life has taken place, one should always consider the possibility of an accidental discharge having taken place. In any event, it is extremely rare for a defendant in a murder trial to admit to having shot somebody deliberately. All manner of other possible reasons will be given for the discharge or multiple discharges by the Defence, and he will be prepared to challenge evidence for the Prosecution assisted by that variable commodity, the Defence firearms expert or experts.

One must therefore, be able to give the fullest accounts of your tests and to back them up in court by non-firing demonstrations which in some instances will require jury participation.

## 4.4   Repeating Arms

Repeating magazine shotguns are not, as previously stated, popular for use on formal game shoots in the UK. A good deal of time has passed since Major Pollard pronounced on such weaponry in the chapter on repeating arms in his 1923 book *Shot-Guns*, and attitudes have softened to some degree. However, there is still a substantial residue of the disdain for the use of this type of arm in the circumstances stated. It would be fair to say that the words he used then would still strike a chord with many traditionalists in the UK today. 'The use of such arms for game shooting in the UK is not good form…but in some of the wild and undeveloped areas of the States and Canada such guns are permissible and popular'. It is true to say that bolt-action, pump-action and self-loading shotguns now have a considerable following in this country, although restrictions have recently been imposed upon their magazine capacity by the Firearms (Amendment) Act 1988 and the Wildlife and Countryside Act 1981. These relatively inexpensive guns are used in the main for wildfowling, vermin control, informal game shoots, clay-pigeon shooting and for the recently introduced sport of practical shooting.

The bolt-action guns are essentially of the same general construction as their rifled counterparts. Apart from a few pump/self-loading guns fitted with detachable box or drum magazines which have been derived from military weapons projects, pump-action and self-loading guns employ a tubular magazine positioned underneath the single barrel, which is capable of holding between two and eight cartridges; 12 gauge is the most common chambering for these weapons as it is for conventional English pattern guns. Some so-called 'practical shotguns' may have extended magazines capable of holding a greater number of cartridges.

Pump-action or slide-action guns are designed to be operated by pulling back the fore-end to the rear and by then pushing it back to its forward location. This action clears the chamber of any previously fired spent cartridge case, which is then thrown clear of the gun, cocks the action, transfers a live cartridge from the magazine tube, elevates it to align it with the chamber and then chambers the cartridge ready for firing by the application of a pull upon the trigger. These actions can then be repeated for subsequent shots at the discretion of the firer or until the magazine becomes empty.

The reliable operation of pump-action and self-loading shotguns is dependent upon the dimensions and form of the cartridge rim and, to a lesser degree, the finish upon the case walls. The first criterion determines how reliably the extractor engages with the rim of the cartridge. The second consideration determines the reliability of feeding into the chamber. Some cartridges, especially those produced some years ago in European and former Communist countries, were not handled reliably by these arms due to non-standard head dimensions. The glossy lacquer finish popular in the past to waterproof English ammunition could scuff on the edge of the chamber mouth resulting in a failure to feed. Most of these problems have now been overcome, although some weapons are more ammunition-sensitive than others, and very old ammunition is frequently encountered in criminal casework. Pump-action guns are fitted with manual safety catches, often in the form of a button located in the region of the trigger guard.

Pump-action shotguns are usually favoured over those of self-loading design by the police because of their ability to deal with all types of loadings, whereas the reliable operation of a self-loading arm is very dependent upon the pressure and the recoil generated by the cartridge, which controls the successful operation of the mechanism. Recent developments by Franchi and Benelli now allow weapons which offer operation in either mode at the discretion of the user; the SPAS 12 is the best-known weapon in this class followed by the SPAS 15 with its detachable box magazine system. Great mechanical advantage is provided by the manual operation of the fore-end, both in the feeding and the extraction operations. Although generally seen as an advantage, this feature can occasionally lead to tragedy. In one such instance I can recall a young owner of such a weapon had purchased some Russian cartridges from a dealer at a very low price because of corrosion on their brass-coated pressed steel heads due to adverse conditions of storage. The youth and his friends had charged the magazine with the rusted cartridges and had then proceeded to work them through its action to demonstrate its mode of operation. This was done with some attendant difficulty, as the rusted heads were effectively oversize for the chamber. The final rearward pull on the fore-end did not cause the extraction of a live cartridge and so created the impression that the gun was unloaded. Unfortunately, a badly rusted cartridge had been forcibly jammed in the chamber by the previous breech-closing operation, and the rearward pull had simply caused the narrow extractor to rip away a piece of the rim of its head. Shortly afterwards, one of them played with the 'empty gun' by closing the breech and pressing the trigger when it was pointing towards a friend's head, with the inevitable tragic consequences.

Semi-automatic (self-loading) shotguns are also made with a manual non-automatic safety catch which operates in a similar manner to those used on pump guns. These weapons are made in the US, Europe, Japan and the Philippines. They utilise either recoil energy or gas pressure for their operation. The combined mass of the barrel and bolt provides the necessary delay in the unlocking of the breech in long recoil self-loading weapons. However, gas-operated guns constitute the most common type of self-loading shotgun. A portion of the relatively low-pressure gases is tapped off through a gas port covered by the front end of the fore-end. The gas is redirected backwards at 180° to exert its force upon a piston, which in turn is linked to the bolt. The rearward movement which releases the bolt lock can only be imparted by the gas pressure after the shot charge and wadding have passed the midpoint of the barrel, thus ensuring that the residual gas pressure has dropped to an acceptable safe level. The bolt then continues its rearward movement, compressing a bolt return spring in the process. The extractor pulls the spent cartridge clear of the chamber until, at a point near to the limit of its rearward movement, the metal cartridge head collides with a fixed ejector to be kicked clear of the gun through the ejection port; this will usually, as is true with most pump guns, throw the spent case to the right of the shooter. A fresh cartridge is released from the magazine tube, elevated to align it with the chamber and then transferred into the chamber by the forward movement of the bolt returning to the locked breech position under spring pressure ready for the next shot. The design and capacities of the tubular magazines associated with these arms are similar to those of pump-action guns.

Self-loading shotguns exhibit similar sensitivities to changes in ammunition as previously described for pump guns. However, their reliable operation is also dependent on the nature of the recoil generated during discharge in the case of recoil-operated arms, and also the intensity of the gas pressure generated and the profile of the propellant time/pressure curve in gas-operated arms. This latter effect is very noticeable in sawn-off gas-operated guns, as this preparatory step for the criminal use of the gun often tends to involve the saw cut being made close to the gas port. Some of these shortened weapons will not operate as self-loading arms with certain brands of cartridges due to the reduction in the gas pressure of the particular loading at the takeoff point, which provides insufficient force upon the piston to allow the normal operation of the self-loading mechanism. It must also be noted that the unloading of the magazines of pump-action and self-loading guns can be something of a chore and, if not carried out with due care, can result in the firing of a supposedly unloaded gun.

## 4.5  Magazine Systems

Repeating arms possess magazines designed to furnish the weapon with a stock of cartridges. Magazines can be an integral part of a weapon or be detachable. Detachable magazines are mostly boxlike devices made of sheet metal or plastic, or in some instances in the form of a circular drum. In rare instances cylindrical helical-feed magazines are used in weapons, an example is the 'Calico' range of pistols, carbines and submachine guns. The Military frequently resort to belt-feed or disintegrating-link belt-feed systems for their machine guns, which can be stored in the original ammunition container. Additionally, use is frequently made of charger clips which are designed to hold a convenient quantity of cartridges, which in turn can be transferred when appropriate to magazines. Partly as a consequence of this, the term 'clip' is often misused to describe a magazine, in the same way as the term 'bullet' is substituted for the correct term 'cartridge'.

The reliability of repeating, self-loading and automatic firearms is greatly influenced by the design and condition of the magazines. Springs can take a 'set' especially if made from inferior materials or if improperly tempered. The long-term storage of fully charged magazines will of course aggravate this problem, as under these conditions the magazine spring is in its maximum state of compression. This fault will cause problems with the feeding of the last one or two cartridges because the weakened spring will not push them up fully to the top of the magazine lips, or will do this so slowly or imprecisely as to cause jams or feed failures with automatic and self-loading arms. It must be said however, that magazines can be made to very high standards where the possible reduction in compliance caused by leaving them fully charged for long periods is difficult to detect. Submachine guns are usually supplied with magazines capable of accepting 30 or 32 cartridges; as a consequence a good deal of finger pressure is required to charge them with the last five cartridges due to the long spring nearing maximum compression. The British Sterling submachine gun uses a relatively sophisticated magazine fitted with roller units at its mouth, which greatly reduces this problem, thus eliminating the need for a separate charging tool. In view of the possible feeding problems, particularly for the last few cartridges in the magazine, associated with spring set, slow bolt closure and incorrect loading methods used by soldiers, older military handbooks often advised charging such magazines with two less cartridges than the design maximum. Modern magazine springs are generally made to higher standards and from superior materials, thus reducing such problems as spring set.

The most critical parts of the majority of box magazines are the lips. This part of the magazine suffers the most wear and abuse in service, especially if the magazine is dropped upon a hard surface, or if improper force or bad techniques are used during its charging. Such defects are the most probable cause of jams and misfeeds, especially in automatic or self-loading weaponry. Dents, dirt or corrosion, in the case of tubular magazines will offer resistance to the normal smooth movement of the cartridges as they are being pushed under spring pressure by the follower. This type of fault will be even more pronounced if the magazine spring has deteriorated, especially when it is near to the limit of its movement during the feeding of the last few cartridges, as the spring will be exerting its lowest possible force. Apart from misfeeds, this can be a cause of accidents where an apparently unloaded weapon is caused to fire when its action is reworked again and its trigger is pulled by a careless or unaware handler. Old pump-action .22 in rim-fire rifles which have been subject to minimal cleaning and maintenance during their life or which have a slight dent in the exposed side of the tubular magazine are the most likely candidates to exhibit this type of fault, which can on occasion result in tragedy.

## 4.6  Bolt-Action Weapons

One of the most common and safest designs of repeating arm is the bolt-action system. This design is used mostly in the construction of rifles, although it is also utilised for the manufacture of relatively cheap shotguns and a few specialist pistols. A great many currently manufactured centre-fire rifles are based upon the Mauser design of the late nineteenth century. Most rifles of this type are furnished with integral or detachable box magazines. The manual operation of the bolt results in the transfer of a cartridge from the magazine to the chamber, the cocking of the striker, followed by the secure locking of the breech. After firing, the bolt handle is manually rotated a short distance upwards to unlock the breech, followed by a rearwards pull to extract and eject the spent cartridge case. Rifles are usually fitted with a manual safety catch which often locks the bolt in the closed position at the same time; some safety catches have a second position which allows the safe opening of the breech when unloading.

## 4.7  Lever-Action Rifles

The simplest form of lever action is that employed for single-shot hinged-block Martini action rifles and guns and other sliding-block designs. Here the downward movement of the hinged lever underneath the action causes the breech block to pivot or drop to expose the chamber ready for manual loading and to cock the action. After firing a similar movement will also eject the spent cartridge case or allow it to be extracted by hand.

When considering repeating magazine rifles employing lever operation, one automatically thinks of the Winchester models of 1866, 1873, 1892 and 1894; the last model is still manufactured today. Tubular magazines located underneath the barrel furnish these old weapon designs with considerable firepower, although in some instances they dictate the need for the use of flat-tip bullet loadings to prevent recoil-initiated discharges of cartridges within the magazine. Many of the older guns were chambered for the same cartridges as were used in the revolvers of the period; the counterpart of this today is reflected in weapons chambered for .357 and .44 in Magnum cartridges. The forward-hinged movement of the lever pulls back the breech block, at the same time causing the extraction and the ejection of any spent cartridge case left in the chamber from a previous firing and the elevation of a fresh cartridge from the magazine. The return movement of the lever causes this cartridge to be chambered and the hammer to be left in the cocked position ready for firing. The manual setting of the hammer at an intermediate safety position is used instead of a safety catch, although many users choose to carry this type of rifle with an empty chamber.

## 4.8   The Revolver

The most prolific repeating arm of both this century and last two must be the 'revolver'. It was first exhibited in the form of pepperbox revolvers and longarms. The introduction of the current design of a separate barrel and cylinder system dates back to the early stages of the nineteenth century and became famous with the introduction of the Colt revolvers both in muzzle-loading and breech-loading forms. It is interesting to note that the present day revolvers are merely design variants of the Smith and Wesson .22 in rim-fire revolver of 1857. In this instance even the .22 in rim-fire Short cartridge system for which it was initially chambered is as current today as it was then and is still manufactured annually in the millions. The preponderance of revolver weapons are handguns, although Colt and others manufactured some revolver rifles and shotguns. In recent years this concept has been revisited in the form of the Dragon 12, the Striker and Streetsweeper 12-gauge revolver smooth-bored guns and shotguns.

## 4.9   Accident by Design

The lever-action rifles of today differ little from the Henry and Winchester designs of the 1860s and 1870s. The pump-action or slide-action system of the late-nineteenth century is used extensively today, particularly in the manufacture of repeating shotguns. Modern revolvers are still manifestations of the old Rollin White patent. Conventional shotguns are based on the Anson and Deeley patent of 1875 and other designs of the period. Bolt-action rifles and self-loading pistols are essentially based upon designs dating from the last decade of the nineteenth century and the first decade of the twentieth century. It is therefore important to remember that many of these old weapons while still remaining viable firearms may have suffered from the effects of considerable wear, or may not contain certain internal safety features found on their modern counterparts, which can render them prone to accidental discharge in certain circumstances.

Ignoring the fact that it is far easier to inadvertently point a handgun at a part of your own anatomy or someone else's than it is to do so with a longarm, it must be said that single-shot weaponry whether in the form of a pistol, rifle or a shotgun, is the simplest and therefore the safest of all designs. Next to this must come bolt-action longarms, followed by lever-action and pump-action longarms. The greatest attendant dangers are associated with self-loading and finally automatic weapons, especially if these are pistols or of some other design of short overall length.

Revolvers, whether of single-action or double-action design (Figure 4.3) are inherently safer to handle than self-loading pistols. Although the vast majority of revolvers lack a safety catch, their design offers the least hazard during handling, especially for novice shooters. The hammer of a single-action revolver must be deliberately cocked before the weapon can be fired. In the case of a double-action revolver two methods of operation are possible. First, it can be operated in the same way as the single-action arm; secondly, it can be fired by the application of a much heavier pull to its trigger, at the same time causing it to be moved through a longer distance of between 10 and 18 mm (0.5 and 0.75 in); this action rotates the cylinder, cocks the hammer and then releases it. It is common for the term 'double-action' to be misused especially when referring to the mode in which the weapon is fired. The meanings of most words in any language tend to change with the passage of time. This effect is caused by the fact that languages are 'living', and like all life forms, tend to change or adapt in general use; an example of this is to be found in the relatively recent hijacking of the word 'gay', which one would now shrink from using to describe a person who is merely full of fun. Most gun users and firearm manufactures now habitually use the expression 'double-action' to describe the second method by which a double-action revolver is fired, even to the degree of referring to some weapons being 'double-action' only (Figure 4.6). This change in the use of the term is now so well established that I have chosen to use it at various locations in this book so as not to appear unduly pedantic.

Modern revolvers have an internal safety block device which interposes itself between the hammer and the frame, thus allowing the weapon to be fired only when the trigger has been pulled. The design of some revolvers utilises a transfer-bar device which moves into place to transfer the blow of the hammer to the firing pin only at the proper moment. Revolvers of older design, and this includes some single-action arms, can be caused to fire if the rear of the uncocked hammer is subjected to a severe impact. Many users

**Figure 4.3**   Solid-frame single-action revolver typified by the Colt Model 1873, hinged-frame Webley revolver and modern solid-frame double-action stainless steel revolver by Sturm Ruger.

of such weapons of the period used to carry them with an empty chamber underneath the uncocked hammer and some people maintain this practice today.

The greatest moment of danger with revolvers and weapons of other designs is encountered if the user decides not to shoot the weapon after the hammer has been cocked and then tries to uncock the hammer to restore it to a safe carrying condition. To achieve this the hammer spur must be held back in place with the thumb before it is gently lowered to its uncocked position after the trigger has been carefully pulled. Carelessness, nervousness, cold or wet fingers can result in an accidental discharge if the trigger is pressed before the hammer has been secured.

The shape of the hammer spur and the degree of knurling upon the pressure face will also influence the degree to which the hammer is susceptible to slipping from the pressure of the thumb in this scenario. Allowing the hammer to slip from a partially cocked position, whether this is caused by the hammer having snagged on something or simply by the thumb slipping off the hammer spur during the cocking or uncocking operations, can lead to an accidental discharge if the weapon involved does not possess some form of internal safety device previously mentioned, or if the rebound safety stop on some old or cheap shotguns is worn or damaged as previously described. In addition, any wear or damage to the sear which may have contributed to this problem, or upon the full cock notch (bent), can also lead to the hammer falling from the cocked position if the gun is subjected to some impact force or jarring action.

In instances of even more severe wear to the sear and bent, the hammer can fail to be held at its fully cocked position after it has been released at the end of the otherwise normal action of cocking it preparatory for firing. These all represent circumstances which could result in an accidental discharge or which could in turn be offered by the Defence in a murder trial as an explanation for how the unfortunate shooting took place. However, it is always the duty of the firearms expert working for the Prosecution to describe all such defects he has found during his examinations of the weapon in his initial written statement.

## 4.10   Safety Catches and Internal Safeguards

The design, operation and effectiveness of any safety catch or internal safety device should always be determined during the firearm examination. The traditional English shotgun is usually fitted with an automatic safety catch of sliding design fitted upon the top-strap of the action in a convenient and highly visible location. This catch is automatically pushed to the rear to become engaged whenever the breech is opened.

However, it should be borne in mind that these safety devices merely bolt the trigger blades to prevent their movement if pulled. Other factors, such as the weapon being subjected to hard jarring forces might still allow a sear to come out of bent if some other defect or damage exists.

To prevent such an occurrence resulting in a discharge, some guns are made with additional intercepting safety devices, which act to arrest the movement of the hammers before the firing pin is struck in circumstances where the triggers have not been pulled; such devices are usually fitted to better quality side-lock guns rather than on weapons of box-lock design. The movement of the safety catch, whether it be of top-sliding or some other design, is also an important consideration. The catch should move between two positive detents to click into place at each end of its movement. A catch which can be moved too freely from its previously chosen position represents a potential hazard, especially if the gun can be fired when the catch is located at some intermediate position so as to just reveal the 'safe' indication mark.

Safety catches fitted to American or Continental shotguns, particularly those sporting guns of pump-action or self-loading design, tend to be of non-automatic, manual, design. In addition, those on repeating arms tend to take the form of a button, positioned behind or in front of the trigger and designed for lateral movement. Once again, these devices usually merely bolt the trigger movement. Such catches have a low visibility both in terms of their location and setting. It is usual however, for the safety to be set when the button is projecting from the right side of the action; such a position allows it to be pushed to the left with the tip of the right index finger, in the case of a right-handed firer, to release it ready for firing.

Safety catches and other safety devices fitted to self-loading pistols vary somewhat both in design and location from one make of weapon to the next. The majority of manually operated catches are located on the rear of the left side of the frame, to allow convenient operation with the thumb, for right-handed shooters. A number of pistols of more recent manufacture recognise the reality that not all people are right handed, and have a catch on each side sharing a common spindle, thus allowing truly ambidextrous operation. Some weapons are fitted with an additional grip safety, which must be depressed by the normal gripping action of the hand before the pistol can be fired; the best-known example of this is the Colt pattern .45 in model of 1911 (Figure 4.4). Colt pistols of more recent manufacture also have an internal safety device which arrests the movement of the firing pin in circumstances other than deliberate firing. This feature adds further security in circumstances of use where the pistol is being routinely carried in the 'cocked and locked' condition. The safety catches of some pistols cause the automatic lowering of the hammer and at the same time cause a rotating metal shroud device to prevent the hammer hitting the striker (firing pin); this design is used in certain pistols of Walther manufacture, such as the PPK pocket pistol and with some other makes (Figure 4.6). Other pistols using this type of feature also include a striker blocking device or a striker retracting system, for example, the Polish Radom P35. Current pistols using hammer-drop safety catches include a number of Smith and Wesson models, the Steyr GB and the Ruger P85.

An additional magazine safety feature, which prevents the weapon from being fired whenever the magazine is removed, is used on a number of self-loading pistols; a well known example is the Browning P.35 9 mm pistol, sometimes referred to as the F.N. Browning High Power. The reasoning behind this particular safety constraint lies in an attempt to make the unloading operation safer. Once the main source of cartridges has been removed by the removal of the magazine, the chamber can be cleared by pulling back the slide without the attendant risk of inadvertently firing the pistol by touching the trigger in the process.

## 4.11  Decocking Devices and Alternative Designs

Some pistols have hammer decocking levers which are intended to avoid the pitfalls associated with the manual decocking of the hammer used to render the weapon safe; in this respect they serve a similar function to the Walther

**Figure 4.4**  Diminutive but potentially lethal Kolibri 2.7 mm self-loading pistol of 1914 next to Colt Model 1911A1 .45 in pistol. Claimed ballistics for the Kolibri loading was a 3 grain (0.2 g) bullet at 650–700 ft/s (198–213 m/s) for a striking energy of 3 ft lb (4 J).

**Figure 4.5**  Even the tiny Walther Model 9 .25 in (6.35 mm) self-loading pistol looks huge next to the 2.7 mm Kolibri.

**Figure 4.6**  Stainless steel Smith and Wesson Model 5946 'double-action only' 9 mm self-loading pistol next to Walther PPK 7.65 mm true double-action pistol with hammer decocking safety catch.

safety catch previously mentioned. A number of pistols take this concept a logical step further by using this feature as a means of eliminating the manual safety catch altogether. An example is some SIG model self-loading pistols which employ a long revolver-style double-action pull for the first shot, after which the normal recoil cycling of firing allows subsequent shots to be taken from the lighter single-action type pull. At the end of the course of fire the pistol is simply rendered safe by the decocking lever. Recently introduced Smith and Wesson self-loading pistols have simplified the system further, and at the same time have tried to respond to the accidental discharge problems encountered by certain US police forces more used to using revolvers, by designing the firing mechanism so that the hammer is left in the uncocked position after every shot, thus causing the user to apply the less accident prone long double-action pull comparable to that of their previous issue service revolvers for all subsequent shots. This of course simplifies things further by allowing the elimination of the manual safety catch.

The Heckler and Koch P7 pistol is unusual in that it attacks this same problem from a different direction, and at the same time also eliminates the need for the usual manual safety catch. This dual function is achieved by fitting a hinged fixture on the front edge of the grip frame which is depressed during the normal action of gripping the pistol ready for firing, causing the striker mechanism to be cocked in the process. If the user decides not to fire the pistol, or if he wishes to make the weapon safe after firing one or more shots, the action of simply relaxing this tight hand grip causes the striker mechanism to decock automatically (Figure 4.7). Other novel features on this pistol are a gas-operated system (Figure 4.8), which delays the unlocking of the breech until the pressure level has dropped to a safe level, and a fluted chamber.

The Austrian Glock range of pistols uses a most unusual and simple-to-use system which bypasses the apparent need for safety catches or double-action mechanisms to achieve better accuracy for the first shot (Figure 4.9). This pistol design employs a two-piece trigger. The hinged lever in the trigger must be pulled back directly to the rear before additional pressure will allow the pistol to be fired; this guards against possible accidental discharge if the trigger is subjected to any unforeseen lateral pressure forces. The striker mechanism remains partially cocked from the previous retraction of the slide during the loading operation or from firing. Only about half of the normal double-action trigger pressure is needed to complete the cocking of the striker and to fire the next shot, which is accomplished through a relatively short trigger movement. The initial part of the trigger pull also causes the depression of a plunger in the slide which unbolts the forward movement of the striker; the rating of the coil spring on this safety unit can also be used to alter the weight of the trigger pull. However, the

**Figure 4.7** Heckler and Koch innovative gas retarded P7 9 mm self-loading pistol which utilises a squeeze-cocking/decocking device built into the grip.

**Figure 4.8** P7 pistol partially dismantled to reveal gas piston arrangement attached to front end of the slide.

**Figure 4.9** The Austrian Glock 17, 9 mm self-loading pistol challenged many of the rules for firearm design and construction which had preceded it.

introduction of these large-magazine-capacity pistols in place of the conventional revolvers previously used by some police forces in the US, in an attempt at meeting the perceived need for additional firepower, resulted in a number of accidental discharges. The trigger pulls on Glock pistols can be altered by fitting special components to suit the needs of individuals or police department specifications. The pistols can thus be ordered up from the factory or distributor with trigger pulls increased at the factory to be more in line with the 8-lb-plus double-action revolver trigger pulls the US police officers were more accustomed to. Even higher trigger pulls are used on some special order batches, which are referred to as the 'New York' trigger pull or the 'New York-Plus' trigger pull.

## 4.12   Hazard Indicator Devices

A number of firearms have cocking indicators upon them to make the user aware of their status. However, another interesting safety feature is to be found on a number of self-loading pistols, for example, Walther pistols and some longarms. This feature takes the form of a loaded chamber indicating pin, which usually projects from the rear of the slide to warn the user of its condition whenever there is a cartridge present in the chamber. It is fairly common practice for some people to carry, or in the case of the military, to be instructed to carry, self-loading arms with a loaded magazine fitted to them but with an empty chamber, to help guard against accidental discharges. The Luger pistol has a more obscure feature which is intended to serve the same purpose. In this case the side of the extractor claw, which is pushed upwards and thus exposed to view when it is engaged in the rim of a cartridge, is marked 'geladen'.

## 4.13   Bolt-Action Rifle Safety Catches

Most military-style bolt-action rifles have turning or hinged safety levers situated close to the rear ends of their bolts. These are positive safety catches because they constrain the movement of the cocking-piece. On modern sporting rifles, which these days are usually fitted with telescope sights, the safety catches are sometimes moved to a more convenient location, such as upon the top strap or near to the trigger. This is often done in order to allow the telescope sight to be mounted lower and thus closer to the axis of the barrel. Generally speaking, the setting of the safety catch also prevents the bolt from being opened. Some sporting rifles have a second 'safe' setting for the catch which can be used whenever the weapon is being unloaded, as an additional safeguard against accidental discharge when the bolt is being opened in conditions where the chamber is loaded.

## 4.14   Trigger Pulls

During any trial concerned with murder, attempted murder, or wounding, one question will always be asked about the firearm involved, and that is of course the trigger pull required to cause its discharge. There is a perpetual infatuation with the concept of 'light' or 'hair' triggers, which might be used to account for an unfortunate and inadvertent discharge. The range of trigger pulls determined to be appropriate over the years by firearms manufacturers generally reflects the results of considerable experience concerning the use to which a particular class of weapon is likely to be put. A person intending to use a .22 in pistol for precision slow-fire target shooting in the secure conditions of an indoor range will usually want the minimum trigger pull allowed for that discipline. This is likely to be about 1 kg (2 lb). In a centre-fire target pistol the trigger pull will be in the 1.5 to 2 kg (3 to 4 lb) range. On the other hand, weapons of all types intended for military service use will exhibit heavier trigger pulls, generally in the region of 3 to 3.5 kg (6 to 7 lb). The reason for these heavier pulls is that in service use the arms will often be used in considerably less favourable conditions.

Firearms manufacturers over the years have all arrived at generally similar trigger pulls appropriate for each particular type of weapon. These trigger pulls are, in effect, compromise settings so as not to be so heavy as to affect unduly accuracy of fire or constrain the normal use of the weapon, yet not so light as to lead to its accidental discharge during normal conditions of handling. The majority of sporting shotguns are made with trigger pulls in the 1.6 to 2.3 kg (3.5 to 5 lb) range. A good quality double-barrelled gun of British manufacture will be set with a pull of between 1.6 and 1.8 kg (3.5 to 4 lb) for the front (right barrel) trigger and a slightly heavier pull upon the rear (left barrel) trigger, this increase being in the region of approximately 0.2 to 0.4 kg (0.5 lb) or slightly more. It is interesting to consider what the various authorities on firearms have said on the subject of correct shotgun trigger pulls over the years:

- Charles Lancaster refers to the correct trigger pulls for a sporting shotgun in his book *The Art of Shooting*, as follows: '...The gunmaker has devoted much time to the highly skilled work of making the pulls of the correct weights, which should be about three-and-a-half pounds for the right lock and four pounds for the left'.

- In his book *Letters to Young Shooters,* Sir Robert Payne-Gallwey comments: '…The usual pull for the triggers is, right barrel 4 lb, left barrel 4 3/4 lb; and the way to test them is with an ordinary spring balance…The triggers of a gun, whatever their resistance, should pull off short and sharp, without any draw'.
- In his book *Shooting and Gun Fitting,* Arthur Hearn recommends: '…Trigger pulls should be sweet and crisp, there should be no long drag or take up…. Normal pulls are, for the right barrel 4 lb, for the left, 4 3/4 lb. Pulls can be adjusted to suit individual requirements, but pulls below 3 lb are dangerous, and above 5 lb too heavy for most people'.
- W.W. Greener comments in his famous book *The Gun and its Development:* '…The weight of the pull-off of the triggers is usually 4 lb. (Spring balance measurement)'.
- Major Sir Gerald Burrard states in his book *The Modern Shotgun:* '…As a general rule the trigger of the right barrel has a pull of from 3 1/2 to 4 lb, and that of the left from 4 to 4 1/2 lb. These weights have been found by long experience to be the most satisfactory, and all shooters will be well advised not to have their pulls set outside these limits'.
- Elmer Keith comments in his book *Shotguns:* '…Shotgun trigger pulls even on fine trap guns should never be less than 3 1/2 lb as a safety feature, and on two trigger guns it is well to have the first barrel, that is the one bored the more open, to fire at about 3 1/2 to 4 lb. So long as the trigger pull is clean and sharp it makes relatively little difference if it be 4 lb or less as one soon becomes accustomed to its weight, the thing is to have it heavy enough for safety'.
- In his book *Shotguns and Cartridges* Gough Thomas recommends that: '…The ideal trigger pull, as has often been said, should resemble the breaking of a glass rod. For the average man, a 3 1/2 to 4 lb pull for the right trigger and 4 to 4 1/2 lb for the left is about right'.
- Robert Churchill used to recommend a right barrel trigger pull value which was approximately equal to half the weight of the gun. He reasoned that a pull of 1.4 kg (3 lb) on a 3 kg (6.5 lb) 12-bore gun, felt the same as a 2.7 kg (6 lb) trigger pull on a 5.9 kg (13 lb) eight-bore wildfowling gun, or a 1.1 kg (2.5 lb) trigger pull on a 2.3 kg (5 lb) 20-bore gun. In his book *Game Shooting* he admits to using considerably lighter pulls on a gun made without a safety catch which he used for competitive clay pigeon and live pigeon shooting, where there was a perceived need for very fast shooting after the release of the target. For a period he admits using a right trigger pull of 0.8 kg (1.75 lb) which was so light that he had to close the breech of the

gun gently to guard against an accidental discharge. He advises against the use of such light pulls, even for such specialist use, for persons not possessing the most sensitive sense of touch. In one murder and suicide incident I dealt with recently, the finely made Belgian FN over-and-under trap gun owned by this person, who had previously been a well-known top-class clay pigeon shooting champion, had locks set at comparable trigger pulls to those previously used by Churchill; despite the lightness of its trigger pulls it was not however, prone to accidental discharge by bumping or jarring.

The majority of repeating shotguns of American manufacture exhibit trigger pulls which I have measured using the dead-weight technique over the years, of approximately 1.8 kg (4 lb) which is in the middle of the generally recommended range previously mentioned. Most sporting rifles exhibit trigger pulls of between 1.4 and 2.3 kg (3 and 5 lb).

Some sporting rifles, particularly those of Continental manufacture, are fitted with 'set triggers'. Such triggers can be used in the conventional way, or in special conditions of use they can be set to the optional much lighter setting for fine shooting. On some rifles this is achieved by pulling a second rear trigger to set the mechanism, on others this action is achieved by pushing upon the rear of the single trigger. The 'set' or 'hair' trigger can be adjusted to a level of 0.3 kg (8 oz) or less on most rifles.

## 4.15   Blow-Back and Locked Breech Designs

Self-loading pistols and rifles designed to fire low-powered cartridges, and some old Winchester self-loading rifles designed to fire relatively low-powered cartridges such as the .351 and the .401 in centre-fire cartridges, operate on the simple blow-back principle. These weapons rely upon the slight delay in the opening of the breech afforded by the inertial resistance of the mass of the slide or bolt to the rearward recoil forces. As the slide or bolt moves to the rear the extractor claw, which is engaged in the cartridge rim, extracts the spent cartridge case from the chamber. Almost at the limit of the rearward movement, the cartridge case collides with a fixed-ejector rod situated approximately opposite the extractor, this causes the cartridge case to be kicked out of the ejection port clear of the weapon. The slide, or bolt, is then free to return into battery, picking up a live cartridge in the process, which can then be fired by a further trigger pull. Some small .25 in ACP (6.35 mm) pocket pistols utilise the projecting striker to serve the additional function of the ejector; other small pistols dispense with the need for an extractor, relying on residual gas pressure or momentum to free the cartridge case from the chamber. Colt used to manufacture a self-loading pistol which was similar to the Smith and Wesson Model 52, in that it was designed to fire .38 in Special wadcutter target ammunition. The chamber of this pistol had a series of shallow rings cut in it. The intention was that, at the peak pressure for this relatively modest loading, the swelled cartridge case would tend to grip hold of the chamber walls more substantially than normal, thus inducing some element of delay in the breech opening.

On weapons designed to fire powerful cartridge loadings which generate dangerously high pressure levels, it is important that the breech does not open prematurely. A delay is essential to allow the necessary drop in the very high gas pressure levels generated by the firing of these high-intensity loadings. This momentary delay, when the slide or bolt remains locked to the barrel, can be achieved by various techniques. The Browning pistol system is the most common. In this system the barrel and slide move back locked together a short distance, before the barrel tips downward fractionally to allow the disengagement of the locking lugs on top of the breech end of the barrel from a series of recesses in the underside of the top of the slide. After this the barrel is arrested and the slide moves back in recoil, causing the extractor to pull the spent cartridge case from the chamber, followed by its ejection and the return of the slide under the pressure of the compressed mainspring along with the stripping of a fresh cartridge from the magazine. Some pistols operate in essentially the same manner but dispense with the obvious locking lugs by replacing them with a formed section of the breech which engages into the cut-away ejection port for the initial stage of rearward movement.

The French Mab Model R and P.15 9 mm pistols use a rotating barrel system resembling that used on an earlier pistol made by Savage. The barrel has a lug protruding from the top and bottom of the chamber end, the uppermost of which is engaged in a slot cut in the slide. The bottom lug is located in a cam surface in the recoil spring rod guide mounting. As the bullet moves up the barrel engaged in the rifling, the top lug remains in the locked position. After the discharge of the missile the barrel is free to rotate and thus release the breech lock.

A number of pistols utilise the short recoil system of the Walther P.38. This design causes the barrel and slide to recoil back a short distance when still locked together. At this point a falling block is cammed downwards to unlock them when the breech pressure has dropped to a safe level, thus allowing the slide to continue its rearward movement as in the Browning action.

An intricate elbow-like 'toggle' joint fitted to the breech block of the Luger pistol serves the same mechanical delay; the barrel and block move back together a short distance to allow a short interval for the pressure level to drop before the joint hinges open allowing the block to move freely to the rear.

Heckler and Koch use a type of roller locking system on their rifles and some of their pistols; an extremely simple gas delay system on the P7 pistol; and a combination of a heavy slide and a strong recoil spring in the VP70. The VP70 is unusual in a further respect in that it can be provided with a shoulder stock which can be clipped onto the pistol, thus converting it into a form of carbine, and at the same time allowing the use of a three-shot burst-fire facility. A number of Heckler and Koch firearms also use a fluted chamber system similar to one introduced during World War II for improving the extraction reliability on machine guns by effectively floating most of the cartridge case on a layer of high pressure gases. The distinctive P7 pistol made by this same firm employs an unusual, yet incredibly simple gas-operated retardation device for its recoil operation. Here, gas is tapped off through a port situated in the underside of the barrel near to the breech. The gases are directed forwards onto the head of a small piston linked to the front end of the slide. The force of these gases on this piston prevents the slide from opening until the breech pressure has dropped to a safe level, thus providing the necessary period of delay (Figure 4.8). This unusual form of hesitation lock has been taken up on the South African Vektor CP.l compact 9×19 mm pistol. This system also allows both weapons to use slides of relatively low mass, thus reducing their overall length and weight.

Generally speaking, however, the .380 ACP (9 mm Short), or the slightly more powerful 9 mm Ultra or Police and Soviet Makarov loadings represent the bench-mark limit for simple blow-back pistols, although as with all things there will be exceptions, for example, the Heckler and Koch VP70 selective-fire pistol/carbine, and the old Spanish Astra Model 400 pistol are both simple unlocked blow-back designs utilising robust coil springs which are able to accommodate the powerful 9×19 mm cartridge. Automatic-fire submachine guns use the inertia of a heavy bolt and a long recoil spring to tolerate the high pressure levels of the ubiquitous 9×19 mm cartridge and, at the same time, reduce the cyclic rate of fire to the generally accepted norm of approximately 600 rounds per minute. More compact automatic weaponry such as the Ingram MAC 10, the Mini-Uzi and the Micro-Uzi, exhibit cyclic rates approximately twice the normal rate for a submachine gun. Some miniature automatic weaponry such as the 7.65 mm Czech Skorpion have a rate reducer incorporated into their action to lower the cyclic rate of fire (Figure 4.11).

## 4.16  Gas-Operated Arms

Many high-power self-loading rifles, a number of self-loading shotguns, and a few pistols such as the Israeli Desert Eagle utilise gas-operated systems, although some shotguns use a long recoil system of operation, relying on the

**Figure 4.10** Unusual Yugoslav Agram 2000 sub-machine gun chambered for 9×19 mm ammunition was intercepted by port controls before arriving with other arms at its intended destination in a Northwest city. The longer barrel which incorporates an integral silencer unit can be screwed in to replace the standard barrel.

combined mass of the barrel and bolt and a stiff coil spring to produce the necessary delay before the unlocking of the breech. The vast majority of these gas-operated weapons tap off some of the gases generated by the burning of the propellant through a gas port fitted approximately at the midpoint of the barrel, where the pressure level has dropped to an acceptable level for safe breech unlocking and gas utilisation. The gases are directed backwards through 180°, usually to act on a piston head fitted to an operating linkage to the bolt carrier. The breech is thus unlocked at the correct time, and some of the otherwise wasted gas pressure is utilised to open the action, extract the spent cartridge case and cause its ejection as before. The Armalite AR15 rifle and its clones use direct gas impingement upon the bolt carrier via a tube linked to the gas port leading to the bolt-carrier. This system performs the same functions but uses less components and dispenses with an additional reciprocating mass. The Desert Eagle pistol is designed to fire a range of very powerful pistol cartridges. Here the breech is locked by a multilug rotating bolt, similar to that used on some rifle designs. Some of the gas pressure is tapped off via a port positioned just in front of the chamber. The gases move forward along a channel positioned underneath the bore of the barrel towards the muzzle, at which point they are deflected downward and

**Figure 4.11**   One of six cases recovered from a burnt out flat previously occupied by Middle Eastern students. Each case contained a Czech Skorpion VZOR 61 compact sub-machine gun, a holster, spares kit and package of 7.65 mm (.32 ACP) ammunition. Originally designed for tank crew, but later favoured as a concealable automatic arm for terrorist use along with the Polish WZ 63, which is chambered for the 9 mm Makarov cartridge. A Skorpion was used by the Red Brigade in the assassination of Andre Moro, the former Italian Prime Minister.

backwards onto a piston which is propelled to the rear to unlock the breech and carry out the extraction, ejection and reloading operations.

The mechanism of the recently introduced Russian Avtomat Nikonov AN94, 5.45x39 mm assault rifle, utilises a combination of both recoil and gas operation, described as 'Gas Operated Blowback Shifted Pulse'. The barrel is integrated with its receiver to form the firing mechanism that travels inside the carrier-stock composed of glass-fibre reinforced plastic. When fired in its two-shot burst mode, a very high cyclic rate of fire of approximately 1,800 rounds per minute is realised. This extremely high cyclic rate is also achieved for the first two shots when used in its automatic-fire setting, after which subsequent discharges take place at a decreased cyclic rate of approximately 600 rpm, as long as the trigger is held to the rear. In doing this, the barrel assembly performs two cycles inside its receiver before travelling fully to the rear to produce the slower rate of automatic fire. An unusual cable and pulley mechanism causes cartridge feed to be accomplished in two stages, thus shortening the cartridge chambering operation by preloading a round on a feed tray; this eliminates the need for the bolt carrier having to move fully to the rear, beyond the rear of the magazine, in order to pick up a live

**Figure 4.12**  Heckler and Koch trigger grouping with fire selector to suit all tastes. Pictorial markings which minimise any language barrier indicate—safe, single-shot, three round burst or full—automatic modes of operation. Optional groupings calling up burst-fire operation involving a different number of cartridges are available.

cartridge. It is claimed that the new rifle is more reliable than the current Kalashnikov AK-74 assault rifle, and that greatly improved accuracy is achievable during burst-fire and the initial stages of automatic-fire due to a delay in perceived recoil until after the first two bullets have cleared its barrel.

## 4.17  Gas and Air Weapon Designs

Air weapons have existed in the form of blow-pipes for a considerable period of man's history, and are still used and manufactured to this day along with weapons employing mechanically compressed or precompressed air. Today, however, most air weapons employ a charge of mechanically compressed air to propel the missile. The most common method of compressing the air is to utilise the power provided by the release of a compressed coil spring upon a column of air swept through a transfer port by a piston. The coil spring can be compressed by hand, using a barrel which is hinged at its breech end, linked to draw back the piston to the point of maximum spring compression. The natural forward movement of the spring is arrested by a sear system, which is in turn linked to the trigger. An alternative system is to use a built-in cocking lever to accomplish the same task. One air weapon manufactured by 'Theoben' in Cambridgeshire uses a gas piston system filled with inert nitrogen gas in place of a coil spring; a piston transfers the power released by the sudden expansion of this gas when the trigger is pressed, to act upon a charge of air as previously described.

Pneumatic air weapons use some system to place a charge of compressed air into a reservoir, from which it can be released in whole, or in part, to propel a missile. The release of a charge of compressed air is usually achieved by the impact of a spring-loaded striker upon the head of a valve. This system has been used for a considerable period, often to produce large calibre weapons which were suitable for killing game or, as previously mentioned, even for use in warfare.

Walking stick air guns of various designs were made in considerable quantities in the nineteenth century, and even as late as 1914. These were mainly rifled weapons, the most popular calibre being .31 in (8 mm), capable of firing 15 consecutive balls through a 25 mm (1 in) thick plank of wood, after the reservoir had been charged to a pressure of 400 to 500 psi using about 260 strokes of a handpump. After charging the reservoir which is built into the handle section, it is screwed back onto the gun, a ball is muzzle-loaded or in some instances introduced via a tap-loading device in the breech and the striker is cocked by turning a key placed in a square hole at the side of the breech. The round end-knob of the cane is rested upon the cheekbone to allow the sighting of the weapon and a projecting button which is pushed out of the side of the gun during the act of cocking the striker is pressed with the thumb to fire it. The rifling sleeve can often be removed from the barrel thus converting the weapon to a smoothbore gun of larger calibre, approximately .44 in (11 mm), which could then be used with charges of small-size lead shot wrapped in paper as a shotgun to kill birds at modest ranges.

The majority of modern pneumatic arms are designed to fire conventional air rifle pellets of 4.5, 5.0, 5.6, 6.3 and 7.62 mm (.177, .20, .22, .25 and .30 in). Many of these arms, with the exception of the last two largest calibres, have the handpump built into the gun and are designed to empty their reservoirs in the firing of a single shot. Although some specialist .177 in pistols use a single stroke of the pump to charge their internal reservoirs, the majority of these pneumatic arms use anything between 3 and 20 strokes of the pump in their preparation for firing. As the reservoir is normally emptied upon firing, the use of a greater number of pump strokes will increase the velocity and consequent energy of the discharged pellet, which could be advantageous if the rifle is being used to kill vermin or small game, although it must be said that some owners can damage these weapons by attempting to overcharge them in a pursuit of even greater velocities. In many instances overcharging these weapons reduces the ability of the spring-loaded striker to fully open the release valve, so that performance actually drops off after a certain point and eventually declines.

An alternative system used particularly upon repeating BB pellet guns of US manufacture and some specialised .177 in target weapons, is to use replaceable reservoirs filled with compressed/liquefied carbon dioxide gas, similar to the bulbs used with soda water syphons; this again is not a new invention, as carbon dioxide powered weapons were made by Giffard in the nineteenth century. Canisters containing Freon gases are sometimes used, particularly on low-powered 'soft air guns', although one higher-powered continuous fire pistol called the 'M19 Annihilator' was made to discharge BB pellets using this same gas. It must be said at this stage that, strictly speaking, these compressed gas-powered weapons are not true air weapons, this difference is currently recognised in British law, although the legislation in most other countries allows them to be dealt with as air weapons.

An increasing number of UK-manufactured air rifles now use the compressed air from a diver's air bottle to charge up their large capacity built-in reservoirs to allow anything up to 90 high-velocity shots to be fired from a single charging. The air cartridge system has also become popular, particularly with revolver-type air weapons. These use brass air reservoirs resembling .38 in revolver cartridges, which are loaded into the chambers and fired in a similar way to a conventional breech-loading arm. The cartridges are precharged with compressed air in advance using a handpump, and a .177 in or .22 in pellet is inserted into an opening at its front end. The firing pin strikes the cartridge valve head which is situated in the same position as a conventional cartridge primer.

## 4.18   Crossbows

Crossbows constitute the final class of arm to be described in this chapter. Although crossbows were used for several hundred years before finally being discarded in favour of firearms, they have enjoyed an upturn in popularity in recent years. Modern crossbows use metal alloy or fibreglass composite structures in the construction of the bow (prod), which in turn is attached to a body that extends to form a rifle-like shoulder stock. The bow is normally drawn back by hand to cock it by causing a sear to lock the tensioned string in the rearward position. After placing a bolt in the open-top channel and releasing the automatic safety catch, usually fitted to this type of weapon, a pull upon a trigger will release the string to discharge the bolt.

The majority of crossbows cannot be described as firearms as they do not possess barrels, although a few are made with a tubular barrel unit which can be used to fire ball ammunition in place of the more usual bolt; in British law such weapons can be classed as 'lethal barrelled weapons' and hence 'firearms'. In all cases however, the forensic testing of crossbows is little different from that of conventional firearms. Trigger pulls can be measured, the operation of any safety catch can be checked, the weapon can be subjected to jarring tests, the velocity of the missile can be measured, and its range and accuracy can be determined. I have dealt with a number of cases of wounding and murder over the years which have involved the use of modern crossbows. The weapons involved in the fatal incidents exhibited bow draw weights of between 68 and 100 kg (150 and 220 lb) and the bolts discharged completely pierced the torsos of the victims (Figure 4.13, Figure 4.14 and Figure 4.15).

## 4.19  Processes Used in the Manufacture of Firearms

The machining processes used in the production of the component parts of firearms obviously involves the use of a number of tools, which will leave

**Figure 4.13**  Although not classifiable as a 'firearm', modern high-power cross-bows such as the above fitted with a prod of 150 pound (68 kg), and higher draw-weights, are occasionally used in acts of murder and wounding. In this incident, the first one involving such a weapon dealt with by the author, three triple-edged 'broad-head' bolts, similar to those shown above, were fired through a man's chest, pinning him to a steel filing cabinet. The laboratory tests such as chrono-graphing discharged missiles, measurement of trigger pull, security of safety catch, and determining any tendency towards accidental discharge, are conducted in a similar manner to the testing of a conventional firearm.

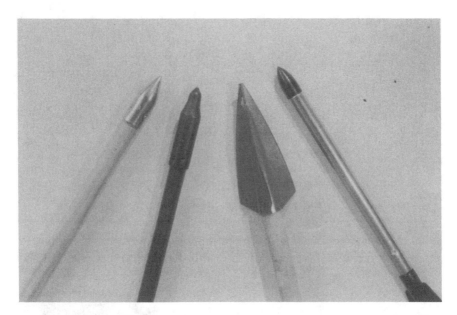

**Figure 4.14**   The different shapes of target and game shooting projectiles used with conventional bows and crossbows have implications as to the nature of the entry wounds and the actual wound tracks.

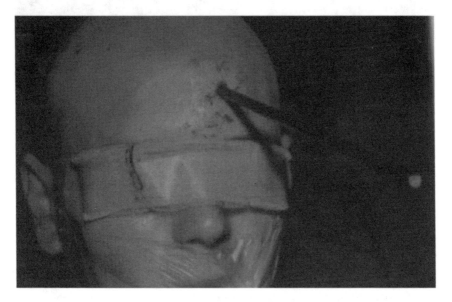

**Figure 4.15**   A pointed target bolt damages less tissue and induces far less haemorrhage than its 'broad-head' hunting counterpart. Apparently severe injuries, as in the instance above, to some parts of the human brain can prove to be survivable.

**Figure 4.16**   Russian four-barrelled under-water pistol for use by special forces. The cartridges used with this pistol are loaded with harpoon projectiles

both class and individual tool-marks upon these same components. However, these firearm components will in turn impart negative impressions of these features upon the softer material components of the cartridge loaded and/or fired in the particular gun. In doing this, the components of the firearm are in themselves acting as tools, thus leaving behind upon the cartridges, cartridge cases, primers and in some instances plastic shotgun wads, what may be described as tool-marks. It is necessary therefore, to possess some understanding of the various machining processes that may be used in the production of firearms, and the nature of the tool-marks they might produce, especially bearing in mind that manufacturers may employ different machining techniques for the same operation.

### 4.19.1  The Rifling of Barrels

A smooth-bore barrel is first produced by drilling and reaming a barrel blank. This process leaves behind circular scratches set at 90 degrees to the axis of the bore. In some applications after the rifling grooves have been formed, the blank is cut into sections which are then subjected to further machining processes so as to produce a number of short gun barrels. This factor should be borne in mind, as although the bores of these barrels will possess individual characteristics, they will tend to exhibit some sub-class characteristics. The chamber is then reamed out and its cone section polished. A chamfer is cut into the muzzle end of the bore to increase its diameter slightly during

**Figure 4.17** High-speed photograph of Beretta 92F 9 mm pistol being fired. At this point the slide has recoiled backwards with the barrel to the point where the breech will begin to unlock, so as to allow the slide to move to its rearmost position to cause the extraction and ejection of the spent cartridge case, followed by the return of the slide and the stripping of a fresh cartridge from its 15-shot magazine.

the 'crowning' process to help protect this critical area of rifling from possible impact damage. It is usual also to radius the exterior of the barrel wall to finish it off. After the rifling process the bore is polished by a lapping process using a lead plug and a slurry containing a fine abrasive material, or is burnished by driving a tightly fitting hard steel ball through the bore. The bores of military automatic weapons may be finished with a thin electro-deposit of hard chromium after the rifling process to help reduce bore erosion in service. The spiral pattern of rifling grooves may be imparted by a number of machining methods:

- **Hook** — A single hook-shaped hard cutting tool, mounted on a rod is pulled through the bore as the barrel is rotated so as to cut a shallow, single groove. The process is repeated after increasing the height of the cutting tool a number of times, so as to produce a groove of the desired depth. These processes are then repeated to produce the de-sired number of grooves. This process leaves longitudinal scratches in the cut grooves.
- **Broach, gang** — All of the grooves can be cut simultaneously in a single pass of a cutting tool consisting of a series of hard discs of increasing diameter machined with the profile of the rifling. This process leaves longitudinal scratches in the cut grooves
- **Broach, single** — A series of non-adjustable single broaches of in-creasing diameters are used to cut all of the grooves simultaneously until the desired groove depth is achieved.

**Figure 4.18**   Russian special purpose 9 mm pistol with barrel assembled with integral silencer.

- **Button** — A hardened metal button, machined with the complete rifling profile, is pushed or pulled through the bore to cold form the rifling by a swaging process. The circular scratches left within the bore during the initial drilling and reaming processes are pushed into the surfaces of the grooves, leaving these marks behind on both the lands and the grooves.
- **Scrape** — A tool machined with the profile of two rifling cutters is scraped through the bore to produce two opposing grooves in each operation.
- **Swage or hammer** — An extremely hard and polished mandrel possessing the desired rifling form is passed through a bore of slightly greater diameter than that eventually desired, while the external surface of the barrel is subjected to a process of hammer forging or the application of hydraulic pressure. Afterwards the rifled bore is left behind virtually free of any striations. The barrel will also exhibit a

spiral pattern upon its exterior due to the displacement of metal during this process. In most instances these spiral projections are removed on a lathe, although the firm of Steyr-Mannlicher leaves it on the barrels of their sporting rifles to signify the quality nature of the manufacturing process.

- **Electrolytic and gas** — There has been some limited use of electrolytic and gas cutting rifling processes. Smith and Wesson are currently using this process to rifle many of their revolver barrels. In the electrolytic process an applied direct electric current causes the barrel to act as the anode, whilst a slightly under-sized partially screened rod inside the electrolyte filled bore serves as the cathode. During the operation, metal is stripped from the desired areas of the barrel bore. In the process in use at Smith and Wesson, the cathode consists of a two-inch long plastic cylinder with metal strips countersunk into the plastic in a spiral approximating the desired rate of twist. The barrel and electrode are immersed in a sodium nitrate based electrolyte, which is pumped through the bore as the electrode passes through it rotating at the desired rifling pitch. Typically, the rifling process takes about 60 seconds per barrel, and each electrode is capable of rifling approximately 3000 inches (77m) of barrelling before requiring servicing. This process tends to produce lands possessing distinctly rounded shoulders and a pockmarked pattern of etching inside the grooves.

## 4.19.2 Machining Processes

Many of the machining processes set out below can be incorporated in the tasks carried out by Computer Numerical Control (CNC) machinery. Some manufacturers will use such automated processes to rough out the components prior to hand finishing, whilst other manufacturers will use them in a reverse manner or may use them for the entire operation.

- **Turning** — The work-piece is spun rapidly on a lathe whilst a chisel-shaped tool is applied parallel to the work-piece. The tool is then traversed across its face, cutting away the metal at a predetermined depth, leaving behind fine helical turning marks. Several passes are usually required until the desired depth of metal has been removed. If used in a facing operation, the tool is brought into contact at right angles to the work-piece.
- **Milling** — This process uses a rapidly rotating multi-point cutting tool, possessing equally spaced teeth around its circumference. Each revolution of the tool causes numerous cuts to be made as the work-piece is fed into contact with it. In 'conventional milling' process the cutter rotates in the direction opposite to the feed movement, whilst

in 'climb milling' the cutter rotates in the direction of the work-piece. A fluted multi-point cutting tool resembling a reamer is used in 'end milling' processes, leaving behind semi-circular, evenly spaced lines across the machined surface, or widely separated ridges if the side cutting edges of the cutting tool are used to face a surface.

- **Boring** — An existing hole can be enlarged or reshaped using a single-point cutting tool upon a rotating work-piece. 'Horizontal boring' involves a rotating cutting tool being fed into the work-piece to leave behind helical tool-marks.

- **Drilling** — A fluted tool possessing a V-shaped cutting point and a spiral pattern of multiple cutting edges about its length is rotated with applied pressure to the work surface. The rate of rotation of the drill bit and its feed rate will determine the roughness of the helical tool-marks and the amount of burrs left inside the hole. 'High-speed' drill bits are made from a steel alloy better able to withstand the high temperatures that can be generated during drilling, whilst specialised drill bits, capable of dealing with very hard materials, have extremely hard tungsten carbide or tungsten alloy inserts fitted to the ends of the bit.

- **Reaming** — A fluted multi-point cutting rotating tool is used in a similar process to drilling to remove only a small amount of material inside a hole left by a previous drilling process. The rough finish from the previous process is made smoother, and at the same time the hole is accurately sized to the desired diameter.

- **Broaching** — A tool possessing a series of teeth or cutters, of increasing height or diameter, set in a line, produces parallel tool-marks possessing the features of the final cutter. This process can be used to size, shape or finish a surface.

- **Grinding** — A rotating wheel with an annular shaped hard abrasive material bonded to it used in finishing processes to produce flat or shaped surfaces, leaving behind irregular contoured tool-marks. **Ultrasonic** techniques use the hammering effect created by the very rapid agitation of fluid borne abrasive particles against the work-piece. **Jet** processes use a high velocity air stream, projected from changing positions and directions at the work-piece, carrying particles of abrasives such as sand, carborundum, corundum and boron carbide. a moving tool projecting loose slurry containing abrasive particles is used to produce a fine finish in **abrasive lapping** processes.

- **Stamping** — Components or holes can be punched out of sheet metal by applying a shearing force. Two tools are involved moving in opposite directions to impact the work material, so as to pass each other at the end of the machining stroke.

- **Forging** — Metal is compressed to the desired shape by the application of high impact pressure. When squeezed into a **cold forming** die, a thin 'flash' of surplus metal is squeezed out at the edges. Wire is compressed into a cavity die to produce a desired shape in **cold heading.** A red-hot metal billet or casting is forged to the desired shape in **drop forging.** In **upset forging** a heated rod of metal moved into a cavity die is shaped by the opposing impact force of a punch.
- **Deep drawing** — A sheet metal blank is stretched and drawn into a die by the application of pressure by a punch. This process is used in the production of cartridge cases.
- **Impact extrusion** — A single high-speed impact of a punch applied to cold metal causes metal to flow up around the punch or down through a die.
- **Swaging** — Reduction of a piece of metal to the desired size and shape by the repeated impacts of 'hammers' whilst held in a rotating or stationary die.
- **Extrusion moulding** — Used in the production of shotgun cartridge cases, where heated plastic is shaped into a tube around a mandrel positioned inside a tubular die, by pressure applied by a helical screw. **Injection** moulding involves the forcible injection of molten plastic into a cavity die. The material is allowed to harden by cooling before the removal of the shaped product. Marks left by the injection sprue and the die seams are usually evident.
- **Casting** — Patterns of the desired object are compressed within a two-part frame filled with 'moulding sand' that contains a proportion of clay. The frame is then turned over and opened to allow the removal of the patterns and the dusting of the eventual joint face of the half-mould so produced with clay-free 'parting sand'. The top half of the frame is then filled with more moulding sand, which is rammed home as the frame is closed. Metal is then poured through the sprues into the cavity and allowed to solidify before removal. A ceramic slurry is applied to patterns made from wax or plastic during the process of **investment** casting, sometimes referred to as 'the lost wax process'. After thorough drying, the patterns are removed by melting them, leaving behind precisely shaped cavities. After the cast metal has solidified the outer mould material is broken away. Components of great dimensional accuracy and high surface finish can be produced by **shell-moulding,** where the traditional foundry sand used in the two-part frame is replaced by clay-free fine sand incorporating a 5% addition of a phenol-formaldehyde or urea-formaldehyde plastic bonding agent. The shell-mould halves are heated to 250°C to cause the bonding agent to 'set', after which the faces of the half moulds are

coated with a silicone oil to facilitate subsequent removal of the patterns. The second half of the shell mould is produced as in the previous process but using the same special moulding mixture and heating. The pattern plate is removed from the frame with the shell still attached to it prior to a 'curing' process for two minutes at 315°C. The pattern is stripped from the shell by means of ejector pins built into the pattern plate to allow repeated use in casting quality components. **Powder-metallurgy** techniques allow the compaction and cold welding of metal and carbide powders, or the metal injection moulding (**MIM**) under pressure of wax and metal powder, before going through a high temperature **sintering** process which also induces a controlled degree of shrinkage as the metal powder fuses together and the wax is expelled as vapour.

• **Soldering, brazing** and **welding** — These processes are used in place of pinning or bolting together component parts. **Soft soldering** was traditionally used for such processes as the joining together of the barrels and ribs of a double-barrelled gun. The traditional and complex barrel blueing processes allowed the use of this method of fixing. However, the high caustic soda content of modern rapid barrel blacking processes attacks soft solder joints, thus necessitating the change to **silver solder** or **braze.** The pressed sheet metal bodies, particularly of military arms, are often held together using **electric spot, stitch** or **seam welding** processes; aluminium alloy components in particular require the use of **metal inert gas (MIG)** or **tungsten inert gas (TIG)** welding techniques. **Electric arc, gas, MIG** and **TIG** welding techniques are also used by some gunsmiths when repairing or customising firearms.

## 4.19.3 Finishing Processes

It is customary to apply external protective finishes to firearm components prior to their assembly, these are often intended also to confer a pleasing external appearance. External surfaces of most firearms will be subjected to polishing processes prior to the application of decorative or protective finishes. **Blueing**, the most common finish for ferrous articles, is a very thin, oiled and uniform blue or black (formerly brown) protective oxide coating. Traditional processes required skilled operatives, relatively complex rusting solutions, and a great deal of time, to produce a beautiful blue or blue-black coloured finish. Most modern, mass-production finishing processes yield a black oxide finish within about ten to thirty minutes, depending upon the particular steel alloy, using a hot concentrated aqueous solution of sodium nitrate and caustic soda or tri-sodium phosphate.

Rust-inhibiting phosphate coatings can be applied to steel components using hot aqueous **Parkerising** treatment baths. **Electroplated** metal coatings, typically under a thousandth of an inch thick (less than 25 microns) of nickel, chromium, silver, copper, brass and gold can be applied to firearm components. Copper, nickel and copper alloy deposits are sometimes applied to shotgun pellets and to BB air gun pellets and to lead bullets (e.g., Winchester 'Lubaloy'). Very thick copper electrodeposits are applied to Speer 'Total Metal Coated' (TMC) bullets. Nylon and PTFE coatings have also been applied to, e.g., 'Nyclad' and 'KTW' metal piercing bullets. **Electroless nickel** coatings are sometimes applied to such items as pistol frames, particularly during customising operations. **Anodising** of components made from aluminium and its alloys produces a hard, thin and continuous protective aluminium oxide coating, using an electrolytic anodic treatment in aqueous sulfuric acid or chromic acid based treatment baths. After the anodising treatment is finished the components are steeped in a boiling water bath to seal the pores in the coating. Water-soluble colour dies are usually added to this boiling water bath so as to impart a permanent colour finish, usually black, to the coating. This process is used on aluminium alloy frames, trigger guards, actions, and upon telescopic sights and their mounts.

## Further Reading

Bartocci, C.R. 2001. New Russian assault rifle. The AN-94. *AFTE Journal*, **33** (3) 275–276.

Burrard, Major Sir G. 1950. *The Modern Shotgun*, London: Herbert Jenkins.

Cardew, G.V. and Cardew, G.M. 1995. *The Air Gun from Trigger to Target*, Birmingham: Cardew.

Churchill, R. 1955. *Game Shooting*, London: Michael Joseph.

Garwood, G.T. 1969. *Gough Thomas's Gun Book*, London: A.C. Black.

Garwood, G.T. 1975. *Shotguns and Cartridges for Game and Clays*, London: Black.

Greener, W.W. 1910. *The Gun and Its Development*, New York: Bonanza.

Hearn, A. 1945. *Shooting and Gun Fitting*, London: Herbert Jenkins.

Higgins, R.A. 1987. *Materials for the Engineering Technician* (2nd Ed.), London: Edward Arnold.

Hogg, I.V. 1993. *Jane's Infantry Weapons*, Coulsdon, Surrey: Jane's Information Group.

Keith, E. 1950. *Shotguns*, Harrisburg PA: Stackpole and Heck.

Lancaster, C. 1942. *The Art of Shooting*, London: McCorkdale.

Moltrecht, K.H. 1981. *Machine Shop Practice*, Vol. 1 and 2, New York: Industrial Press.

Nelson, T.B. 1963. *The World's Sub-Machine Guns,* Cologne, Germany: International Small Arms Publishers.

Nelson, T.B. and Musgrave, D.D. 1967. *The World's Assault Rifles and Automatic Carbines,* Alexandria VA: TBN Enterprises.

Nelson, T.B. and Musgrave, D.D. 1980. *The World's Machine Pistols and Sub-Machine-Guns,* London: Arms and Armour Press.

Payne-Gallwey, Sir, R. 1899. *Letters to Young Shooters,* London: Longman Green.

Payne-Gallwey, Sir, R. 1986. *The Crossbow* (8th Ed.), First published 1903, London: Holland Press.

Pollard, Major H. 1923. *Shot-Guns, Their History and Development,* London: Sir Isaac Pittman.

Smith, W.H.B. 1960. *The Book of Rifles,* Harrisburg PA: Stackpole.

Smith, W.H.B. 1968. *Book of Pistols and Revolvers,* Harrisburg PA: Stackpole.

Smith, W.H.B and Smith, J.B. 1973. *Small Arms of the World,* London: Arms and Armour Press.

Todd, R.H. 1994. *Fundamental Principles in Manufacturing Processes.* New York: Industrial Press.

Todd, R.H and Allen, D.K. 1994. *Manufacturing Process Reference Guide.* New York: Industrial Press.

Walter, J. 1984. *The Air Gun Book,* London: Arms and Armour Press.

Whelen, Colonel T. 1945. *Small-Arms Design and Ballistics,* Vol. 1, *Design,* Plantersville SC: Small-Arms Technical Publishing Co.

Wilson, R.K. 1943. *Textbook of Automatic Pistols,* Plantersville SC: Small-Arms Technical Publishing Co.

# Internal Ballistics 5

## 5.1 Basic Principles

Internal ballistics concerns what happens within a time span of in the region of 2 ms between the impact of the firing pin or striker and the exit of the bullet or shot charge from the muzzle end of the barrel. This short span of time has profound implications for the forensic scientist. I have also decided to include within this chapter the consequences of events immediately before and after this prestated time span within the firearm. As previously stated, all modern firearms are, in reality, heat engines of Victorian design. They burn a fuel within them to produce a momentary emission of extreme heat and high-pressure gases. The energy so released is utilised to accelerate a single missile or a number of projectiles down the barrel to exit from the muzzle at high velocity. The kinetic energy of the bullet or missiles so discharged is a function of their velocity and, in turn, is a manifestation of a portion of the energy released by the powder charge.

The material ejected from the firearm will, in the case of simple impulse-launched designs, exhibit its highest velocity at the moment of its release. The energy carried by the missile or missiles is usually referred to as the kinetic energy. This is usually expressed in units of the kinetic energy terms 'ft·lb' or 'joules'. However, as with all heat engines, not all of the energy released by the burning of the fuel is transferred to the intended work function.

## 5.2 The Efficiency of Energy Transfer

Even with a modern well-balanced loading such as the 7.62 mm Nato loading (Figure 5.1), or its civilian counterpart the .308 in Winchester, a large proportion of the potential energy of the burning of the powder charge is lost

**Figure 5.1**    The cartridge loading at the heart of the firearm heat engine. Nato 7.62×51 mm rifle and machine gun loading. However, not all of the available energy contained in the powder charge is imparted to the projectile.

during the process of firing. Tests I have conducted with my own .308 in Sauer bolt action rifle, which I use for deer stalking and target shooting, using Norma cases, CCI primers, 150 grain (9.72 g) Nosler Ballistic Tip bullets, and a charge of 46.3 grains (3.0 g) of Hercules (Alliance) Reloader 15 double-base smokeless powder, yield average missile chronograph values of 870 m/s (2853 ft/s) from its 600 mm (23.6 in) long barrel.

According to official Hercules data the combustion of Reloader 15 powder results in the following combustion products: 42.9% carbon monoxide, 22.5% water, 10.7% carbon dioxide, 11.1% nitrogen, 12.3% hydrogen, 0.5% other gases, and 952 calories of heat per gram when completely consumed. It follows therefore that the powder energy yield of my 3 g loading must be 11,958 J (2856 calories) assuming 100% combustion. The kinetic energy carried by my bullet from such a discharge is provided by the formula:

$$\text{Kinetic energy} = \frac{MV^2}{2}$$

The calculated kinetic energy comes out at 3672 J (2709 ft·lb). The bullet is therefore carrying only 30.7% of the potential energy of the powder charge, which is in fact a respectable efficiency ratio for a firearm. Other functions account for the 69.3% of the energy that has been effectively lost, the bulk of which will have been used to heat up the barrel and cartridge case or released as muzzle blast. Previously published figures from the Royal Military College of Science at Shrivenham in Wiltshire indicate that about 0.2% of the energy will be used to provide the rotational spin to the bullet; about 3% of the energy will be consumed by friction in the bore; a further 3% will be used in the work of moving the gases along the bore; and approximately 0.1% of the energy will be released as recoil. The remainder, approximately 63% of the powder energy, will be released as heat, with heating of the barrel and the cartridge case accounting for approximately 20% of the energy and with the violent release of approximately 40% of the energy as a blast of highly energetic hot gases at the muzzle. The major part of the missing energy has thus been wastefully released as a violent blast of extremely hot gas at the muzzle and as transfer of wasted heat to the nearest heat sink, the barrel and cartridge case. The bulk of the energy from the burning of the powder charge has been distributed in wasteful and undesirable work functions. All shooters are aware of the violent effect of muzzle blast and the heating up of a rifle barrel during firing. The former effect is caused by the hot gases exiting the muzzle at several thousands of pounds per square inch pressure, the latter effect is caused by the barrel having been exposed, albeit briefly, to a temperature of approximately 2500 K. This is well above the melting point of the best barrel steel (1800 K) which serves as the pressure vessel. The barrel is not, of course, melted entirely by this effect, no more than your hand will be consumed if you pass it briefly across a flame. Some metal is eroded away however, especially in the region of the rifling leade at the breech end of the barrel. Energy losses in these areas are even higher in the case of certain grossly 'over-bore-capacity' Magnum load-ings, causing short accurate barrel life and the rapid onset of deafness if suitable hearing protection is not worn. This is, of course, one of the predictable con-sequences of the law of diminishing returns and the natural tendency for an increase in the entropy of the universe to occur from any spontaneous reaction. Energy is not released cleanly in a single convenient form; rather its release is manifested in a number of different forms, all of which can interact in different ways upon their surroundings.

The brass cartridge case associated with the original loading has fulfilled a number of vital functions. It has served as a convenient weatherproof, impact-resistant, fire-resistant package for the propellant and the primer. During the firing process it swells with gas pressure to ensure a gas-tight seal for the pressure vessel (the barrel), so that no flash or dangerous high-pressure gases can in normal circumstances compromise the integrity of the firearm or the safety of the firer. It also acts in conjunction with the barrel as the heat sink. In the case of self-loading or automatic weapons the cartridge case extraction thus usefully serves to remove a portion of the undesirable heat of the discharge away from the firearm.

The Law of Conservation of Energy does not allow energy to be 'lost', in the normal understanding of the term. The First Law of Thermodynamics derived from the above states: The total energy of a system and its surroundings must remain constant, although it may be changed from one form to another. The Second Law of Thermodynamics states: Heat cannot be completely converted into an equivalent amount of work without causing other changes in some part of the system or its surroundings. It follows therefore, that the energy released by the combustion of the powder is simply manifested in different other work functions, the bulk of which end up as relatively small contributions of heat to the universe through conduction, convection and radiation. The original orderly constructions of the powder grains, the bullet and the target, have all suffered irreversible decomposition, damage and change. Various gases of combustion have been released into the atmosphere along with the disturbance produced by the blast wave of discharge. The entropy of the universe, and as a consequence the degree of its general disorder, has also suffered a modest increase.

## 5.3   Powders and Pressures

Generally speaking, the pressure levels which are generated during the firing of a high-power, centre-fire rifle cartridge loading will be higher than those appropriate for pistols or shotguns; mean peak pressure values in the region of approximately 3450 bar (50,000 lb/in²) will represent a common value measured by crusher systems expressed in cup (copper units of pressure), or an equivalent value of 4140 bar (60,000 lb/in²) when measured using piezoelectric techniques. Rifle barrels are longer and more robustly constructed than pistol barrels and are designed to withstand far higher pressures than their pistol or shotgun counterparts. The bolt or breech block will also be securely locked to the breech end of the barrel at the moment of firing to contain the forces generated by the high breech pressures, which in modern loadings will be in excess of 3000 bar (45,000 lb/in²). As a consequence the velocity of a rifle bullet is likely to be two or possibly three times that of a pistol bullet or shot charge.

The burning rates of modern smokeless powders are varied to suit particular applications. Pistols will require fast-burning powders for use in their short barrels. Shotguns will also require relatively fast-burning powders, as they are only intended to produce relatively modest velocities and pressures, and to cater for the empty swept volume left in their large-diameter bores behind the shot charge and wadding as they are accelerated down the barrel. As previously stated, most smokeless propellants are single or double base, that is to say that they are composed predominantly of either nitrocellulose, or a combination of nitrocellulose and nitroglycerine; these are both explosive substances in their own right. The addition of nitroglycerine is used to increase the energy content of the powder, and can range from a few percent in the case of some rifle powders, all the way up to 40% in the case of the popular Hercules Bullseye pistol powder. By way of contrast, black powder is an intimate mixture of an oxidising agent potassium nitrate and two fuels, sulphur and charcoal, which react together by way of rapid burning upon ignition. In their original forms nitrocellulose and nitroglycerine are too violent in operation to be used as propellants. By dissolving them in ether and alcohol they are converted to a colloidal form. This plastic material can then be extruded in the form of a thin stick or other shapes, which in turn can be chopped up into suitable lengths. Ball powders are manufactured by an aqueous slurry process to produce the powder in small individual particles which are converted using ethyl acetate solvent. Retardants and stabilisers are added to propellants during their manufacture. Diphenylamine is a common stabiliser; potassium sulphate will reduce the visible flash when the firearm is discharged in conditions of dusk; a graphitised coating will assist the free running of the powder grains through the metering devices used during the loading of ammunition; other deterrents, retardants and coatings can be used to produce further changes in the ballistic characteristics of the particular powder, for example, methyl and ethyl centralite, and dinitrotoluene.

Smokeless powders are often described as being 'slow burning' or 'fast burning', although such terms are misnomers. The value for 'Relative Quickness' (RQ) for a powder is the rate at which the burning gunpowder yields its latent energy relative to some other powder being used as a reference standard. The RQ scale used for Du Pont's propellants uses their 'Improved Military Rifle' powder IMR 4350 to represent 100 units on the relative burning quickness scale (Table 5.1).

Powders manufactured by other companies can be compared in order of decreasing relative quickness (Table 5.2).

**Table 5.1    Relative Quickness of IMR Powders**

| IMR Powder | RQ Value | IMR Powder | RQ Value |
|------------|----------|------------|----------|
| 5010 | 70.0 | 4064/4895 | 120.0 |
| 4831 | 89.9 | 3031 | 135.0 |
| 4350 | 100.0 | 4198 | 160.0 |
| 4320 | 110.0 | 4227 | 180.0 |
| 4895 | 115.0 | | |

**Table 5.2  Relative Quickness of Powders**

| Vihtavuori | IMR | Hodgdon | Norma | RWS | Alliant | SNPE | W-W |
|---|---|---|---|---|---|---|---|
| | | | | P805 | | | |
| | | | R1 | | | | |
| N310 | | HP38 | | P801 | | BA10 | |
| | | | | | Bullseye | | 231 |
| N320 | 700X | Trap 100 | | | Red Dot | | 452AA |
| | PX | | | | GreenDot | | |
| | SR7625 | | | P804 | | | 473AA |
| | | | | | Unique | | |
| | | HS-6 | | P803 | | BA9 | 540 |
| | SR4756 | | | | Herco | | |
| N340 | | | | | | | |
| | | | | | Blue Dot | | |
| 3N37 | 800X | HS-7 | | | | | 571 |
| | | | | | 2400 | | |
| N350 | | | R-123 | | | | |
| | SR4795 | H110 | | P806 | | | |
| N110 | 4227 | H4198 | | | | Tubal 1 | 296 |
| | | | | | | | 680 |
| | | H4227 | 200 | R901 | | | |
| N120 | 4198 | H322 | | | Reloder 7 | | |
| | | BL-C(2) | | | | Tubal 2 | |
| | 3031 | | | R902 | | | |
| | | | 201 | | | | |
| N133 | | | 202 | | | | 748 |
| | | H335 | | | | SP10 | |
| | | | | R903 | | | |
| | 4064 | | | | | | |
| | 4895 | H4895 | | | Reloder12 | | |
| N135 | | | | | | Tubal 4 | |
| | 4320 | | | | | | |
| N140 | | H380 | | R907 | Reloder15 | Tubal 5 | |
| | | H414 | | | | Tubal 6 | 760 |
| | | | | R904 | | | |
| N150 | 4350 | H4350 | | | | Tubal 7 | |
| | | H450 | 204 | | | | |
| | | | | | Reloder19 | | 785 |
| N160 | 4831 | | | | | Tubal 8 | |
| | | H4831 | | R905 | | | |
| | | | MRP | | Reloder22 | | |
| N165 | 7828 | | | | | | |
| | | H870 | | | | | |

*Source*: 1992 Vihtavuori Oy Reloading Guide.

Elevated temperatures tend to increase the pressure generated by a cartridge during its firing, and hence produce a consequent increase in bullet velocity. In the case of IMR propellants used for the loading of .30-06 rifle cartridges, the velocity increase is approximately 1.7 ft/s for each 1°F rise in temperature (0.52 m/s per 0.56° C increase).

## 5.4   Control of Powder Burning Rates

The burning rates of smokeless powders are determined mainly by the dimensions and shapes of the individual powder grains, and to a lesser degree by the use of surface coatings (Figure 5.2). Pistol and shotgun powders tend to be in the form of thin discs or square flakes, which offer a large surface area for burning to take place and which, at the same time, maintain the same exposed surface area before they are completely consumed. Most rifle powders are made in the form of small solid cylinders, cylinders with a hole bored down the long central axis, or in some cases, the grains can be near-spherical. Solid cylinders and spheres expose a

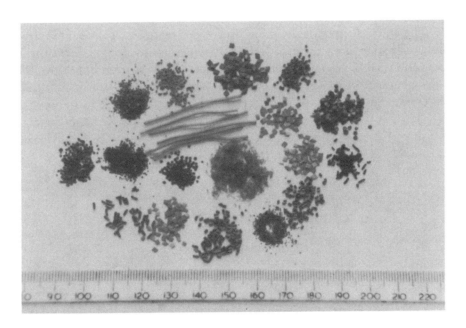

**Figure 5.2**   The different shapes of nitrocellulose powder grains influence their burning rates. The spaghetti-shaped double-based propellant in the centre of the picture is cordite, a hot-burning high-nitroglycerine double-base propellant, favoured by the British for many years.

reduced surface area for further burning as their diameters suffer reduction during the burning process; such shapes will tend to produce a slower burning powder due to this regressive feature, all other things being equal. The pierced cylinder form of powder grain will burn both on the outside and on the inside, with consequent changes taking place in each of the critical diameters, thus tending to produce a consistent exposed surface area; such powders will be faster burning than the solid cylinder shape, but slower burning than simple disc or flake propellants.

During combustion the burning rate in a direction normal to the surface is uniform over the entire exposed surface (Piobert's Law). The thickness of the flake, ball, or the wall of a tubular powder will affect the burning time of the powder. This thickness is sometimes referred to as the 'web'. High-intensity Magnum rifle cartridge loadings will need to exhibit the broadest time/pressure curves to allow very high velocities to be generated without exceeding maximum permissible barrel pressures (Figure 5.3). This is achieved by using heavy charges of slow-burning powders which are consumed in a longer period inside the bore, thus providing a longer period of effective acceleration to the bullet. Although the energy transfer is not as efficient as the burning of faster powders, the velocity gains are considered to have been achieved at an acceptable cost.

The entire surface of the grain of powder regresses at the same rate, as previously stated for Piobert's Law. The powder grains are therefore burning away about all their exposed surfaces in parallel layers from both sides. The rate of reduction in size is referred to as the burning rate or the rate of regression. Superimposed upon the effects of powder grain morphology is the fact that with smokeless powders, the burning rate increases with the pressure of the surrounding gases

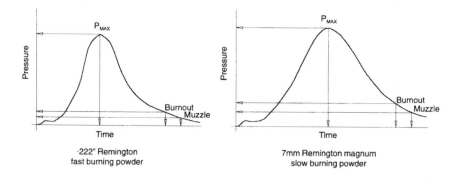

**Figure 5.3**  The different shapes of time—pressure curves.

$$\text{Buring rate,} \frac{ds}{dt} = BP^a$$

where $s$ is the size of the powder grain, $t$ is the time in seconds, $P$ is the gas pressure, $a$ is the pressure index of the particular propellant and $B$ is the burning rate constant of the propellant.

What can be seen from the above formula is that the rate of burning and, hence, the build-up of pressure in turn increase with pressure. If attempts are made to work up high-velocity loadings, especially by using fast-burning powders which tend to produce narrow peaked time/pressure curves, it is extremely easy to create conditions which will result in barrel bursts.

There are a number of significant differences between the black powder (gunpowder) charges used in earlier loadings and modern smokeless powders apart from the obvious ones of their relatively smoke-free burning, less fouling and higher energy contents. Black powder is far easier to ignite and, once lit, burns at a constant rate, leaving behind copious amounts of solid residues, referred to as 'fouling' in the bore. The burning rate of smokeless powders, on the other hand, increases greatly with increasing pressure, and the powders will stop burning if the pressure level within the barrel drops below a critical value. If too much powder is used in a particular loading, and especially if its normal burning rate is too fast for the particular application, the inevitable consequence of the exponential increase of the burning rate with increasing pressure will result in the catastrophic failure of the pressure vessel.

## 5.5   Drachms and Drams

It is of interest to note that in the black-powder period most powder charges were measured out by volume, both during the muzzle-loading period and during the use of this propellant in the reloading of ammunition. Disaster overcame people when first trying the new smokeless powders, which of course required considerably smaller charges to produce the same ballistic effect. Charges thrown by conventional powder measures resulted in burst guns, injury and sometimes the death of the would-be firer. For a few decades, the new powders were bulked out to allow their safe use in old powder measures. A residue from this period is still to be seen on shotgun cartridges of American manufacture which still refer to the dram (drachm) equivalent of the modern low-density powder charges used. The dram/drachm weight used in times past is different from that used by pharmacists, which has added to the confusion. The powder dram weighs one-sixteenth of an ounce, which corresponds to 1.772 g (27.34 grain).

## 5.6   The Residues of Combustion

The above factors are of interest to the forensic scientist because, apart from the different pressure effects he will observe on the spent cartridge cases, powder charges are not completely consumed during the discharge of a firearm, in the same way as unburnt coal or wood will be left behind in the fireplace from the previous day's fire. Unburnt grains or fragments of powder grains will often be found in the bore or other parts of a gun. Similar materials will be forcibly ejected from the gun barrel with the fatal bullet or shot charge and at close confrontational ranges will be found embedded in the clothing or tissue of the victim. Such effects upon the victim will be used at some stage for the estimation of the range of firing, to determine the probable brand of ammunition used from powder grain morphology and composition and from the nature of the primer-generated residues.

Unburnt or partially consumed powder grains and other discharge residues can be recovered during the examination of the weapon, the clothing of the victim or from the tissue of any wound sample submitted or requested from the postmortem examination. The size and morphology of the powder grains can be compared with the laboratory database of propellants, and they can also be analysed to determine their composition along with any primer-generated residues. Such work will yield information which can be used to determine the type or likely brand of loading used, and may be significant if similar materials are found in ammunition possessed by a suspect.

## 5.7   Primer Formulations

The primers used in the manufacture of smokeless ammunition are more energetic and are made to more exacting standards than those used with black powder loadings. The particular primer used in the cartridge loading will generate materials of interest to the investigating scientist, as proprietary brands of primers can vary greatly in their formulation. Early primer formulations were based upon the use of mercury fulminate, $Hg(CNO)_2$, which is a sensitive explosive material in its own right, potassium chlorate which can also explode if subjected to severe impact force and is at the same time a powerful oxidising agent, antimony trisulphide which acts as a fuel, and powdered glass which acts as an abrasive friction material. Unfortunately, mercury fulminate-based primers deteriorate during storage, thus leading to misfires; in addition, mercury is an element which can cause embrittlement or 'season cracking' in brass formulations normally used in the manufacture of cartridge cases (an alloy of 70–72% copper and 28–30% zinc), and the potassium chloride residues produced as a reaction product from the potassium chlorate are a powerful promoter of subsequent barrel corrosion, if adequate cleaning is not carried out soon after the particular gun has been used.

During World War I, in an attempt to avoid the problems caused by mercury fulminate, the US Frankford Arsenal moved to a primer formulation based upon potassium chlorate, antimony trisulphide and sulphur; this formulation also avoided the use of ground glass which was thought at the time to be injurious to the bore. After encountering unexplained problems with misfires they were forced to change to a Winchester formulation which was based upon potassium chlorate, antimony trisulphide, lead thiocyanide and TNT. In Germany, a chlorate-free non-corrosive primer formulation was in use from 1911 which was based upon mercury fulminate, barium nitrate, antimony trisulphide, picric acid and ground glass.

Various other attempts were made over the years to produce non-corrosive ammunition primers, and for a period a primer formulation based upon barium nitrate and red phosphorus was used in certain US military loadings. Eventually however, most formulations moved to the use of barium nitrate as an oxidiser in place of potassium chlorate and substituted lead styphnate (lead tri-nitro resorcinate) in place of mercury fulminate, with the occasional use of tetracene to increase its sensitivity, and antimony trisulphide as the fuel. A range of other materials can be used, such as powdered glass as a friction agent and calcium silicide and other materials which will cause hot incendiary sparks to pass into the powder charge. The German 1921 Sinoxid formulation is an example of one of the earliest 'modern' primer formulations:

Lead styphnate, 20–73%
Tetracene, 1–40%
Barium nitrate, 6–49%
Lead dioxide, 0–10%
Calcium silicide, 0–16%
Antimony trisulphide, 0–27%
Powdered glass 0–16%

The priming mixtures used in the manufacture of some modern .22 in rimfire cartridges sometimes omit the use of antimony trisulphide. A typical range of modern proprietary primer formulations is shown in Table 5.3.

In a response to problems encountered with high lead levels in the atmosphere in indoor ranges, RWS of Germany have recently introduced a lead-free priming formulation called *Sintox*. This formulation is based upon tetrazine, diazole (2-diazo4, 6, dinitrophenol) as the primary metal-free explosive material, zinc peroxide as an oxidiser, and titanium to burn so as to produce a shower of white hot incendiary sparks. A similar priming com-

**Table 5.3   Some Modern Proprietary Primer Formulations**

| Component | Composition (in%) | | | | |
|---|---|---|---|---|---|
|  | A | B | C | D | E |
| Lead styphnate | 36 | 41 | 39 | 43 | 37 |
| Barium nitrate | 29 | 39 | 40 | 36 | 38 |
| Antimony trisulphide | 9 | 9 | 11 | 0 | 11 |
| Calcium silicide | 0 | 8 | 0 | 12 | 0 |
| Lead dioxide | 9 | 0 | 0 | 0 | 0 |
| Tetrazine | 3 | 3 | 4 | 3 | 3 |
| Zirconium | 9 | 0 | 0 | 0 | 0 |
| Pentaerythritol tetranitrate | 5 | 0 | 0 | 0 | 5 |
| Nitrocellulose | 0 | 0 | 6 | 0 | 0 |
| Lead peroxide | 0 | 0 | 0 | 6 | 6 |

position recently introduced by CCI for use in their lead-free 'Clean-Fire' range of ammunition uses the same primary initiator along with strontium nitrate as a replacement for the more usual barium nitrate oxidiser. The bullets used in these loadings are similar to those used in their lead-free 'Blazer' ammunition in that their lead bullets are totally encapsulated in an electrodeposited pure copper coating 0.25 mm (0.010 in) thick, intended to reduce airborne lead levels in firing ranges further. Winchester has recently introduced pistol cartridges loaded with 'Win-Clean' primers declared to be free of lead, barium, antimony and strontium, which also employ totally encapsulated bullets to reduce airborne lead in indoor ranges. A similar line of lead-free primers and totally encapsulated pistol bullets has recently been announced by Remington. The Federal Cartridge Company has responded with the introduction of 'Ballisti-Clean' ammunition and copper jacketed bullets filled with zinc cores. Federal also produce heavy-metal-free .22 inch Long Rifle ammunition loaded with 27 grain (1.75g) tin bullets. The US military have developed a special purpose 5.56x45 mm lead-free loading using a jacketed bullet filled with a tin/tungsten core. Commercial ammunition is now being manufactured at Muron in Russia, based upon diazodinitrophenol, potassium styphnate and a glassy frictionator material containing potassium, aluminium and silicon, along with traces of sodium, magnesium, titanium and iron.

## 5.8   Gunshot Residue Analysis

When a cartridge is fired in a gun combustion, products from both the primer and the propellant will be released at the same time. Although nitrocellulose is a relatively common material, often used in paints and lacquers, the finding of traces of this material in conjunction with nitroglycerine and perhaps dinitrotoluene on hand swabs, hair or the clothing of a suspect, would support the likelihood that he had had either fired a firearm recently, or had been in close proximity to one being fired, using a cartridge loaded with a double-base powder.

The scanning electron microscope, when used with a microprobe facility (energy dispersive X-ray fluorescence detection) can also be used to check for the presence of gunshot residues. These residues tend to be approximately spherical in shape, and range in size between 0.5 and 10 μm diameter. An automatic computer program can be used to search swabs, discs or tapings overnight or at weekends, to avoid the chore of searching through the jumble of dirt and detritus also present. Gunshot residue particles are likely to contain elements from the priming mixture. Typically, lead, barium, antimony, calcium, silicon and sulphur, in the case of ammunition of recent manufacture, together with traces of iron from the erosion of the bore and copper and zinc vaporised from the primer cup and the cartridge case. Some individual particles detected may contain all of these materials, others may contain only a few of these elements. However, the finding of a characteristic range of such materials can be considered to constitute definitive proof for a firearm use association to be made. Although gunshot residues will be almost non-existent on a person's hands after a few hours of normal activity, they will be retained for a longer period on hair and face swabs and may be retained for weeks on the clothing of the firer. The finding of some of the more unusual elements previously stated to be used in some brands of ammunition can be much more specific, especially if these same materials are found to be present in any ammunition possessed by a suspect, or which are found to be present in fouling recovered from the bore of a suspect weapon. The presence of mercury and potassium immediately signal the use of old corrosive ammunition, and it is notable that modern military ammunition made by former members of the Soviet Bloc also tend to contain potassium chlorate in the primer formulation.

## 5.9   The Transfer of Marks to Missiles and Cartridge Cases

During the loading and firing of a firearm marks both of a family and an individual nature will be left upon the spent cartridge case, the bullet and in some instances shotgun cartridge wadding. Finding such marks together with other features will allow the firearm examiner to provide the police investigative team with information as to the calibre or gauge of gun involved, the type of weapon used along with the brand and likely age of the ammunition used in the incident (Figure 5.4). By comparison against exhibits contained in the

**Figure 5.4**   Conventional felt, wood-fibre and card shotgun cartridge wads used by different manufacturers. The wads with holes in their centres are employed in loadings containing a tracer capsule.

laboratory Outstanding Crimes Files the forensic scientist will also be able to inform the police if the weapon has been used in some previous shooting incident. At some later stage, if a suspect weapon is recovered, the comparison of the marks produced upon test-firings will normally allow it to be positively linked to the shooting incident or eliminated, as may be the case.

The formation of these characteristic marks upon a bullet, cartridge case or plastic cartridge wad is achieved by a variety of actions and effects. In the case of a rifled arm, the bullet will be engraved with the pattern of rifling contained in the bore and by defects at the muzzle. Over the years firearms manufacturers have come to use different forms of rifling to achieve the same stabilising rotational spin on the bullet (Figure 5.5). The spiral pattern of rifling in the barrel can be manufactured by various engineering techniques. These rifling methods, along with other firearm manufacturing processes and their implications during the examination of casework exhibits, are comprehensively described in Chapter 9.

The groove depth of most rifling measures approximately 0.1 mm (0.004 in). The high points in the bore are referred to as the lands. These effects are less easy to see or measure in polygonal pattern rifled barrels, but are evident as a regular pattern of distortion when the bullet is viewed at its base end. The barrels of the vast majority of commercially produced or modified firearms are 'crowned' at their muzzle ends, by means of rounding off both the inner and outer exposed edges. Revolver and pistol barrels are frequently cut to length from a longer piece of rifled tube or from a single forging intended to make up two pistol barrels. During all of these manufacturing processes

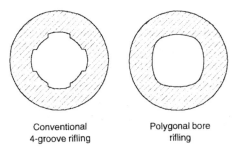

Conventional
4-groove rifling

Polygonal bore
rifling

**Figure 5.5**    Rifled barrels.

small imperfections of a random nature are left behind in the bores due to
tool wear and the nature of the cutting processes. These imperfections are
added to by the effects of use, rough handling or careless cleaning practices.
It follows therefore, that a bullet passing through the barrel of a rifled arm
will pick up both the normal intended pattern of rifling upon its exterior,
and also a pattern of fine lines or striations from the chance imperfections
contained in the bore and at the muzzle. These imperfections and the normal
pattern of rifling will of course be seen upon the bullet in a negative form.
It has long been established that such randomly produced imperfections,
which can be seen under the microscope as a pattern of fine parallel lines
similar to supermarket packaging bar codes, are as unique as a person's
fingerprints.

During the firing process, the pressure of the powder gases causes the
rapid release of the bullet from the mouth of the cartridge case held in the
chamber. The bullet must then jump some distance before it enters the leade
of the rifling in the barrel. There is always some tendency for skidding to
occur before the rifling fully engages its control upon the bullet to induce its
rotational spin. In the case of revolvers, the bullet has to jump a greater
distance under acceleration than with other arms before clearing the cylinder
gap and entering the slightly enlarged barrel throat and then the rifling. As
a consequence it travels on in a straight line for a short distance before the
rifling is able to impart a rotational spin. This tendency for initial skidding
is therefore, more pronounced in this type of weapon. These effects can be
observed on the parallel section of the bullet immediately behind its ogival
nose section at the beginning of the rifling land impression, on the side
opposite to the direction of bullet rotation. Useful features can often be
observed here that can be used for matching purposes. Colt muzzle-loading
percussion revolvers were machined with "gain twist" rifling that gently
imposed the rifling spin to the soft lead balls and conical bullets used with
them in the mid-nineteenth century, and some modern rifled tank barrels,
where very high missile velocities are achieved, also use this same old concept

of gain twist rifling. However, most arms manufacturers perceive no real need for such complications.

Soft lead bullets also tend to strip during their passage through rifled barrels if driven at high velocities. Using lead alloys hardened with tin and/or antimony, coupled with lubrication bands will prevent this to a generally acceptable degree and will minimise the deposits of "leading" left within the rifling. Some hand-loaders using hard cast lead alloy bullets for use with magnum revolvers and medium velocity rifle loadings, may also seek the benefit of crimping brass gas-checks to the heels of the bullets, made in the form of a very short cup, to help prevent gas-cutting damage from the bullet base. Generally speaking, jacketed bullets are used for loadings generating missile velocities above about 1500 ft/s (460 m/s). The non-deforming smooth ogival noses of jacketed bullets are also beneficial in eliminating feeding problems with self-loading arms.

Randomly produced imperfections occur on all of the other machined parts of a firearm, which can in turn be supplemented by the effects of corrosion, minor impacts and improper cleaning techniques; such marks are also uniquely individual in nature. As the cartridge case is forcibly thrust against the recoil face of the gun, and the primer sets back from its pocket due to the effects of headspace, useful marks will be imparted upon the primer and the remainder of the cartridge head. Such marks will best be produced if the cartridge loading generates a relatively high pressure, or if the primer cup is thin or easily deformed by impact. The primer will of course also bear an impression of the firing pin or striker, which for similar reasons will contain imperfections of a unique nature.

Marks will be left on the sides of the cartridge case by the lips of box magazines as the cartridges are stripped from them during the loading of a manually operated arm, the self-loading action of the pistol slide or the self-loading rifle bolt-carrier. The cartridge stop device normally present at the breech end of the tubular magazine of a pump-action or self-loading shotgun prevents a cartridge being released from the magazine except at the correct moment for its transfer when the fore-end is pulled to the rear. The considerable recoil generated upon the firing of the chambered round will cause the column of live cartridges in the magazine to shift and the next cartridge head will, in turn, strike the cartridge stop device, thus picking up a characteristic mark.

Chambering marks will also be left upon the cartridge cases if there is a projecting edge or any roughness on top of the loading ramp or edge of the chamber mouth. In conventional shotguns fitted with spring-loaded ejectors, ejector marks will be left on the underside of the cartridge rim from the 'kick' of the ejector. Marks will be left in a similar location along with an ejector mark some distance away on the edge of the cartridge head if a repeating, self-loading, or automatic arm is involved. The nature and disposition of these marks together with the profile of the firing pin and its location relative to the extractor in the rim-fire arms, will be used along with breech face marks and the rifling pattern, if appropriate, to help determine the manufacture and possible model of weapon used in a shooting incident. Marks are also left on the sides of ejected cartridge cases in the case of certain firearms which have a propensity for their cartridge cases to clip the edge of the ejection port on their way out.

Some of the marks found on reloaded ammunition can be attributed to the sizing dies and moulds used to cast lead bullets. Sawn-off shotguns can sometimes leave matchable marks upon certain types of plastic cartridge wadding if the inner barrel edge at the muzzle end is left in a rough state from the crude barrel shortening process generally used by criminals.

## 5.10   The Microscopy of Air Weapon Missiles

It often comes as a surprise to some police officers and the person subsequently charged with an offence, that pellets discharged from air weapons can be matched up in the same way as conventional rifle and pistol bullets. I have dealt with a number of cases over the years where air weapon missiles have inflicted serious or sometimes lethal injuries upon individuals. Offences have also included the air weapon being used in the commission of an armed robbery or a rape; in such instances the ability to match the weapon to the incident is just as important as it would be in the case of the use of a conventional firearm in a similar offence. One case I dealt with some years ago involved the use of an air rifle being fired from a parked car at the windows of houses thought to be unoccupied by their normal residents. The breakages were in the region of the opening catches of the windows. After the relatively quiet breaking of the window, the firer would merely wait a short while to ensure that no one had been disturbed before he continued with the act of burglary. A number of such burglaries had been carried out in a city area using the same MO. Eventually matching up the damaged pellets recovered from the various locations by the scene of crime officers with the rifle subsequently recovered from the suspect put an end to this particular career.

## 5.11   Recoil and Barrel Flip

The question of recoil is sometimes brought up in a trial of murder or attempted murder. It is sometimes suggested that the high level of recoil of the weapon in question caused the gun barrel to move so that a shot intended to miss the victim was accidentally realigned by chance to one which in fact struck him (usually in the centre of the chest). The most common scenario is for a shot said to have been directed at the ground or near to the feet of the victim being redirected by the upward movement of the recoil kick, so as to strike the body of the victim.

When considering what happens during the firing of, for example a .38 in revolver in such an incident, it is important to bear in mind that the mass of a bullet and any other ejecta is only a small fraction of that of the gun used in its discharge. A typical Smith and Wesson .38 in M&P revolver weighs approximately 1.9 pounds (approx. 850 g). A .38 in Special cartridge will be loaded with a 10.2 g (158 grain) bullet and approximately 0.26 g (4 grain) of powder. The nominal muzzle velocity of the bullet will be in the region of 244 m/s (800 ft/s). Newton's Third Law of Motion will allow the calculation of the recoil force. Allowances must be made for the momentum imparted to the powder gases by accelerating them out of the barrel and the jet effect as they are released into the atmosphere at the muzzle. As a general rule, a figure of one-and-a-half times the bullet velocity is assigned to the weight of the exiting powder gases (0.26 g (4 grain) in this instance).

Recoil velocity = (Bullet mass × velocity) + (Mass of powder gas × 1.5 × bullet velocity). The resulting value obtained is divided by 7000 (the number of grains in a pound), and then by the weight of the revolver, also expressed in pounds weight.

$$\text{Recoil velocity} = \frac{(158 \quad 800) + (4 \quad 1.75 \quad 800)}{7000 \quad 1.9} = 9.92\,\text{ft/s}\,(3.03\,\text{m/s})$$

The kinetic energy of a moving body is given by the formula:

$$\text{Kinetic energy} = \tfrac{1}{2}\,MV^2$$

To convert this value to terms of ft/lb of energy it is necessary to divide the resultant value by a local value for the acceleration due to gravity; here we will use a typical value of 32.19 ft/s² (9.81m/s²).

$$\text{Recoil energy} = \frac{0.5 \quad 1.9 \quad 9.92^2}{32.19} = 2.9\,\text{ft lb}\,(3.93\,\text{J})$$

This is only a small fraction of the 224 ft·lb (304 J) of energy possessed by the bullet.

However, the considerable differences between the mass of the revolver and the mass of the ejecta cause that other property, inertia, to impose its presence. The axis of the revolver barrel is also positioned above the axis of the arm holding it. As a consequence the recoil forces act to pivot the revolver barrel upwards where it is gripped in the hand as well as pushing directly backwards. The mass of the revolver is slow in taking up this movement, and as a consequence the bulk of the recoil movement occurs after the bullet has left the barrel. The front sight of the revolver in question is approximately 1.5 mm (0.060 in) higher than the rear-sight to compensate for the portion of upward movement anticipated during the barrel time of the bullet. Although this is of consequence to a target shooter firing at a small mark positioned 25 yd or 25 m distant, it will be of little consequence at the short confrontational ranges of most shooting incidents, in any event the major portion of the upward movement of recoil occurs after the bullet has left the barrel. (Figure 4.17)

## 5.12   Choke Boring of Shotguns

The last topic in this chapter concerns the influence of the constriction or 'choke' normally present in the last 2 in (50 mm) of the barrel of a sporting gun. In sawn-off shotguns this section of the barrel will have been discarded. Choke is a restriction or reduction in the bore of the shotgun which is intended to reduce the degree of shot spread at sporting ranges. Some barrels intended for use at close ranges are bored without chokes and are referred to as being bored 'true cylinder'. The lightest choke in the English system, and one which is frequently used for the right barrel of a double-barrelled gun, is referred to as 'improved cylinder', and involves a restriction of about 0.005 in (0.12 mm). 'Quarter choke' consists of a constriction of about 0.010 in (0.25 mm); the constriction of 'half-choke' is about 0.020 in (0.50 mm); the constriction of 'three-quarter choke' is about 0.030 in (0.75 mm); and full choke constriction is in the region of 0.040 in (1.0 mm), which is the maximum constriction normally employed (Figure 5.6 and Figure 5.7).

American and Continental choke designations are slightly different. The following dimensions are taken from specifications used by the Ithaca Gun Company of Ithaca, New York:

- Cylinder bore diameter 0.729 in (18.5 mm), choke length 0
- Improved cylinder/skeet choke diameter 0.720 in (18.3 mm), choke length 0.625 in (15.9 mm)
- Modified choke diameter 0.711 in (18.1 mm), choke length 1.25 in (31.8 mm)
- Improved modified choke diameter 0.702 in (17.9 mm), choke length 1.875 in (47.7 mm)
- Full choke diameter 0.693 in (17.6 mm), choke length 2.50 in (63.6 mm)

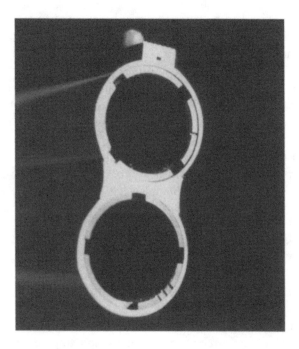

**Figure 5.6**    Modern screw-in choke tubes are a convenient alternative to conventionally choke bored barrels. Rifled choke tube units are also available to increase the accuracy of single slug loadings. The four shallow square cut recesses at the end of the choke tubes allow the use of a special tool for their removal or fitting. The narrow grooves cut in the end signify the degree of choke boring. A single slot in the upper tube signifies 'full choke', whilst the three in the lower tube signify 'modified choke'.

**Figure 5.7**    Polychoke device of the type frequently seen on American repeating shotguns. This device consists of a ring of short, narrow steel strips separated from each other by a small gap. The twisting of the constrictor ring closes up the gaps so as to decrease the bore diameter and hence produce an increase in the degree of choke.

As will be explained in Chapter 6, pattern spread is affected by other variables, and for these reasons the best English gunmakers would bore the gun to compensate for the effects caused by a particular cartridge loading upon the patterning characteristics to suit the particular customer requirements. The chokes of guns of larger boring would need a slightly greater degree of restriction to achieve similar full choke patterning properties (e.g., 0.045 in (1.1 mm) in the case of the Super 10), and a lesser restriction in the case of the smaller bores (e.g., 0.030–0.033 in (0.76–0.84 mm) in the case of a 20-bore gun).

The shot charge, typically consisting of between 200 and 400 pellets, accelerates down the smooth bore to enter the choked section at a velocity in the region of 1200 ft/s (370 m/s). The pellets are suddenly forced together, suffering some deformation in the process, both from friction with the barrel walls and by their interaction with each other. This is, ballistically speaking, an undesirable change. The relatively high antimony contents of modern lead alloys used in the manufacture of shotgun pellets is an attempt to reduce the degree of pellet deformation. The bulk of modern shotgun cartridges are also loaded with plastic cup-shaped wads which serve the normal function of a gas seal and at the same time afford significant protection to the pellets by keeping them away from the steel barrel walls (Figure 5.8). The large pellets used in buckshot loadings are particularly prone to deformation, and some manufacturers put soft buffer materials with these large pellets to afford them even greater protection.

Alternative forms of choke boring have been employed in the past, and it is interesting to note that in some forms of short-range game and clay pigeon shooting referred to as 'skeet shooting' certain adaptations both to gun and cartridge can be employed to increase the shot spread above that which would be produced by a cylinder-bored gun. Special slow twist rifled barrels, sometimes referred to as canon rayé are made for such purposes. Special shot spacers can be used in the cartridge loading, or cube-shaped or disc-shaped (plomb disco) shot employed in the loading to produce 'dispersante' loadings. Devices can also be fitted to the muzzle end of a police type shotgun in order to change the shape of the pattern from circular to that of an ellipse; the notion being that the increase in lateral spread will give a higher probability of hits on figure targets (Figure 5.9).

## 5.13   Gauges and Bore Sizes

Frequent reference has been made in the last few paragraphs to the term 'bore' or 'gauge' of shotguns and smooth-bored weapons. In the early days of gun manufacture the actual internal diameter of a finished gun barrel

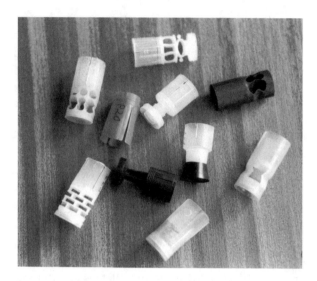

**Figure 5.8** A few of the many different designs of plastic cup wads used in the loading of shotgun ammunition. The construction of the wadding has implications in respect of close range wound effects and the identification of the brand of cartridge used in an offence.

could vary somewhat from that which might have been intended, and this was especially true in the muzzle-loading period. The scale of gun bore sizes was based upon the number of spherical lead balls contained in 1 lb weight (454 g) which would exactly fit the particular gun bore. It follows therefore, that this would constitute 12 balls in a 12-bore gun, 16 in a 16-bore gun, 20 in a 20-bore gun, and so on (Figure 5.10).

Above 3-bore a mixed system of letters starting at 'P' is used, along with the addition of 2-bore and 1-bore, until the largest listed bore of nominally 2 inches diameter is given the designation 'A-bore'. At the other end of the scale, the smallest bore sizes are listed in the form of nominal inch diameters (viz., .410 in and .36 in). To add to the confusion some European arms manufacturers refer to the .410 in as '36-bore', which is both misleading and incorrect, while the European cartridge manufacturers refer to it as '12 mm'. Shotguns and cartridges in obscure bore sizes are still manufactured in Continental Europe including the 32-bore, where the designation '14 mm' is often used.

## Further Reading

Ackley, P.O. 1970. *Handbook for Shooters and Reloaders*, Vols. 1 and 2, Salt Lake City: Publishers Press.

**Figure 5.9** Special shotgun muzzle attachment to change the normal circular shot spread to one of oval form considered by the designer to be better suited for use against human targets.

**Figure 5.10** Disassembled 12 bore, .410 and 9 millimetre rim-fire shotgun cartridges loaded with conventional shot loads and fibre wadding.

Farrar, C.L. and Leeming, D.W. 1982. *Military Ballistics: A Basic Manual*, Oxford: Brassey.

Hatcher, Major General, J.S. 1966. *Hatcher's Notebook*, Harrisburg, PA: Stackpole.

Hercules Staff. 1988. *Reloader's Guide for Hercules Smokeless Powders,* Wilmington, DE: Hercules Inc.

Hornady Staff. 1991. *Hornady Handbook of Cartridge Reloading,* Grand Island, NE: Hornady Manufacturing Co. Inc.

Keith, E. 1950. *Shotguns by Keith,* Harrisburg, PA: Stackpole.

Marshall, A. 1917 and 1932. *Explosives,* London: Churchill.

Speer Staff. 1966. *Speer Manual for Reloading Ammunition,* Kansas City, MO: Glenn Co.

Tenny, L.D. 1943. *The Chemistry of Powder and Explosives,* Hollywood, CA: Angriff.

*Textbook of Ballistics and Gunnery.* 1987, London: HMSO.

Whelen, Colonel T. 1945. *Small-Arms Design and Ballistics, Vol. 2. Ballistics,* Amworth, T.B. (Ed.), Plantersville, SC: Small-Arms Technical Publishing Co.

# External Ballistics and Cartridge Loadings

# 6

## 6.1  Basic Principles

External ballistics is concerned principally with the flight of the bullet or shot charge after leaving the barrel. This will of course involve the missile trajectory, the arclike flight path which is the resultant of the effects of gravity and air resistance. In shot charges fired from smooth-bored guns, it will also be concerned with the changes in the spread of the shot charge with range. Missiles will also be affected by crosswinds which will push them off their original course. One other aspect of external ballistics must also be covered, as it is extremely important to the forensic scientist. This is the flight and the influences of the other materials which are discharged, almost as unintentional secondary missiles. Cartridge wadding and unburnt particles of propellant will produce significant effects at close range upon the victim of a shooting, as will the flash and high-pressure powder gases nearer to the muzzle.

## 6.2  Bullet Stability and Instability

As the bullet emerges from the barrel of the gun, it is suddenly released from the rigid constraining action of barrel walls and is immediately acted upon by the forces of air resistance which will attempt to destabilise it further. The bullet will only have its long axis perfectly in line with the bore by chance at this point due to the disturbing effects caused by its sudden release. Any condition of yaw will allow the cyclone-like wind which opposes the bullet to act against its sides, thus acting to slow it down and increase its angle of yaw further. These forces will act upon a point in the bullet referred to originally by Leonardo da Vinci as 'the centre of pressure', which in most bullets will lie somewhere between the bullet tip and its centre of gravity. This is when the powerful gyroscopic spin imparted upon the bullet by the rifling in the barrel acts to restabilise the missile by forcing its point back into its original alignment just before it leaves the muzzle. Throughout its flight through the atmosphere the bullet will continue to suffer the buffeting effects of air resistance, and periodic lesser irregularities will occur during its flight (Figure 6.1). However, assuming that the bullet's construction is sound and that the correct rate of rotational spin has been imparted upon it, then the bullet's flight will follow on a normal trajectory within conventional conditions of use. Insufficient spin upon the bullet will lead to unstable flight, eventually resulting in the bullet tumbling end over end with the loss of all hope of accuracy. I have dealt with instances in which crude improvised smooth-bore barrels have been fitted to firearms subsequently used with bulleted ammunition. The effects are apparent during the examination of damage at the scene of the incident or upon the body in the form of abnormal elongated bullet entry holes, and in some instances the bullet hole has clearly resembled the profile of the bullet.

## 6.3   The Bullet's Flight

The other major forces which exert their influence upon the bullet include the force of gravity which acts to pull the bullet downwards towards the earth at a rate of acceleration of approximately 32.2 ft/s² (9.81 m/s²); the resistance of the opposing wind forces previously mentioned which slow the bullet

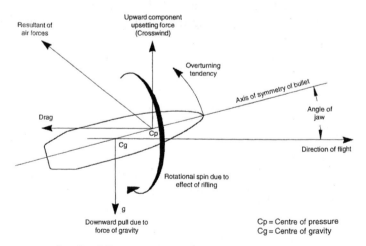

**Figure 6.1**   Bullet yaw and stability in flight.

down, thus stripping from it both velocity and retained kinetic energy, and crosswinds which will push the bullet sideways from its intended course.

The effects of air resistance and buffeting are, of course, a natural consequence of our not existing in a vacuum; a bullet would travel considerably further in a vacuum environment and would not be tormented by crosswinds. However, as this is an uninviting option for humans to live in, other methods are used to lessen the effects of air resistance. The degree of retardation of a bullet can be influenced by its velocity, shape and weight. One only has to look at the typical shape of the hull of a boat to realise the shape which will work best, especially if one considers how much more resistance is offered by the denser medium water.

## 6.4   Bullet Shape, Sectional Density, and Ballistic Coefficient

Modern sleek pointed boat-tail bullets designed to reduce both forebody and base drag are clearly not a newly invented shape. These pointed ('Spitzer') bullets will clearly suffer less air resistance than those of flat or blunt-nose design. Once again, if we look at high-speed, ocean-going yachts or naval frigates it appears obvious that increasing the effective length of the bullet and at the same time reducing its diameter, should also increase the ability of the missile to cheat the effects of air resistance. However, the effective stabilisation of such bullet shapes necessitates faster and faster rates of spin, in the region of 300,000 rev/min in some current military rifle loadings. The continual reduction in the bore sizes of rifles over the years from those which would have been normal in the first half of the nineteenth century has been the inevitable result of years of trial and experimentation. If one were to maintain a particular desired bullet weight but reduce its diameter, then this effect on its own would increase a property referred to as its sectional density (SD).

$$\text{Sectional density} = \frac{\text{Weight of the bullet in lb}}{\text{Square of bullet diameter in in}}$$

Clearly, by constructing the bullet from a convenient and dense material such as lead, and by selecting a diameter which is substantially less than that of the length of the bullet, then a missile of high sectional density should be ensured. By changing the uniform cylindrical shape so that the intended nose is of a rounded or pointed ogival shape or form, the bullet can be improved further. A modest reduction in the diameter at the base will also be useful if the bullet is intended for long-range military application. These alterations have now increased another bullet property referred to as the ballistic coefficient (BC or C).

$$c = \frac{SD}{I} \text{ where } I \text{ is a coefficient of form.}$$

Typical values for/the coefficient of form are as follows:

Round nose = 1.00
Three-calibre head = 0.72
Four-calibre head = 0.62
Five-calibre head = 0.60
Six-calibre head = 0.56
Eight-calibre head = 0.49

The effect of changes in the ballistic coefficients of bullets fired from rifles within the velocity range 1750 to 3750 ft/s (530–1140 m/s), and up to firing distances of 600 yards (550 m), can be predicted within a maximum error of 5–10% (Table 6.1).

## 6.5 External Ballistics and Their Calculation

Most external ballistic tables provided by the various cartridge manufacturers have been calculated using a single simple value for C, the ballistic coefficient of the bullet, and generally provide satisfactory solutions over realistic hunting ranges (within 300 m).

The military will, of course, be interested in the external ballistic performances of some of their missiles over much greater ranges, and as a consequence will need to utilise more complex methods of calculation. These calculations use drag coefficient $C_D$ values of the bullet appropriate for the different velocity regions (Mach bands) through which it passes during its flight.

The majority of bullet manufacturers now provide information in their published literature which contains the simple ballistic coefficient values for

**Table 6.1  Effect of Ballistic Coefficient upon Retained Velocity**

| Ballistic Coefficient C | % Velocity Loss per 100 Yards (90m) Travel |
|:-----------------------:|:------------------------------------------:|
| 0.223                   | 16                                         |
| 0.252                   | 14                                         |
| 0.290                   | 12                                         |
| 0.340                   | 10                                         |
| 0.410                   | 8                                          |
| 0.536                   | 6                                          |

each bullet type, calibre and weight. They frequently provide additional information in the form of tables which indicate the likely performance of their bullets over hunting distances, although the values given above 300 yd or 300 m will tend to be over-optimistic because of the method of calculation used in their derivation. Manual use can also be made of the original Hodsock and Ingall tables; the latter can be found at the back of *Hatcher's Notebook,* along with representative worked-out examples of ballistic calculations, such as retained velocity at various ranges, time of flight, height of trajectory, determination of ballistic coefficient from velocity data, and the determination of the angle of departure. In recent years, with the advent of home computers, various ballistic programs have become available to the public. These programs are generally based upon the above material and will give reasonable results up to the range limits previously mentioned.

All things being equal, the higher the ballistic coefficient for a particular bullet, the flatter shooting and more efficient it will be, in that it will retain a greater measure of its original velocity and energy. As an added bonus, the bullet of greatest ballistic coefficient will be less affected by the influence of range crosswinds. For example, reloaded .30 in-06 cartridges can be assembled using two bullets of similar weights but of different shapes, to produce the same muzzle velocity and consequent muzzle energy levels, but very different down-range performances. The Hornady tables indicate that in the first instance the round nose soft point (RNSP) 180 grain (11.7 g) bullet has a sectional density of 0.271 and a ballistic coefficient $C$ of 0.241. In the second instance, the boat-tail soft point (BTSP) Spitzer bullet of similar sectional density, has a ballistic coefficient of 0.452 because of its sleek wind-cheating shape. The retained velocities and kinetic energies of the two bullets are given in Table 6.2, together with values for the bullet drop from the intended aiming mark, for rifles with telescope sights fitted 1.5 in (38 mm) above the line of the bore, sighted for bullet impact at 100 yards (91 m) and 200 yards (183 m), respectively.

In addition to the improvements in retained velocity, energy and bullet drop, the bullet with the highest ballistic coefficient is also caused to move less laterally from its intended path by the effects of crosswinds. In the case of a modest 10 miles/h (16 km/h) breeze blowing at 90° across the range, the deflection at 200 yd will be 6 and 4 in (152 and 102 mm), respectively. At a distance of 300 yd, deflections of 16 and 9 in (406 and 229 mm), respectively, will be realised.

In both cases the bullets have travelled along normal shaped trajectories, in which the shallow curved track has its highest point situated at a distance which is somewhat greater than the midrange position. The bullet's flight will be flattest during the initial stages of its flight, the downward curvature in its flight path becoming more pronounced with increasing range after it

**Table 6.2   Exterior Ballistics for the Two Bullet Examples**

| Bullet Type | | Range in Yds. | | | |
|---|---|---|---|---|---|
| | | 0 | 100 | 200 | 300 |
| RNSP | Velocity | | | | |
| | ft/s | 2700 | 2338 | 2005 | 1703 |
| | m/s | 823 | 713 | 611 | 519 |
| | Energy | | | | |
| | ft.lb | 2913 | 2185 | 1607 | 1159 |
| | J | 3950 | 2962 | 2179 | 1571 |
| | Bullet Drop | | | | |
| | in | −1.5 | 0.0 | −4.9 | −18.5 |
| | mm | −38 | 0.0 | −124 | −470 |
| | in | −1.5 | +2.5 | 0.0 | −11.2 |
| | mm | −3.8 | +64 | 0.0 | −284 |
| BTSP | Velocity | | | | |
| | ft/s | 2700 | 2504 | 2315 | 2135 |
| | m/s | 823 | 763 | 706 | 651 |
| | Energy | | | | |
| | ft.lb | 2913 | 2505 | 2142 | 1822 |
| | J | 3950 | 3396 | 2904 | 2470 |
| | Bullet Drop | | | | |
| | in | −1.5 | 0.0 | −4.1 | −14.6 |
| | mm | −38 | 0.0 | −104 | −371 |
| | in | −1.5 | +2.0 | 0.0 | −8.5 |
| | mm | −38 | +51 | 0.0 | −216 |

drops from its highest point. Table 6.2 shows the bullet initially rising in order to pass through the line of sight, in this case the axis of the telescope sight mounted above the line of the bore. It then climbs upward to the highest point in its trajectory after passing the midrange position. After a brief period of near-level flight its path curves downwards so as to fall at an ever-increasing rate due to the downward accelerative pull of gravity and the continual loss of forward velocity due to the effects of air resistance, eventually striking the intended target or the ground. When considering the case of small arms, the maximum distance of firing will be achieved when the barrel is elevated approximately 30° from the horizontal. In the absence of an atmosphere the optimum elevation would be 45°; values quite close to this are appropriate for heavy artillery shells due to the greater ballistic coefficient values of the missiles employed.

## 6.6   Accuracy

The *Oxford English Dictionary* (1993 edition) defines the term accurate as meaning 'Careful, precise, in exact conformity with a standard or with truth'.

In court, the expert witness will sometimes be asked difficult questions such as, how far can this gun discharge a missile, or how easy or difficult would it have been for the accused to have fired a shot in order to hit a person in a particular part of the body at a given range. The expert witness will have to answer in a manner which will be understood. The answer to the first question is of course confused by the difference between the normal range of use of the particular type of weapon and its ultimate range if it is fired with the barrel inclined upwards at an angle of approximately 30° from the horizontal. Answering the second question would require information as to the skill of the firer. It is true to say that the intrinsic accuracy of most firearms exceeds the abilities of their firers. However, it has long been recognised that some firearms and loadings are more accurate than others when used by a firer possessing a high level of skill. It is also true to say that some weapons or loadings are easier to use with best effect than others. However, the question of intrinsic accuracy and end-user skill has been a matter for debate for a great many years.

The following words were written by Ned Roberts, rifleman and self-made ballistics expert, born in Goffstown, New Hampshire, USA on 21 October 1866. His favourite Uncle Alvaro gave Ned his first muzzle-loading percussion rifle on his ninth birthday. When instructing Ned in the use of a rifle Uncle Alvaro proclaimed that a 'real rifleman' should be able to keep his bullets in an 8 in bullseye at 40 rods offhand shooting (20 cm group fired from a distance of 220 yd/201 m), or in a 4 in (10 cm) ring at that same distance when shooting with a rest, using a rear peep and pinhead front sight, *if the rifle was a really accurate one*. If the accurate rifle had a telescope sight, the sharpshooter should be able to keep his bullets in a 2.5 in (6.35 cm) circle at that range when shooting from a rest, using a rifle with a false muzzle. The false muzzle he refers to was a device used to assist with the initial loading stage of the bullet with such muzzle-loading target rifles. In later years Ned went on to develop his own high-velocity cartridge loading the .257 Roberts. Rifles chambered for the .257 in Roberts, which was based upon a necked-down 7×57 mm Mauser cartridge case, were made in 1928, followed by the commercial manufacture of the loading by Remington in 1934. But even then he went on to proclaim that the tight groups shot with heavy muzzle-loading Morgan James rifles back in 1859 would be hard to beat with 'the latest craze' (back in 1940) rifles such as the .220 in Swift and the .22 in Varminter (later to be christened the .22/250).

In his book *The Muzzle-Loading Cap-Lock Rifle* Ned describes how the target groups were measured in string length. In this system a wooden peg was placed in each bullet hole, after which a piece of string held at one end at the centre of the aiming crossmark, was then passed around each of the wooden pegs in turn, back to the centre cross, and then cut off; the target group with the shortest string measure was the winner.

These days it is customary to measure the distance between the centres of the two bullets positioned on opposite sides of the extreme edges of the bullet group. This then represents the maximum dispersion of the bullets in the group fired from a given distance: the smallest group size being the winner. In the English-speaking world most sportsmen will check the sighting of a rifle and loading at 100 yd (91 m), as this is a convenient distance and represents in most instances the anticipated sporting distance for shooting deer or other game. Subsequent groups can then be fired if necessary at greater distances, although most sporting users will make use of the data available in the ballistic tables. By way of an example, if the sportsman is interested in shooting game at longer distances on open ground rather than in the forest, he might choose a 200 yd (182 m) zero. With most modern sporting loadings and a rifle fitted with a telescope sight he can achieve this if the centre of his 100 yd group is positioned approximately 2 in (5 cm) above the bullseye. Similar 100 yd bullet impact settings can be obtained for zero values at greater distances from the ballistic tables, provided that the height of the bullet's trajectory above the line of sight at intermediate ranges is acceptable for the intended quarry. Pistols are normally sighted in at distances of between 20 yd (m) and 50 yd (m), although specialist pistols used in long-range target shooting are sighted in at distances comparable to those of rifles.

One interesting and significant fact is directly available to the shooter using Imperial rather than metric measurements. Target shooting accuracy or sight adjustments are often expressed in terms of 'minutes' or 'minutes of angle' (MOA). A circle is composed of 360°, and in turn each degree can be broken down into 60 min. By chance, a minute of angle subtends an arc very close to 1 in length at a range of 100 yd. It follows therefore, that a 1 in group can be described as a one minute group and so on. The shooting described by Uncle Alvaro in Roberts' book (2 1/2 in at 40 rods) corresponds to approximately 1 1/8 minute of angle, which by most standards represents very accurate shooting with today's weaponry, especially if we are to accept that the sharpshooter is expected to achieve this high standard on every occasion.

The Military use the expression 'mil', where the mil is the angle with a tangent of 1/1000. It follows therefore, that a mil subtends an arc of 1 m in length at a distance of 1000 m. A circle is therefore composed of 6283 mils, sometimes referred to as the 'Infantry Mil'. To make it easier for the soldier to divide this into simple multiples it is rounded up to 6400 parts and referred to as the Artillery Mil, which in turn corresponds to 3.375 MOA.

Another British military system for expressing the accuracy of a batch of ammunition is referred to as its Figure of Merit and is now perhaps only of historical interest. This elaborate procedure involved the firing of .303 in Mark Seven British Service rifle ammunition in machine-rested Short

Magazine Lee Enfield (SMLE) rifles over a distance of 600 yd (549 m). For 8 to 12 targets, 20 shots were obtained. The accuracy was then determined by calculating the average distance, measured in inches, of the 20 shots from the mean point of impact (MPI). The average figure obtained from all of the targets was called the Figure of Merit (FOM). The lower the value of the FOM then the more accurate was the batch of ammunition. For .303 in service ammunition, the batch passed proof if the FOM did not exceed 8 in (20.3 cm). This yields an average diameter of bullet spread of 16 in at 600 yd range, which corresponds to 2 2/3 MOA, but as this is an average value, it follows that many bullets fired in the groups were dispersed outside this measurement.

## 6.7   Fin and Aerodynamic Stabilisation

There is of course another and much older method of imparting stability to a missile than rifling, and this system can be used in situations in which a barrel is not involved in the discharge or release of the missile. By bringing the centre of pressure behind the centre of mass so that it is positioned at the trailing end of the missile, and at the same time moving the centre of mass closer to the front, it is possible to exert a considerable degree of stability and self-righting properties to the missile to ensure that it remains pointing nose-forward in its flight. The tufts of hair or fibre on the end of a blow-pipe dart, or the feathered flights at the end of an arrow are the earliest and best-known examples of this technique. If the missile yaws in flight, the pressure of the air through which it is passing pushes against the exposed side of the flight, thus forcing the missile back into its correct alignment. Some firearm designs also employ this system, the best known of which are the large calibre smooth-bore guns used on a number of heavy tanks such as the German Leopard or the American M1 main battle tanks. The finned missiles used in the 120 mm guns of the two examples are capable of being fired accurately to very long ranges. The majority of fin stabilised loadings employ discarding sabot wrappings on the missiles to protect them in the bore during the force of acceleration and also to provide the necessary obturation. This is true even in the case of the diminutive rifle flechette loadings the military have toyed with in recent times. Multiple flechette loadings have also been perfected for military combat shotgun loadings.

Rifled shotgun slug loadings are also in reality aerodynamically stabilised in flight, although most manufacturers claim some additional rotational spin stability being contributed by the simulated rifling impressed upon the sides of these missiles (Figure 6.2). It is notable however, that rifled barrels are available for a range of popular US repeating shotguns to improve the accu-

**Figure 6.2** An assortment of shotgun slugs, which include Balle Blondeau diabolo shaped missiles, rifled and unrifled hollow Foster slugs, the ever-popular Brenneke slug, the Sellier and Bellot S-Ball, spherical and lethal ball and a barricade penetrating Ferret CS bomblet.

racy of conventional rifled slug loadings. The common Foster hollow-based slug seen in the majority of US shotgun loadings, along with a variety of ingeniously designed counterparts from other countries, all bear more than just a passing resemblance to the shuttlecock used in the game of badminton. The BRI Sabot subcalibre missile used in some current Federal loadings utilises a discarding sabot and a diabolo missile configuration. This system is reported to be capable of impressive accuracy, and at the same time, the increase in missile length and the reduction in its calibre both serve to increase the ballistic coefficient and hence the down-range performance of this loading.

## 6.8   The Question of Range

The maximum ranges for birdshot-sized lead alloy shotgun pellets will lie between 200 and 300 m. The formula devised by Journé for predicting the approximate maximum ranges of shotgun pellets when fired at an angle of approximately 30° from the horizontal, can be used with reference to the standard tables for pellet diameters:

Maximum range = 2200 times pellet diameter in in

Another formula of German origin is as follows:

Maximum range = 100 times pellet diameter in mm

If we were somehow able to live on this planet without an atmosphere, i.e., in a vacuum, then a projectile fired from a conventional rifle would travel to a very great distance due to the elimination of air resistance. As a general principle in the real world, however, the heavier a body is, or the less its cross section, then the greater will be its sectional density and ballistic coefficient, and hence its ability for passing through the air. Relatively low-velocity large-calibre missiles fired from military weaponry such as trench mortars will give maximum ranges similar to those which would be realised in vacuum conditions when fired at departure angles of 45°. An approximate and very basic calculation derived from the Parabolic Formulae described on pages 278 and 309 of *The Textbook for Small Arms—1929* is useful when considering the maximum range for rifle grenades or trench mortar bombs when fired at a departure angle of 45 degrees. Here the muzzle velocity of the projectile in ft/s is equal to, or greater than, ten times the square root of the range expressed in yards.

$$R \text{ yds} = (V \text{ ft·s}^{-1}/10)^2$$

Thus a large and heavy projectile fired at a velocity of 100 ft/s would have a maximum extreme range of 100 yds, while the same projectile launched at 1000 ft/s would have a maximum range of 10,000 yds. If we were foolish enough to apply the above calculation and the correct units of measurement demanded by it to normal rifle bullets such as the diminutive .22 inc rimfire bullet fired at 1145 ft/s in the real world we exist in possessing an atmosphere, then we would end up with an estimate for its maximum range of 13,110 yds (3,996 m), which bears no comparison to the actual measured maximum range of this same missile, shown in Table 6.3, of a meagre 1,500 yards (1,370 m). Some slow, heavy, large-calibre pistol bullets can achieve impressive percentage values of the vacuum range value; e.g., the .455 in Webley bullet weighing 265 grains (17.2 g) at a muzzle velocity of 600 ft/s (183 m/s) will travel about 1300 yd (1190 m), which is about 36% of the vacuum value. Modern, light, high-velocity rifle bullets will experience considerable air resistance due to the speed at which they are travelling, and as a result will only achieve between 4 and 10% of the vacuum value. Magnum bullet loadings will suffer great resistance during the initial stages of their flight, which is why they do not travel appreciably further than their more modest counterparts.

Table 6.3   **Absolute Maximum Ranges of Firing for Various Cartridge Loadings in Still Air Conditions**

| Cartridge | Bullet Weight | Velocity | C | Max. Range |
|-----------|---------------|----------|------|------------|
| .22 in LR | 40 grain | 1145 ft/s | 0.128 | 1500 yd |
| – | 2.6 g | 349 m/s | – | 1370 m |
| .45 in ACP | 234 grain | 820 ft/s | 0.16 | 1640 yd |
| – | 15.2 g | 250 m/s | – | 1500 m |
| .30 in M2 | 152 grain | 2800 ft/s | 0.40 | 3500 yd |
| – | 9.9 g | 853 m/s | – | 3200 m |
| .30 in M1 | 172 grain | 2600 ft/s | 0.56 | 5500 yd |
| – | 11.1 g | 792 m/s | – | 5030 m |
| .50 in AP.M2 | 718 grain | 2840 ft/s | 0.84 | 7275 yd |
| – | 46.5 g | 866 m/s | – | 6650 m |

A typical .22 in Long Rifle bullet will have a maximum range in the region of 1400 m. Bullets fired from high-velocity centre-fire rifles will travel between 3000 and 5000 m; the maximum ranges being achieved with long slender pointed bullets, and those of boat-tail design will travel further than their plain-based counterparts due to suffering the least air resistance during the subsonic portion of their flight. This is a useful property for the military to enjoy as the use of boat-tailed bullet loadings greatly extends the suppressive fire capability of machine guns.

## 6.9   The Spent Bullet Myth

One often hears the terms spent or falling bullets. Tests have shown that military rifle bullets fired vertically up into the air will return in a period of approximately 50 s, the actual period depending upon whether they fall point-first or base-first. After travelling to a height of between 9,000 and 10,000 ft (2,740 m) they strike the ground at a velocity of approximately 300 ft/s (90 m/s). Under the same conditions, shotgun pellets will fall to earth at speeds of between 70 and 160 ft/s (20 to 50 m/s), depending upon the particular pellet size.

The approximate terminal speeds of shotgun pellets can be calculated using the Ingalls-Siacchi expression for the retardation R of a projectile in a standard atmosphere:

$$R = A_n V^n / C$$

Where n is some power of velocity V representing relationship for a given narrow band of velocity; $A_n$ is a very small number determined by previous experiment using the standard projectile; and C is the ballistic coefficient of the projectile. Spherical shotgun pellets are only able to achieve very low free-

**Table 6.4  Terminal Velocities of Falling Shotgun Pellets**

| Shot Size | Diameter in Inches | C | V in Ft/S and M/S |
|---|---|---|---|
| 9 | 0.08 | 0.008 | 74/22.6 |
| 6 | 0.44 | 0.011 | 87/26.5 |
| 4 | 0.13 | 0.013 | 94/28.7 |
| 2 | 0.15 | 0.015 | 103/31.4 |
| BB | 0.18 | 0.018 | 111/33.8 |
| No 4 Buck | 0.24 | 0.025 | 131/39.9 |
| No 1 Buck | 0.30 | 0.031 | 146/44.5 |
| 00 Buck | 0.33 | 0.034 | 153/46.6 |

fall velocities, for which the value of n is approximately 2. Terminal velocity is reached when the deceleration of the missile due to air resistance is balanced by g, the accelerating downward pull of gravity. The simplified expression for determining such terminal velocities can be obtained using the formula:

$$V_{terminal} = 830C$$

Values of ballistic coefficients, diameters in inches, and approximate terminal velocities for US shotgun pellets are contained in Table 6.4.

A British Number 6 pellet will strike the ground at a calculated velocity of 83 ft/s (25 m/s), and the largest buckshot pellet LG or its American equivalent '000' at a velocity of 160 ft/s (50 m/s), the kinetic energies of the pellets in these instances being 0.025 and 3.976 ft·lb, respectively (0.033 and 5.39 J). However in real-life conditions pellets and bullets usually return to earth with some additional forward component of velocity which can allow the missiles the ability to inflict a serious injury or even a fatal wound. I recall calculations done some years ago in connection with a fatal incident which had taken place at the extreme edge of a military firing range. Given the assistance of a 20 mph (32 km/h) tailwind, it was estimated that the 7.62 mm Nato loading rifle bullet fired at 33° elevation would return to earth at 400 ft/s (122 m/s) after travelling up to a maximum trajectory height of 3840 ft (1170 m). A missile of this weight travelling at such a speed would be capable of inflicting a lethal injury, especially if it were to strike a vulnerable part of a person's body. The striking energy would be in the region of 50 ft·lb (68 J) at a range of 4460 yd (4080 m).

## 6.10 Secondary Ejecta

As previously mentioned, the bullet or the shot charge are not the only materials which are forcibly ejected from the muzzle end of the gun barrel

when it is fired. Other ejecta-related materials such as shotgun cartridge
wadding, unburnt powder grains, buffering materials used in buckshot loadings, and in certain specialised loadings, the discarded sabot or the fragments
of a discarded sabot can also be discharged at high speed. All of these unintentional or secondary missiles will be discharged at the muzzle at a velocity
of at least that of the primary missile or missiles. However, these materials
tend to be light, of low mass and of poor ballistic shape and, as a result, suffer
severe retardation by air resistance, thus greatly limiting their range. However,
as the majority of criminal or casework incidents take place at short confrontational distances their influence can be significant and, therefore, of
interest to the forensic scientist.

Close to the muzzle end of the gun, the heat and visible flash of the
discharge can cause burning or blackening effects, and some synthetic fibres
can be melted. At even closer ranges or in the case of contact or near-contact
shots, the high-pressure gases will also enter the wound track into tissue,
carrying with them the other secondary materials of discharge. At muzzle-
to-target distances of 2 to 12 in (5 to 30 cm) unburnt powder grains can still
be travelling at speeds sufficient to embed themselves in the fabric of the
clothing worn by the victim or to cause tattoo injuries to exposed tissue. All
of the effects mentioned will be greatly influenced by the particular cartridge
loading used in the shooting incident.

## 6.11   The Behaviour of Shotgun Wadding

When a shotgun is fired the cartridge wadding can travel 30 yd (30 m) or
further and, due to its shape, can deviate from the centre of the flight path
of the shot charge, particularly at greater distances. Initially, the wadding will
emerge from the muzzle along with the shot charge as a compact mass and
can remain effectively associated with the dense shot charge up to ranges of
a few yards and as a result can frequently be found inside the wound track.
At greater distances compound wadding charges can separate, resulting in
the lighter elements, which suffer the greatest effects of air resistance, travelling to a shorter distance. The leaves of the commonest types of plastic cup-
wads start to open up a short distance from the muzzle in order to release
the shot charge. This action is progressive and thus range dependent for the
particular type or brand of wad used in the loading. Most cupwads have two
or four leaves, which after fully opening can turn back upon themselves or
can become detached from the base unit, especially in two-leaf designs. Up
to distances of a few yards wadding, whether of fibre or plastic construction,
will still be travelling at sufficient speed to cause damage or inflict injuries,
which in the latter case will be evident upon the body. Observations of close-
range blackening, powder tattooing, and these latter effects produced by

cartridge wadding will allow the forensic scientist to conduct suitable firing tests in order to determine the range of firing. The estimation of the firing range, usually expressed from the muzzle end of the gun barrel to the damage or the wound site, will always be of great significance during the investigation or at any subsequent court hearing. The high muzzle pressures associated with sawn-off shotguns can also leave their influence upon the base sections of certain types of plastic cup-wads, in some cases causing the hollow-base section, which normally rests upon the powder charge in the loaded cartridge, to be forcibly blown back upon itself, thus leaving it in an everted condition (Figure 9.42).

At greater distances, where the effects of air resistance have retarded the powder grains or wadding to a degree where they are not capable of causing damage or injury, their influence can still be detected. Low-velocity strikes can still leave visible bruising upon the skin and can, in addition, leave traces of firearms discharge residues upon the clothing at the impact sites. A simple chemical test using a saturated aqueous solution of sodium rhodizonate can reveal traces of lead and barium left upon blood-free areas of clothing. Such materials have been deposited upon the powder grains or the wadding from the primer. Lead can also be vaporised from the base of the bullet and then transferred to the powder grains. Finally, traces of lead, usually in significant quantities, will be left upon the margins of any holes caused by the passage of a bullet or an individual shotgun pellet, thus allowing discrimination of firearm-related damage to clothing from that caused by other mechanisms.

## 6.12   Sabot Loadings

The Remington Accelerator range of rifle cartridge loadings allow the owner of a large-bore rifle to fire a .22 in (5.56 mm) jacketed bullet at a very high velocity (Figure 6.3). The .30–06 loading drives a 55 grain (3.6 g) bullet at a muzzle velocity in the region of 4000 ft/s (1220 m/s). The bullet is loaded into the cartridge in a multileaved plastic sabot which is of sufficient diameter to form a gas-tight seal in the bore and also to transfer the spin imparted by the rifling to the bullet. Once again the severe effects of air resistance cause the plastic leaves of the sabot to open up shortly after leaving the muzzle so as to release the bullet and be left behind. At short distances the plastic sabot is still capable of inflicting a star-shaped area of damage or injury. With this type of loading true rifling impressions will only be left upon the sabot.

Sabot loadings are also used with the sub-calibre armour-piercing kinetic energy missiles fired from the 120 mm rifled gun on the current British battle tank, with all of the fin-stabilised missile loadings used in the smooth-bore US and German tank guns of similar calibre, and with certain sub-calibre

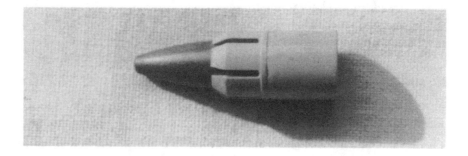

**Figure 6.3**  Remington .30–06 accelerator allows the firing of a .224 in (5.56 mm) projectile from a popular deer rifle. The plastic sabot is discarded by the effects of air resistance a short distance from the muzzle. Manufacturers claimed muzzle velocity of just in excess of 4000 ft/s (1220 m/s).

shotgun slug loadings. Sabot loadings are not a new concept, as they were used with the Dreyse needle-fire Zündnadel-Jägerbüchse rifles issued to the German military forces during the mid-nineteenth century. A sub-calibre discarding sabot pellet is also available for use with .22 in air rifles. The Prometheus range of air rifle pellets use non-discarding plastic sabots, as did the Sellier & Bellot 'S-Ball' 12-bore shotgun loading.

## 6.13  Choke Boring — Shotgun Pellet Spread and Velocity

In Section 5.12, reference was made to the choke boring of shotguns. The presence of the restriction in the last few inches of the muzzle end of the shotgun barrel exerts a powerful influence upon the degree of pellet spread at normal sporting ranges. However, it is true to say that the majority of criminal cases I have dealt with over the years have involved ranges in the region of 1 yd (1 m). At such short distances there is very little difference between the patterning of a sawn-off shotgun possessing no choke in the remaining portion of its barrel and a fully choked barrel of conventional length. There will of course be some reduction in the muzzle velocity of the shot charge fired from a sawn-off gun, although it will not be noticeable in terms of the nature of the wounds inflicted upon the victim. The degree of velocity reduction will also be affected by the cartridge loading and the shape of the time/pressure curve produced by the particular propellant used, as was explained in Chapter 5. The actual measured reduction in velocity is often less than one might imagine, as is revealed in some tests I conducted a number of years ago, in which I shortened the barrels of a 12-bore and a .410 in gun by degrees and measured the velocities in each instance (Table 6.5).

**Table 6.5   Changes in Muzzle Velocity Due to Progressive Shortening of the Barrel of a 12-Bore Shotgun\***

| Barrel Length | Muzzle Velocity | Average Velocity Loss |
|---|---|---|
| 29 in | 1239, 1248, 1241 ft/s | 0 |
| 737 mm | 378, 380, 378 m/s | 0 |
| 24.9 | 1127, 1210, 1195 ft/s | −68 ft/s |
| 632 mm | 344, 369, 364 m/s | −21 m/s |
| 20.9 in | 1176, 1160, 1192 ft/s | −66 ft/s |
| 531 mm | 358, 354, 363 m/s | −20 m/s |
| 15.9 in | 1119, 1145, 1112 ft/s | −117 ft/s |
| 404 mm | 341, 349, 339 m/s | −36 m/s |
| 11.9 in | 1076, 1097, 1101 ft/s | −151 ft/s |
| 302 mm | 328, 334, 336 m/s | −46 m/s |
| 8.1 in | 991, 1009, 978 ft/s | −249 ft/s |
| 206 mm | 302, 308, 298 m/s | −76 m/s |

\* Russian Baikal single barrelled 12-bore gun. Chamber length $2^3/_4$ in (70 mm). Bore diameter 0.727 in (18.5 mm). Choke diameter 0.684 in (17.4 mm). Original barrel length 29 in (737 mm). Cartridge type Eley Grand Prix, Standard Velocity, $1^1/_{16}$ oz (30 g) Number 4 (UK size) shot.

In the 12-bore tests, the average velocity loss per inch (25.4 mm) of barrel reduction was 11.9 ft/s (3.6 m/s). Over the entire shortening process the kinetic energy of the shot charge was reduced from 1591 ft·lb to 1228 ft·lb (2157 J to 1665 J). The variations in recorded velocity from shot to shot are typical of those one would record when testing 12-bore shotgun cartridges (Table 6.5).

After about one yard (1 m) the pellets on the edges of the compact mass of shot start to separate, and this process continues with increasing range (Figure 6.4). The degree of spread of the shot charge can also be influenced by the type of wadding used, the nature of the loading and the size of the pellets in the shot charge. It is always very notable how large buckshot pellet loadings tend to produce patterns of lesser diameter than normal, and how erratic these patterns can sometimes be with the largest pellet sizes. It was, and still is, customary for the makers of quality handmade British shotguns to ensure that the stock dimensions and form best suit the needs of the purchaser, in the same way as a tailor would make and fit a suit of clothes to an individual. At the same time they would ask the purchaser what cartridge and shot size would be used with the gun. During the choke boring stage the gun would be test-fired with cartridges of this same loading to produce sufficient 40 yd shot patterns to allow, with some degree of confidence, the most probable percentage of pellets within a central 30 in circle to be determined. If the customer had ordered the right barrel to be of 'Improved Cylinder' boring, and the left barrel 'Half Choke', then the degrees of choke in the barrels would be adjusted as necessary, until the percentages

**Figure 6.4**  12-Bore shot charge and associated fibre and card wadding captured a short distance in front of the muzzle of the gun associated with their discharge. The range here of just over one metre is quite common in criminal shooting incidents. The compact mass of pellets and the wadding are just starting to separate, and would be likely to produce the damage depicted in Figure 9.4 and 9.5, depending upon whether the barrel of the gun was sawn off or not.

**Table 6.6  Changes in Muzzle Velocity Due to Progressive Shortening of the Barrel of a .410 In Shotgun***

| Barrel Length | Muzzle Velocity | Average Velocity Loss |
|---|---|---|
| 25.5 in | 1181, 1192, 1142, 1181, 1164 ft/s | 0 |
| 648 mm | 360, 363, 348, 360, 355 m/s | 0 |
| 20.0 in | 1111, 1211, 1143, 1274, 1117 ft/s | 0 |
| 508 mm | 339, 369, 348, 388, 340 m/s | 0 |
| 16.0 in | 1056, 1081, 1134, 1105, 1101 ft/s | −77 ft/s |
| 406 mm | 322, 329, 346, 337, 336 m/s | −23 m/s |
| 12.0 in | 1069, 1079, 1039, 1030, 1046 ft/s | −119 ft/s |
| 305 mm | 326, 329, 317, 314, 319 m/s | −36 m/s |
| 8.0 in | 916, 923, 980, 987, 970 ft/s | −217 ft/s |
| 203 mm | 279, 281, 299, 301, 296 m/s | −66 m/s |
| 6.0 in | 802, 862, 809, 793, 873 ft/s | −344 ft/s |
| 152 mm | 244, 263, 247, 242, 266 m/s | −105 m/s |
| 4.0 in | 773, 689, 800, 732, 808 ft/s | −412 ft/s |
| 102 mm | 236, 210, 244, 223, 246 m/s | −126 m/s |

* Webley and Scott bolt-action .410 in gun. Original barrel length $25^1/_2$ in (648 mm). Chamber size $2^1/_2$ in (65 mm). French manufactured Eley Fourlong cartridges loaded with 7/16 oz (12.4 g) of UK Number 6 size shot.

of pellets enclosed in the 30 in circles during subsequent test-firings averaged 50 and 60%, respectively. Such refinements are not possible during the manufacture of modern mass-produced guns, where restrictions approximating to the choke restrictions listed in Section 5.12 are used directly, often by a swaging technique on the muzzle end of the barrel blank, and without any subsequent test-firing and measurement of shot spread. In the same way, gunstocks are made to suit the average man with no regard to the length of his neck, the width of his chest, and whether he is right or left handed. Nominal values can be attributed to the diameter of the spread of the bulk of the shot charge at various ranges for each degree of choke.

A cylinder bore gun should place 40% of the pellets in its shot charge inside a circle of 30 in (76 cm) diameter at 40 yd (37 m); an improved cylinder 50%; $1/4$ choke 55%; $1/2$ choke 60%; $3/4$ choke 65%; and full choke 70%. Useful tables of the anticipated spread of the bulk of the pellets in a shot charge are provided in Table 6.7.

When patterning a shotgun it is always advisable to use the same cartridge brand and shot loading as that used in the shooting incident, or the nearest available alternative loading. All tests should be conducted using the 'crime' weapon. Bearing in mind the variations in patterns which can occur, it is advisable also to carry out a sensible number of test-firings. To a degree this can be done to suit particular conditions, as some guns and loadings will pattern more uniformly and with greater regularity than others. It is not uncommon for 'fliers' from the shot charge to increase the actual pattern diameter to twice that of the bulk of the shot charge; when measuring the diameters of patterns it is usual to quote the diameter of spread at a given range for the bulk of the shot charge; all distances are quoted from the muzzle end of the barrel to the patterning sheet.

A great deal has been said and claimed to be true concerning the patterning qualities and the effective range of various choke borings since their

**Table 6.7 Diameter of Shot Pattern vs. Range for Different Choke Borings**

| Boring of Gun | Spread in cm at Ranges in Metres | | | | | | |
|---|---|---|---|---|---|---|---|
| Range in metres | 10 | 15 | 20 | 25 | 30 | 35 | |
| True cylinder | 54 | 71 | 88 | 105 | 122 | 140 | |
| Improved cylinder | 38 | 55 | 72 | 89 | 106 | 124 | |
| $1/4$ choke | 34 | 49 | 64 | 80 | 97 | 115 | |
| $1/2$ choke | 31 | 44 | 58 | 73 | 90 | 108 | |
| $3/4$ choke | 27 | 39 | 52 | 66 | 82 | 101 | |
| Full choke | 23 | 33 | 45 | 59 | 75 | 94 | |
| Boring of Gun | Spread in Inches at Ranges in Yards | | | | | | |
| Range in yards | 10 | 15 | 20 | 25 | 30 | 35 | 40 |
| True cylinder | 20 | 26 | 32 | 38 | 44 | 51 | 58 |
| Improved cylinder | 15 | 20 | 26 | 32 | 38 | 44 | 51 |
| $1/4$ choke | 13 | 18 | 23 | 29 | 35 | 41 | 48 |
| $1/2$ choke | 12 | 16 | 21 | 26 | 32 | 38 | 45 |
| $3/4$ choke | 10 | 14 | 18 | 23 | 29 | 35 | 42 |
| Full choke | 9 | 12 | 16 | 21 | 27 | 33 | 40 |

general adoption in 1875. I have already mentioned the real variations in pattern quality and spread that will be observed upon the patterning plate or witness card. Variation can occur from shot to shot using the same cartridges, variations induced by oil in the barrel, change of shot size, propellant, cartridge type, cartridge batch, wadding, choice of pellet material and the use of shot buffer materials. The length of the choke section and the choke profile can also influence the nature of the patterns likely to be produced. Shotgun patterning results are normally obtained as two-dimensional images, while in reality the shot cloud is of three-dimensional form, with some pellets travelling in front of others to produce 'shot stringing' effects. In his book *Volume III The Gun and the Cartridge,* Burrard describes how the results displayed on shot patterning plates can be deceptive when thinking of the effectiveness of a particular loading when used on a crossing shot at a fast moving bird. The crossing game bird occupies a particular place for a very short period of time, during which there might be a hole in the moving three-dimensional strung-out shot cloud. He mentions how Sir Ralph Payne-Gallwey had described his own rather simple experiments to determine the extent of shot stringing in his book *High Pheasants in Theory and Practice,* and how in 1857 R.W.S. Griffith had conducted tests when firing at a 12 foot diameter steam-driven disc moving at a rim velocity of 200 feet/sec and connected electrically to a chronograph. Burrard describes his own tests conducted when firing his gun at a patterning plate fixed to the side of a fast-moving vehicle driven by his intrepid assistant C.E. Allan.

In 1996, the Department of the Environment published the results of a study conducted by the University College London, entitled *"A Ballistics Measurement System to Assist the Development and Evaluation of Non-Toxic Shot,"* by R.A. Giblin and D.J. Compton. A test facility was set up at the Holland & Holland Shooting Grounds in 1994 using a special test gun employing various chokes, and a 3.6 m square array of electronic impact detectors on a trolley of 1000 kg total weight, that could be moved along a 50 m length of railway track. Eight chronograph skyscreens were also employed during tests conducted using at least ten firings of each cartridge loading for each chosen choke setting. The following results obtained in such tests using a 36 g loading of UK Number 3 lead shot and a three-quarter choke constriction (0.030 in/0.76 mm), reveal some interesting findings for the length of the shot cloud, and the velocities of pellets at both its leading and trailing edges at various ranges (Table 6.8).

John Harradine of the British Association of Shooting and Conservation (BASC), raised these same factors in a notice sent out in April 2001 concerning findings of their research department, concerning the influence of various choke borings upon loadings of different pellet sizes and composition, conducted by Roger Giblin and David Compton of the former Ballistic Research Laboratory of the London University College. All test-firings were conducted

**Table 6.8   Pellet Shot Cloud Properties with Increasing Range**

| Range (m) | Leading Edge Flight Time (ms) | Trailing Edge Flight Time (ms) | Leading Edge Velocity (m/s) | Trailing Edge Velocity (m/s) | Pellet Energy (J) Leading Edge | Pellet Energy (J) Trailing Edge | Shot Cloud Length (m) |
|---|---|---|---|---|---|---|---|
| 20 | 60.8 | 68.4 | 293 | 250 | 8.0 | 5.9 | 1.9 |
| 25 | 78.7 | 89.2 | 293 | 230 | 6.6 | 4.9 | 2.5 |
| 30 | 98.4 | 111.8 | 242 | 213 | 5.5 | 4.2 | 2.9 |
| 35 | 120.0 | 136.2 | 223 | 198 | 4.6 | 3.7 | 3.3 |
| 40 | 143.3 | 162.4 | 206 | 185 | 4.0 | 3.2 | 3.6 |
| 45 | 168.4 | 190.3 | 192 | 173 | 3.4 | 2.8 | 3.9 |
| 50 | 195.3 | 220.0 | 180 | 163 | 3.0 | 2.5 | 4.1 |

at 40 yds (36 m) using a standard 12-bore test barrel fitted with linear chokes varying from 'Cylinder' bore up to 'Super Full Choke' of 0.050 in constriction (1.27 mm). Ten cartridges from the same batch were fired through each choke, because fewer firings were not found sufficiently reliable to characterise the pattern of a given choke. Three different lead shot loadings were used with pellet sizes running from No. 7 (2.4 mm) up to BB+ (4.25 mm), one loading of Bismuth No. 4 (3.1 mm), two loadings of Steel No. 5 (2.8 mm) and No. 3 (3.3 mm), and one approximate No. 5 (2.9 mm) Zinc loading (Figure 6.5).

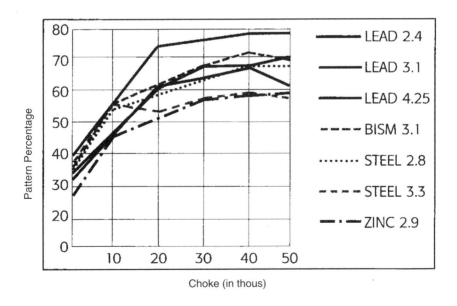

**Figure 6.5**   Change in pattern percentage as choke increases.

The patterning results shown in Figure 6.5 indicate that actual pattern percentage in these particular tests did not, as was generally thought, increase consistently with an increasing degree of choke, with the test gun fitted with widely used linear tapered chokes. The results here showed that after 'Half Choke' the improvement was, at most, only slight. In some instances pattern percentages decreased from 'Full Choke' to 'Super Full Choke'. In addition, the results are based on the average of ten firings of each cartridge with each choke. Although this is the correct approach to take, it does not reveal the considerable shot-to-shot variations in the patterning results. Taking account of the considerable degree of overlap of results obtained for 'Three Quarter', 'Full' and 'Super Full' chokes, there was little real difference between them. An individual pattern of 70% could have been fired from a 'Half', 'Three Quarter', 'Full' or 'Super Full' choke. Relying on just three patterning results with the Lead 4.25 mm loading using 'Quarter Choke' could produce pattern percentages of between about 25 and 62%, as revealed in Figure 6.6, caused largely by the random behaviour of the pellets in the shot cloud as it travels down range.

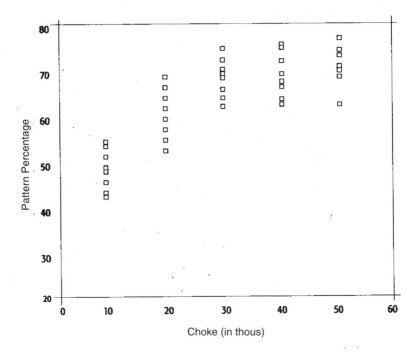

**Figure 6.6**   Scatter of pattern percentage firing results from quarter choke using lead 4.25 mm pellet loadings.

## 6.14 Pellet Deformation within the Bore

The charge of shot travels down the barrel, eventually being accelerated to a velocity in the region of 1250 ft/s (381 m/s) in the case of a conventional gun and cartridge. The pellets immediately next to the wad are in effect trying to travel faster than the bulk of the charge, thus exerting considerable forces of compression upon it. The longer the shot column, the greater this effect becomes. The pellets on the outside of this compact mass of shot are abraded or distorted by the hard barrel walls. Increasing the hardness of the shot by the use of high antimony alloys, using electrodeposits of copper or nickel upon the pellets, using plastic cup-wads to separate the pellets from the barrel walls or the incorporation of buffering materials, are all methods used by the cartridge manufacturers to reduce barrel leading and pellet deformation (Figure 6.7 through Figure 6.9). Deformed pellets will suffer greater effects from air resistance and will not retain as much speed and energy, and will deviate from the normal flight path so as to become 'fliers' from the main pattern. Large buckshot pellets, in particular, suffer greatly from such deformation; some manufacturers use soft buffering materials with the pellets in an attempt to address this problem. Long-shot columns aggravate the conditions described, thus leading to increased pellet deformation and hence a greater incidence of 'fliers'. The recently introduced use of steel shot has reversed this problem to the point where heavy plastic wads are used to reduce the tendency for bore damage caused by the friction of the hard pellets, particularly when they pass through the choke constriction. One method of

**Figure 6.7** A few of the many gauges of shotgun cartridge loadings, from the huge 4-bore down through 12, 16, 20, .410 in and 9 mm rim-fire to the diminutive .22 in rim-fire shot cartridge.

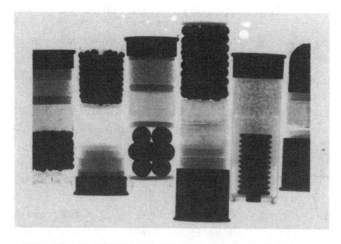

**Figure 6.8 and Figure 6.9** X-ray views of different 12-bore cartridge loadings show the arrangement of both fibre and plastic wadding. Loadings include
conventional birdshot, buckshot, Foster rifled slug and Sellier and Bellot 'S-
Ball'.

addressing this issue has been to overbore the barrel of a gun chambered for
12-bore cartridges to approximately 10 bore. It is essential however to use
plastic cup wads with such guns which have a hollow base of sufficient design
to ensure the necessary degree of obturation. The hazards associated with
poor obturation were recognised many years ago. Wadding which affords
poor gas sealing properties can allow hot powder gases to pass through the
shot charge, causing pellets to fuse together. The 'balling' of shotgun pellets
in the earlier days of cartridge manufacture has been blamed for persons
being injured at long ranges by the heavy irregular missiles produced, which
can of course travel much further than conventional small sized birdshot.
The incidence of 'balling' of shot was usually attributed to the use of poor

wadding materials, open-bored guns, and the firing of cartridges shorter than those for which the gun was chambered.

## 6.15   Choke Operation

In 1866 Roper in the US patented a removable choke device for use on single-barrelled guns, and choke boring in its present form was commonplace after 1875. It must be said, however, that choke-like devices or adaptations go back as far as 1781. It has often been said that the cone-shaped reduction in the barrel bore imparted an inwards component of motion to the pellets, thereby reducing their natural tendency to separate in flight. A more recent explanation is centred around the choke section of the barrel enforcing an elongation in the shot column, thus increasing the velocity of the pellets at the front of the shot charge. The disconnection of the pellets in the shot charge during the 1/10,000 part of a second during their transit through the choke section adds about 80 ft/s (24 m/s) to the velocity of the front pellets caused by their acceleration through the cone. An estimated pellet separation in the region of 0.004 in (0.1 mm) defeats the main cause of pellet spread (the outward pressure upon the bulk of the shot charge caused by the pressure exerted by the pellets at the rear of the shot column, as previously mentioned in Section 6.14). It follows that the length of the cone section of the choke must also affect the effectiveness of the choke, as must the degree of smoothness of the choke or the presence of oil in the bore, as these will act against the pellet capturing effect, thus reducing the effective choke. The fact that changes in pellet size will change their stacking characteristics at the muzzle is another factor which has been recognised for years by the best English gunmakers (see Section 5.12). It is interesting to note that the apparent reduction in choke effectiveness caused by oily bores was commented upon by Oberfell and Thompson many years ago in their article entitled 'The mysteries of shotgun patterns'.

Table 6.9 provides useful information concerning the retained velocity and energies of UK pellet sizes at various ranges. Note that in many other instances the 'nominal velocities' quoted in Eley data refer to the mean velocity over a distance of 20 yd (18 m). This is of course lower than the actual muzzle velocities and represents the traditional presentation of velocities as measured by the now outmoded Boulengé's chronograph.

## 6.16   Soft and Hard Shot — Shotgun Pellet Ballistics

Shotgun pellets consist of small lead alloy spheres containing between approximately 0.5 and 8.0% antimony, which is added to increase the hard-

**Table 6.9    Pellet Striking Velocities at Different Ranges in Metric and Imperial Units**

| Shot | Striking Velocity in M/S and Striking Energy in J at Ranges in M | | | | | |
|------|------|------|------|------|------|------|
|      | 20 | 25 | 30 | 35 | 40 | 45 |
| BB | 284/16.5 | 269/14.8 | 254/13.4 | 238/11.7 | 226/10.4 | 212/9.3 |
| 3 | 272/7.62 | 253/6.60 | 236/5.74 | 219/4.94 | 203/4.25 | 188/3.68 |
| 4 | 269/6.14 | 249/5.26 | 231/4.53 | 214/3.89 | 197/3.30 | 181/2.78 |
| 5 | 265/4.62 | 244/3.91 | 224/3.30 | 205/2.76 | 188/2.32 | 171/1.92 |
| 6 | 261/3.65 | 239/3.06 | 219/2.57 | 199/2.12 | 180/1.73 | 163/1.42 |
| 7 | 257/2.81 | 234/2.33 | 212/1.92 | 191/1.55 | 172/1.26 | 154/1.01 |
| 9 | 247/1.52 | 220/1.19 | 196/0.96 | 171/0.75 | 150/0.55 | 128/0.40 |

| Shot | Striking Velocity in Ft/S and Striking Energy in Ft.Lb at Ranges in Yd | | | | | |
|------|------|------|------|------|------|------|
|      | 20 | 30 | 35 | 40 | 45 | 50 |
| BB | 942/12.4 | 860/10.3 | 815/9.24 | 770/8.25 | 729/7.38 | 688/6.56 |
| 3 | 915/5.79 | 804/4.48 | 753/3.92 | 704/3.43 | 657/2.99 | 612/2.59 |
| 4 | 905/4.68 | 788/3.54 | 735/3.08 | 683/2.66 | 635/2.30 | 587/1.97 |
| 5 | 893/3.52 | 768/2.60 | 711/2.23 | 656/1.90 | 604/1.61 | 555/1.36 |
| 6 | 883/2.80 | 752/2.03 | 691/1.71 | 634/1.44 | 579/1.20 | 528/1.01 |
| 7 | 871/2.16 | 731/1.52 | 667/1.27 | 606/1.06 | 549/0.86 | 496/0.70 |
| 9 | 840/1.18 | 680/0.77 | 608/0.62 | 537/0.48 | 475/0.38 | 412/0.28 |

ness. A trace of arsenic was traditionally used to aid spherocity. For many years shot was traditionally made by allowing molten droplets of lead alloy to fall in air down a tall shot tower into a bath of water to break their fall. In recent years systems such as the Bleimeister process have eliminated the need for these very tall shot towers. Traces of other elements will also appear as impurities in commercial shotgun pellets which will vary in composition depending upon the source of the lead used as well as the antimony content specified for the particular application. Small lead spheres typically 2 to 3 mm in diameter have a poor ballistic coefficient and, as a result, will suffer severe retardation due to air resistance. This factor tends to limit the killing power of the weapon compared with that of a rifled arm. Even when used with rifled slug loads severe velocity losses are observed over relatively short ranges, due to their poor shape and hollow-based construction. As an example, the old 7/8 oz (25 g) 12-bore Foster slug would lose approximately 26 per cent of its muzzle velocity of 1590 ft/s (485 m/s) after travelling only 50 yd (46 m). The resultant loss in kinetic energy over this same distance comes to a staggering 45%. Smaller, lighter conventional pellets slow down rapidly, shedding a large portion of their original kinetic energy in the process as is shown in Table 6.9 using data derived from Eley ammunition tables for English pellet sizes.

## 6.17   Steel Shot Loadings

All of the values in Table 6.9 are of course for low antimonyl lead alloy pellets. In recent years the use of non-lead shot has become mandatory in wetland areas of the US, and there are moves to extend this to other upland shooting areas. Some European countries have implemented similar legislation, and there are plans for other EC members to follow the same course. The predictable rush to introduce non-toxic steel shot loadings in Denmark resulted in disaster for their specialist timber industry. The long thin and very sharp blades used to machine logs to produce thin veneers were chipped, or sometimes broke away dangerously when they encountered a steel pellet embedded in the timber. This resulted in a ban on steel loadings in Denmark in timber producing areas, and a move to alternative softer alternatives such as Bismuth/Tin alloy pellets. In the UK a voluntary ban on the use of lead shot was started for the 1995 wildfowling season in designated wetland areas. Since then a mandatory ban in such areas has been introduced in England. It is hoped that this will reduce the incidence of lead poisoning in wildfowl, which is caused by the birds picking up spent lead pellets lying in shallow water instead of the grit used as a part of their normal digestive process. Lead poisoning occurs due to the pellets being digested when ground in the extraordinarily harsh conditions of the bird's gizzard.

Steel shot, or more correctly low-carbon-content soft iron shot, has been used in the US for some years and this is likely to remain the primary alternative material. Processes have been perfected to produce pellets from wire which is cut to length and then rolled to shape with a rust inhibitor. However, its use is not without attendant problems. The hardness of these pellets is approximately 90 DPH as against 30 DPH for conventional shot, and the density of the pellets so produced is approximately 30 per cent lower. This harder, less dense material causes a predictable reduction in the ballistic coefficient of the pellets and at the same time causes problems with the available loading space within cartridges of conventional length. One response to the latter problem has been to introduce a 3 1/2 in (87 mm) 12-bore cartridge for use in suitably chambered guns. This problem is also addressed by eliminating the buffer section at the base of the plastic wad to increase the volume of the cup, which in turn adversely alters the recoil characteristics. The arithmetic remains the same however; a one ounce load of US Number 4 shot consists of 134 lead pellets and 192 steel pellets. In order to use missiles of similar performance it is usual to choose a steel loading containing pellets two sizes larger than the corresponding lead shot loading. As steel loads tend to pattern tighter than their lead shot counterparts it is recommended that a lesser degree of choke is used. Unless the gun is of a type which uses screw-in choke tubes or an adjustable polychoke, this of course entails the reboring of the barrel chokes.

A special plastic high-density polyethylene cup-wad utilising thick walls is required to protect the barrel walls from grooving or choke deformation effects caused by the use of these relatively hard pellets. Such heavy wads constitute an undesirable long-lived environmental hazard in their own right, although research is being conducted to perfect plastic wads made from materials such as maize cellulose which will biodegrade after firing when in contact with the soil. Additional hazards to the firer or to other persons are a consequence of the high propensity for ricochet of these pellets.

American manufactured steel shot cartridges produce higher pressure levels than conventional loadings, and in an attempt to offset the reduction in killing range caused by the poor ballistic properties of this material unusually large pellet sizes are often employed. Such loadings are not approved by the European CIP Proof authorities for use in European guns, which tend to be lighter and less robust than their American repeating counterparts. The barrel walls near to the muzzle ends of a traditional English or English-style double-barrelled side-by-side gun are extremely thin. Problems can be encountered with choke deformation, barrel bulging, the loosening of the barrel ribs and the cracking of actions. All of these problems are of course worse with older guns which have been made from relatively soft unalloyed steels. The CIP steel shot standards appropriate for European guns stipulate lower velocities and pressures than the US counterparts, place limits upon the degree of choke used and include additional specifications to ensure that the hardness and the diameters of the pellets do not exceed recommended standards. The standards apply to the CIP member signatories Austria, Belgium, Chile, the Czech Republic, Russia, Finland, France, Germany, Hungary, Italy, Spain and the UK. For normally proved guns at the time of writing, the standard steel loading shall exhibit a maximum velocity of 400 m/s (1312 ft/s) measured at a distance of 2.5 m, a maximum pressure of 740 bar, a maximum shot momentum of 12 Ns and a maximum pellet diameter of 3.25 mm (0.128 in). Guns marked with the special European steel shot proof mark for a high-performance loading allow a maximum velocity of 430 m/s (1410 ft/s), a maximum pressure of 1050 bar, a maximum shot momentum of 13.5 Ns, and a maximum pellet diameter of 4.00 mm (0.157 in) unless fired in barrels of less than half-choke (0.020 in/0.5 mm). It is possible that changes will be made in the future to these specifications.

## 6.18   Alternative Non-Lead Materials

Other softer non-lead materials have been tried or used recently in an attempt to increase the ballistic performance of the shot and at the same time eliminate the use of heavy wads, high pressure, over-hard pellets and special proof

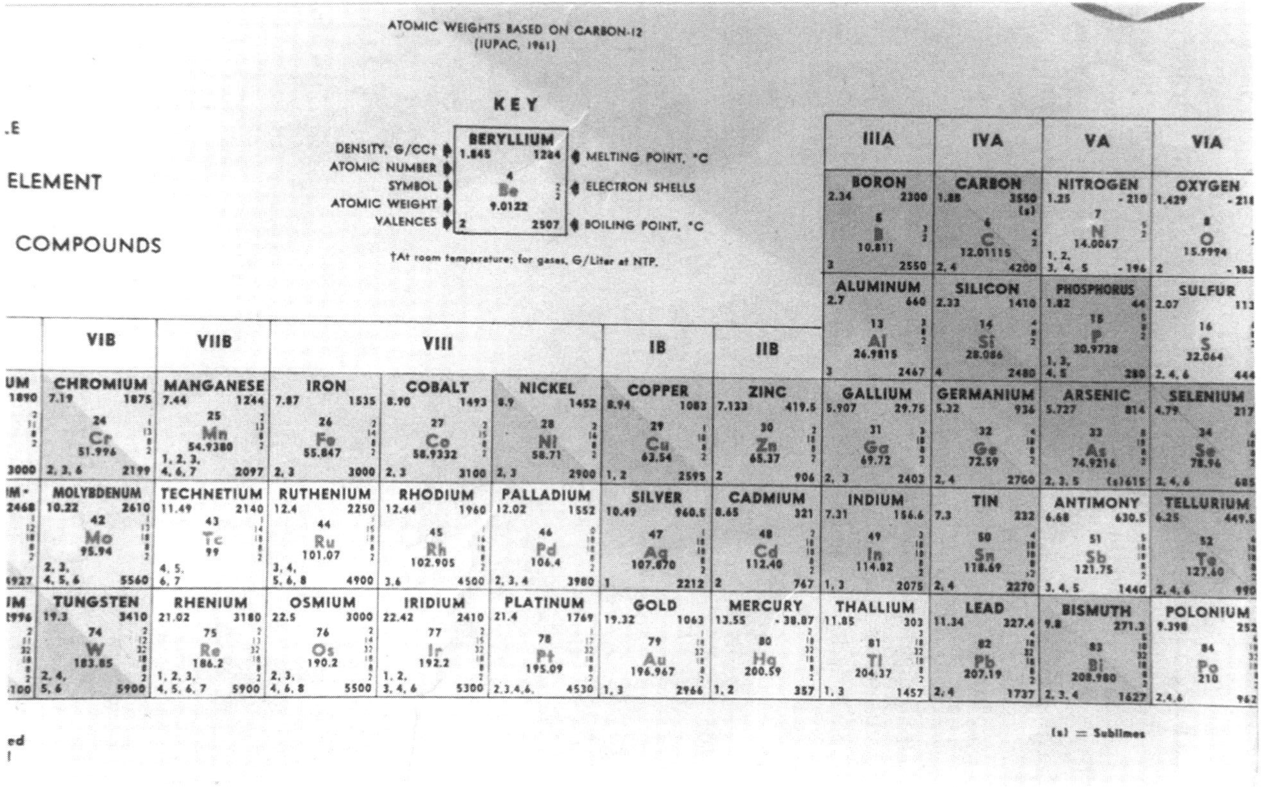

**Figure 6.10** A section of the Periodic Table of the Elements, showing the relative densities of a number of metallic elements of interest for use as replacement materials for toxic lead (Pb-Plumbum) shotgun pellets.

testing (Figure 6.10). Eley Black Feather cartridges use pellets made from tungsten in an organic polymer (Figure 6.11), and the Gamebore Company has introduced Impact Tungsten Matrix (ITM) shot loadings possessing a density close to that of lead, although this latter type of material is relatively hard, thus necessitating the need for a protective plastic wad. Tungsten is a denser material than lead (19.3 g/cc), but when made up in this polymer it forms a soft material possessing a density comparable with that of lead shot alloy (11.1 g/cc). Eley Hawk have also introduced a bismuth/tin alloy possessing a density of 9.7 g/cc, which is closer to that of lead and appreciably higher than that of steel shot (7.96 g/cc). The Kent Cartridge Company attempted to market a loading based upon another high-density element molybdenum (10.2 g/cc), and also offered zinc alloy shot loadings for short range skeet shooting and other applications, although this was discontinued after it was also found to be toxic to waterfowl. Shot made from 39% tungsten, 44.5% bismuth and 16.5% tin has also been tested, as has shot made from tungsten-iron (Federal Cartridge Company). Tungsten-iron offers greater

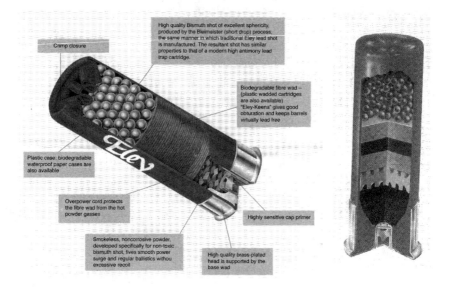

**Figure 6.11** Cut-away images of modern shotgun cartridges. Eley cartridge with choice of drawn plastic tube or traditional paper case, alongside Winchester cartridge using injection moulded case with solid head. Both cartridges shown here employ traditional biodegradable compressed fibre wadding and star crimp end closures. The Eley cartridge contains a loading of non-toxic Bismuth alloy pellets, produced by the German 'Bleimaster' short drop process.

density, but has the disadvantages of being harder than steel and more expensive than Bismuth. A relatively soft, non-toxic shot loading using tin is also being marketed, even though it is relatively expensive and its density (7.3 g/cc) is slightly lower than that of iron. To the forensic scientist such differences are good news because analysis of shotgun pellets recovered from a body may now produce significant additional data.

## 6.19  Pellet Sizes and Weights

Shotgun pellets are usually graded in size and checked for sphericity at the shot tower or other producing centre. However, it is true to say that some manufacturers operate to higher standards than others, or may be forced to cut some inspection standards in order to produce shot to the price the customer is prepared to pay. It is always wise to weigh a significant number of the pellets recovered from the crime scene or body so that such differences can be detected. Such data will prove useful if compared with the pellets found after dismantling any cartridges recovered from the suspect. Such features as wide weight range scatter along with the analysis results for antimony content and the finding of any significant impurities will often prove to be useful. For the same reasons it is unwise to assume that the indicated shot loading upon a particular batch of cartridges is actually representative of the contents. Mistakes in shot selection, both in weight and antimony content are not unusual. Such features are often found upon dismantling ammunition along with a high incidence of out-of-round pellets or the presence of twin pellets fused together.

Shotgun pellet sizes are graded using number and letter systems, the origin of which is now lost or confused. At one time different cities in the same country would use different grading systems. Confusion still exists today despite attempts at rationalising the scales of sizes within individual countries. When I was younger almost all shotgun ammunition used in the UK was of domestic manufacture. I suspect that today the figure would be in the region of 50%, with the remainder coming predominantly from West European countries, Russia, the US and former Eastern Bloc countries. All manner of pellet loadings are now to be found printed on the sides of cartridges and cartridge boxes. Using data from Eley literature it is possible, with a little modification, to provide a useful listing for British shotgun pellets from the largest buckshot pellet down to the smallest popular size of skeet pellet. One must always bear in mind, however, that the typical weights stated correspond to conventional soft-alloy pellets containing approximately 0.5% antimony as a hardening agent. Hard shot containing higher antimony levels (average value 4%) (Figure 6.12) will be slightly lighter due to the lower

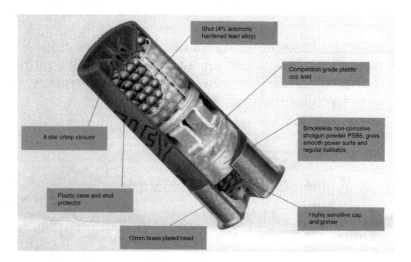

**Figure 6.12**  Cut-away image of trap shooting cartridge containing plastic cup wad containing charge of high antimony content lead shot. The 'Olympic 2000' loading uses 4% antimony lead shot, whilst the 'VIP' premier competition cartridge uses lead shot of 8% antimony content. Hard high antimony content lead pellets are intended to minimise pellet deformation within the bore of the gun, so as to ensure more consistent shot patterns with less 'fliers'.

density of the alloy used in their manufacture, which in turn should produce a small increase in the number of pellets contained in a given charge weight of shot of the same specified size (approximately 2% more in the case of a shift in antimony content from 0.5 to 4.0%). Similar adjustments both for pellet weight and count must also be made in the case of steel or other non-lead loadings by the factors previously indicated (Table 6.10).

The majority of Western European and former Eastern Bloc countries have now, mercifully, taken up the practice of marking the shot size in millimetres as well as their own shot number; in addition it is not uncommon for the British and American equivalent sizes also to be marked upon the cartridge. For these reasons I am not choosing to provide comprehensive listings of pellet sizes, although the data for American pellet sizes (in Table 6.11 and Table 6.12) should prove useful.

## 6.20   The Propensity for Ricochet

This topic concerns the effects of ricochet or the influence of intermediate targets. All firearm missiles can ricochet if they strike a suitable surface at a

**Table 6.10  British Shotgun Pellet Data**

| Designation | Diam. (in) | Diam. (mm) | Weight (g) | Pellets/oz |
|---|---|---|---|---|
| LG | 0.36 | 9.1 | 4.54 | 6 |
| SG | 0.33 | 8.4 | 3.54 | 8 |
| Special SG | 0.30 | 7.6 | 2.58 | 11 |
| SSG | 0.27 | 6.8 | 1.89 | 15 |
| AAA | 0.20 | 5.2 | 0.81 | 35 |
| BB | 0.16 | 4.1 | 0.40 | 70 |
| 1 | 0.14 | 3.6 | 0.28 | 100 |
| 3 | 0.13 | 3.3 | 0.20 | 140 |
| 4 | 0.12 | 3.1 | 0.17 | 170 |
| 5 | 0.11 | 2.8 | 0.13 | 220 |
| 6 | 0.10 | 2.6 | 0.10 | 270 |
| 7 | 0.095 | 2.4 | 0.08 | 340 |
| 7½ | 0.090 | 2.3 | 0.07 | 400 |
| 8 | 0.085 | 2.2 | 0.06 | 450 |
| 9 | 0.080 | 2.0 | 0.05 | 580 |

low angle of incidence. However, some missiles are more prone to ricochet or deflection than others. Bullets travelling at very high velocity, and particularly if of soft-point or hollow-point construction designed to expand in tissue, will have a propensity to break up, almost explosively in some instances (Figure 7.23 and Figure 7.24). By way of illustration, I recall many years ago doing some limited tests in which missiles of comparable calibre were fired at a shallow angle at a concrete surface, the incidence of ricochet being recorded by the presence of a large sheet of cardboard positioned upright beyond the impact zone. Tests conducted using .22 in Long Rifle loadings repeatedly produced the ricochet effects for which this particular round is so noted. Tests using 55 grain (3.6 g) soft-point bullets discharged from a .22 in-250 rifle at a muzzle velocity in the region of 3700 ft/s (1130 m/s) disintegrated completely on impact with the concrete leaving fragments of copper jacket and lead core adhering to, or sticking in the thin sheet of cardboard. Most deerstalkers who have hunted deer in woodland conditions soon become aware of the effects caused by the bullet striking a thin branch or twig, especially if they chose to use high velocity lightweight bullet loadings such as those offered in the .243 in Winchester range.

Even when the bullet does not break up, as in the case of a heavier missile moving at a moderate velocity, the bullet can still suffer substantial deflection if it chances to strike a twig or even heather, in the case of hill stalking when taking a prone shot (Figure 6.12 and 6.13). This is most severe if the unintentional impact occurs at some point near to the firer, as the effects of even a minor deviation from intended course will be greatly magnified at the

**Table 6.11  American Shotgun Pellet Data**

| Designation | Diameter (in) | Diameter (mm) | Pellets/Oz Lead | Pellets/Oz Steel |
|---|---|---|---|---|
| No. 000 Buck | 0.36 | 9.1 | 6 | |
| No. 00 Buck | 0.33 | 8.4 | 8 | |
| No. 0 Buck | 0.32 | 8.1 | 9 | |
| No. 1 Buck | 0.30 | 7.6 | 11 | |
| No. 2 Buck | 0.27 | 6.9 | 15 | |
| No. 3 Buck | 0.25 | 6.4 | 19 | |
| No. 4 Buck | 0.24 | 6.1 | 21 | |
| FF | 0.23 | 5.8 | 24 | |
| F | 0.22 | 5.6 | 27 | 40 |
| TT | 0.21 | 5.3 | 31 | |
| T | 0.20 | 5.1 | 36 | 52 |
| BBB | 0.19 | 4.8 | 43 | 62 |
| BB | 0.18 | 4.6 | 50 | 72 |
| Air rifle | 0.175 | 4.4 | 55 | |
| B | 0.17 | 4.3 | 59 | |
| 1 | 0.16 | 4.1 | 71 | 103 |
| 2 | 0.15 | 3.8 | 87 | 125 |
| 3 | 0.14 | 3.6 | 106 | 158 |
| 4 | 0.13 | 3.3 | 130 | 192 |
| 5 | 0.12 | 3.0 | 170 | 243 |
| 6 | 0.11 | 2.8 | 220 | 315 |
| 7 | 0.10 | 2.5 | 290 | 422 |
| $7^{1}/_{2}$ | 0.095 | 2.4 | 340 | |
| 8 | 0.09 | 2.3 | 400 | |
| 9 | 0.08 | 2.0 | 570 | |
| 10 | 0.07 | 1.8 | 850 | |
| 11 | 0.06 | 1.5 | 1350 | |
| 12 | 0.05 | 1.3 | 2335 | |
| Dust shot | 0.04 | 1.0 | 4565 | |

greater distance at which the intended target is positioned. At a distance of 100 yd (91 m) a deflection of a meagre one degree will cause the bullet to strike a point 5 ft (1.5 m) from the intended aiming point, which is sufficient to miss even the largest of deer.

One must always bear the above factors in mind when dealing with casework submissions, as it is extremely unusual for the accused person in the case of a murder or wounding incident to admit to shooting the victim deliberately. The recovered missile should always be subjected to initial examination under a low-power stereo microscope to check for the presence of ricochet damage, paint, plaster or anything else which might be relevant before proceeding to comparison microscopy. In addition, the scene can also be examined to determine the presence of any bullet strikes which might

**Table 6.12 Shot Size Equivalents (Nominal)**

| English | Diam(mm) | American* | Canadian | French | Belgian** | Italian | Spanish |
|---|---|---|---|---|---|---|---|
| LG | 9.1 | 000 Buck | — | — | — | — | — |
| SG | 8.4 | 00 Buck | SSG | — | 9G | 11/0 | — |
| Spec.SG | 7.6 | 1 Buck | SG | C2 | 12G | 9/0 | — |
| SSG | 6.8 | 3 Buck | AAAA | C3 | — | — | — |
| AAA | 5.2 | 4 Buck | AAA | 5/0 | — | — | — |
| BB | 4.1 | Air Rifle | Air Rifle | 1 | 00 | 00 | 1 |
| 1 | 3.6 | 2 | 2 | 3 | — | 1 or 2 | 3 |
| 3 | 303 | 4 | 4 | 4 | — | 3 | 4 |
| 4 | 301 | 5 | 5 | 5 | — | 4 | 5 |
| 5 | 2.8 | 6 | 6 | 6 | 5 | 5 | 6 |
| 6 | 2.6 | — | — | — | 6 | 6 | — |
| 7 | 2.4 | 7$^1/_2$ | 7$^1/_2$ | 7 | 7 | 7$^1/_2$ | 7 |
| 7$^1/_2$ | 2.3 | 8 | 8 | 7$^1/_2$ | 7$^1/_2$ | 8 | 7$^1/_2$ |
| 8 | 2.2 | — | — | 8 | 8 | — | 8 |
| 9 | 2.0 | 9 | 9 | 9 | 9$^1/_2$ | 9 | |

\* Also Swedish
\*\* Also Dutch

have been associated with such a ricochet; a simple direct chemical test for the presence of lead using sodium rhodizonate reagent will differentiate between bullet damage and damage caused by other effects.

## 6.21 Gunfire and the Sounds Made during the Flight of Missiles

The loud sound produced when a gun is fired is caused by the sudden explosive supersonic muzzle blast of high velocity gases produced from the burning of the propellant charge. A loud 'crack' produced by the escape of high velocity air will also be produced when a powerful air rifle is fired. The propellant gases will, however, travel only a short distance before dissipating into the atmosphere. The noise of the discharge will travel a considerable distance, depending upon its intensity, the prevailing atmospheric conditions and the nature of ground cover. The peak impulse sound signal is only of very short duration, although it can be reflected back a number of times by surfaces offering it little attenuation, and so lengthening its duration. The measurement of such sounds are covered in Section 9.3. Health and Safety Regulations now make mandatory the use of earmuffs and shooting glasses to protect the firers of guns in the ballistics laboratories. The lining of the laboratory range walls with acoustic panels containing sound-attenuating materials such as a mineral fibre like 'Rockwool', will reduce the level of

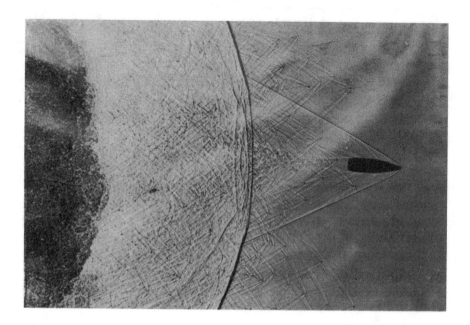

**Figure 6.13**  High-speed photograph of 7.62 mm Nato rifle bullet a short distance from the muzzle end of the barrel just in front of the 'bubble' of emerging powder gases. The shape of the shock wave attached to the nose of the bullet indicates a velocity of approximately Mach 2.5. At this early stage the unburnt powder grains seen travelling with the bullet each have their own characteristic angled shock waves signifying individual velocities ranging from Mach 1 to Mach 1.5. The turbulence at the base of the bullet caused by the filling of the vacuum its passage has created is reduced by the use of a boat-tail bullet shape.

reflected sounds and, thus, the duration of the sound signal. If a gun is fired in a room with reflective tiled walls, then the duration of the sound signal will be considerably lengthened, and the level of potential hearing damage to the firer will be correspondingly increased. I recall measurements being made of gunfire signals produced in a section of caves used for test-firing guns at the laboratory during the early stages of my career. Depending on the type of gun used, the initial impulse signal could sometimes exceed 160 decibels (A-weighted), but due to the nature of the location, measurements indicated that hazardous sound levels existed for as long as 500 milliseconds.

The sound produced by the discharge of a gun will travel away from it at the prevailing speed of sound, which is in the region of 1,100 ft/s (335 m/s). The actual speed of sound decreases with increased altitude, increases with increased temperature, and increases very slightly with increased relative humidity (Table 6.13).

**Table 6.13   Variation of Speed of Sound with Temperature and Altitude**

| Variation at Sea Level in Dry Air | Variation of Speed with Altitude |
|---|---|
| 0°C 331.4 m/s (1087 ft/s) | 0 metres 340.29 m/s (1116 ft/s) |
| 10°C 337.5 m/s (1107 ft/s) | 1000 metres 336.43 m/s (1104 ft/s) |
| 20°C 343.4 m/s (1127 ft/s) | 2500 metres 330.56 m/s (1085 ft/s) |
| 30°C 349.2 m/s (1146 ft/s) | |

An observer listening to the sound of the flight of a missile travelling towards him in stable flight will hear what he might describe as a hissing noise or a z-z-z-z-z-z noise, with a Doppler shift as it approaches and then passes him. An unstable, missile will be accompanied by an erratic flurry of sound as it constantly tumbles over in flight. The unsafe practice by some wild-fowlers of desperately firing charges of large buckshot pellets at distant geese flying above them, has coined the term 'blue whistlers', to describe the sounds of the flight into the sky of deformed buckshot pellets fired from heavy choke barrels using un-buffered shotgun cartridge loadings. A ricochet of a bullet off a hard surface will be signified by a whistling or whining noise due to its unstable flight.

Modern centre-fire rifle loadings usually generate bullet velocities in the Mach range 2.5–3.3 (Figure 6.13). The arrival of a supersonic bullet close to an observer, such as a target marker in the range butts, will be accompanied by a sharp 'crack' sound, due to the shock wave being associated with the bullet. Some short time afterwards the observer will hear the less intense, lower frequency sound of the rifle's discharge. If the missile is discharged from the gun at a muzzle velocity below the speed of sound, then the sound of the discharge will travel in front of the bullet at the constant speed of sound, and the bullet's arrival will not be accompanied by a supersonic 'crack'. The bullet on the other hand will be constantly decelerating during its flight due to the effects of air resistance, thus causing the lag between the sound of discharge and the arrival of the bullet to increase with increasing range. Magnum revolvers, black powder cartridge loadings and muzzle-loading rifles will usually generate muzzle velocities a little above the speed of sound, typically in the range 1,200–1,500 ft/sec (366–457 m/s). In these instances the sound of the discharge will initially travel behind the bullet. However, the bullet will rapidly decelerate due to the effects of air resistance, and at some point downrange the two events will arrive together. Further on downrange the sound of the gun's discharge will overtake the bullet to an increasing degree.

# Further Reading

Braun, W.F. 1973. *Aerodynamics Data for Small Arms Projectiles,* Ballistics Research Laboratories Report No. 1630, Exterior Ballistics Laboratory, Aberdeen Proving Ground, MD.

British Proof Authorities. 1993. *Notes on the Proof of Shotguns and Other Small Arms: The Gun Barrel Proof Houses,* London and Birmingham.

Burrard, Major Sir G. 1921–1932. *The Modern Shotgun: Volume I. The Gun, Volume II. The Cartridge, Volume III. The Gun and the Cartridge,* London: Herbert Jenkins.

Eley Shooter's Diary. 1995. 90th Edition, Birmingham: Eley Hawk Ltd.

Farrar, C.L. and Leeming, D.W. 1983. *Military Ballistics—A Basic Manual,* Oxford: Brassey.

Federal Ammunition Brochure. 1995. The Federal Cartridge Company, Anoke, MN.

Haag, L.C. 2002. The sound of bullets. *AFTE Journal,* **34** (3), 255.

Hatcher, Major General, J.S. 1966. *Hatcher's Notebook,* Harrisburg PA: Stackpole.

Hornady Staff. 1991. *Hornady Handbook of Cartridge Reloading,* Grand Island, NE: Hornady Manufacturing Co. Inc.

Products Brochure. 1992. Remington Arms Co. Inc., Wilmington DE.

Roberts, N.H. 1958. *The Muzzle-Loading Cap-Lock Rifle,* Harrisburg, PA: Stackpole.

*Textbook of Small Arms.* 1929. War Department, London: HMSO.

*Textbook on Ballistics and Gunnery.* 1987. London HMSO.

Warlow, T.A. 1988. A question of accuracy, *Journal of the St. Hubert's Club of Great Britain,* October, 4–8.

Whelan, T, 1945, *Small Arms Design and Ballistics,* Vols. 1 and 2, Plantersville, SC: Small-Arms Technical Publishing Co.

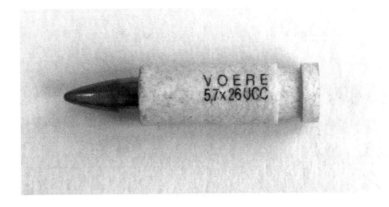

**Figure 6.14** Austrian Voere 5.7 mm caseless ammunition. Here the bullet is embedded in a shaped cake of propellant which is ignited electronically by the rifle.

**Figure 6.15** 1.5 in/37 mm riot control baton rounds. The original shaped black rubber bullet was replaced by an ivory coloured plastic polyurethane bullet in an attempt at reducing the incidence of fatalities in service use in Northern Ireland.

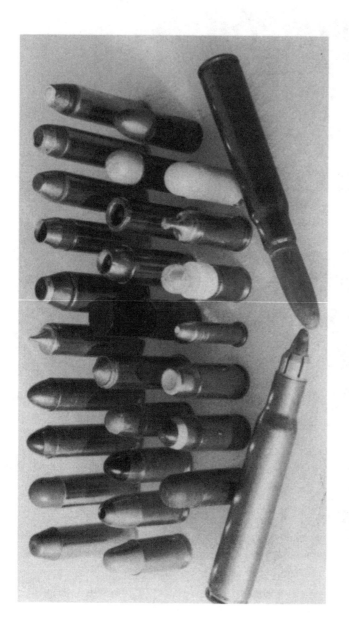

**Figure 6.16**  An assortment of special and exotic cartridge loadings. Starting at the left side of the back row: .38 in Special tungsten polymer bullet loading. MBA .38 in Special Short-Stop. Israeli .357 in Magnum CBAP armour piercing. Israeli CBX Cavity-Wounding. French SFM THV. Velet .44 in Special Mercury filling. PMC .38 in Special Tubular. National .357 in Magnum Tracer. Velet .357 in Magnum explosive. Bingham .38 in Special explosive. KTW 9 mm armour piercing. Geco 9 mm Action 3. Israeli 9 mm CBAP. Geco 9 mm Effect Nose. .38 in Special Quad. Speer Target 44 Plastic primer-powered training. Federal 10 mm Hydra-Shock. .38 in Special Scorpion. SNC-FX .38 in Marker. Geco 9 mm Action Safety. TEC 9 mm Frangible. Israeli 9 mm CBAP. Glaser 9 mm Safety Slug. Bingham .22 in LR Devastator explosive. SNC-FX 9 mm Simunition. SFM 9 mm THV. Geco 9 mm Plastik Training. Remington .30–06 Accelerator. 7.92 mm Mauser wooden bulleted rifle blank.

**Figure 6.17**  5.56×45 Nato versus the Soviet 5.45×39 loading. The use of a slightly smaller calibre and a steel core bullet enhances the ballistic shape of the Soviet loading as well as conferring a significant improvement in its ability to defeat light screening cover. The relatively new Nato SS109 bullet configuration which has replaced the original plain lead core loading, includes a part steel core and an increased weight to achieve similar enhanced downrange performance and penetration.

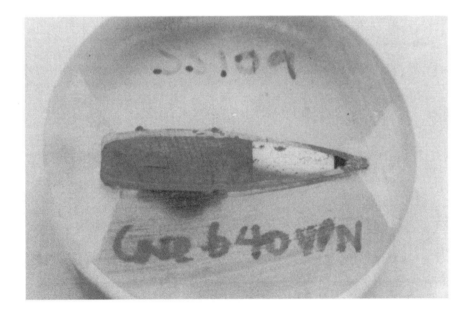

**Figure 6.18**  Microsection of Nato SS109 5.56 mm bullet showing truncated cone shaped hard steel core in front of the plain lead alloy filling.

# Terminal/Wound Ballistics and Distance of Firing

# 7

This chapter deals with what takes place when the bullet, missile, or shotgun pellets strike the target, which can constitute living tissue or some other material. During this brief period of interaction the missile tends to suffer some degree of deformation, or disintegrates, and the target is pierced or otherwise damaged. The degree of destruction which takes place is dependent upon the mass of the projectile, its striking velocity, its design and construction and the nature of the target. Much has been written upon what a bullet or shot charge will do upon a human target, even to the degree of stating the precise volume of the anticipated temporary cavity or the quantity of haemorrhagic tissue which will be found within the wound track for each unit of kinetic energy expended by the bullet. However, over the years I have seen so many atypical or, some would say, freak effects, that I would hesitate to predict exactly how a missile will perform beyond stating generalisms. The human body is not a homogeneous block of material such as that typified by a block of 10% ordnance gelatine. In reality it contains hard bones exhibiting curved surfaces which can deflect a bullet or cause it to break up at velocity levels where one would expect penetration. Fatty tissue or liver will not offer the same resistance as would muscle. The lungs constitute a cavity within the body filled with air, which, in contrast to the tissue surrounding it, is compressible. On top of all this there is an overlying tendency for the unexpected to happen during these extremely brief, sometimes high-energy change interactions, which at times has caused me to wonder what exactly constitutes normality. A bullet can be deflected off a rib on a person's back so it is directed along a circular path in the tissue covering the rib cage leaving the victim with a relatively trivial injury. A bullet can be deflected or break up on striking a relatively modest item of screening cover interposed between

169

the firer and the intended victim, or some article inside a pocket of the coat worn by the victim. A heavy sheepskin coat and sweater can greatly reduce the lethal capabilities of a charge of birdshot fired from a shotgun even from a relatively short distance. A man can die after being struck by a low-energy air rifle pellet, if it chances to strike a vulnerable exposed part of his body, while another man can survive extensive injuries to the body and head inflicted by a high-powered rifle or sawn-off shotgun.

You can go to a scene of a suicide where the victim has placed the muzzle end of a 12-bore gun under his chin before firing it, and find the shot charge and wadding lodged inside his head during the post-mortem examination, rather than the more usual explosive type of injury from such a discharge. However, much work has been done by other researchers, who do not always concur with each other's findings, which I will attempt to cover later in this chapter.

## 7.1   Mass, Momentum and Kinetic Energy

This section attempts to address the misconceptions concerning the actual meaning of the above terms. The expression 'mass' is frequently confused with the expression 'weight'. Debate concerning the other two terms, when attempting to predict the potential of a moving object to influence other bodies, can be traced back to the seventeenth century when a protracted controversy took place between two eminent mathematicians, Liebnitz and Descartes. The curious property under discussion was given the rather vague title 'the efficacy of moving bodies'. The great dispute arose because each attributed to it a different meaning. Liebnitz maintained that the efficacy of a moving body was its Kinetic Energy, or its capacity to do work. Kinetic energy is energy associated with motion. He maintained that this kinetic energy was proportional to the square of the velocity of the body. He was of course correct, as scientists now know that the kinetic energy of a moving body with mass $m$ and velocity $v$ is given by the long-established and universal formula:

$$\text{Kinetic energy} = \tfrac{1}{2}\, mv^2$$

Descartes, on the other hand, declared that the efficacy of a moving body was directly proportional to its velocity. In this respect he was equally right, for he was thinking of what we now know by the term Momentum, which is provided by the formula:

$$\text{Momentum} = mv$$

The expression Momentum represents the quantity of motion that a force can impart to a body in a given time. Around the same time, a young student attending King's School, Grantham, in Lincolnshire, England, regarded as a dull and unimpressive academic by his superiors, went on to enter Trinity College, Cambridge, to study mathematics and science, where he achieved many great things. Although the popular and much remembered myth claims that Isaac Newton discovered gravity after watching an apple fall from a tree, one of his most notable scientific insights is contained in his famous three Laws of Motion, which are named after him as "Newton's Laws of Motion." His First Law states that *a body continues in a state of rest or continues to move with a steady velocity in a straight line if it is not acted upon by other forces.* The tendency of a body to remain at rest or to move with unchanged velocity is due to what is called its Mass or its Inertia. A massive body has a large mass and one will find it difficult to change its motion or to start its movement. Try kicking a tennis ball and then a large iron cannon ball to appreciate the difference.

The mass and the weight of a body are, however, entirely different properties. Strictly speaking, this is why, particularly when using Imperial Units, one should describe the unit of mass as the lb. and the unit of weight (or force) as lb.wt. Away from the physics of Einstein, who as a student was also described by his headmaster as being a dull and unimpressive student who would never amount to much, we can regard mass as being a constant quantity, but weight can only be measured in a gravity field, which on planet Earth pulls the object toward its centre. The acceleration due to gravity at sea level is approximately $9.81$ m/s$^2$, but it in fact increases as one moves from the poles towards the equator. It decreases with increasing elevation and varies due to the nature of the mineral deposits in the ground under the location where it is being measured. The variation due to latitude is nearly 1 part in 200 between the equator and the poles. A standard value of $32.174$ ft/s$^2$ ($9.80665$ m/s$^2$) relative to the value for $g$ measured at Potsdam is generally used. So, when an object of one pound mass is hung on a spring balance, it is being pulled downwards by this same downward force, and the scale indicates a value of one lb.wt. If we were to take that same object and spring balance to the moon and repeat the exercise, the scale would indicate a value for its weight approximately one sixth of the earth value, due to the lesser gravitational force existing on that body. Its mass however, would remain the same. An astronaut up in the International Space Station may float around virtually weightless in zero-g conditions (free fall). However his mass will remain the same as that on Earth. This property will be obvious to an aggrieved colleague, if the same astronaut should collide feet first into his teeth while showing off his zero-g acrobatic skill. Although he will be able to lift objects of greater mass and potential weight than he could if back on

Earth, he will still perceive the differences in mass (inertia) of different bodies when starting to move them or to arrest their motions. For example, he would not be able to stand in front of, and then stop an incoming shuttlecraft, without some consequence to his own well being, due to its huge momentum, even if it were travelling at a very modest velocity.

Because mass and weight are not the same, it is necessary to express the measured weight of a bullet in terms of its mass before attempting to calculate its kinetic energy at a given velocity by the basic formula. In the case of calculation in Imperial ft.lb units, and if one has measured the bullet weight in grains (avdp), then it is necessary first to convert this grain weight into lb.wt by dividing by 7000 (the number of grains in a pound (avdp)), and then to divide by the acceleration due to gravity of 32.174 feet per second per second to convert the lb.wt into pounds mass. In the case of a .243 inch 100 grain bullet travelling at a muzzle velocity of 3000 feet per second:

$$KE = \tfrac{1}{2}\, mv^2 = (100 \times 3000 \times 3000) / (2 \times 7000 \times 32.174) = 1998 \text{ ft.lb}$$

Some people choose to divide by an approximate factor such as 450,700 or some similar number, which does the same thing and also eliminates the need to halve the mass for the energy equation; this is a time saving technique especially if one is involved in doing many such calculations. The metric energy values for cartridge loadings indicated in some older European ammunition catalogues will be listed in "kilogram.metre" units, sometimes indicated as "kpm," instead of the current expression "Joules" or "J." These values can be converted to ft.lb by multiplying by the factor 7.233. This factor is produced by multiplying the conversion units from metres and kilograms into feet and pounds (viz. 2.20462 x 3.28084). To convert ft.lb of kinetic energy into kilogram.metre units it is necessary to multiply by the factor 0.138255, the factor produced by doing the reverse conversion of mass and weight (viz. 0.3048 x 0.4536). In the calculation of kilogram.metre units of energy the kilogram weight value of the projectile has been divided by the acceleration due to gravity of $9.80665 m/s^2$ in order to convert it into a mass value.

Most scientists however, will use the International Metric System (SI) for their calculations that utilises metre, kilogram and second units (MKS System). Here energy units are expressed in Joules (J) named after an English cleric and physicist Dr. J.P. Joule (1818–89) who noted the great amount of heat generated when cannon barrels were being bored out. He realized that a considerable portion of the work energy of the drilling process was being wastefully converted into heat, rather than doing the desired mechanical work, and this led to the determination of the mechanical equivalent of heat. The metric unit, the Joule, is a convenient term used in the metric system for expressing heat or energy. It is equivalent to the work done in one second by a current of one ampere against a resistance of 1 ohm. As this would require a pressure of one volt, it becomes one watt.second (the passage of a current of one amp at a pressure of one volt for one second). The Joule is also equivalent to the work done when a force of one Newton advances its point of application by one metre. All units in the SI (MKS) system here must be introduced as metres, kilograms and seconds. In currently published European cartridge catalogues the bullet weights are usually given in gram weights for convenience. For example, a bullet listed as being 10 grams in weight would weigh slightly over 154.3 grains. This must be converted to kilograms by dividing by 1000 to give a bullet weight of 0.01 kilograms, and half of this is 0.005 kilograms. A convenient aspect of the current metric system is that the kilogram weight value measured here on Earth can be used directly in the basic equation as a unit of mass, without the need to divide by the value for the acceleration due to gravity of 9.80665 m/s². Bullet velocity must of course be introduced as metres per second. If the bullet mentioned had a muzzle velocity of, say, 1000 m/s (3281 ft/s) then:

$$KE = \tfrac{1}{2}\, mv^2 = 0.005 \times 1000 \times 1000 = 5000 \text{ Joules}$$
(5 kilowatt seconds or approximately 3687 ft.lb)

The Second Law of Motion states that *when a force acts on a body it produces an acceleration which is proportional to the magnitude of the force.* Force equals mass times acceleration (F = ma). Imagine a moving body of mass $m$ and velocity $u$ striking a body of similar mass so as to accelerate it to the velocity $v$, then

Acceleration or impulse = mv − mu (i.e., the change in momentum)

However, when calculating momentum changes it is imperative that all the velocities are taken in the same direction. If they are in the opposite direction then the lesser one must be assigned a negative value. The reason for this is that unlike kinetic energy, momentum is a vector quantity. All momentum must be accounted for at the end of each interaction. It follows that in an incident where two objects of equal mass and velocity, collide directly against each other so as to stop, then as one is assigned a positive value for initial momentum, and the other an equal but negative value, then their vector assignments have been recognized correctly, so as to result in them both ending up with zero momentum. When one considers the actual momenta of bullets fired from commonly encountered centre-fire sporting and military rifles, and the fact that in many instances the bullet exits from a live target, thus taking with it a portion of its original kinetic energy and momentum, one can understand why outside Hollywood movies so-called 'knock down power' is simply a myth. Although a rifle shot fired by a hunter into the body of a deer may cause it to drop immediately to the ground, in many instances an unalerted deer standing broadside on to the shooter will often show no immediate reaction to a correctly placed bullet strike in the heart-lung area that does not impact with the spine or some substantial bone. The actual sound of the shot is so short-lived that, unless the shooter gives his position away by moving or generating further sound, the beast, though mortally wounded by a correctly placed shot, will often carry on with its normal deer activity, before falling to the ground as the oxygenated blood supply to its brain becomes depleted. If on the other hand, it chances to fall to the ground immediately after the bullet strike, it can fall towards the direction of the firer just as frequently as one might fall away from him. The momentum transfer, or impulse, from the bullet to the body of the deer is so slight as to be insignificant, even if it lodges within the animal so as to transfer all of its momentum to it. This is because the mass of the bullet at, for example 10 grams weight (0.01 kg) is tiny when compared with, for example that of a 100 kilogram deer. In this instance the velocity of the stationary deer is zero, and that of the bullet is 1000 m/s. As here the bullet lodges in its body, its mass becomes coupled to that of the deer, and all of its momentum and kinetic energy imparted to it. To calculate the potential velocity $v$ imparted to this combined mass:

Momentum after impact = momentum prior to impact

$$(100 + 0.01)\ v = 0.01 \times 1000$$

$$v = (0.01 \times 1000)\ /\ (100 + 0.01)$$

$$v = 0.1\ \text{m/s}\ (0.328\ \text{ft/s})$$

This trivial momentary impulse would be accommodated by an indiscernible sway imparted to the body that would in turn be accommodated by flexion of the deer's leg joints. The so-called knock-down effect of a typical pistol or revolver bullet of similar weight travelling at a substantially lower velocity in the region of 200 to 400 m/s, would of course be considerably lower than the above value.

The Third Law states that if a body A acts upon a body B, the body B always exerts an equal and opposite force on A, or action and reaction are equal and opposite.

This simple statement explains why your rifle kicks your shoulder when you fire it. It is usual for the bullet to weigh considerably less than the rifle, so that even when taking account of the weight of the powder charge and rocket effects, the kick is well within our tolerance zone of about 15 foot pounds for the average rifle. Everyone who has tested their rifle with bullets of different weights will know that, all other things being equal, the heavier bullet loads generate greater recoil. Any ex soldier who has fired the heavy Energa anti-tank bomb from a .303 inch rifle utilizing a blank cartridge as the means of propulsion, will be able to testify to the potentially bone break-ing experience of the consequences. If the weight of the total ejecta (projectile plus powder charge gases and discharge residues) was the same as that of the rifle being fired, then due to the additional rearward rocket effects of muzzle blast gases, the recoil rearward velocity and recoil energy of the gun would be slightly greater than that of the projectile, which in turn would be far lower than that of the discharge of a conventional loading. A less extreme example would be the experience of test-firing a sawn-off English-pattern 12-bore shotgun, where the loss of the bulk of the barrels and butt-stock results in a considerable weight reduction and a consequent substantial increase in its recoil.

Newton's three laws of motion are capable of dealing with any problem in dynamics, i.e., problems dealing with the motion of bodies and the forces involved. When solving certain problems however, it is convenient to use the energy and momentum equations deduced from Newton's Second Law of Motion. (F = force, s = distance travelled, v and u = initial and resulting velocities, and t = time of application.)

1.  Newton's Second Law of Motion. Force equals mass times acceleration:

$$F = ma$$

2.  The Principle of the Conservation of Energy. Work done equals the change of kinetic energy:

$$Fs = \tfrac{1}{2} \, mv^2 - \tfrac{1}{2} \, mu^2$$

    Energy can neither be created or destroyed; this law is analogous to the Law of Conservation of Momentum. When energy appar-ently disappears it has merely been changed into some other form of energy, usually via a number of work functions. This should be remembered when kinetic energy is lost, for example during wound formation. This apparently "lost energy" reappears during the work functions as other forms of energy. Most of this energy is eventually realized in the form of heat, which in turn is dissi-pated by the effects of conduction, convection and radiation back to the universe.

3.  The Momentum Equation for Imparted Impulse. Impulse (Ft) equals the change of momentum:

$$Ft = mv - mu$$

When two or more bodies act on each other (provided no external force acts on the whole system), there is no total change of momentum.

Here, all of the velocities must be taken in the same direction. If any of them is in the opposite direction, then it must be expressed as a negative value in the calculation.

Terms such as 'knock-down power', 'relative stopping power' or 'relative incapacitation index' and the like have been coined to describe or to predict the effectiveness of a particular firearm missile upon an aggressive adversary. The poor performance of the .38 Long revolver loading used by US forces against fanatical Moro attackers in the Philippines around the turn of the nineteenth century caused handgun effectiveness tests to be conducted in 1904 by Thompson and La Garde. The tests were not particularly scientific in nature, but did lead to the introduction of the .45 inch Colt Model 1911 service pistol. Observations were made concerning the visible impact effects upon the unclaimed bodies of "John Does" obtained from the local mortuary, suspended in the air with wire. The degree of sway induced upon the suspended body, and its duration, after each shot was recorded, and live steers were shot at in a stock yard with various handgun loadings in order to record their response to each shot, the time elapse until death, or the number of shots necessary to produce this end result. Large calibre, heavy bullets seemed to perform the best, if fired at sufficient velocity. The test results were later summarised by Major General Julien S. Hatcher in his famous formula to predict the relative stopping power of a handgun/cartridge loading combination. It was based upon the bullet mass (in pounds), its velocity (ft/s), its frontal area (in²), and a factor representing its frontal shape:

$$RSP = M.V.A.SF$$

Values for the bullet shape factor are 0.9 for a jacketed round nose bullet; 1.0 for a jacketed flat point or lead round nose; 1.05 for a lead bullet possessing a small flat point (e.g., .45 Colt revolver); 1.10 for a lead bullet possessing a large flat point (e.g., .44/40 Winchester); and 1.25 for a Keith pattern semi-wadcutter or a wadcutter lead bullet. The frontal areas of bullets of the following diameters: .22, .25, .30, .38, .40, .41, .44 and .45 inches are entered as 0.039, 0.049, 0.075, 0.100, 0.126, 0.129, 0.146 and 0.160 square inches, respectively. The resultant values of RSP are multiplied by 1000 to convert them to whole numbers, and are sometimes divided by two. The resulting values of RSP for a .45 ACP standard pistol loading are approximately twice that of a standard .38 Special lead round nose bullet loading, indicating that the .45 inch pistol loading can be expected to be twice as effective in 'stopping' an adversary than the .38 inch revolver loading. The original tests did not involve hollow-point expanding loadings.

A later study by Di Maio entitled "Law Enforcement Standards—LESP-RPT-0101.01" using X-ray flash photography to measure the volume of the temporary cavity produced by a particular bullet loading fired into 20% ordnance gelatine, allowed the Relative Incapacitation Index (RII) to be assigned to a variety of handgun loadings, that included the use of hollow point and soft point bullet loadings. The temporary cavity shape and volume were compared against a 'computer man' target, using a strike mid-point between the armpits, and an assumption that the most sensitive parts of vital organs lie at a penetration of only 1.75 inches (4.45 cm). The results generally favoured high velocity expanding bullet loadings, giving very high values for frangible lightweight .38 Special and .357 Magnum 'Safety slug' loadings, of 37.5 and 50.0 RII units, respectively. Interestingly, the .45 ACP loading previously referred to scored a miserable 6.5 units of effectiveness, barely greater than the 5.0 units achieved by the .38 Special lead round nose loading. This caused great consternation and disbelief amongst the many advocates of the .45 inch 1911 service issue pistol and loading. The Relative Incapacitation Index was based upon the simplistic belief that bullet effectiveness could be determined solely upon the relatively modest and momentary volume of the temporary cavity it could produce in ordnance gelatine, without regard to the survivable elastic nature of most human tissue.

Both attempts to assign 'scientifically determined' relative handgun bullet effectiveness values are flawed, and are best compared to the concept of 'the curate's egg', i.e., something of which (optimistically) parts are excellent.

## 7.2   Incidence of Ricochet

The way in which a particular missile interacts with the target is to some degree dependent upon the angle of impact. Numerous tests have shown that firearm missiles striking the smooth surface of water at an angle of incidence of less than 7° result in ricochets; in this instance the surface of the water has acted in effect as a firm surface. Tests have shown that the angle of departure of these same missiles is considerably less than the angle of incidence due to the bullets hydroplaning before turning sufficiently to depart. Bullets striking the surface of rougher bodies of water, such as the sea, can ricochet at angles up to about 20° from the nominal horizontal. Ricochets can occur from all manner of surfaces, although the texture of the surface and the velocity and construction of the missile can exert considerable influences. Soft yielding surfaces tend to capture missiles, hard smooth surfaces tend to promote ricochet. Stony or frozen surfaces usually lead to an increase in the incidence of ricochets. Full-metal-jacket military style bullets will tend to produce more ricochets than expanding hunting bullets. The greatest tendency for ricochet in any given situation is provided by low-velocity loadings, especially if they employ heavy bullets. Studies of the ricochet effects of shotgun pellets off concrete surfaces up to angles of incidence of 26° again tend to show a considerably lower angle of departure. As previously stated, very high-velocity lightweight expanding bullets exhibit the lowest tendency towards ricochet, frequently breaking up on impact with many surfaces.

Even relatively soft, yielding materials can cause deflection or deviation in the flight of a missile during the period of penetration. During this period of interaction the velocity of the missile is also reduced. High-velocity, lightweight expanding bullets can break up when impacting the relatively light screening cover typically encountered by woodland deer stalkers, or suffer sufficient deviation from their intended course to miss the quarry completely. In an attempt to counter the first of these problems some hunters use relatively low-velocity, large-calibre heavyweight bullet loadings, often using blunt-shaped bullets, in the belief that these so-called brush busting projectiles will plough their way through twigs and branches to their target; test results reported in *The American Rifleman* some years ago indicated that these missiles do not tend to break up but they can still suffer substantial deflection from their intended course in the process of passing through such screening cover. The effects of such deflections on any type of loading will be greatest if the inter-action takes place close to the firer. Even at a modest range of 50 yd/m a thin branch causing a bullet deflection of just one degree near to the firer will result in a complete miss on a deer-sized target. The non-homogeneity of thin twigs and leaves can also cause deviation in the flight of shotgun pellets, although here the relatively low initial energy levels of such small missiles results in their suffering considerable retardation after a few interactions.

## 7.3 Consequences of Impact and Penetration

The penetrating capability of a missile is also more complex than one might imagine. A harpoon fired from an underwater spear-gun is launched at a trivial velocity compared with normal firearm missiles, and yet is able due to its shape and sectional density to kill at a distance useful to the user. Yet tests conducted in the past by the US Ordnance Department have indicated that when fired at 90° to the water, a powerful .50 in machine gun bullet will only inflict a wound upon a person submerged at up to a depth of about 5 ft (1.5 m), and only 4 ft (1.2 m) at a firing angle of between 45° and 60°. Navy tests reported by Hatcher (1966), revealed that at an angle of firing of 90° a man would be safe from a .30 in-06 M2 bullet fired at a muzzle velocity of 2770 ft/s (844 m/s) when at a depth of 4 ft (1.2 m), and at a depth of 2.5 ft (0.76 m), at a firing angle of 30°, which would approximate the angle of attack by aircraft.

High-velocity bullets tend to be deformed more readily on impact with material than identical missiles travelling at lower velocities. In addition, as previously stated, the early stages of a bullet's trajectory through the air coincide with its least stable period of flight; any bullet yaw exhibited in the early stages of penetration will result in the greatest retardation and consequent energy loss. As a result a bullet will often exhibit a greater degree of penetration in a given material at longer ranges, when it is in more stable flight and when its velocity has moderated somewhat. US Army tests reported by Hatcher (1966) for the .30 in-06 M1 loading are as shown in Table 7.1.

Hatcher also reported a straight-line penetration in oak of 32.5 in (826 mm) at 200 yd (183 m) for a 150 grain (9.7 g) .30 in-06 bullet fired at a muzzle velocity of 2700 ft/s (823 m/s). The penetration of the same bullet fired from a distance of 50 ft (15 m) was only 11.25 in (286 mm), the bullet track varying in direction due to the effects of bullet yaw.

The penetrative properties of a bullet fired at a hard target material, such as steel or armour plate, is affected greatly by the incidence velocity, the bullet construction and the angle of attack. A bullet travelling at a very high velocity is capable of penetrating a substantial thickness of steel plate even if the bullet is light in weight and of a flimsy soft-point design. I recall some crude tests conducted when I was a young man using different rifle loadings upon a 3/8 in (9.5 mm) thick steel plate. A 50 grain (3.2 g) soft-point bullet fired from a .222 in Remington rifle loading at a muzzle velocity in the region of 3150 ft/s (960 m/s) 'burned' a clean hole through the plate alongside a hard penetrator core left stuck in the plate from a .303 in armour-piercing loading fired previously which had possessed approximately twice as much kinetic energy upon impact, albeit at a substantially lower velocity.

Table 7.1  Average Penetration in Inches

| Material | 200 yd | 600 yd | 1500 yd |
|---|---|---|---|
| Dry sand | 6.5 | 7.1 | 8.2 |
| Moist sand | 7.3 | 9.6 | 8.7 |

Table 7.2  Skin Penetration Threshold Velocities for a Range of Different Missiles

| Missiles | Mass | Threshold Velocity |
|---|---|---|
| .177 in/4.5 mm | 8.2 grain/0.53 g | 331 ft/s/101 m/s |
| .22 in/5.6 mm | 16.5 grain/1.07 g | 246 ft/s/75 m/s |
| .38 in/9 mm | 113 grain/7.3 g | 190 ft/s/58 m/s |

One aspect of missile penetration which is often ignored or discounted is that of the initial penetration of human skin before the main wound is formed in the under-lying tissue. US Army medical studies, conducted to explain wound effects observed during World War II and the Korean War, produced threshold velocity criteria for skin penetration of 170–180 ft/s (52–55 m/s) for lightweight missiles, and 125–150 ft/s (38–46 m/s) for a 150 grain (9.7 g) bullet. More recent studies by Di Maio and other researchers have come up with higher threshold values necessary for skin penetration using diabolo air rifle pellets and a solid lead round-nose pistol bullet fired into the skin of freshly severed human legs (Table 7.2).

The thickness of the skin, and hence its resistance to penetration, varies at different sites upon the body, which results in considerable variations in the threshold velocity necessary for perforation. The toughness of the skin of a small child or very old person will also be lower than that of a healthy man in his prime of life. Differences will also be likely where the skin is shored up by an underlying bone just below the surface. The nose shape of a missile will also affect its ability to perforate skin. Clearly, a 4.5 mm (.177 in) pointed air gun dart will perforate human skin at a lower velocity than a flat-nosed waisted lead pellet of the same diameter. Substantial shot-to-shot differences in threshold velocity can be encountered for skin from the same source (Table 7.3 through Table 7.5).

Table 7.3  Threshold Velocities for Human Skin Perforation: Children vs. Adults (Missliwetz)

| Projectile | Weight | | Threshold Vel.—Adults[a] | | Threshold Vel.—Children[a] | |
|---|---|---|---|---|---|---|
| | grs | g | ft/s | m/s | ft/s | m/s |
| 4.5 mm/0.177 in Lead Spheres and Waisted Pellets | | | | | | |
| Lead sphere | 8.3 | 0.54 | 361 ± 39 | 110 ±12 | 292 ± 31 | 89 ± 9.4 |
| Spire point | 8.6 | 0.56 | 358 ± 39 | 109 ± 12 | 272 ± 36 | 83 ± 11 |
| Flat nosed | 7.6 | 0.49 | 446 ± 56 | 136 ± 17 | 364 ± 28 | 111 ± 8.5 |
| Hollow point | 6.8 | 0.44 | 436 ± 59 | 133 ± 18 | 354 ± 22 | 108 ± 6.7 |

[a]  Skin of upper thigh; adults aged 18–90 years; children aged 1–38 months.

**Table 7.4  Threshold Energy per Cross-Sectional Area for Human Skin Penetration[a]**

| Projectile | Energy Density | |
|---|---|---|
| | J/cm² | ft-lb/in² |
| Standard steel BB | 18 ± 2 | 86 ± 16 |
| Pointed lead .177 in pellet | 25 ± 5 | 119 ± 24 |
| Flat-nosed lead .177 in pellet | 30 ± 2 | 143 ± 16 |
| Pointed lead .22 in pellet | 26 ± 2 | 124 ± 16 |
| Flat-nosed .22 in lead pellet | 39 ± 9 | 186 ± 43 |

[a] Buttocks, thigh and calf skin (Rathman).

**Table 7.5  Threshold Velocity and Energy Density for Human Skin Perforation[a]**

| Composition | Weight | | Sectional Density | | Threshold Velocity | | Energy Density | |
|---|---|---|---|---|---|---|---|---|
| | gr | g | lbs/in² | g/mm² | ft/s | m/s | ft.lb/in² | J/cm² |
| 4 mm — 0.157 in Spheres | | | | | | | | |
| Glass | 1.2 | 0.08 | 0.0089 | 0.0064 | 650 ± 75 | 198 ± 23 | 46 | 9.7 |
| Steel | 4.0 | 0.26 | 0.030 | 0.021 | 413 ± 46 | 126 ± 14 | 62 | 13.1 |
| Brass | 4.8 | 0.31 | 0,035 | 0.025 | 397 ± 43 | 121 ± 13 | 69 | 14.5 |
| 4.5 mm —.177 in Lead Pellets | | | | | | | | |
| Sphere | 8.3 | 0.54 | 0.048 | 0.034 | 361 ± 39 | 110 ± 12 | 98 | 20.7 |
| Spire point | 8.6 | 0.56 | 0.050 | 0.035 | 358 ± 39 | 109 ± 12 | 99 | 20.9 |
| Flat-nosed | 7.6 | 0.49 | 0.044 | 0.031 | 446 ± 56 | 136 ± 17 | 134 | 28.3 |
| Hollow point | 6.8 | 0.44 | 0.040 | 0.028 | 436 ± 59 | 133 ± 18 | 116 | 24.5 |

\*   Adult upper thigh skin (Missliwetz).

Various attempts have been made to find replacements for human skin for ballistic testing, with the idea being that a sheet of such material can then be placed against the front of the gelatine test block prior to ballistic testing. Fresh abdominal pigskin of 3–4 mm thickness has been shown to produce the most comparable results, but difficulties are encountered in controlling its thickness, in storage, and in obtaining convenient supplies. In his paper 'Skin Perforation and Skin Simulants', Haag found that car inner-tube rubber of 0.050–0.080 in (1.3–2.0 mm) thickness gave the next best results. This material is also easy to obtain and offers no difficulties in its storage. In his tests he found that other simulants such as 0.050 in (1.3 mm) chamois and 0.070 in (1.8 mm) thick artificial chamois skin gave missile threshold velocity results which were too high and too low, respectively. Tests both by Haag and by Salziger have shown that the reduction in missile penetration in ballistic gelatine when using such thin barriers in front of the gelatine test blocks are only significant, in the case of standard 9 and .38 in handgun bullets, at velocities below 100 m/s. Such projectiles will either be stopped or will have considerable remaining velocity after perforation of the interposed barrier has taken place.

The threshold velocity for penetration of the eye is rather less than that required by skin, and of course will be influenced by the shape of the missile. Using steel spheres of between 0.040 in and 0.25 in diameter (1.0–6.4 mm), of masses between 0.06 and 16.0 grain (0.004–1.037 g), threshold velocities ranged between 230 and 154 ft/s (70–47 m/s).

Dzimian conducted tests for the US Army in 1958 with small spherical steel missiles on 20% gelatine. An article by Ed Lowry in the October 1988 edition of *The American Rifleman* considered the implications of the results obtained at typical downrange shotgun pellet velocities of less than 1000 ft/s (300 m/s). This allowed a simple formula to be proposed which would indicate the degree of penetration of a pellet in exposed tissue for a given striking velocity. However, this formula necessitates a correction to be made to the effective diameter of the pellet as it travels through this water-rich medium due to the boundary effect which causes a thin layer of the medium to travel with the pellet. A correction was made by adding 0.033 in (0.84 mm) to the pellet diameter. A value for a constant 'T' for 20% gelatine of 0.233 was also derived. In the simple formula $P$ refers to the penetration in in; $U$ is the striking velocity in ft/s less 200 ft/s to allow for the threshold velocity for skin penetration; this overlarge correction to the velocity appears to be based on the misconception that the velocity loss after penetrating the skin is the same as the initial threshold velocity for its penetration, and in any event the 200 ft/s value for such small, blunt and light projectiles is not consistent with more recently determined values of approximately 350 ft/s (107 m/s) for birdshot-sized shotgun pellets. $S$ is the sectional density of the pellet expressed by the weight of the pellet in pounds divided by the square of the corrected pellet diameter in inches:

$$P = S \times U \times T$$

The skin barrier to penetration is overcome once it has been ruptured by the projectile, and as stated above, the full value of the penetration threshold velocity is not deducted in full as the projectile begins its passage through the underlying tissue. On page 242 of the publication *Bullet Penetration* by MacPherson, the effective velocity loss of typical bullets with striking velocities of between 600 and 1000 ft/s (183–305 m/s), after their initial penetration of skin, is quoted as being between 1 and 8 ft/s (0.3–2.4 m/s). At normal handgun velocities this initial resistance has very little effect in terms of the depth of subsequent tissue penetration. However, it is quite common to see bullets or buckshot pellets lying just underneath the skin at what would have been their potential point of exit after passing through a body (see Figure 7.1 and Figure 7.2). On a number of occasions I have observed tears in the clothing worn by such victims, particularly in thin underlying garments or the thin lining of jackets, which covered these failed exit zones. It was clear that the non-exiting bullets had momentarily and forcibly poked a stretched pocket of skin outwards close to the limits of its elasticity, so as to create this damage. The skin once again acts as a barrier to the passage of a missile, but this time at the point of exit after it has been slowed down considerably after generating the long wound track. On other occasions I have found bullets retained inside layers of clothing worn by the victims that had clearly possessed insufficient retained velocity to rip through the outer garments. On other occasions I have observed bullets lying on the ground close to the body of the victim. In these instances the bullets had lost most, or all of their velocity after passing through the exit skin barrier. MacPherson describes these same effects in the publication *Bullet Penetration*, along with tests performed by Fackler, where swine skin was supported against the bullet exit face of short ballistic gelatine blocks. The unbroken skin was shown to be a significant barrier to bullet exit. The exit velocity of the .45 inch ACP JHP bullet used in these same tests from the length of gelatine block used in the test was determined to be approximately 360 ft/s (110 m/s). It follows that the skin resistance must have necessitated a bullet velocity of at least this value. From the results of other tests involving various missiles, previously determined or published, it follows that the resistance offered by skin during bullet exit is in fact somewhat greater than that at the bullet entry site, as the skin at this point lacks the shoring effect afforded by the body of the victim, thus reducing the stress concentration in the skin.

## 7.4 Armour-Piercing Ammunition

Military armour-piercing bullets, which are frequently also of an incendiary loading, usually employ hardened steel, hard tungsten alloy or tungsten carbide pointed cores. These bullets are intended to defeat light armour or other screening materials, with the added benefit, if also of an incendiary nature, of setting fire to fuel if they chance to strike a gasoline tank or fuel line. The dense and weakly radioactive uranium isotope $^{238}$U, usually referred to as depleted uranium (DU), is used in armour defeating tank gun loadings and also in the electrically-operated 30 mm Gatling-gun housed in the nose of the American A-10 "Tankbuster" ground attack aeroplane. This element

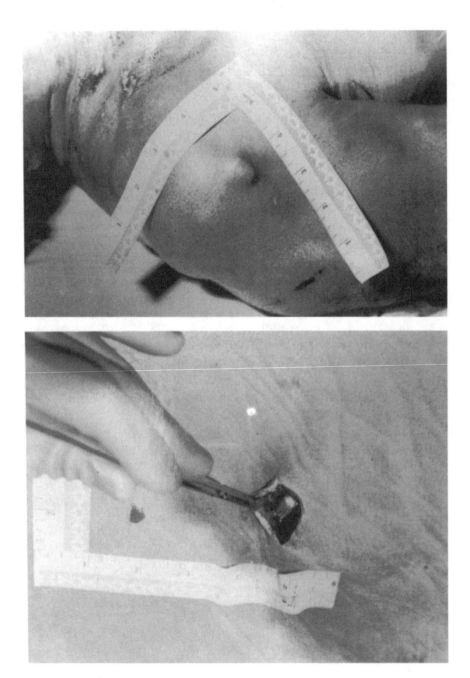

**Figure 7.1** and **Figure 7.2**  Human skin offers significant resistance to the passage of a bullet both at the entry and the exit sites. It is not uncommon to see a bullet lying under the skin having just failed to exit; in some instances the clothing covering the failed exit point can be damaged. The jacketed 9 mm bullet is easily recovered during the post-mortem examination.

also bursts into flame upon impact, thus producing the same desirable incendiary effects.

Small-arms ammunition not specifically designated as being armour-piercing can contain hard bullet core materials. A good example of this is to be found in the bulk of former Soviet Bloc 7.62×39 mm M.43 ammunition (Figure 7.3 through 7.7). The bullet used here consists of a truncated steel cone fitted with a minimal lead binder inside a copper-coated steel jacket; just prior to the break-up of the Communist Bloc the East Germans started to incorporate tempered-steel cores in their standard ball ammunition presumably to serve as a compromise between the standard ball and the more exotic armour-piercing loadings. A similar bullet is used in the loading of the more recent 5.45×39 mm ammunition, which exhibits considerable greater destructive capabilities on hard steel plate than older Nato 5.56×45 ball ammunition which employs a soft lead core bullet enclosed in a conventional tombac jacket. These loadings however lack the thin copper ballistic cap used on the 7.62 mm BZ armour-piercing incendiary loading, although in the case of the 5.45 mm loading it has been suggested that the copper-coated steel envelope with its air space in front of the penetrator provides a similar function.

In recent years the 5.56 mm Nato loading has been modified in an answer to criticisms concerning its down-range performance, and in particular its unreliability in defeating the standard battlefield helmet penetration test at 300 m. The current loadings employ a composite bullet core fitted inside a tombac jacket (Figure 6.18). The frontal core section comprises a hardened steel truncated cone shaped penetrator, behind which resides the rear lead alloy core unit. The resulting missile, which is longer and about seven grains heavier, has a higher ballistic coefficient which as previously described assigns to it better retention of velocity and energy at longer ranges, less influence from crosswinds, and a considerable improvement in defeating lightweight body armour, the standard military helmet or light screening cover. The use of this longer, sleeker bullet has necessitated a considerable increase in the rate of spin needed to stabilise it in flight, resulting in a change of rifling pitch from one turn in 12 or 14 in, to one turn in 7 in (180 mm), resulting in a rate of spin for the bullet in the region of 300 000 rev/min. These recent changes in bullet construction, which utilise hard core materials, have in effect blurred the distinction between standard ball ammunition and designated armour-piercing loadings, without the need for exotic materials.

## 7.5  Explosive Anti-Armour Munitions

I have had to advise and help with the drafting of legislation for all manner of weaponry and munitions over the years, including heavy weaponry of the

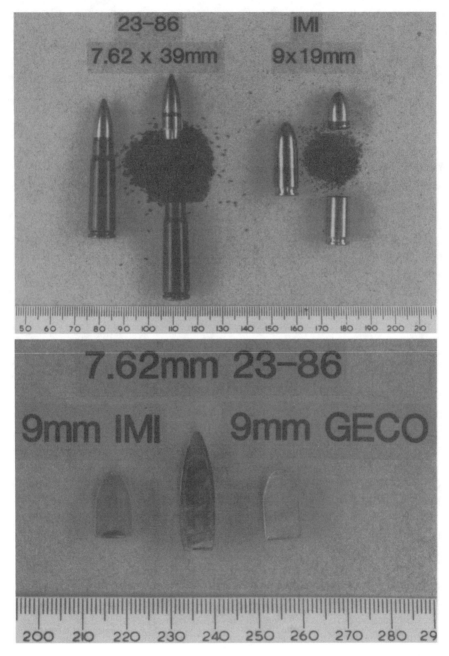

**Figure 7.3 and 7.4** The Kalashnikov 7.62×39 M43 and the IMI 9×19 mm pistol loadings used in the Hungerford incident. The microsections of the bullets show the plain lead alloy jacketed core construction of the 9 mm ammunition and the steel core construction of the copper plated steel jacketed 7.62 mm ammunition.

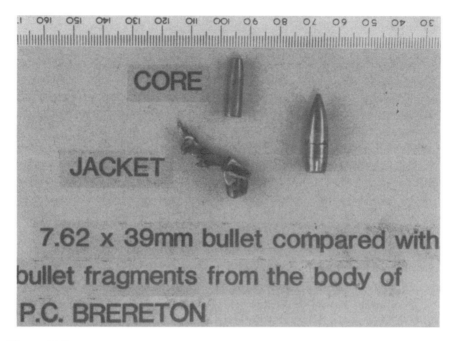

**Figure 7.5**  Damage was caused to the envelopes of the 7.62 mm bullets as they passed through motor vehicle bodywork. The bullet fragments recovered from the fatal injury site show the steel core in an undamaged condition after striking the top of the spine.

type used by all three military forces. Although this is to some degree outside the general work activity of most firearms-reporting forensic scientists it is useful to have knowledge extending beyond one's normal field rather than be caught short in some unforseen situation. Armour-piercing ammunition is identified and dealt with in British, European and American legislation. On a number of occasions I have had to deal with LAW and RPG anti-tank rocket-launching weapons in routine casework. Greater armour-defeating characteristics are provided for use against tank armour by the kinetic energy bolt fired from subcalibre armour-piercing disposing-sabot loadings used in large calibre tank guns; with such loadings velocities well in excess of those generally encountered with small-arms munitions are realised. Other armour-defeating loadings are also employed, the most common of which utilises a shaped explosive charge which effectively directs a focused ultra-high velocity jet of high temperature gases upon the target. Such HEAT (high explosive anti-tank) projectiles utilise a thin metallic liner upon the cone-shaped cavity on the charge of explosive in the missile, which is detonated at the optimum distance away from the armour by means of an extended impact fuse. About 20% of the metallic liner goes into the focused jet which is directed at the surface of the armour. The jet has a velocity gradient of

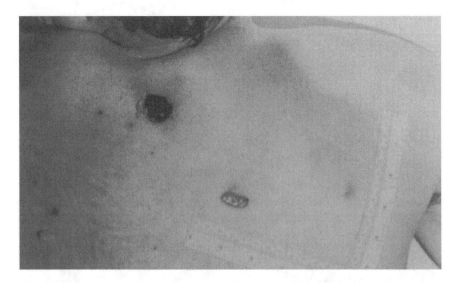

**Figure 7.6**   The large upper entry wound shows where the bullet core and the jacket entered the back to inflict the fatal injury. The damaged jacket was found just under the surface. Below this injury is an entry wound caused by a tumbling steel bullet core separated from its jacket by the effects of penetrating car body-work from another discharge.

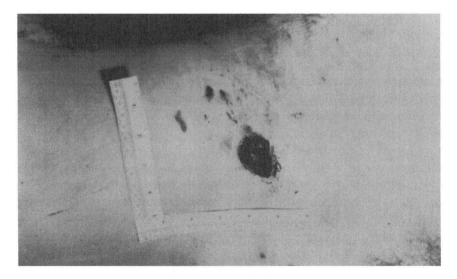

**Figure 7.7**   Atypical rifle bullet entry wound caused by the entry of a damaged M43 bullet core along with its ragged previously damaged jacket; small satellite injuries caused by the impacts of jacket and core material fragments are also evident.

between 26,000 and 30,000 ft/s (8000–9000 m/s). The remainder of the liner follows the jet at about 1000 ft/s (300 m/s) as a plug. The armour-defeating concentration of kinetic energy at the tip of the jet exerts a pressure of approximately 200 ton/in$^2$ (3050 MPa). Any diffusion or disruption of the jet reduces its efficiency, and it is for this reason that it is generally used in unrifled weapons using fin-stabilised missiles such as large calibre smoothbore tank guns or rocket launchers. In the case of rifled tank guns, such as those used by the British Services which are required to fire a range of other loadings, a slipping driving band is used for the fin-stabilised missile.

Another system, referred to by the titles High Explosive Squash Head (HESH) or High Explosive Plastic (HEP), used in anti-armour loadings employs a large charge of plastic explosive behind an inert shell filling. In this system the compressive stress waves from the explosion, which is initiated without the use of a stand-off device, are reflected back off the inner surface of the armour as a rebounding tension wave, thus encountering other incoming stress waves which combine to defeat the tensile strength of the plate, causing the forcible detachment of a large scab of material from the inside surface into the crew compartment.

## 7.6 Shotgun Missile Injuries

Normal small-sized shotgun pellets used in the loading of game or clay-pigeon shooting cartridges have relatively low penetrating power in most materials, including human tissue, once the pattern has spread so that pellets impact the target separately. Table 6.9, providing details of pellet striking energy versus range, shows that the individual pellets carry only modest amounts of kinetic energy due to their low mass and relatively low velocities.

The majority of criminal shootings take place within confrontational ranges of up to 6 ft (2 m), and in most of these instances the actual range, measured from the muzzle end of the gun to the victim, will be about half this value. At ranges of within 3 ft (1 m) the pellets in the shot charge will still be travelling as a compact mass even if fired from a sawn-off shotgun (Figure 6.4 and Figure 7.8). The shot in effect, strikes the body of the victim as a single large calibre missile measuring approximately 1 in in diameter (2–3 cm). Such a missile has considerable initial penetrating power due to its relatively high velocity and large mass. At such short distances a charge of shot can blow a hole through a heavy door and still be capable of inflicting lesser injuries to a person on the other side. An entry hole of similar dimensions will be created upon the body of a victim when struck directly by a shot charge fired from such a short range (Figure 7.9). However, once inside

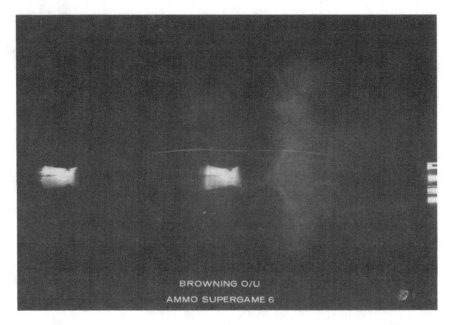

**Figure 7.8**  High-speed twin flash photograph show the shotgun pellets still retained inside the cup section of the plastic wad at these short distances (up to approximately 30 cm) from the muzzle.

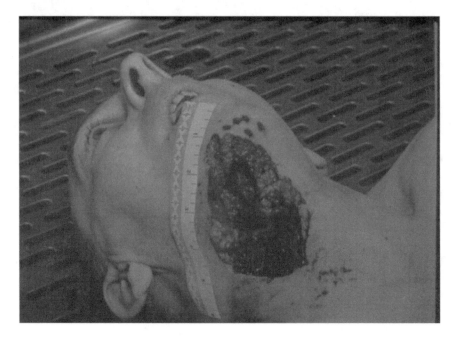

**Figure 7.9**  Close range shotgun wound to the throat.

the body of the victim the pellets within the shot charge will separate to allow a dispersed pattern of injury tracks caused by individual pellets. The initial X-ray plates taken of the torso of the victim will show pellets spread over a considerable area (Figure 7.10). Once again, the penetrating ability of these individual pellets will be limited and it is most rare for birdshot sized pellets to exit after inflicting a direct chest injury upon an adult.

The larger buckshot pellet sizes are another matter, due to their greater individual mass. I remember attending the scene of a double shooting some years ago, where the firer used SG buckshot loads in a pump-action shotgun against two men in a factory office. One man, an ex-police officer, tried to escape via a passageway on the other side of a low dividing wall made out of acoustic screening partitions. The nine pellets in the loading passed through the screen at a range of approximately 30 ft (9 m) and then struck him in the back as he ran. He was a heavy man weighing about 270 lb (120 kg). When I looked at the injuries during the initial stages of the post-mortem examination I was able to see some of the pellets lying just under the skin at the front of his stomach. In another incident involving the close range discharge of LG shot, the largest size buckshot pellets passed through the chest

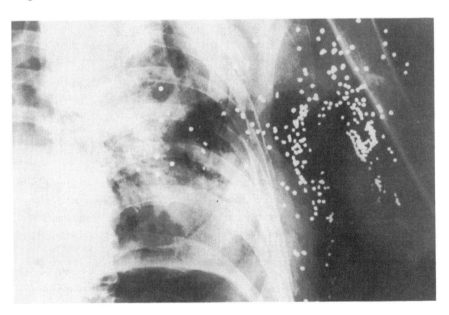

**Figure 7.10** Typical X-ray plate of close range shotgun injury to human torso. At close range the pellets and wadding have struck the chest as a compact mass, after which the individual pellets follow divergent paths and as a consequence exhibit different degrees of penetration. Birdshot loadings will generally remain inside the chest. Larger buckshot pellet loadings can result in the complete penetration of the chest of a man.

of the victim and then embedded themselves in the plasterwork of a wall on the other side of the stairway.

At the short confrontational ranges mentioned charges of ordinary sized birdshot are capable of inflicting massive injuries when they strike a limb as a compact mass. Major bones such as the tibia or the femur can be shattered in the process and the femoral artery severed, resulting in the death of the victim. In one incident reported to me a charge of Number 4 buckshot, fired from a distance of approximately 4 ft (1.2 m), across a thigh at its midpoint, caused the fracture of the femur due to the temporary cavity effect; this also resulted in stellate wounds at both the entry and exit sites due to the momentary containment of the same temporary cavity inside the relatively confined area of the limb. At most of the short ranges under discussion in the above examples, it is usual for the cartridge wadding to be found inside the wound track or the chest cavity.

At distances greater than the 1 to 2 m range previously mentioned, the shot charge spreads and a greater number of injuries are caused by the impacts of individual pellets. At these distances the cartridge wadding, which at this stage of its flight is travelling a little distance behind the shot charge due to its greater rate of deceleration, is more likely to rebound back off the victim and fall to the ground. In the process of doing this it is still capable of causing damage to clothing and of inflicting bruises or abrasion injuries to tissue. Such injuries due to wadding strikes should be noted during the initial stages of the examination of the body and duly photographed. The visible damage to the clothing will be noted during the subsequent examination of the relevant garments later at the laboratory. The presence of non-damaging wadding impacts is frequently detected by the simple sodium rhodizonate test previously mentioned, conducted upon filter paper pressings from the areas in question.

As previously stated, the wadding decelerates rapidly and frequently moves away from the line of fire due to the greater effects of air resistance and due to the changes in shape occurring during its brief flight, as a result the wadding can sometimes miss the victim or strike some distance away from the bulk of the pellet strikes. In addition the leaves of plastic cup-wads open up progressively in the early stages of their flight, and at some stage can turn completely back upon themselves or even become detached from the base unit of the wad (Figure 9.42). The impact effects of two- or four-leaf wads can be detected upon the clothing and the body. The rate at which the wad leaves peel back or become detached is often reproducible. Simple tests conducted using the same type of ammunition in the crime weapon conducted upon sheets of card placed at measured ranges, will provide a permanent record of the effects of blackening, powdering impact marks, pellet spread, and the impact characteristics of the wadding, which in turn can be compared with the damage or the wound under consideration. The wadding strike effects can sometimes be extremely reproducible, thus allowing range estimates to be expressed in 2 in (5 cm) steps with certain types of wadding. Because of the differences in the behaviours of the many types of wadding used in shotgun cartridges and the differences in pellet sizes and propellant pressure characteristics, it is important that tests be conducted with the incident weapon and with cartridges of identical loading, or better still, with any live cartridges recovered from the suspect (Figure 9.43 through Figure 9.46).

In all incidents involving death or injury caused by the discharge of a shotgun firing tests should be conducted in order to determine the actual pellet spread at different ranges. It is of course not necessary to conduct firing tests at ranges greatly dissimilar to that likely to be involved in the incident. It is however, important to do sufficient tests so that the necessary level of confidence in the incident range estimate can be attained. Ideally all tests for pellet spread, wad strike effects, or the close range discharge effects described in detail at the end of Section 7.8 (concerning injuries inflicted by single missiles), should be conducted with the incident weapon and any live ammunition recovered from the suspect. In certain situations it may be necessary to use a laboratory gun and stock ammunition. If this is the case, a weapon of similar barrel length and choke boring should be employed along with stock cartridges of similar shot size and comparable loading. Sheets of white card are best used for witness cards of pellet spread, and these can be retained conveniently in many cases with one's file or collection of retained materials (Figure 9.5 and Figure 9.26). The ranges in all tests, measured from the muzzle end of the barrel to the witness card, should be marked upon the card together with the case reference number, the date, any other information thought to be relevant and then signed. All range estimates provided in statements are best made if they provide maximum and minimum likely ranges of firing in the particular incident.

## 7.7  Expanding Bullets

Low-velocity missiles such as shotgun pellets or pistol bullets tend to produce simple and unremarkable wound tracks in tissue. Military jacketed spitzer-style rifle bullets will often produce wound tracks comparable to those of low-velocity pistol bullets, provided that they do not strike some intermediate target such as a car windscreen first, or if they travel through an insufficient depth of tissue to promote yaw in normal circumstances. The performance of a pistol or rifle bullet can be greatly increased if it is designed to expand in tissue in a predictable manner to increase its effective diameter in the process. Such expanding bullets, often incorrectly referred to as 'Dum Dum', are usually of soft-point, hollow-point or capped-hollow cavity design. The hard metal jacket of a soft-point bullet is open at its nose to expose the soft lead bullet core. A hollow-point or hollow-cavity bullet has a hole drilled partway down the central long axis of the bullet from the nose (Figure 7.11). A ballistic cap or hard wedge fitted in the end of the hole is used on certain loadings (Figure 7.12). High-velocity rifle loadings, with their greater attendant kinetic energies, can be transformed in their wounding performance, simply by moving from a fully jacketed design to one of soft-point or hollow-point design. In turn, a change from one design of expanding bullet to another, better suited to the velocity range or the intended quarry, can again transform the performance of the rifle.

The ideal performance of an expanding bullet is achieved when the nose material peels back upon itself to form the classic mushroom shape at the correct depth of penetration in the particular target, and that this expansion

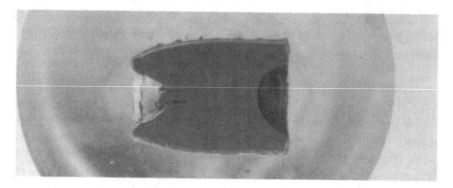

**Figure 7.11**    Hollow-point pistol bullet designed to reduce over-penetration and increase wounding performance.

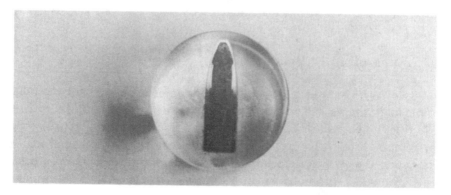

**Figure 7.12**    Winchester Silvertip capped expanding jacketed rifle bullet design.

is achieved without the bullet breaking up or suffering an unacceptable degree of weight loss. In this ideal situation the bullet either stops under the skin on the other side of the living target, or falls to the ground completely de-energised after just clearing the target. In the scenario described the expanded bullet has utilised its potential for tissue destruction at the optimum point of penetration to cause the maximum destruction in the internal zone likely to contain vital organs, and at the same time eliminating the danger of undesirable over-penetration and consequent danger to objects or persons beyond the intended target. Achieving all of these things on every occasion is a difficult or impossible process, especially if the same bullet is employed in different loadings producing very different muzzle velocities. Not all expanding rifle or pistol bullets behave in real-life situations in the manner described in ammunition manufacturers' advertisements (Figure 7.13). I remember reading somewhere that the marketing departments may show the reader of a sporting magazine an impressive picture of the classic perfectly mushroomed bullet to demonstrate the capabilities of their wares, but they do not show pictures of all of the other bullets fired in order to achieve this one perfect result. Tests conducted with the best performing loadings using ballistic gelatine or ballistic soap will show that a large portion of the bullet's momentum has been transferred to the tissue simulant at the optimum depth of penetration, bearing in mind the nature of the intended target, thus creating a significant temporary cavity about the axis of the permanent cavity, followed by a lesser degree of overall penetration Figure 7.14 through Figure 7.21).

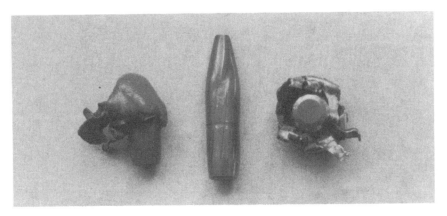

**Figure 7.13** Not all expanding design rifle bullets produce the classic mushroom shape when used in the field. A combination of a rigid laminated steel jacket and a relatively low velocity allowed this Swedish bullet fired from the author's 6.5 mm Mannlicher Schonauer carbine to pass through the entire length of a red stag without expansion. The effect of the rifling spin has however left a corkscrew pattern of distortion upon the bullet.

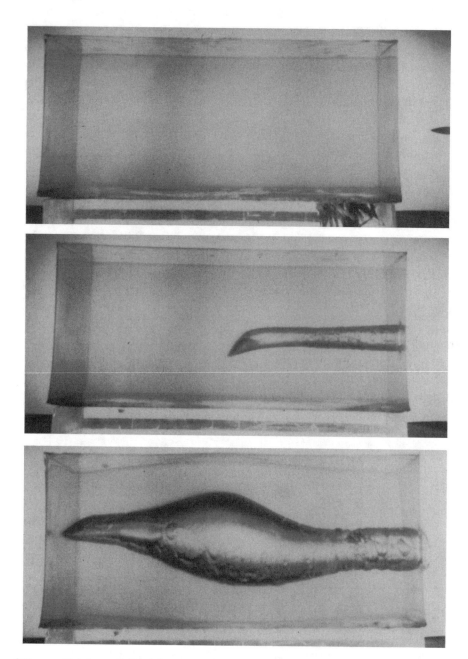

(**Figure 7.14 to 7.16** (this page) and **Figure 7.17 to 7.19** (next page) Series of high-speed photographs of Nato 7.62 mm rifle bullet passing through a block of ordnance gelatine. As can be seen, the violent temporary cavity is set up in the region where the undeformed hard jacketed bullet tumbled. This enhanced wounding effect will not be observed, as is often the case with military bullet designs, if the undamaged missile exits prior to this point of destabilisation.

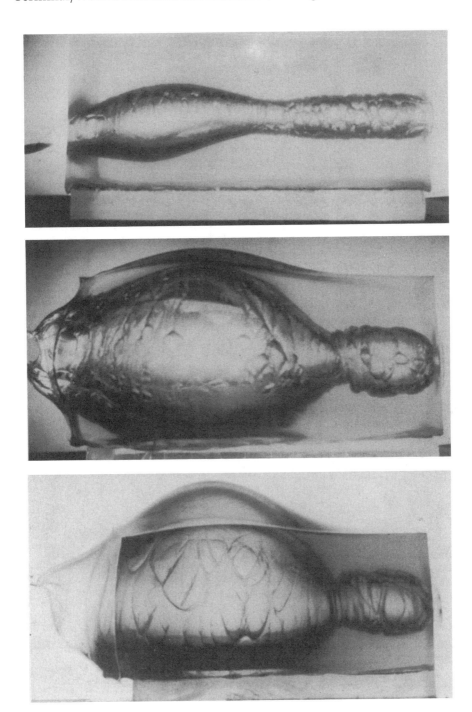

**Figure 7.17 to 7.19** (see caption on page 196).

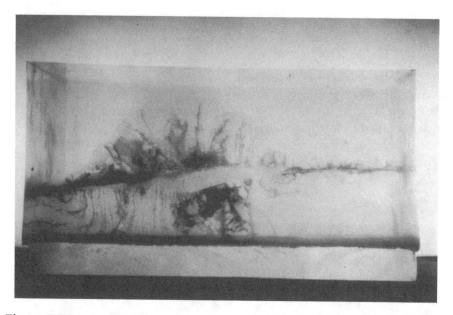

**Figure 7.20** The smaller permanent cavity left behind after the passage of the bullet surrounded by damaged material from the brief but violent temporary cavity formations.

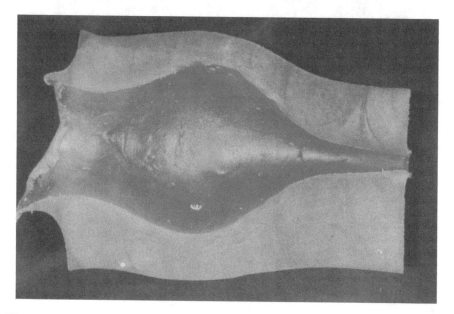

**Figure 7.21** The use of a suitable ballistic soap allows a form of the temporary cavity to be frozen for inspection.

Many expanding bullet designs are very sensitive to changes in cartridge loading specifications. The same bullet can often be used in loadings of very different intensity. A good example of this is the use of a bullet in a high performance .357 in Magnum revolver loading, followed by the same missile used in the loading of a standard .38 in Special revolver cartridge. It may give excellent performance in the Magnum loading but fail totally to expand when used in the loading of the standard cartridge. The hollow points of some pistol bullets can become plugged with fragments of material during their initial penetration of the clothing worn by the victim, and as a result can fail to expand during their passage through underlying tissue. In another example a light .30 in (7.62 mm) bullet intended for shooting small-sized vermin may produce shallow surface blow-up wounds upon the shoulder of a stag when fired from a .30–06 rifle at the very high velocity generated by this type of light bullet loading. The .220 Swift and the .22/250 Remington loadings can produce shallow surface wounds on deer with certain bullet designs better suited for varmint shooting, if the shot is taken at relatively short range where the velocity is very high and where the bullet is still suffering some of the initial instability effects in the early stages of its flight, but produce good kills at greater distances where the bullet has become more stable and its velocity has moderated.

Similarly, a bullet designed to produce rapid expansion in a soft target can expand prematurely if the intended human target is wearing heavy winter clothing or can break up or be greatly de-energised if the bullet strikes an intermediate target such as glazing, screening materials or motor vehicle bodywork. I recall one incident associated with the Hungerford massacre which took place in the summer of 1987 and resulted in major changes in the firearms legislation. After murdering a woman out picnicking with her two young children in the Savernake Forest situated some distance to the west of Hungerford, Michael Ryan stopped at a garage on the way to his home in Hungerford. He fired a shot from the forecourt at the cashier inside the shop of the petrol station from a .30 in M1 carbine, using a Geco soft-point loading intended for use on small game. The bullet struck the laminated plate glass window fronting of the store between him and the female cashier. The woman received no injury, but when I examined the range of goods around her till area, I found tiny fragments of bullet jacket and lead core material just barely sticking in the paper wrappers of the chocolate bars on display. More recently, I examined the scene of an incident in which an armed police officer fired his Heckler and Koch 9 mm carbine at a man who had the barrel of a rifle poking out of a section of the shop window he had broken during the initial stages of the siege. The Winchester 95 grain (6.2 g) bullet struck a wire security grille on the front of the 6 mm thick laminated window, breaking up prematurely in the process. Examination of the X-ray plates of the injured person at the hospital confirmed the extensive degree of bullet break-up. At the same time I was able to see the injured party sitting up in his hospital bed drinking a cup of tea while talking to police officers. He was stripped to the waist so I could clearly see the superficial injuries consisting of a shotgun-like pattern of damage on the front of his chest; none of the fragments had penetrated into the chest cavity. In another case in which the police shot a man using a 5.56 mm soft-point loading, the bullet broke up into small fragments after passing through his arm which he was holding in front of his chest, resulting in a similar pattern of trivial injuries to the chest, as in the case above (Figure 8.31).

Another more rigid expanding bullet better able to deal with such situations may expand indifferently in the body of an exposed and lightly clothed target. The higher the velocity of the pistol bullet then the greater will be its interaction with the target, thus resulting in greater expansion, more explosive energy interchange, and thus less penetration or a lower propensity for over-penetration. The original Police 158 grain (10.2 g) .38 in Special round-nose solid lead bullet loading travelling at a muzzle velocity in the region of 800 ft/s (240 m/s) was renowned for poor stopping power, over-penetration, and ricochet. This bullet generally suffers little in the way of deformation in its passage through tissue and as a result often exits possessing a substantial proportion of its original velocity thus endangering persons well beyond the intended target.

I recall a case I dealt with many years ago where the police had been summoned to deal with a heavily armed and deranged person. It was a cold January night, snowing, and the man was wearing numerous layers of unusually heavy clothing, over which he was wearing two 12-bore cartridge belts crossed over his chest. The .38 in round-nose bullet passed through a leather loop of the belt and the cartridge held in it, through the back of the belt and the other belt crossed underneath it, through a padded parka, a combat jacket, body warmer, heavy sweater, shirt and vest, before passing completely through the chest. The bullet exited, after passing through the same garments on the other side, another cartridge belt and cartridge held in a loop, and then travelled on never to be recovered. The man died because of good bullet placement as the wound track resembled a rapier thrust. I examined the entry and exit wounds and found them both to be of identical form, apart from a slight abrasion ring on the entry hole, measuring about 3 mm in diameter; the reduction being attributable to the elastic nature of the skin as the round-nosed bullet passed through it (Figure 7.22).

When a bullet penetrates the skin and passes into tissue, its effect inside depends upon a number of variables, some of which I have already described. Human skin offers a surprising degree of resistance to the initial penetration of the missile. The critical threshold velocity for penetration will depend

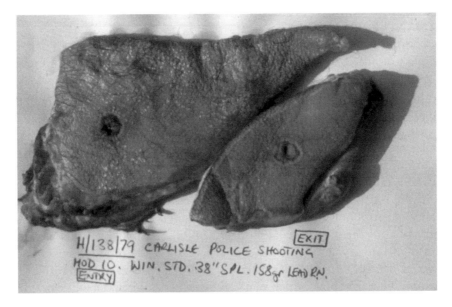

**Figure 7.22** Entry and exit wound samples from the front and back of a heavily clothed man killed by a police .38 in Special 158 grain (10.2 g) lead round nose bullet in the incident described in the text.

upon the weight and the shape of the missile rather than its kinetic energy. The nature and severity of the wound produced is a function of the forcible crushing action of the bullet with tissue, supplemented in some instances by the consequences of bullet fragmentation, the splintering of internal bones and damage due to the displacement of tissue during the formation of the temporary cavity. The composition of a human body varies considerably from one part to another. Some parts are relatively soft or elastic, the bones are hard and offer considerable resistance and, if shattered, can be turned into secondary missiles capable of inflicting separate wound tracks. On average, a man's body is composed of approximately 68% water, which is about 800 to 900 times as dense as air. The relatively fast spin imparted upon the bullet by the rifling in the gun barrel is sufficient to stabilise it in the atmosphere, but it is far too slow a rate of spin to stabilise it in this denser medium. There will be a tendency for the bullet to yaw as it strikes the target, and any damage or tendency for deformation will tend to increase the degree of yaw to the point of complete instability or tumbling within the target. The point at which significant yaw takes place in a high-energy loading will determine the location of the temporary cavity, or cavities and hence the location of the greatest degree of tissue damage. In many instances, military bullet loadings exit before these effects can be exhibited.

## 7.8   High-Velocity Wound Effects

As previously stated, low-velocity pistol bullets tend to produce relatively simple wound tracks with damage being caused mainly by penetration and crushing forces. Within limits the performance of the bullet can be optimised by the use of well-chosen expanding bullets designed to perform within the anticipated parameters of operation.

Incapacitation or death tends to be caused, if one discounts the psychological aspects of the victim's state of mind, by damage being caused to vital organs or major blood vessels or by impact with the spine. However, when one considers the nature of injuries which can be caused by missiles fired from the much more powerful loadings used with most rifles, the performance of pistol bullets is put into perspective. This has in turn caused many authorities in the past to speak in terms of 'high-velocity wounding effects' as if high velocity alone was the sole criterion for the production of severe injuries. Threshold values are often quoted of between 2000 and 2300 ft/s (610 to 700 m/s) above which one can expect such high-velocity wounding effects can take place. In turn, this has caused some well-known rifle manufacturers to create products promoted as being a realisation of such ultra-high-velocity flat-shooting lightning-strike kill weapons. In reality, setting aside the consideration of flatter trajectories, the mechanism of wound formation is as much a function of the mass and the construction of the bullet as it is of its velocity. By their very nature, rifles are capable of driving a bullet of a given mass at a greater velocity than would be the case for a handgun. A small-calibre spitzer-shaped lightweight rifle bullet can only produce such effects if it is of a suitable expanding design for the velocity range and the intended target, if the wound track is of sufficient length to allow significant yaw to occur in instances in which the bullet does not expand or otherwise become deformed, if the bullet is deformed as a result of striking a significant bone, or if the missile is so constructed as to suffer significant yaw soon after entering the target.

Anyone who has read accounts of early experiments with ultra-high-velocity small-calibre rifle loadings (muzzle velocities well in excess of 3000 ft/s (900 m/s)) should be aware that velocity alone does not exert the greatest influence upon bullet wounding characteristics, even upon woodchuck and other small animals. Attempts were sometimes made to produce super-accurate, streamlined, perfectly balanced small calibre bullets in order to improve the flat shooting performance and accuracy of the rifles at extended ranges. An article produced by Elmer Keith in 1937 describes the results of one failed experiment using a rifle chambered for the .220 inch Swift cartridge and cartridges loaded with sleek, needle-pointed, solid bronze bullets of .90 inch (22.9 mm) overall length. The theory being that, due to the greater retained down-range velocities of these bullets (estimated to be in the region of 3000 ft/s at 300 yards), they should have excellent killing power on small animals such as gophers or rabbits due to their high velocity alone. Although these loadings proved to be very accurate, their destructive performance on the bodies of rabbits was abysmal. Unless shot in the head or spine they jumped initially before running away, then carried on feeding, showing no other signs of having been hit, although they would probably have died eventually. Some jack rabbits received between two and four such body hits before slowly toppling over, when shot at ranges of between 60 and 350 yards. In all instances the bullet exit holes were so small that they were difficult to detect. Subsequent body hits from the same rifle but using conventional 48 grain soft-point factory loadings demolished jack rabbits at ranges up to 200 yards. Very similar results will be encountered by persons who have used a .22 in centre-fire rifle, such as the .222 or .223 in Remington with loadings utilising cheap surplus 5.56 mm military projectiles, in an attempt at bringing back rabbits fit for presentation for the kitchen. On the odd occasions where two rabbits are lined up the destabilised bullet exiting from the first apparently unconcerned rabbit can wreak havoc upon the second one. It is clear from this that unless the bullet is specifically designed for rapid expansion, or if some chance effect causes it to yaw prematurely, high velocity alone will not bring about the much talked about explosive tissue destruction. Correct bullet construction, bearing in mind the toughness and thickness of the intended target, is the critical criterion for efficient translation of kinetic energy into wound performance.

Expanding bullet loadings were first reported upon at the British arsenal at Dum Dum in India during the period of the Raj as a response to the disappointing performance of the newly issued .303 in Mark II service ammunition, which employed a 215 grain (13.9 g) round-nosed, cupro-nickel jacketed bullet discharged at a velocity in the region of 2000 ft/s (610 m/s), in stopping onrushes of fierce Pathan tribesmen on the Northwest Frontier. The 500 grain (32 g) soft lead bullets fired from the previously issued .577 in Snider and .577/450 in Martini-Henry rifles at muzzle velocities of approximately 1250 and 1350 ft/s, respectively (380 and 411 m/s), had not given rise to such complaints despite their markedly lower velocities. A reference to this in the *Textbook of Small Arms,* explains the situation: 'Even against fanatical tribesmen the Snider and Martini-Henry bullets were satisfactory. But the .303 bullet with its diminished cross-section area and greater velocity had a power of penetration which made its impact hard to feel in many cases, and its track through the tissues was a clean puncture without circumferential damage of any kind'. The original loading made at the Dum Dum Arsenal in India referred to as Cartridge SA Ball .303 in Cordite Mark II Special was of similar weight to the standard service ball round, but had a 0.5 mm opening in its jacket to expose the nose; it was based upon a design patented by a Major General J.W. Tweedie in 1889 and 1891. Although discharged at a slightly lower velocity, it was found to be far more effective than the standard Mark II ball round at the Chitral and Tirah expeditions on the Northwest Frontier in 1897 and 1898. Later development work at the Royal Laboratory at Woolwich resulted in improved hollow-point loadings up to Mark IV design. Although several million rounds of Dum Dum ammunition were issued in India it was not approved for general use elsewhere, although good reports of its effectiveness were received from the Sudan. Fackler reported tests which indicated that the temporary cavity produced by the old Italian Vetterli Service round using a 300 grain (19.4 g) soft lead bullet, was comparable to that produced by an M16A1 5.56 mm rifle firing a 55 grain (3.6 g) jacketed bullet at 3100 ft/s (945 m/s). Here, the soft lead Vetterli bullet expanded rapidly in the gelatine block. Bullet fragmentation has been identified as being responsible for a major part of the tissue damage which can be inflicted by the high-velocity 5.56 mm bullet. Jacketed bullets must of course be used with high-velocity rifle loadings, otherwise the rifling impressions imparted upon them will be stripped off in the bore. Whether the bullet is of expanding design or of military configuration, any tendency for expansion, deformation or disintegration within tissue will be greatly increased with increasing velocity and made more rapid in action.

During the initial stages of interaction with tissue the bullet tries to compress the relatively incompressible water-laden material in front of it, thus setting up a compression wave of spherical form which passes outwards into the body at a velocity approximating to the velocity of sound in water, 4800 ft/s (1500 m/s), generating peak pressure changes in the region of 100 atmospheres lasting about 1 μs. This extremely brief interchange cannot overcome the inertia of the tissue, although it has been claimed that nerves have been stimulated or in some cases damaged at considerable distances away from the point of initiation. It must be said however, that real damage is created by the consequences of temporary cavitation rather than by these sonic pressure waves, and even then, this will be dependent upon the relative elasticity of the tissue involved and the energy release within the target. The permanent cavity has resulted from the direct action of the missile upon the tissue, while the temporary cavity is formed as the walls of the permanent cavity are displaced outwards by way of reaction. Fackler likens this outward displacement of tissue to that of a splash in water. In this scenario, the sleek pointed military jacketed rifle bullet moving normally within tissue produces as little splash as an accomplished diver executing a neat dive into a swimming pool. In turn, the expanded, deformed, or tumbling rifle bullet interacts like a belly flop from a less able swimmer. In the latter situation, the more energy available to be used in destructive work functions inside the target, all other things being equal, then the greater the potential for tissue destruction.

The momentum transferred to the tissue from the passage of the bullet causes it to move and oscillate, generating a temporary cavity which can be considerably larger than the permanent cavity caused by the initial injury which in turn is related to the effective diameter of the missile. This large temporary cavity can be rapidly formed and then caused to collapse several times within the next few milliseconds. Most of this violent activity will occur after the bullet has been arrested within, or exited from, the target. The temporary cavity will be ellipsoidal in shape if the bullet has failed to tumble during its passage through the tissue. In instances where the bullet has tumbled base over apex great changes will have occurred in this area caused by the missile interacting with the tissue. This can cause changes to occur in the direction of the wound track and also in the shape of the temporary cavity, the largest zone, or in some instances zones of temporary cavitation tending to occur when the tumbling bullet is moving through the tissue sideways-on at high velocity in the case of a non-expanding military fully jacketed bullet. A commonly repeated misconception concerning injuries caused by bullet tumbling is that the bullet tumbles in flight towards its target. As previously mentioned in Chapter 6 on exterior ballistics, to achieve the accuracy necessary to be able to hit the intended target at any real distance the bullet must be in stable flight, few people are killed by misses; wound forming tumbling activity occurs, if at all, when the bullet is inside the target.

All bullets entering soft tissue will create what is referred to as a temporary cavity; this work function, provided by the kinetic energy of the bullet during its rapid passage through tissue, exerts sudden lateral forces throwing tissue outwards to produce the cavity. The kinetic energy of this accelerated and elastic tissue is momentarily transformed into strain energy, which is at its highest when the maximum cavity size is reached. This strain energy, or potential energy, then causes rapid inward movement of the tissue, causing the cavity to collapse. The volume of the temporary cavity is a function of the amount of strain energy temporarily stored in the dislodged tissue, which is a function of the bullet drag force, and also of the relative resistance of the particular region of tissue involved. However, most tissue, with the exception of organs such as the liver, spleen, pancreas and the kidneys or regions where tissues are constrained, can suffer a significant amount of such strain without suffering permanent damage. Fragmentation or splintering of the bullet during the formation of the wound, a relatively common effect with high velocity expanding rifle bullets and with close range shots from certain military bullet loadings, will induce concentration of the stress forces at these points, and can lead to severe permanent tissue disruption (Figure 7.23). High velocity expanding bullet rifle bullet loadings, or military bullets which have been

**Figure 7.23**   A .223 in soft point bullet similar to the one on the left disintegrated inside the head of an 8-year-old girl in a close range shooting accident without exit taking place. The destruction to the head was of course extensive and explosive in nature.

caused to yaw, are able to generate large diameter temporary cavities that can cause significant wound trauma on the body of a man or animal of similar size. On small animals, high velocity lightweight rapid-expansion bullets are able to generate temporary cavities larger than the animal itself, thus resulting in its almost explosive destruction. The modest velocities of bullets fired from typical handguns will not result in temporary cavities large enough to overcome the elastic limit in most tissue and so contribute to wound trauma incapacitation.

The violent formations and collapses of the temporary cavity within the span of these few milliseconds can lead in some instances to local tissue destruction, the rupturing of organs and blood vessels, and in some instances the fracturing of bones. Some parts of the body are more resistant to these effects than others. The lungs containing air offer substantial resistance to damage from these forces, while the soft and relatively weak material of the liver can suffer damage even when the bullet has passed through the body on the other side of the diaphragm.

A fully jacketed military bullet, or a sporting soft-point bullet which is too rigid in construction for the velocity of the loading or the nature of the target, which has passed through the target tissue before inducing the formation of a

**Figure 7.24** The composite form and the design of the current Nato 5.56 mm bullet loading frequently leads to missile blow-up effects at close ranges. The truncated cone steel penetrator from the core is shown in the centre right of the field.

significant temporary cavity, can exit at a very high velocity wastefully taking a large portion of its initial striking velocity with it. However, the same projectile, if subject to yaw and tumbling within the wound track, will tend to have a greater wounding potential. A military bullet which becomes badly deformed or which breaks up will tend to produce a more severe injury, and in some instances where the missile remains in the body will use its wounding potential to disrupt far more tissue. Similarly, a bullet which strikes a substantial bone will itself suffer considerable deformation or can even fragment in the process of initiating a shower of bone fragments, which act as high-velocity secondary missiles to inflict their own wound tracks. One authority has claimed that the current Russian 5.45 mm bullet discharged at a muzzle velocity of around 2950 ft/s (900 m/s), tends to suffer nose deformation in tissue, thus enhancing its wounding effect in tissue, due to the presence of an air space inside the bullet tip situated on top of the steel penetrator core; this claim however, sounds remarkably similar to those put out many years ago in respect of the British .303 in Spitzer bullet loadings which employed an aluminium filler in the nose section in front of the lead core to improve the ballistic shape of the bullet without adding appreciably to its weight. Tests conducted by other

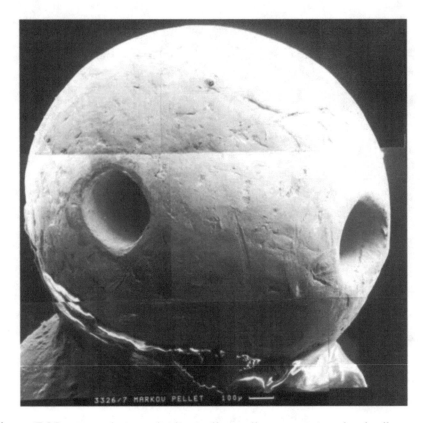

3326/7 MARKOV PELLET    100μ ——

**Figure 7.25** Tiny platinum/iridium alloy pellet containing the deadly castor bean toxin Ricin, removed from the leg of the body of the Bulgarian BBC World Service radio reporter Markov. The poison pellet used in his assassination was thought to have been fired from close range by an agent working for the then Communist government of Bulgaria, armed with an air weapon disguised as an umbrella.

authorities have failed to reproduce such external distortion, although asymmetric internal bullet changes have been observed caused by the shifting of the small amount of lead filler material from around the steel core into the frontal air space, which can cause shifts in the bullet track at greater depths of penetration in ballistic gelatine. Likewise, the original American M.193 5.56×45 mm was criticised by some when first introduced on the basis that the 14 in (356 mm) rifling pitch only just stabilised the bullet in air, thus increasing its propensity to yaw during the initial stages of target impact. In reality, few of these claims in respect of the original M16 rifle loading have been substantiated in medical feedback from the fields of battle.

The proposed diminutive bullet for the G11 4.7 mm caseless ammunition assault rifle, which at one time was intended to be the next German military

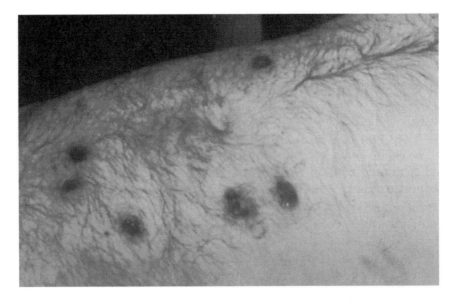

**Figure 7.26** 12-Bore shot to stomach of police officer using cartridge loaded with six 'LG' buckshot pellets of nominal 9.1 millimetre diameter. Large size buckshot loadings often give poor or 'cartwheel' patterns, as above.

rifle, was made with a spoon-tip shaped depression in its nose so as to promote the type of instability in tissue previously described. The current Nato 5.56 mm M-855 full metal jacket bullet is based upon the Belgian SS.109 missile, which as previously described employs a two-piece core using a hard-steel cone penetrator and a lead base core. The junction between the two core units coincides with a deeply formed cannelure in the tombac jacket, thus encouraging shearing action at this point in the missile's construction (Figure 6.18). I have dealt with a number of close range fatal shootings involving the current British service rifle and the light support weapon using this type of ammunition. In almost every instance, which included head and chest shots, the bullets broke up inside the bodies thus resulting in zero exits. It is likely however that at greater ranges when the velocity of the bullet has moderated and the bullet is travelling with a greater degree of stability, this tendency would be greatly reduced.

Enhanced wound formation is achieved with less luck or guile in the case of sporting or police loadings where there is no legal requirement to abide by military conventions. As previously explained, expanding bullets of various constructions can be employed to better guarantee the desired level of performance in any particular application. The type of bullet used on a thin-skinned animal, or for that matter a human target, will be different from that intended for use on elk or a cape buffalo. Bullets can be selected which will ensure the required degree of penetration, and which at the same time will almost guarantee optimum expansion at the correct depth inside the target for maximum effect. Such bullets, when used on human targets, will tend to produce the majority of their temporary cavitation a short distance inside the target, and exit at modest velocities. The early onset of the formation of a large temporary cavity will be confirmed both in tests using 10% ballistic gelatine or when the wound tracks are examined directly during the post-mortem examination of the body or when the carcase of the deer or other quarry is being gralloched by the shooter.

Recent research has indicated that the wound profile of a particular loading can be predicted, in the absence of the other chance effects previously mentioned, using 10% ordnance gelatine. It has been suggested that the gelatine must first be 'calibrated' by firing a BB air gun pellet at the block at a standard velocity of 590 ft/s (180 m/s); the pellet penetration standard being 8.5 cm, with a deviation each side of 1 cm. It is claimed that the dimensions of the wound profiles produced using this medium closely match the dimensions of the wounds measured during autopsies of gunshot victims, and a mathematical predictive model of bullet wounding shots was published in 1994 (MacPherson, 1994).

## 7.9    Range Determination of Single Missile Injuries

When examining pistol or rifle bullet injuries we are not of course able to use pellet spread measurements to determine the range of firing. However, bear in mind that even when weapons of this type are used in criminal shootings, the attack is usually confrontational in nature. As previously stated, not all of the propellant is completely burned in the gun barrel, resulting in a portion of it being forcibly ejected at supersonic speed from the muzzle, so as to travel towards the target as a cloud of unintentional secondary missiles. Due to the rocket effect of emerging high-pressure powder gases there is an initial tendency for the powder grains, or fragments of grains, to overtake the bullet. However, their speed is quickly checked by air resistance due to their low weight and poor ballistic coefficient, and as a result, they rarely travel with significant damaging properties above a distance of about 6 ft (2 m). However, this coincides with the range limits of many of the shootings likely to be investigated.

When the muzzle end of the gun barrel is in contact, or near-contact with the victim, the heat of the flash of discharge and the energetic nature of the emerging high-pressure gases have a profound effect upon the target. It is likely that the margin of the wound will be charred, and there can be sooty deposits of combustion if the muzzle was not in direct and firm contact so as to form an effective gas-tight seal. The high-pressure gases and unburned powder will follow the bullet into the target where their effects will be seen during the post-mortem examination. The high-pressure gases often try to escape forcibly back near their initial point of entry causing rips in clothing and damage radiating from the bullet hole which is of a stellate shape. Gas and blackening can try to escape at 90° to the line of fire between the layers of clothing, where it can again be detected. A similar escape path for the gases can result in the blackening of the outer surface of large bone structures such as the skull or the sternum; such effects are initially screened by the overlying tissue in the early stages of the examination (Figure 8.3).

High-pressure gases entering the wound can also cause a violent ballooning action of the tissue in this region. This action can sometimes cause a bruise to be left upon the skin where it has been forced back against the firearm used in the firing. In a number of such instances I have seen a near-perfect impression of the muzzle end of the gun which in some instances is sufficiently characteristic in nature to allow tentative identification of the model involved. In one instance the high Baumar foresight impression from a Smith and Wesson .357 in Magnum was clearly outlined on the skin in the wound area, and in another the complicated shape from the muzzle end of a .22 in Beretta target pistol (Figure 8.23).

At a muzzle-to-target distance of about 2 in (5 cm), the unburned propellant will just be starting to diverge from the central path of the bullet, inflicting punctuate injuries around the wound margin along with the charring or blackening effects. Rifle loadings will of course be more energetic than magnum revolver loadings, which in turn will be more energetic than standard pistol or revolver loadings, resulting in different intensities of the effects described. Lead revolver bullets, which utilise wax or grease type lubricants to reduce their tendency for barrel leading, tend to generate on average, more sooty deposits than jacketed pistol bullets due to the burning of part of the exterior bullet lubricant displaced by the rifling lands within the bore. However, it is unwise to guess or generalise too much as differences in the propellant and other loading features can greatly influence the nature of the effects described. The presence of a flash eliminator on the weapon used in the shooting can leave tell-tale effects upon the skin in the wound area, due to the fanlike forward escape of high-pressure gases and other discharge products, to produce a characteristic star-shaped pattern of tattooing corresponding to the number of slots cut in the body of the flash eliminator attached to the barrel muzzle (Figure 8.5).

At greater muzzle-to-target distances the level of blackening will diminish and will eventually cease (Figure 9.6 through Figure 9.8). Tattooing effects, caused by punctuate injuries formed by the impacts of powder grains, will be perceived over a wider area and will lessen in intensity with increasing firing distance as the influence of smaller particles of debris are checked due to the greater effects of air resistance and consequent disproportionate velocity loss. Thin flake type powder grains suffer severe velocity loss due to the greater effects of air resistance upon their poor ballistic shapes. Stick and ball powders are able to travel greater distances due to their higher sectional densities and better ballistic shapes. Ball powders tend to produce some of the most dramatic effects, especially when used as heavy charges in magnum revolver loadings. One can often find complete grains of ball propellant embedded in the exposed tissue of the victim, and on a number of occasions I have noted the effects produced by this same propellant caused by its lateral escape from the cylinder gap of the revolver. Examination of an excised wound sample back at the laboratory under the microscope will allow recovery of powder grains and larger fragments embedded in the tissue. As previously stated the size, morphology, and composition of these items recovered from the damaged tissue or from the fabric of the clothing of the victim can provide useful additional information.

Examination of any associated clothing involved at these firing distances will normally be supplemented by the use of simple chemical detection techniques for residues from the discharge. A saturated solution of sodium rhodizonate is the most useful method, provided the clothing is not heavily bloodstained in the area under examination. This can be done by pressing filter paper, previously moistened with 1% hydrochloric acid, firmly down upon the area of the garment being examined when it is placed upon a smooth firm surface. The paper is then removed and oversprayed with the saturated aqueous solution of the reagent. The initial purple coloration for lead changes to blue with additional or 5% hydrochloric acid; the presence of barium leads to a reddish coloration. Such tests will allow the range of detection of powder strikes to be extended just beyond the distance at which they can damage or become embedded in the weave of the fabric. In addition the test allows the elimination of any spurious damage on the clothing being mistaken for that which has been produced by a firearm, and discriminates between entry and exit damage due to the detection of the lead wipe effects left upon the margin of the hole on the entry side.

Tests should then be conducted in the firing range using sheets of card, or in some instances card covered with fabric, which in an ideal situation will involve fabric taken from an undamaged part of the clothing so as to ensure a similar degree of fabric/powder residue interaction. As an example of this, an open weave fabric will retain or capture powder particles better than a strong-fine weave fabric, particularly at longer ranges. All testing should be done using the incident weapon and any unfired ammunition. Failing this, a laboratory reference weapon of similar manufacture and barrel length should be used along with comparable ammunition from the laboratory store. All witness cards should be marked with the firing range, measured as accurately as possible from the muzzle end of the barrel to the target, with the case reference number and other relevant data, signed and dated. The witness cards can then be compared directly with the damaged clothing, wound sample, or photographs or sketches taken during the post-mortem examination. Additional rhodizonate tests for retained discharge residues can also be conducted upon the fabric-covered test cards. Always be aware that changes in the cartridge loading used in the tests can influence the test results significantly. In all range tests it is best to bracket the likely range and conduct additional tests if in doubt. In the statement it is usual to describe the likely minimum and maximum possible distances in your range estimate. Always check these results against details contained in witness statements describing recollections of events, especially any statement made by the accused. In addition, try to see if the likely scenario you are about to describe can be fitted within the area noted in the scene plan or your own notes of distances, points of damage, apparent lines of fire, and blood splashes observed during a scene visit. If something does not fit, check your test results again, always taking advantage of the second opinion of a colleague, and if necessary visit or revisit the scene of the incident and attempt additional reconstructions.

## Further Reading

Ackley, P.O. 1970. *Handbook for Shooters and Reloaders* Vol. 1, Salt Lake City, UT: Publishers Press.

Amato, J., Syracuse, D., Seaver, P.R. and Rich, N. 1989. Bone as a secondary missile: an experimental study in fragmenting of bone by high-velocity missiles, *Journal of Trauma*, **29** (5), 609–612.

Di Maio, V.J. 1982. Minimal velocities necessary for perforation of skin by air gun pellets and bullets. *Journal of Forensic Science.* **October,** 894–898.

Di Maio, V.J.M. 1985. *Gunshot Wounds,* Oxford: Elsevier.

Fackler, M.L. 1994. The wound profile and the human body: Damage pattern correlation, *Wound Ballistics Review,* **1** (4), 12–19.

Fackler, M.L. 1995. Wound ballistics and soft-tissue treatment, *Techniques in Orthopaedics,* **10** (3), 163–170.

Fackler, M. (President of the International Wound Ballistics Association, Florida, USA) 1995, 1996. Private communication.

Fackler, M.L. 1988. Wound Ballistics—A Review of common misconceptions. *The Journal of the American Medical Association*, 259, 2730–2736.

Fackler, M.L. and Malinowski, J.A. 1988. Ordnance gelatin for ballistic studies. *The American Journal of Forensic Medicine and Pathology*, **9** (3), 218–219.

Fackler, M.L. and Malinowski, J.A. 1988. Internal deformation of the AK-74; a possible cause for its erratic path in tissue, *Journal of Trauma*, **28** (1), S72–75.

Fackler, M.L. and Roberts, G.K. 1992. Failure to expand: federal 7.62 mm soft point bullets, *Wound Ballistics Review*, **1** (2), 18–20.

Fackler, M.L., Surinchak, J.S. and Malinowski, J.A. 1984. Bullet fragmentation: a major cause of tissue disruption, *Journal of Trauma*, **24,** 35–39.

Fackler, M.L., Surinchak, J.S., Malinowski, J.A. and Bowen, R.E. 1984. Wounding potential of the Russian AK-74 assault rifle. *The Journal of Trauma*, **24** (3), 263–266.

Farrar, C.L. and Leeming, D.W. 1982. *Military Ballistics A Basic Manual*, Oxford: Brassey.

Gander, T.J. and Hogg, I.V. 1993. *Jane's Ammunition Handbook*, Coulsdon Surrey: Jane's Data Division.

Gold, R.E. and Schecter, B. 1992. Ricochet dynamics for the nine-millimetre parabellum bullet, *Journal of Forensic Sciences*, **37** (1), 90–98.

Haag, L.C. 1994. Falling bullets: Terminal velocities and penetration studies. IWBA Wound Ballistics Conference.

Haag, M.G., 2002. Skin perforation and skin simulants. *A.F.T.E. Journal*, **34**, 3.

Hatcher, Major General, J.S. 1966. *Hatcher's Notebook*, Harrisburg, PA: Stackpole.

Keith, E. 1937. Solid bronze bullets in the .220 Swift. *American Rifleman*, July 1937.

Labbett, P. and Mead, P.J.F. 1988. *303 Inch: A History of the .303 Cartridge in the British Service*, Michigan: Forensic Ammunition Service.

LaGarde, L.A., 1916. *Gunshot Injuries*. Second Rev. Ed. Mt. Ida, A.K. 1991: Lancer Militaria.

Lowry, E. 1988. Shot penetration in soft targets, *The American Rifleman*, **136,** 24–40.

MacPherson, D. 1994. *Bullet Penetration – Modelling the Dynamics and the Incapacitation Resulting from Wound Trauma*, El Segundo, Ca: Ballistic Publications.

McConnel, M.P., Triplett, G.M. and Rowe, W.F. 1981. A study of shotgun pellet ricochet, *Journal of Forensic Sciences*, **26** (4), 699–709.

Office of the United States Surgeon General. 1962. *Wound Ballistics*, Washington, DC: Department of the Army.

Ordog, D.J., Wasserberger, J. and Balasubramanium, S. 1988. Shotgun wound ballistics. *The Journal of Trauma*, **28**, 624-31.

Owen-Smith, M.S. 1981. *High Velocity Missile Wounds*, London: Edward Arnold.

Rathman, G.A., 1987. *The Effect of Shape on BB and Bullet Penetration*. A.F.T.E. Journal, October, **19**, 4.

Salziger, B. and Strobele, M., 1999. Eindringtiefe von 9 mm Luger Geschossen in Gelatine. *Der Auswerfer*, March 1999 pp. 29–31, BKA, Wiesbaden, Germany.

Sciuchetti, G. 1989. What's best in the bush, *American Rifleman*, **137** (9), 42–7; 79.

Sellier, K.G. and Kneubuehl, B.P. 1994. *Wound Ballistics and the Scientific Background,* London: Elsevier.

*Textbook of Small Arms.* 1929. War Department, London: HMSO.

Warlow, T.A. 1994. The choice of rifle and loading for use in the management of deer, *Deer— Journal of the British Deer Society,* **9,** 307–14.

# The Scene of the Shooting Incident

# 8

If you've got a nice fresh corpse, fetch him out!

**Mark Twain**

*Innocents Abroad*

## 8.1 The On-Call Rota System

In an ideal world the forensic scientist is called out to the scene during the earliest part of the investigation. This decision will, however, be left within the discretion of the senior police officer in charge of the investigation. For many years I have worked within a department offering a 24-h, 365-day on-call service for the 41 police forces in England and Wales, and the London area in more recent years.

During evenings or other out-of-hours periods it has been usual to operate personnel, on a rota basis, who in turn are furnished with a nation-wide electronic paging device and a mobile telephone. Although it is not particularly pleasant to be dragged out of one's bed at 2 am on a cold January morning to travel to a scene 200 or more miles away, what can be achieved by examining the body and the scene when it is in an undisturbed, or relatively undisturbed form can make it all worthwhile. In other circumstances the scientist will have to depend on the efficiency of the scene of crime officers and the observations made by the pathologist, which in some instances may be of limited assistance.

One can consider the incident scene to be rather like a partially completed jigsaw, which is far easier to solve in its partially assembled undisturbed form than will ever be possible after it has been dismantled, packaged and then

217

sent to the laboratory. In addition, when giving evidence to the court at some future date, it is always a source of comfort and strength when being subjected to cross-examination to be able to speak from one's own personal experience and scene visit notes.

## 8.2   Arrival at the Scene

On arrival at the scene, the senior officer in charge should be contacted as soon as possible in order to identify yourself and to establish during these critical initial stages, the proper working relationship between yourself and the police investigative team. At scenes of major incidents the situation on the ground can be in an apparent state of confusion, and this can also be the perception of some of the participants. It will be normal for the scientist to be briefed by the senior investigating officer or the senior scene of crime officer as to what has happened or is thought to have happened. It is wise to make notes during this briefing, at the same time noting the names of the deceased and those of all key officers. At the end of this briefing, which can sometimes also include a brief view of the points of interest at the scene, it is best if you can present the senior officer with an outline of what you wish to do and, at the same time, make this an integral part of the official plan of action. In this way you can then use the scene of crime staff on behalf of the senior officer to best effect.

## 8.3   Scene Examination

At this stage it is important that you seek advice regarding fingerprint or footprint examination at the scene. It is usually a wise decision at this stage to don surgical gloves, plastic overshoes and other garments deemed necessary such as the all-enveloping 'moon suit' to prevent scene contamination and for your own protection from health hazards such as blood and body tissue. If the scene of crime officers have laid protective plates on the floor in order to preserve any footprints, it is important that you do not move from this protected route without permission or the installation of additional floor coverings.

It will be normal for you to make a rough sketch of the scene, including the position and location of the body or bodies, the locations of any weapons, cartridges, cartridge cases, wadding, shot, bullets, blood splashes and firearm-related damage. The scene of crime officers will already have taken some photographs prior to your arrival and may also have recorded it on video. In these days this will usually be a digital recording machine with instant playback facility, allowing you to observe the initial condition of the scene during your briefing. However, now is your opportunity to add to this by using your specialist firearms knowledge to spot things that may have been missed or discounted. You can then arrange for the photographic staff to record what you think to be key findings, and this is often done to advantage by insisting on camera angles which mimic your own viewpoints used when taking notes.

A marker, which in some instances will be numbered, will usually be placed next to the object in question, and where it is relevant a scale should also be placed next to or on the object being photographed, to allow better interpretation of the picture in court or back at the laboratory. Dimensions which you think are critical or which will be useful should always be recorded in your notes, together with heights of bullet strikes, the locations and dimensions of articles of furniture, or any other details you feel are relevant. Your notes should also indicate the times of arrival and departure at the various locations you will be required to visit, along with the names of the senior police or scene of crime officer with you or whom you meet at each stage.

It is important to have all the equipment you think you might need in your scene visit bag, as you can never be sure that the police will have all the tooling and equipment at the scene. I usually carry a steel tape measure in my pocket, along with a magnet, a pocket knife, a Mini-Maglite or torch of similar design which allows you to focus the beam on a particular object, and a small folding ×10 magnifier. In my kit I carry a 30 m surveyor's tape, a folding 2 m rule, a ball of twine, some lengths of 3 mm welding rod to use as probes when evaluating bullet damage, a small device for use in the measurement of angles, a wallet containing scissors, forceps, scalpel, plastic exhibit bags and markers, surgical gloves, plastic overshoes and a kit containing filter papers and reagents for conducting sodium rhodizonate tests on suspected bullet strikes. I also use a pocket-size digital camera of my own to take the images to supplement my notes and to insert into my statements.

A comprehensive photographic record should be made of all relevant features at the scene and all of the findings made during the post-mortem examination. In the past this was done in black and white. Colour photographs now allow far easier discrimination between such things as bloodstains and powder blackening effects, and a video recording overview can often be of great advantage at a later stage in the investigation or even for use as a court exhibit. One can always file away unnecessary or surplus photographs, but if things come unstuck at a later stage of the investigation the lack of such recordings can prove disastrous.

It will be necessary at some stage for any firearm at the scene to be made safe. This will be done by the visiting firearms expert, or in his absence by a police firearms officer considered competent for the task. This must always be done after discussion with the senior officer, as fingerprinting will also be a consideration. Before the weapon is opened the position of safety catches or single-trigger shotgun barrel selector switches should be noted together with the setting of the polychoke in the case of certain American repeating shotguns. As you are at this stage unaware of the mechanical condition of the gun, it is essential that it is handled carefully and pointed in a safe direction during the unloading operation. In the case of self-loading pistols and other removable magazine arms, the magazine should be removed first and its condition noted. The breech should then be opened in the manner appropriate for the particular arm in question. The finding of a spent or live cartridge should be noted and photographed *in situ*. This is especially appropriate in revolvers where the fired chamber should be positioned in the 12 o'clock position so that the photograph correctly shows the positions of any live and spent cartridges in its cylinder (Figure 8.1). Great care should be taken when checking and removing cartridges from tubular-magazine repeating arms. The cartridges and cartridge cases can then be packaged and labelled by the scene of crime officers. In the case of revolvers I often place

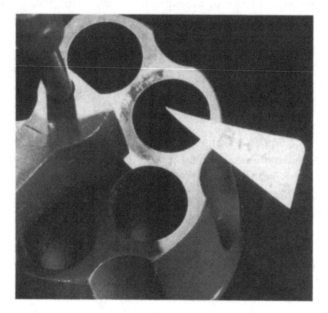

**Figure 8.1**    .38 in Smith and Wesson revolver found concealed under floor boards at murder scene residence. Initial examination showed a halo of recently discharged residues at the end of one of the chambers. This chamber was marked to identify it and photographed. This was very important later on when it was confirmed by microscopy of test bullets to be the murder weapon, as mechanical faults in the cylinder timing caused very great differences in the double action trigger pull from one chamber to another.

a mark on the outside of the cylinder to indicate the location of the chamber which was aligned with the barrel. The scene of crime officers can also take swabs from the insides of any spent cartridge cases found at the scene *before* they are submitted to the firearms laboratory for further examination. The moistened cotton swabs should then be placed back in their protective plastic sheathes before being sent separately to the laboratory facility which will use them as control samples of propellant and primer generated residues. The information gained from the brief examination of firearms and cartridge cases recovered at the scene of the shooting incident will be of great use to you when attempting to interpret damage at the scene or the wounds upon the body during the post-mortem examination.

Although the main examination of any recovered firearm will be done at a later stage back at the laboratory, it is always useful to conduct a brief examination of it at the scene, as this will give you information as to what you might expect to find at the scene or during the examination of the body. Make of the weapon, the rifling pattern, the presence of discharge residues in the bore and the type of cartridge loading used are all important features. If the arm is of pump-action or self-loading design you will then expect to find spent cartridge cases at the scene, which in the initial viewing may well have fallen out of sight. Spots of blood on the forward-facing parts of the weapon may well be associated with a close-range firing where blood has backspattered onto the firearm (Figure 8.2). Blood inside the bore and the extent of its travel, will be a function of bore size, the intensity of the loading, and the distance of firing. Research work by MacDonnell and Brooks (1977) indicated that such effects will be more marked with large calibre pistols or shotguns. Blood deposited at distances of up to 5 mm down the barrel were found at ranges of up to 5 in/12 cm) in large gauge shotguns, and 1 to 1.5 in/2.5–3 cm in .22 in rim-fire arms. However, as in all things it is best not to generalise too much, and in a few instances of contact head shots with .22 in arms that I have dealt with, blood was absent upon the end of the barrel as well as inside the bore, although the finding of other discharge effects upon the wound margin and inside the wound track confirmed without doubt the true nature of the injuries. In contact or near-contact firings, some of the high-pressure gases will enter the wound track and will usually escape back through the entry wound, often ripping the wound margin in the process, thus providing backspatter effects. Where a substantial area of bone is covered by a thin layer of tissue, as in the case of a shot to the skull, tissue in the wound margin can be ripped by the interaction of the bullet or shot charge with this hard surface after the initial penetration of surface tissue (Figure 8.3).

In some instances of suspected suicide which involve the use of a long-barrelled gun such as a conventional shotgun, one will sometimes find a loop of cord or leather strap hooked around the trigger. Such improvisations allow

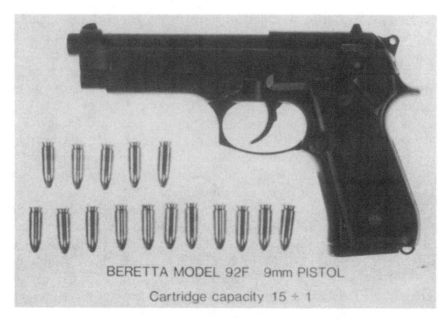

**Figure 8.2**    Beretta model 92 9 mm pistol used in the Hungerford incident along with Kalashnikov rifle. Blood is present on the muzzle end of its barrel and also upon the grips after its final use in the suicide of Michael Ryan.

the victim to fire the gun with a downward movement of the foot placed inside this stirrup-like device, while at the same time allowing the alignment of the gun with the intended target area. This will usually be the centre of the chest in such instances as the length of the gun would otherwise make such an alignment difficult to achieve. The presence of any such device should be noted and photographed. Without such an improvisation, the normal elective site for a deliberate self-inflicted injury with a longarm, is to place the muzzle end of the weapon inside the mouth or in contact with the underside of the chin (Figure 8.5). Shots to the chest do occur without the assistance of such a device if the person has a long reach or if the barrels are not too long. One sometimes see botched suicide attempts using this method, however, where the gun has been misaligned when straining to reach the trigger with the right thumb. In one such instance I dealt with, the initial firing resulted in a massive shallow raking injury to the left side of the rib cage. A second shot was then successfully fired with the muzzle end of the gun inside the mouth, after the victim had to go back inside the house to find a further cartridge. Misalignment can sometimes occur even when the muzzle end of the shotgun is placed against the underside of the chin or inside the mouth. In one case I dealt with a man tried to kill himself in this manner after the police arrived at the murder scene. He was dazed, but remained conscious despite the loss of a large part of the side of his head

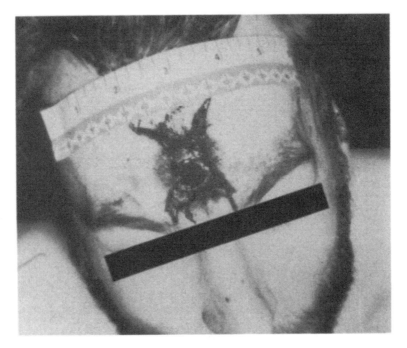

**Figure 8.3** Stellate injury with burning and blackening caused by self-inflicted injury with pistol barrel in hard contact with the forehead. In this type of injury one should expect to find powder blackening on the exterior of the skull during the post-mortem examination of this part of the body.

and one of his eyes. He threatened the police with the gun, took a police car, and drove it at night a distance of approximately 30 miles along narrow twisting country lanes. He then held up the occupants of a police station with the gun before collapsing after a woman fainted when she saw his condition. Some months later he was able to stand trial for the killing. In the case of handguns, the preferred elective site is the temple or the side of the head, although a shot to the mouth, the underside of the chin, or even to the forehead, is not uncommon.

Always remember, that in instances of suicide which involve the firing of a shotgun or other weapon likely to generate a high level of recoil, the way in which the gun is being held by the firer can in turn lead to unusual or unexpected effects at the scene. The gun is not being supported against the shoulder and it will not usually be gripped firmly at the instant of firing. This can result in the gun being flung some distance away from the firer by the forces of recoil. For example, a person seated in a chair on a woodblock or linoleum-covered floor, will have the butt end of the stock in contact with the floor at an angle. Upon discharge the gun can skid along the floor several feet or in some instances, yards. On initial examination by investigating

**Figure 8.4**    Classic self-inflicted entry wound caused by a contact shot from 9 mm Beretta pistol to the right temple of perpetrator of Hungerford incident. The bullet had exited from the left side of the head, tumbling in flight before hitting the classroom wall sideways on. The recovered bullet and cartridge case were microscopically associated with the pistol which was still in his hand, attached by a lanyard to his wrist, when I examined the body *in situ*. Despite this, the presence of blood on the muzzle end of the pistol and the fact that the bullet entry wound was in a preferred self-elective site for a suicide attempt, 'expert opinion' later appeared in some press reports that he had been murdered by a shot fired from outside the window by Special Forces, and that the trajectory of fire of the bullet track (from right to left across the head) would be 'impossible' for a right-handed person to achieve with a pistol.

officers this can appear to be an incident of murder, where the firer has abandoned the gun at the scene. In one incident the old double-barrelled hammer shotgun was caused to fire its other loaded barrel when the back of its hammer spur struck the edge of a wall some distance away in its flight. In this incident an area of pellet damage was present on the wall above the suicide victim, a few feet to the left of the main spray of blood and tissue from the upward directed explosive head injury. Careful examination of the scene revealed the impact impression of the back of the hammer spur of the left barrel in the plasterwork of the wall. In addition, there were traces of plaster present on the back of the hammer spur.

When examining a scene of a fatal shooting upon rough ground or farmland, always carefully examine every feature of the area, as a hole or

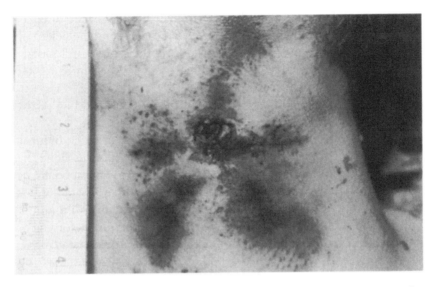

**Figure 8.5** Distinctive fan shaped pattern of tattooing and blackening due to slots in flash eliminator on FN 7.62 mm self-loading service rifle used to fire this underchin self-inflicted injury. One of the preferred self-elective sites for the use of a longarm in a suicide.

ridge in the ground might have caused a person to stumble or trip, thus leading to the discharge of the firearm. In one incident a farmer was found dead with a head injury in his tractor at the end of the field of peas he had been rolling. The shotgun which he normally carried in the cab was found in a damaged condition about 100 yd away. I arrived at the scene at first light and was able to examine the body *in situ*. It was clear that the shot charge had been fired from a range of a few feet in an upwards direction to strike him at an angle of approximately 45°. I found that the left barrel of the old hammer gun which had been discharged also had a defective rebound safety, which would allow it to be fired if the back of the hammer spur received a firm blow. He must have seen a fox or some other animal he wished to shoot and there were also geese about. So as not to alert the animal by stopping he had stood up and opened the cab door of his slow-moving tractor. Something had caused him to drop the gun, which fell butt-first towards the ground. In its fall the back of the hammer spur of the defective lock had struck the edge of one of the exterior steel foot treads, causing the gun to discharge. The gun then fell to the ground where it was damaged as the roller being towed by the tractor rolled over it, and the tractor continued on its way down to the end of the field.

Structural damage caused by bullets should be confirmed if necessary using the sodium rhodizonate test. The angle at which the bullet or shot charge has impacted should also be determined, along with the direction of fire, the spread of the pellets in shotgun-related firings, and the height of the bullet strike, or the centre of the shot spread from the ground or floor. Always bear in mind that some of the shots may have missed their intended target, causing damage in sometimes obscure locations at the scene. Always try to account for all of the spent cartridge cases or items of wadding recovered with corresponding injuries or damage.

A thin probe can be placed into a bullet hole in a wall or article of furniture to determine the angle of impact and the line of firing. I often use long lengths of 3 mm welding rod for such exercises, these thin rods are especially useful when reconstructing what has taken place when shots have been fired at the occupant of a car. The rods can be left in place and fitted with a numbered card in cases of multiple bullet damage, to allow photographic recording of the findings which can be used to assist in the preparation of your statement and for use as exhibits in court(Figure 8.6 and Figure 8.7). The angles made by the rods can then be measured and projections made on the scene plan to indicate the reconstructed lines of fire. Small laser-projector theodolite units can also be used in these instances to help determine the position of the firer and the lines of fire. In one instance where I was reconstructing the course of fire used in the wounding of an officer in his patrol car, I acquired long thin canes from a local garden centre for this purpose. In this incident which involved the use of a Colt pattern .45 in self-loading pistol, an entire magazine was fired resulting in shots striking the vehicle in different locations from different angles. Here I was able to get the use of a fire tender so that the scene of crime officer could photograph, with good effect, the numbered witness rods from above the vehicle (Figure 8.8 through Figure 8.10).

The locations of splashes or pools of blood or other body fluids and tissue should also be recorded and photographed. In some instances a biologist will be on hand to help deal with these matters. In any event samples will be taken for DNA matching purposes as some of the blood may well have been associated with the murderer if he has been injured during the incident. The height and directional effects of blood splashes and spattering can often assist greatly with determining the locations of the firer and the victim, and also the likely positions they were adopting at the time of the shooting. Information gained here will also indicate the possibility of the biologists finding blood splashes upon the clothing of the firer. Although the presence of clothing will reduce such effects, additional shots fired at blood-stained locations can generate a spray of fine droplets. Head shots usually tend to produce copious bleeding, and in the case of close range or self-inflicted injuries to the head using a centre-fire rifle or shotgun, extensive injuries of an almost explosive nature often occur, causing a spray of tissue, blood and skull fragments over a wide area (Figure 8.11). Such effects do not

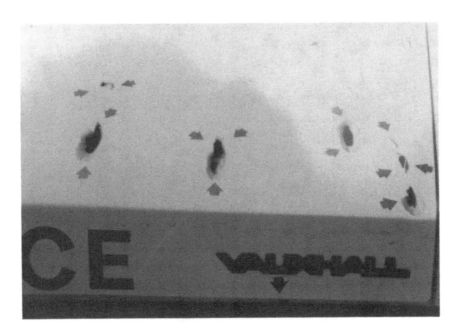

**Figure 8.6 and Figure 8.7** In contrast with the initial ineffectual shots fired at a police vehicle in Southview Hungerford from the 9 mm pistol, the M43 Kalashnikov loadings were particularly effective against the police car and other persons inside vehicles. Here the firer has run in a half circle around the vehicle emptying the magazine into it from waist height after first firing a number of ineffectual 9 mm pistol shots at its front end.

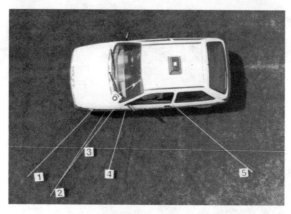

**Figure 8.8 to Figure 8.10**      Reconstruction of shooting incident involving six hits from a .45 in Colt pattern self-loading pistol on a police vehicle. Here, canes have been passed through the holes in the car bodywork to indicate the lines of fire in each instance. Although the officer sustained an injury to his left thigh the reconstruction indicates his narrow escape from one bullet which must have passed close to his head.

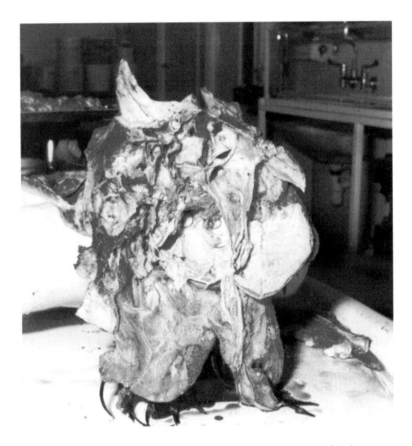

**Figure 8.11** Explosive injury caused by self-inflicted shot fired in an upward direction when the muzzle end of a 12-bore gun was in contact with the underside of the chin. However, not all such shots result in the complete rupture of the head.

occur in every instance however, as there is always a measure of uncertainty as to how a bullet or shot loading will interact with the human body.

Where a bullet or shot charge has passed through a window or other partition, it is useful to reproduce the missile track using a length of light-coloured twine which will show up in the scene of crime officer's photographs. It is sometimes possible to remove bullets from furniture or walls relatively easily. In other instances it will be appropriate to cut out a piece of wood or remove a door for this work to be done at leisure in the laboratory on your return to avoid obliterating the fine-bore details on the bullet. Bullets in plasterwork of walls should be removed with great care using a probe to determine their location and depth, followed by the slow removal of plaster with a mallet and wood chisel, starting a safe distance to the side of where you believe the bullet is resting. Do not rush this job as it is very easy, especially when dealing with lead revolver bullets, to damage them further, thus making them less useful for subsequent microscopy. Always be prepared to return to the scene at a later time or another day if necessary. This will often be the case if you have to go immediately to the post-mortem examination. Revisiting the scene can also be used with good effect to attempt reconstruction of what you believe may have taken place. All such reconstructions, which will usually involve scene of crime officers acting out scenarios or standing in position, in some instances holding the unloaded gun in the process, should be photographed and video recorded for possible use in court. Bearing in mind the stature of some police officers, do make a point of choosing persons who will best represent the height of the victim and the suspect. Bloodstained furniture or bedding can be covered with sheets to protect the participants without unduly upsetting the visual aspects of the recording. The mechanical aspects of the operation of the weapon and its test-firing can also be recorded if thought appropriate back at the laboratory.

### 8.3.1    The Pathologist at the Scene

The majority of scene investigations will involve attendance by the Home Office appointed pathologist, or his equivalent in other countries. The main duty of the pathologist is to determine the cause of death for the Coroner's inquest which will be held at a later date. In earlier times, it was usual for this person to attempt to interpret all of the crucial technical parts of the scene investigation, even when this required specialist knowledge lay outside his normal field. Most of the Home Office pathologists will now expect, or even request, scene attendance by the forensic scientist specialising in firearms examination, followed by his assistance in the interpretation of firearm-related aspects of the post-mortem examination. The two specialists thus work together, as a team within the main investigative team, to provide the optimum contribution to the senior police officer; this activity can sometimes also involve the forensic biologist.

### 8.3.2    Roles

In order to function efficiently, it is important that all of the players understand both their own roles and those of other participants. This is relatively easy to achieve and can even become automatic in nature, if the participants have functioned together in the past, because then the rules of play are implicit. The firearms expert and the pathologist will both want to see the layout of the scene, preferably in its undisturbed form, and both will want to see the disposition of the corpse and to take notes. It is at this stage that significant potential findings are put at hazard as the preliminary examination of the body is undertaken.

## 8.4   Initial Examination of the Body

It is usual to conduct a brief examination of the body prior to its removal in order to determine the nature and disposition of injuries. This is an extremely useful procedure as it will then help you to understand what has taken place during the incident and in turn will help you to interpret other effects which might otherwise have been missed, or instigate a search for other likely exhibits or effects which will be of evidential value. The pathologist will also want to check the body temperature by means of a rectal temperature measurement to help him determine the time which has elapsed since death, and there will always be a perceived need by others for the body to be transferred to the mortuary at the earliest opportunity. In all of these activities it will be necessary for the body to be moved or rolled over, possibly putting at hazard a textbook pattern of powdering and blackening marks on the front of the white shirt worn by the deceased as it becomes immersed in a pool of blood. It is unlikely that circumstances will allow a complete examination of the clothing and relevant parts of the body at this stage. In many instances the examination will be taking place at night, in bad weather conditions, or in cramped conditions. All that is necessary at this time to help interpret the scene should be accomplished without the need for extensive activities as the full examination will be better carried out at the mortuary under more ideal conditions. The firearms expert and the pathologists are the only persons who should have access to the body; otherwise critical features or exhibits can be lost, although one must accept the realities of the prior involvement of paramedics at the scene. In one scene I attended some years ago where a youth shot his own father with a pump-action shotgun, a knife I found behind a sofa at the other side of the room was eventually found to have been removed from the hand of the deceased by one of the paramedics and then flung by him across the room; needless to say, this aspect of the incident had a profound effect upon the possible course of legal action.

If all parties understand each other's needs to work to an agreed prioritised plan of activity, then all should go well. It is usual at the end of this stage for the two parties to discuss their findings and to come to a consensus before transmitting their initial interpretation of the scene findings to the senior investigative officer. In most instances agreement will be reached regarding the areas of priority to be dealt with at the subsequent examination in the mortuary. The pathologist will discuss these matters with the coroner's officer so that arrangements can be made for the transfer of the body to the mortuary and for the availability of prior X-ray examination of the body at the hospital before the post-mortem examination is started.

## 8.4.1   The Post-Mortem Examination

The first things to observe when entering the mortuary concern health and safety. One should always don plastic overshoes or mortuary dedicated Wellington boots to prevent pick-up of blood or tissue on your normal footwear, followed by protective clothing, surgical gloves and a disposable plastic apron. When assisting with the examination of the wounds or handling bloodstained bullets, wadding, or other bloodstained exhibits it is imperative that surgical gloves are worn. When taking notes during individual examinations, it is quite usual for these to be dispensed with and replaced by another pair before continuing with the next stage. The duty of the ballistics examiner is to supplement the skills of the pathologist who is identified as being the person in charge of the examination of the body. Unless you enjoy the trust of the pathologist from working together previously you should conduct yourself in a way which will engender his trust and cooperation. In the UK many pathologists simply do not have the experience to properly interpret firearm wound characteristics and missile types, or to know how many elements of cartridge wadding are to be expected associated with a close-range shotgun discharge, due to the relatively low level of firearm-related serious crime they are likely to have experienced previously. In addition, it is in these crucial initial parts of the examination that the ballistics expert can provide the senior police investigative officer with vital information concerning the type and number of weapons involved, details of the ammunition used and details concerning approximate distance of firing and likely location of the firer at the scene. In many instances I have been able to provide the police with details of the likely make and model of weapon used, together with information as to its previous use in an incident in their area. Such initial findings must always, of course, be subject to confirmation after examining the exhibits or the wound samples more closely during their subsequent examination back at the laboratory. It is quite usual also for you to give a verbal presentation of your scene and post-mortem findings to all of the officers in the investigative team at a wash-up session back at the police station; this will always cause questions to be raised by individual officers which you will be expected to answer.

## 8.5   X-Ray Examination

In the early stages of my career, I was always surprised when a pathologist about to conduct an autopsy on the body of a gunshot victim did not give automatic consideration to prior X-ray examination. Many items of great evidential value must often have been missed as a result. Things have moved on, and it is now customary for X-ray plates to be on hand and studied before the examination of the body is contemplated. The portable fluoroscope with digitally recorded images can prove to be a very useful instrument giving near-instantaneous images, albeit of a slightly reduced quality. It is important to obey due precautions from the radiology staff present, and in the use of the fluoroscope this will usually entail wearing lead-filled aprons. A small amount of time spent studying the photographic plates or images will often eliminate untidy, and sometimes frantic, searches for lost missiles at a later stage of the examination. Bullets can often end up in the most unexpected places, and in the case of the smaller calibres such as .22, .25 in (6.35 mm) or even .32 in (7.65 mm), be most difficult to find. X-ray plates of shotgun victims can often allow pellet counts to be determined back at the laboratory, which in turn can indicate the likely cartridge loading if viewed in conjunction with the cartridge wadding. It is always good policy to have the plates hung on the light-box on display during the post-mortem examination, particularly if one is dealing with a case involving multiple missile injuries.

## 8.6   The First Samples and Observations

During the initial stages of the examination of the body when the clothing is being removed, bagged and recorded, it is good policy to make notes on any firearm-related damage to help you identify those garments which should be submitted to the laboratory for further examination. The scene of crime officers should be instructed to dry the articles of clothing properly in their drying room when spread out and placed upon sheets of brown paper. The clothing should not be allowed to dry when rucked up in the shot-damaged areas as this will lead to difficulties in examining these areas later on at the laboratory. Afterwards, the clothing should be packed when folded flat between sheets of brown paper, which in turn are placed in a sealed paper sack or other form of paper wrapping, labelled and bearing a health hazard warning sticker. Nothing is worse than receiving wet clothing sealed up in a plastic bag, especially if it has been stored for some time during hot weather.

The next thing to check for is the possible presence of bullets or cartridge wadding in the clothing or the body bag or other wrapping. Shotgun cartridge wadding can often be caught up in the clothing of the victim, and the restraining influence of human skin previously described, can often decelerate exiting missiles to cause them to be left in the clothing near to the exit wound. Such items can slip out into the body bag or some other location in the clothing during the process of removing the body from the scene, or during the removal of the clothing.

The pathologist will carry out his own external examination of the body, during which he will note the locations of old and fresh injuries, bruises and any other unusual features. He will also want to examine the hands, take scrapings from under the nails and take intimate body samples before the main examination. It is at this stage that the ballistics expert should also examine the hands. During close-range confrontational shootings, it is not uncommon for powder blackening or even gunshot injuries to be left upon the hands or forearms of the victim if he has instinctively raised them in a defensive posture just prior to the shot being fired (Figure 8.12). Any features of this nature should be noted, and in the case of blackening effects the presence of lead can be confirmed by means of the simple sodium rhodizonate test. One can often find residues of this nature on the index finger, thumb, and web of the non-firing hand, where a person has supported the muzzle end of the barrel of a long-barrelled shotgun to his chest or to the underside of the chin prior to committing suicide.

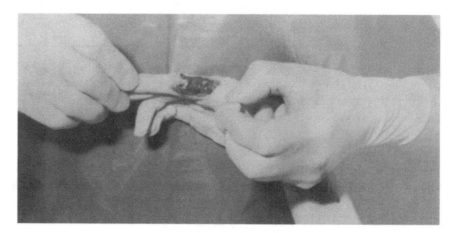

**Figure 8.12**    Gunshot damage to one of the hands of victims of close range shootings is quite common, presumably caused by raising the hands in front of the face and body as a defensive posture. These effects, or other minor effects such as powder blackening or tattooing should be noted during the post-mortem examination to assist with range determination and the reconstruction of the incident later back at the laboratory.

## 8.7 The Wound Sites

It is at this stage appropriate to conduct the detailed examination of the firearm related injuries. One should note their locations and dimensions upon a body chart of the type commonly used by pathologists, and determine if they represent entry or exit wounds. Each gunshot injury should be given a number agreed with the pathologist. The height of the wound from the bottom of the heel of the victim should be entered, along with its distance from the body centre-line or other convenient marker. The shape of the wound should be recorded along with any discharge blackening or powdering effects. These features and the dimensions of each injury should also be recorded after being agreed with the pathologist; uniformity is essential if your statement is to knit up with that produced by the pathologist. Each wound site should be photographed with a scale present by the scenes of crime officer responsible for compiling the photographic record of the examination. In shotgun injuries this will be relatively easy if the pellets have started to spread prior to striking the victim, or if there are related wad-strike abrasion injuries near to the main wound site. Very close-range shots will also leave powder blackening and/or powder tattooing effects upon the wound margin (Figure 8.13 and Figure 8.14). All such findings should be noted and discussed with the pathologist. It is important to remember that blue-black marks very similar to powder blackening in appearance can be produced by subcutaneous haemorrhage, and grey bullet wipe effects in the wound margin tend to be left by lubricated plain lead revolver bullets. Before

**Figure 8.13** High-speed photographic image of Austrian 'Glock Model 17' 9 mm pistol being fired. Un-burnt particles of propellant can be seen travelling alongside the bullet. Such high velocity particles are capable of producing punctuate tattooing injuries in the margin of the bullet entry wound, when firing takes place at short distances and before the effects of air resistance slow them down. At this point the slide has moved back sufficiently for the breech to begin unlocking, allowing a flash to be visible in the barrel-slide gap.

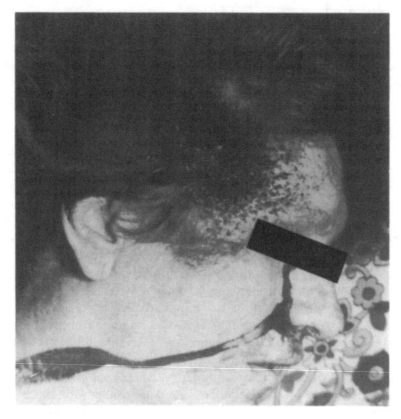

**Figure 8.14**  Powder tattooing effect around margin of close range handgun bullet entry wound.

the wound site is cleaned with a damp sponge a photographic record should be made by the scene of crime staff photographer. All photographs should be taken directly at 90° to the wound site, and it is imperative that a scale should be included to assist any subsequent study. At these times it is usual for colour photography to be used in all such recordings. This represents a considerable improvement over black-and-white pictures, especially in those instances where the ballistics expert has not attended the post-mortem examination, as it allows relatively easy discrimination between bloodstains and powder blackening effects. In such instances of non-attendance, it is appropriate for the pathologist to excise the wound site so that it can be submitted to the firearms expert at the laboratory with the clothing and the rest of the exhibits. Under no circumstances, however, should the wound be preserved in formalin as this will make its subsequent interpretation at the laboratory extremely difficult. Where there is a need to preserve the wound sample for a short period prior to transfer, this can be done by freezing the sample down in a plastic container, skin side up, after draining off any surplus blood.

Entry and exit wounds can be discriminated where a wound has been inflicted by a single missile or a compact mass of shot, even in instances where there are no other visible discharge effects, by examination of the injury sites after cleaning away any surface bloodstaining. The interpretation of missile wound sites on decomposing bodies can however be very difficult. Human skin is very elastic and surprisingly strong. When a firearm missile strikes it the skin attached to the missile nose is pushed into the body before it is perforated. As the bullet passes through this hole in the deformed area of tissue, it effectively rubs against the sides of a collar of skin, which then snaps back into place. Careful examination will reveal a ring-shaped abrasion injury in the wound margin (Figure 8.15). This abrasion ring might be more pronounced on one side if the bullet has struck at an angle. A similar pattern of abrasion injuries will be produced on close range shotgun injuries. Cup-shaped plastic cartridge wadding of the type so common in cartridges of current manufacture act in the same way as the sides of a bullet at close range as the shot charge is still closely associated with the wadding as a compact mass. Abrasion marks of a very characteristic shape will be produced if the leaves of the plastic wad are just starting to open up and peel back (Figure 8.16 through Figure 8.18). At these very close ranges one can expect to find the wadding, often with its leaves detached, inside the body associated with

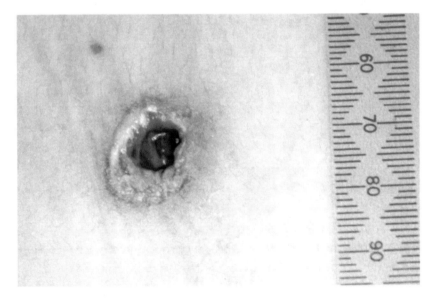

**Figure 8.15**   Classic bullet abrasion ring about entry wound margin.

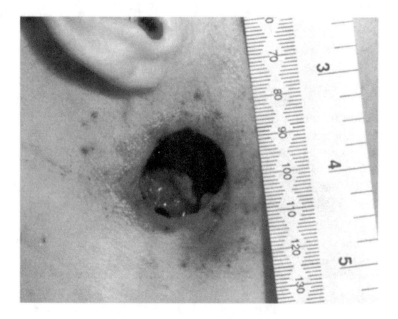

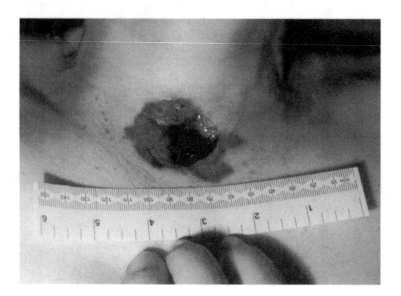

**Figure 8.16 and Figure 8.17** Close range shotgun entry wounds. Here the shot and wadding have entered the wound track as a compact mass. The second firing was at a slightly greater range, resulting in less powdering and blackening effects, and also by the tell-tale abrasion injury in the wound margin caused by the opening of the leaves of the plastic cup wad involved.

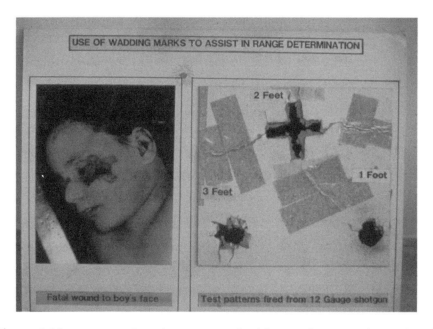

**Figure 8.18** 12-Bore shot charge injury fired from 2 feet range (60 cm) with characteristic abrasion injury in wound margin from open leaves of plastic cartridge wad. Tests showed that the wad leaves opened in a predictable manner with increasing range of firing.

the wound track (Figure 8.19 and Figure 8.20). As previously stated, it is very rare for shot charges to exit from the other side of a human torso where conventional birdshot loadings are used (Figure 8.21). The procedures previously set out will confirm the entry sites where several shots have been fired from the shotgun, which might otherwise be confused with entry and exit shots if the wound tracks merge within the body. In addition, the recovery of items of wadding considered in conjunction with an approximate pellet count conducted on the X-ray plates will resolve such issues if they arise.

The pathologist will explore each injury site to confirm whether or not it constitutes a substantive wound. Any underlying missile wound track and related internal damage will be recorded, as will be the finding of any missile or wadding; the pathologist will assign a unique identity to each exhibit written on the exhibit bag. It is common practice for the pathologist to make use of thin probes to highlight wound tracks during photography, especially if an entry wound can be related by a definite track to an exit wound. It is important that the pathologist takes due care not to use excessive force during such reconstructions, so as to avoid imposing false lines of firing. The direction and line of fire should then be recorded in your notes. You will use all such findings, in conjunction with your range of fire estimates, when com-

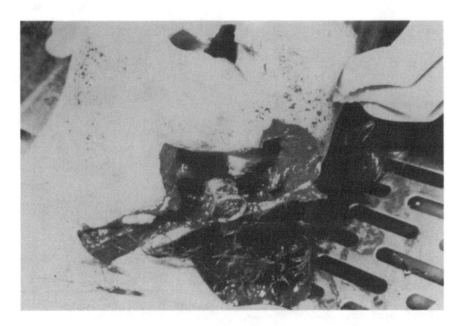

**Figure 8.19 and Figure 8.20**    Shotgun cartridge wadding is frequently found inside close range injuries. Recovered base section of plastic wad minus its cup leaves.

piling your final statement. In these days of digital imagery, a CD-ROM disc of the wound images will prove to be of great assistance to you when preparing your statement.

In instances where the bullet or shot charge has struck an area of the body, such as the skull or the front of the shin where hard bone is covered

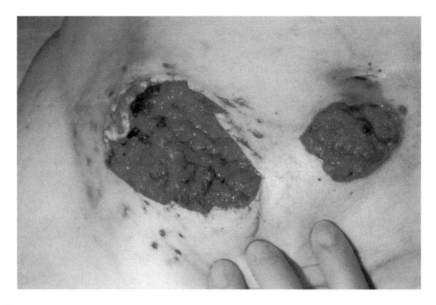

**Figure 8.21**   Relatively rare shotgun through penetration of the torso, here caused by shallow angle of incidence of firing.

by a relatively thin layer of tissue, stellate injuries or severe ripping can take place which might be confused by some with a contact shot, or even an exit wound. Careful examination of the injury site will not reveal the presence of discharge residues previously mentioned, which thus eliminates the possibility of it being a contact shot. In a head shot one should expect to see a cone-shaped enlargement of the hole on the internal exit surface of the skull, an effect sometimes referred to as bevelling, although it may be necessary to reconstruct this part of the skull if it is shattered, as frequently takes place with close-range shotgun injuries. If the flaps of skin are folded back into place, the true size of the entry wound can be determined and the presence of the abrasion ring detected. It is not uncommon with heavier bones for some of the pellets in a shot charge to be deflected to form separate wound tracks, and with all energetic missiles fragmented bone can also be accelerated to form separate secondary missiles, which in turn will be capable of inflicting their own wound tracks. The wadding in a close-range shotgun discharge may end up in the broken bones or damaged tissue of a limb injury, or may form its own exit wound. The penetrating behaviour of plastic cartridge wadding is extremely variable due to the differences in their designs. I have always found the plastic cup-wads loaded into imported Russian shotgun cartridges to be particularly penetrative in nature, even at extended ranges. Although I have not dealt yet with injuries caused by steel shot loadings, I suspect that the heavy-walled, high-density polyethylene wads necessary for use in these loadings should also have considerable penetrative capabilities.

Before leaving the subject of entry wound characteristics one must always be aware of the possibility of other atypical entry wound effects and that of false entry wounds. A bullet striking an intermediate target can partially break up to produce multiple satellite injuries, usually centred around the main defect, or in instances where the bullet has passed through glazing or vehicle window glass, a shower of secondary missiles in the form of glass splinters can be forcibly thrown towards the target, which in turn will produce satellite injuries. False entry wounds, sometimes referred to as shored exit wounds, complete with apparently normal abrasion rings, can be caused if the exit side of the victim is supported by a hard surface, such as a wall or article of furniture. As the tissue is caused to bulge outwards by the bullet on the exit side, an annular shaped area of skin is abraded as the bullet exits and forces it against the supporting surface. It is also possible for similar effects to occur if the bullet exits in a region supported by stiff or tight substantial items of clothing, such as a leather belt. I recall one instance where a murder victim had received seven separate shots fired from a 7.65 mm self-loading pistol. A through-wound to the neck had classic entry site abrasion rings about the margins of both holes. I examined the shirt that had been removed earlier, and found a clear bullet entry hole on one side of the collar, surrounded by discharge blackening effects, and a clear exit hole on collar on the other side, with fibres of material protruding from it. Like many drug dealers, the victim had been dressed only in the most expensive designer clothes. The shirt was made of silk, a very strong material, and there were several layers making up the collar to achieve the correct stiffness. This material had offered a substantial shoring effect during the exit of the bullet.

Shored entry wounds can be produced if a bullet passes through a limb, such as an arm pressed against the chest, that then re-enters the chest. Here, each supporting body acts to shore up the other as the skin in the margin of the chest injury is momentarily forced back against the arm. Figure 8.23 shows the distinctive impression formed by the forcible slap of the skin of the entry wound margin being slapped back against the muzzle end of a revolver barrel used to fire a contact shot. The firm support of an object held inside clothing or a pocket overlaying the bullet entry site can also produce a shored entry wound.

I recall observing unusual entry wound effects upon bodies associated with vehicle-borne victims in the Hungerford massacre. The firing had been conducted using a semi-automatic variant of the Kalashnikov assault rifle using standard ball ammunition of conventional Eastern Bloc manufacture. The 30-round magazines used during the courses of fire resulted in multiple injuries being inflicted in most instances. However, the bullet construction here involved the use of a steel penetrator core, fitted inside a thin copper-coated steel jacket, with only a minimal amount of lead filler used to support the central steel core. As the bullets struck the vehicle bodywork and then went on to pass through seating and internal partitions, the steel jacket broke up and partially disintegrated in the process. The entry wounds on the victims resembled those which might have been produced from the close range discharge of a small gauge shotgun, such as a .410 in. Around the holes produced by the steel penetrator cores, were an irregular pattern of satellite injuries caused by fragmented jacket material. These small pieces of coated steel had produced shallow injuries, as had the bulk of the torn jacket, which by this time had become completely detached from the penetrator core. The hard steel cores had travelled a considerable distance within the body inflicting the lethal injuries. Even when removed from areas of the spine or from joints where some of them had come to rest, they were still in perfect shape. I observed similar effects upon the bodies of casualties repatriated from the 2003 Iraqi conflict, due to the impact of bullets that had been subject to deflection from some prior impact, or which had broken up and tumbled after passing through vehicle bodywork and equipment that had been stored inside them. Some of the missiles involved had been of tracer loading. In one instance, where a tumbled and damaged bullet had inflicted a severe injury to the head of the victim before exiting, analysis of grey combustion residues adhering to a small metal fragment recovered from the wound margin using SEM/EDX, allowed it to be identified as a fragment of a bullet tracer capsule from a specific source. This was important as a bullet core recovered from a wound in a different location could be attributed to fire from the opposing forces.

Bullet exit holes can sometimes be irregular in shape, larger than the entry holes, or of a torn appearance, as the bullet may have deformed or is tumbling during exit. However in many instances, particularly with short slow-moving round-nose handgun bullets, the exit wounds will often be dimensionally similar to the entry wounds. In the absence of blackening or powdering marks it is necessary to differentiate between them by checking for the presence of the abrasion ring. In some instances where powdering effects are only very faint, close examination of the wound margin with a pocket magnifier can provide the necessary information which might otherwise be missed at this stage. In all instances, the examination of the clothing back at the laboratory along with sodium rhodizonate testing will help confirm your findings.

On a number of occasions I have observed apparent missile exit tears on clothing worn by a victim, but with no underlying exit wound. This was caused by missiles that had just failed to overcome the elastic resistance of the skin barrier, but which had momentarily and forcibly poked out a pocket of skin to rip the material before snapping back into position. As explained in Section 7.3, it is usual to find the missiles responsible lying just underneath the skin.

Exit wounds to the head caused by high-velocity rifle bullets or by charges of shot fired from very close ranges, can be almost explosive in nature. Large amounts of the skull and the related tissue can be thrown to considerable distances on the other side, although in many instances the violence of the interaction can cause material to be thrown upwards and even backwards towards the firer. The effects of such an injury will of course have been noted by you at the scene of the shooting.

## 8.8   Arrow and Crossbow Bolt Injuries

Crossbow bolt and arrow injuries are of course self-evident if the missile is still lodged in the body, and the question of entry and exit wounds is also resolved at a glance. However, although these missiles travel at very modest velocities compared with firearm missiles, they do exhibit considerable penetrating properties in human tissue. A broadhead crossbow bolt travelling at a speed of less than 200 ft/s (61 m/s) is capable of piercing a man's chest. In my own experience I have seen a bolt sticking out of the back of a settee upon which the victim had been seated, and in another instance the bolt stabbed a hole in a steel filing cabinet against which the victim had been leaning against after piercing his chest. It is therefore possible for a bolt to pass completely through a less substantial part of the body, or for it to be deliberately removed after the shooting, although I have never experienced such happenings (Figure 4.13 and Figure 4.14).

Sharp blade-like broadhead arrows tend to produce injuries which externally resemble knife stab wounds. Cruciform blade crossbow bolts produce a very characteristic injury which might be confused, in the theorised circumstances mentioned above, with a stellate rip type injury associated with a contact bullet wound. However, powdering or blackening marks will be absent, and these thin smooth contoured slow moving missiles do not produce abrasion ring effects upon the entry wound margin. The metal heads of target arrows or bolts tend to be cone-like in shape ending in a point but with a step or ledge near to the base of the head, resulting in a profile similar to that of a factory .45 ACP mid-range semi-wadcutter bullet. Field archery bolts and arrows, intended for shooting small game or silhouette targets of animals, are blunt ended. Because of their very different shape these latter missiles can leave abrasion ring injuries at the entry site margin which again could be confused with bullet entry wound effects, in the circumstances mentioned. Once again, there will be an absence of powder discharge effects or lead wipe on the clothing, the wound margin or the wound track. I have mentioned these points in an attempt to answer the questions raised by other researchers of arrow and crossbow bolt injuries.

## 8.9   Blank-Operated Tool and Humane Killer Injuries

Captive-bolt guns normally used in abattoirs are sometimes used as murder weapons or in cases of suicide. These guns utilise a blank cartridge to project a steel rod a few inches out of its housing. A shoulder at the base of the rod prevents its being discharged completely away from the gun, and the bolt is usually automatically retracted by a spring, rubber buffer, or gas pressure. On some of these devices the high-pressure gases of discharge are expelled through a vent away from the direct line of fire. There is no direct release of high-pressure gases into the wound track as would be the case with a conventional firearm used in a contact or near-contact shot, although there will often be some leakage or release of discharge materials into the end fitting which will impinge upon the wound margin along with a wipe of dark greasy material from the bolt itself. Cartridges of different power levels are supplied for use with these guns to suit the size of animal to be stunned. The choice of cartridge will therefore change the impact force and the likelihood of finding residues. The rod therefore can be considered to be a short-range reusable missile. The end of the rod is normally circular in shape with a concave or hollowed contact surface. This shape tends to create a wadcutter type injury with an abrasion ring. The extent of the wound track will be limited by the length of the rod, and there will of course be an absence of any missile within it. The muzzle end of the bolt housing is often flat and of a considerably greater diameter. In many instances its edge is formed with ridges, teeth or a pattern of checkering, to prevent the gun slipping on the animals head (Figure 8.22). A characteristic impression of this frontal flange can be left about the wound margin.

Bullet-firing humane killers often have a large hollow bell-like fitting at the muzzle with serrations or a pattern of checkering upon its rim which is again intended to prevent slippage, but in addition allows the free escape of the gases into what is in effect an expansion chamber, thus limiting their intrusion into the wound channel, and at the same time allowing the unimpeded release of the bullet from the muzzle end of the barrel followed by a short period of free flight. Although with this type of gun one will see some discharge blackening, it will be contained within the area of skin encircled by the fitting, which in turn tends to give rise to a distinctive circular pattern of bruising similar to that mentioned above.

Industrial nail or stud guns utilise a rim-fire blank cartridge to fire a nail or fixing stud into timber or masonry. Once again, the cartridges are supplied

**Figure 8.22**    The varied geometry of the muzzle ends of humane killing devices, intended for use in abattoirs, can impart characteristic marks around the wound margins of human victims.

loaded to various power levels to suit a particular task. As there is no real constraint upon the flight in the air of these missiles, it is normal for these tools to be fitted with a safety device which only allows the gun to be fired when it is pressed hard up against a firm surface. With this device in place it is relatively difficult to use the tool as a weapon at a distance, although it is not unknown for this safety feature to be deliberately rendered inoperative or held back with the free hand by the firer. A number of deaths have occurred over the years either by accident or intent with tooling of this nature. The hard-pointed masonry nails or fixing studs do not in any way resemble a firearm missile, and as a result are easily identified. The degree of penetration in a given material will be determined by the power level of the cartridge and by the shape of the head of the nail or the diameter of the washer attached to it.

## 8.10 The Wound Track

In central torso injuries, the pathologist will usually choose to explore these after the removal of the sternum and the opening up of the chest. The wound track can then be confirmed and any firearm-related items present such as shotgun pellets, cartridge wadding, bullets or bullet fragments can be recovered. The pathologist will at this time be principally concerned with the cause of death due to the destruction of organs or blood vessels. However, it is here that the ballistics expert can lock onto other aspects of the injury which might provide important information.

As stated earlier in this book, during a contact or loose-contact shooting much of the powder gases and discharge debris will be forced to travel into the wound itself, leaving unburnt powder, blackening and other discharge effects inside the body. The high-pressure gases will try to escape to the atmosphere, and in most instances they will tear the tissue of the wound margin producing a stellate defect in the process (Figure 8.3). The gases and the sooty debris they carry will suffer lateral deflection off substantial bones, such as the skull or the sternum, the blackened effects of which will be seen as the tissue is pared away from the bone during examination. Sometimes the escaping gases will cause the tissue to bulge outwards in the region of the entry wound, pressing hard against the muzzle end of the barrel of the weapon involved, sometimes leaving a bruise on the skin in the exact form of that part of the weapon used in the firing (Figure 8.23). Lateral gas pump-

**Figure 8.23** Distinctive abrasion mark left on bullet entry site from the effect of a contact shot with the revolver shown. In this instance it would be possible to determine the make of weapon involved solely from the impression left behind.

through effects will often be seen between the layers of clothing covering the wound area, or will be confirmed using the sodium rhodizonate test. In one case of suspected suicide using a .22 in rim-fire pistol, the bullet entry wound to the head did not exhibit visible discharge effects such as powdering, blackening or splitting when I first examined it at the scene of the shooting incident. It was only when the scalp was peeled back from the skull that clear lateral gas pump-through blackening was evident upon a wide area of the outer surface of the skull surrounding the bullet entry hole. In this instance the muzzle of the pistol must have been pressed hard and square on against the head so as to produce a gas-tight seal.

After the initial entry of a charge of shot discharged from a close range, the pellets separate to form a divergent track of damage within the body, as will have been shown on the initial X-rays (Figure 7.10). Many individual pellets will be left a short distance within the body, particularly those pellets at the disrupted edges of the compact entry mass previously described. It is here that one can expect also to find the cartridge wadding, although in some instances it will be recovered later within the blood lying inside the body cavity. The wad may well have broken up during its passage. This will most often be true with plastic-cup wads as their leaves peel back and can sometimes become detached (Figure 8.19 and Figure 8.20). The hardest, heaviest and most substantial parts of the wadding will usually travel the furthest, and in some instances may come to rest almost as far as those pellets most distant from the entry site. As previously stated, one would not normally expect exit injuries upon a direct torso shot upon an adult body in a shooting involving the discharge of conventional birdshot such as that used in clay pigeon or game shooting; exit injuries on torso strikes may well be produced if the larger sizes of buckshot pellets are involved. Close range or contact raking shotgun injuries involving small birdshot loadings may on occasions generate entry and exit wound sites, if there is a relatively short communicating wound track through soft unsupported tissue, such as at the side of the abdomen (Figure 8.21).

All items of wadding should be recovered if possible and washed clean of blood before being placed in the exhibit bag, which in turn should be suitably labelled. The firearms examiner will of course do this to examine the exhibit at the same time. It is at this stage when sample pellets and the cartridge wadding is being recovered that he can advise the senior investigative officer as to the gauge of shotgun involved and the make and likely brand of ammunition involved. The condition of the base of a plastic-cup wad may also indicate if a sawn-off gun is involved. The normally hollow base section may be completely or partially everted due to the unusually high gas pressure and the pocket magnifier may also reveal damage to the sides of the wad which might be caused by its passage through the roughly sawn muzzle end of the shortened barrel (Figure 9.42).

Things are less involved with single missile injuries, although even here the bullet may break up upon striking bone, or break up in the manner previously mentioned due to its striking an intermediate target or to its being of some composite construction. In some instances a jacketed soft-point bullet can shed its jacket inside the body, leaving the two components at two different depths in the wound. This sort of thing will be detected if the firearms expert is present, and in turn he will advise the pathologist; in such situations the initial X-rays may well have prepared you for such an eventuality. Without the firearms expert on hand, a pathologist might easily believe that the recovery of the core alone constitutes the recovery of the fatal missile. The bullet jacket on this type of ammunition is the only part of the bullet which will bear the critical rifling impressions. The firearms expert will wash the bullet and examine it using a pocket magnifier or lens. This examination will allow him to advise the senior investigative officer as to the calibre, type and also perhaps the likely make of gun involved, although it will always be necessary to confirm all of these points once back in the laboratory where the exhibits can be examined more thoroughly. Such initial information can however be crucial at this stage of the investigation, both back at the scene of the incident where scene of crime officers will still be working, or to be passed on to officers conducting searches elsewhere, perhaps even at the homes of suspects.

The resistance of human skin to the passage of a bullet has been mentioned previously. To a degree this resistance will also be experienced by the missile as it attempts to exit from the body. After a pistol bullet has penetrated the bulk of a human torso it will have lost a great deal of its original velocity. In many instances of course, the bullet may still remain somewhere inside the body. However, it is not unusual to find such missiles lying just under the skin on the far side of the wound track, often revealing their presence as a bulge under the skin (Figure 7.1 and Figure 7.2). In these instances the velocity of the bullet has been reduced to a level just below the critical threshold value for skin penetration. The barrier effect to missile penetration of the skin at the unsupported exit site is even higher than that at the potential exit point due to the absence of the shoring effect of the body. On failed exits, the elastic nature of the skin can allow a momentary and forceful projection of a pocket of skin containing the bullet, that can rip light clothing at this point. In other instances where the bullet has possessed just enough velocity to perforate the skin and thus make an exit, one will often find them inside the layers of clothing in this region, sometimes associated with minor fabric damage. Bullets possessing a fractionally higher velocity on exit, will be found lying on the ground close to the body.

The recovered bullet, bullet fragment or item of wadding should be washed immediately to remove blood and tissue adhering to it. After drying it with tissue it can be examined immediately in the mortuary using your pocket magnifier. I use a good quality two-lens loupe carried at all times in my trouser pocket. This useful instrument provides a choice of ×3, ×5 or ×15 magnifications. Cleaning the exhibit at this stage is relatively easy and avoids the problems that can be encountered back at the laboratory in removing dried on blood and adhering tissue. The exhibit can then be wrapped up in tissue to protect it before being put in a plastic pot and then inside a signed and labelled exhibit bag. I have seen many lead bullets over the years which have been dropped straight into a glass jar or vial without any padding. In the case of plain lead bullets this is one of the most effective ways for obliterating the bore markings which have been imparted by the murder weapon, as the bullet rolls around inside the glass container to be polished like some object inside a gem-stone burnishing barrel. Cotton wool wrapping, so popular with many officers, is also a bad choice of material compared with paper tissue, as strands of it tend to get caught up with the torn edges of bullet jackets. Police officers should also be advised against emulating Clint Eastwood in some previously viewed *Dirty Harry* film, in unduly handling recovered bullets, or leaving the scene or the mortuary after having dropped it into their pocket along with the car keys and loose change.

I recall an incident I dealt with some years ago where the initial missile examination proved most useful. After washing the bullet recovered from the head of the deceased, I identified it as being from an obsolete British Service .380 in revolver loading. In addition I tentatively identified it as having been of a type imported from CIL of Canada during World War II. The pattern of rifling was appropriate for it having been discharged from a Smith and Wesson revolver. When I later visited the extensive house set in the grounds where the shooting had taken place, I was told that the murder appeared to have been associated with an armed robbery. A safe had been opened and valuables were missing. The grieving millionaire husband was giving the police descriptions of men he had seen driving a car in the grounds that day. During the search of the main house I was shown two loaded pistols which had been found, which did not appear on the husband's firearms certificate. Although I was able very briefly to eliminate their use in the shooting I was told to assist the officers searching the gun room so that I could make-safe any other loaded firearms. A large gun cabinet held all manner of shotgun and .22 in rim-fire ammunition boxes. I checked these also, and eventually found a .22 in ammunition box which held six rounds of .380 in Service revolver ammunition bearing headstamps indicating their manufacture by CIL of Canada in 1943. I briefly left the room to check the actual murder scene telling the scene of crime officers to find me a Smith and Wesson revolver. A radio call a short time afterwards caused me to return to the gun room, which by then had been searched rather more thoroughly than might otherwise have taken place. The police officers, grinning like Cheshire cats at this stage, had found a further safe underneath the floorboards. On top of the safe was a Smith and Wesson revolver loaded with five live rounds of the same Canadian ammunition and one spent cartridge case of the same type. A few hours later that same night back at the laboratory after test-firing the revolver and carrying out a microscopic comparison of the tests against the murder bullet, I was able to telephone the Police Incident Room with the confirmation that we had the murder weapon. The weapon had of course been hidden in a secure area known only to the house owner, the still, at this stage, heartbroken husband tearfully grieving the loss of his dear wife.

Having noted the locations and the nature of all the firearm related injuries, determined which are entry wounds and which are exits, the pathologist will best advise upon the courses of the individual wound tracks. Many pathologists will make use of long thin probes which will simplify the visual interpretation of the postmortem photographs taken by the police photographer. All experienced pathologists will take due care during these processes to ensure that such reconstructions reflect the reality of the situation, and will usually carry out these activities only after the full examination of the wound track has been accomplished and all missiles of note have been recovered. The determination of the lines of fire supplemented by the range determinations provided after experimentation back at the laboratory will in every instance be of great importance during the subsequent court hearing. The matching up of the recovered bullet with any weapon recovered during the investigation will form the main thrust of the Prosecution case. Even in those instances where the murder weapon is not recovered during the initial stages of the investigation, the information which identifies the likely type of gun used, along with the gauge or calibre and the brand of ammunition used, will all help during the ongoing investigation. Comparison of the recovered bullets, cartridge cases and in some instances, the wadding, will help determine if the weapon responsible has been used in some previous offence held on file back at the laboratory. These recovered exhibits will then be held in the laboratory Outstanding Crimes File for comparison against exhibits received in future submissions.

As previously stated, the recovery of bullets, pellets or wadding is not always a straightforward affair, and it is in these situations that the use of the X-ray facilities really proves their worth. Every pathologist will at some stage in his career suffer the near-panic of wondering if he ever will recover a particularly elusive missile. This is particularly true if the body is decomposed or badly burnt. When examining the bodies of 18 Branch Davidian victims from the siege at Mount Carmel, Waco, Texas, who had been returned for burial in the UK, I recall the constant value of the total body area X-ray plates taken during the initial stages of the examinations. One of my tasks was to view the plates before the two pathologists in the team started their work on each of the bodies. The X-ray plates for some of the victims revealed the presence of staggering quantities of radio-opaque objects within them, most of which were associated with an enormous amount of heat-exploded ammunition present where they had died (Figure 8.24 through Figure 8.26). The plates allowed me accurately to identify the ammunition-related components present where the cases had ruptured when the cartridges had exploded, and also allowed me to determine for the pathologists the locations of missiles of greater significance, such as fired bullets or grenade fragments. Due to the state of some of the bodies, it was not always easy for us to find the items in question even when we knew their approximate location, and in some instances it was necessary for selected parts of the remains to be re-X-rayed before we tracked down all of the objects of interest.

In a drug-related murder case I dealt with some years ago, the victim had escaped from the back door of the house and had then exited the rear garden via a wire mesh gate into the garden next door. During his attempted escape from this garden to the parking area outside, two shots were fired at him from a sawn-off 12-bore pump-action shotgun. The body was recovered in the parking area of the roadway some distance away. It was there that I noted the bright pink content of the blood trail so characteristic of a lung injury. The shots had been fired from the garden area of the first house when the firer was positioned close to the closed heavy wire mesh security gate. The 3 mm wire of the mesh was set in a square pattern at 50 mm intervals. The muzzle end of the gun had been positioned within a few inches of the gate and as a result the compact masses of both shot charges had torn a strip of wire out of the gate as they passed through the mesh. The two charges of shot had spread by the time they struck the victim inflicting normal near-circular patterns of pellet injuries to the top of the left shoulder and to the edge of the right side of the back. When I arrived at the mortuary I was informed that initial examination had also revealed razor slashes to the forearms and the face inflicted during the early stages of the incident, two shotgun injuries, and a long stab wound to the centre of the back. It was clear even at this stage that the two shotgun injuries and the razor slashes should not have been responsible for the man's death. The X-ray plates, taken after some negotiation with the hospital staff, revealed what appeared to be two nail-like objects inside the chest cavity. Initially, I thought that some of the pellets in one of the cartridges had been replaced by nails, as I have seen shotgun cartridges adapted in all manner of ways in the past. However, the recovery of the objects from the lung revealed them to be one of the missing strands of heavy wire from the garden gate, which in turn had been broken into two pieces. When one of the compact masses of pellets had struck this section of the gate, it had torn a strand of wire loose and at the same time

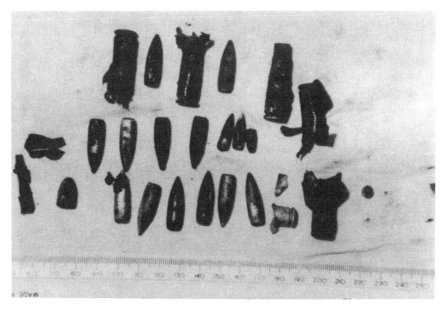

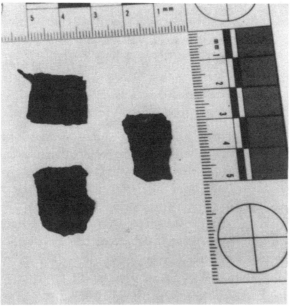

**Figure 8.24 and Figure 8.25**   Some of the fire-exploded cartridge components recovered during the examination of the remains of Waco siege Branch Davidian Cult UK citizens returned to this country for burial. The examination of the many bodies received involved complete X-ray examination for objects of interest before attempting their recovery. Ruptured cartridge cases, bullets and primers from 7.62×39 mm, 7.62×51 mm, 5.56×45 mm, 9 mm and .22 in rim-fire generated items, along with exploded grenade fragments are shown in these photographs.

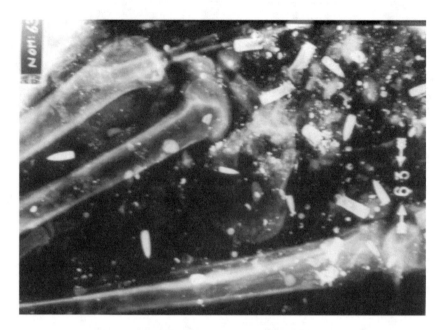

**Figure 8.26**    X-ray typical of a number of the Waco siege victims examined by the author on their repatriation to England. Victim was found lying where approximately three million rounds of mixed calibre ammunition had been stored in church compound of Davidian Cult. The heat of the fire had caused the ammunition to explode, resulting in bullets, ruptured cartridge cases and primers becoming fused into the body remains.

had accelerated it to a velocity comparable to that of the shot charge. When the pellets separated during their flight towards the victim, the wind forces acting upon this unusually shaped and unstable secondary missile, had caused it to deviate in flight from the main charge so as to strike the centre of the back, thus inflicting the fatal injury.

In a recent murder scene investigation I arrived at the mortuary to find that the examination was underway. The deceased had been shot twice with round-nose cast lead hand-reloaded .45 in bullets discharged from a Colt pattern service pistol. I noted a bullet entry hole at the side of his neck, which the pathologist informed me was associated with a downward wound track crossing the body to terminate just below waist level. There was another entry wound at this same location at the side of the back. The pathologist informed me that he had recovered one bullet inside the body cavity associated with the first injury, and a second bullet which had been poking out of the second entry hole on the surface of the skin. I noted two parallel lines of bruising across the small of the back, which had initially been considered to be from a fall against the edge of a table in the bar where the shooting had taken place. However, I pointed out that the abrasion mark associated with the entry wound was elongated consistent with the second bullet having struck the back of the victim at a shallow angle from the left side to travel directly across the waistline of the back. Investigating this area further by opening up the tissue between the two lines of bruising, it was apparent that the bullet had tracked from one side of the back to the other, without striking the spine, in the shallow layer of fatty tissue. The only sensible explanation I could provide was that the movement of the body by the paramedics during initial attempts at resuscitation, followed by the effects produced during the movement of the body from the scene to the mortuary, had created a kneading effect upon the flesh at the back which had pushed the short, smooth, round-nose bullet back along its original wound track (Figure 8.27).

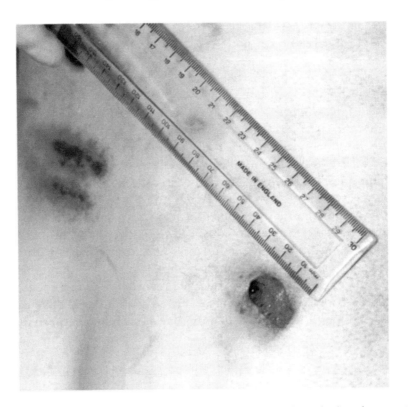

**Figure 8.27**    The apparent 'rebounding bullet injury' described in the text. The abrasion mark on one edge of the .45 in bullet entry wound at the bottom has allowed the cast lead round nose bullet to pass across the back under the fatty layers. The forces generated by the paramedics and other people involved in the attempted resuscitation and the transportation of the body to the mortuary has kneaded the bullet back along the wound track to the entry site where it was recovered. The parallel lines of bruising across the back of the victim give away what actually took place.

Slow-moving revolver bullets can travel great distances inside a body if they manage to miss major bones. The heavy old British .450 in and .455 in bullets are notable in this respect. I remember some years ago carrying out an initial examination of a police officer who had been shot during a bank robbery with just such a loading. This was done in the mortuary prior to the arrival of the pathologist who had to come up from London. The entry wound was in the top of the shoulder, so I asked the Radiography staff to X-ray the chest region. Since no bullet was in sight on this plate and as the bullet had not exited, I asked for additional plates to cover the abdominal region, but again these did not reveal the presence of the elusive missile. A subsequent plate, taken almost in desperation revealed the bullet lying alongside the top of the femur. Fastmoving, lightweight, soft-point magnum revolver loadings, tend to expand and interact with the tissue to a much greater degree, resulting in markedly lesser degrees of penetration than that exhibited by large calibre 265 grain (17.2 g) round-nose bullets travelling at 600 ft/s (180 m/s), or less.

Embolisation of shotgun pellets, air rifle pellets, or of .22 in rim-fire bullets is not unknown, resulting in missiles ending up in locations distant from the original injury. Small-calibre bullet entry wounds can remain unseen in some instances. I recall one post-mortem examination a colleague of mine assisted with, which turned out to be one of a series of post-office murders carried out by a man called Neilson (referred to in the press as the Black Panther). The office manager had been coming down a flight of stairs when he was shot in the arm by a charge of birdshot fired from a sawn-off shotgun. The post-mortem examination took place some years ago when there was still a reluctance to use X-ray facilities, especially as the pathologist in question deemed them to be an unnecessary extravagance. At the end of the main examination and the tentative conclusion that the shot to the arm had been the cause of death, my colleague reported finding a spent .22 in Long Rifle cartridge case at the scene of the incident. It was at this stage that the mortuary attendant mentioned his finding a tiny injury between the cleft of the buttocks of the deceased which was situated near to the anus. A bullet track leading from the tiny entry wound was then explored, but no missile was discovered. Various internal organs which at this stage had been removed, were then placed in a plastic bag and sent for X-ray, resulting in the eventual recovery of a .22 in rim-fire bullet. The killer went on to commit a number of other murders with the .22 in High Standard self-loading pistol he had stolen during the commission of a house burglary.

On a number of occasions my colleagues and I have encountered unusual wounds caused by deflected bullets. One man, who had committed suicide by firing a pistol with the muzzle end of the barrel in his mouth, also exhibited an entry wound to his right temple and an exit wound to the left temple.

Such a finding led the investigative team to think this to be an act of murder, until examination of the interior of the head failed to reveal a through wound track from this firing. The bullet had in fact deflected off the skull, so as to travel in a semi-circular route around the head between the scalp and the skull, before exiting on the other side. The dazed would-be suicide victim then fired a second shot when the muzzle end of the barrel was placed inside his mouth. A similar unusual deflection injury occurred in a case I dealt with which involved a drug-related murder of a young man and the attempted murder of his friend. Examination of the clothing of the injured person revealed an entry hole near to the middle of the back consistent with that which would have been produced by the direct impact of a .38 in Special wadcutter bullet. This missile was recovered just under the skin on the front of the chest next to his right nipple, after it had travelled around the outside of the rib-cage to this point after first deflecting off a rib.

The specialised knowledge of the firearms expert, when at hand to the police senior investigative officer (SIO) during the initial stages of a murder investigation, can help prevent the investigation going badly off-course. Human nature dictates that during these initial stages the SIO will be desperate for any possible lead, and there is sometimes a tendency for some well-meaning person to offer misleading advice to him. In one high profile case I recall, a youth was killed by a close-range discharge to the head from a shotgun fired by a burglar. I did not attend the scene of the incident or examine the body until after the post mortem examination had been completed. The pathologist had recovered a 12-bore fibre cartridge wad from the head of the deceased along with a representative sample of pellets. He eagerly informed the SIO that wads of this type had not been used by cartridge manufacturers for a great many years, and that possession of similar ammunition by a suspect would be a most significant lead. After being informed of this 'valuable finding' by the SIO, I was faced with the unpleasant task of telling him that it was a 'Kleena' fibre compression wad of the type currently used by the Eley Cartridge Company nearby in Birmingham in the loading of tens of millions of their most popular gauge and brand of cartridges sold in the UK each year, using the most common game shooting pellet size. It was clear that he had already made his senior officers aware of the 'breakthrough' and as a result he was reluctant to lose this treasured gem of earlier information. Two of his officers were immediately sent to the Eley factory, where to his considerable dismay I was proved to be right.

## 8.11 Examination of PM Exhibits Back at the Laboratory

The clothing recovered from the victim should always be checked at the laboratory for damage and discharge effects. This is best accomplished using a surgical microscope with a built-in light source to look for traces of propellant or other effects.

Where the relevant area of clothing is relatively blood-free, additional examination using a television monitor and camera set up to view the area with an infrared-rich light source can also be useful in some instances. However, the simple sodium rhodizonate test conducted on both sides of the fabric of the garment in areas corresponding to each of the wound sites will allow confirmation of the direction of fire, and can help confirm the presence of the gas pump-through effects previously mentioned which can occur with contact or loose-contact shots.

In some instances where you have not attended the post-mortem examination, it is here that you will have to work hard to unravel the effects caused in the shooting incident. Colour photographs taken by scene of crime officers both at the scene and during the autopsy will prove useful, as will copies of the X-ray plates, any video-recorded overview and the pathologist's report. You are then able to relate the damage and other effects upon the clothing to the reported injury sites on the body. As previously stated, low-power microscopy and the sodium rhodizonate test will usually allow you to interpret range and line of fire correctly. Examination of the wound samples submitted will be particularly important in instances where the wound site was not covered by clothing. Unburnt propellant particles associated with close range firings can be recovered from the weave of the material or from any punctuate injuries to the skin of the wound sample, or from within the wound track. The size, morphology and chemical composition of these particles can be of great significance. In shooting incidents which are still under investigation and where cartridge cases have not been found at the scene, it may be appropriate for the victim's clothing to be sampled for discharge residues to allow analysis to be made for both propellant and primer residues; after this has been done away from the potentially contaminating influences of the firearms laboratory, the clothing can then be transferred to the firearms laboratory so as to allow the remaining work to be concluded.

All of the findings relating to the examinations of these exhibits should be rechecked against the pathologist's report. At this early stage it is appropriate to contact the pathologist if any inconsistencies are spotted, particularly those relating to incorrect attribution of entry and exit wounds. Such matters can be discussed between the two experts, and if necessary the pathologist can recheck the body or the excised wound samples. It is normal for the murder weapon to be test-fired using ammunition similar to that used in the offence. The close-range firearms discharge effects, shot spread, or the effects produced by shotgun cartridge wadding, can then be used to determine the likely range or ranges of firing. Your own notes made during the post-mortem examination, or your examination of the damage to the clothing considered in conjunction with the pathologist's report, wound samples, scene photographs and scene plan, will then allow you to compile the necessary information for this section of your statement.

## Further Reading

Broome, G., Butler-Manuel, A., Budd, J., Carter, P.G. and Warlow, T.A. 1988. The Hungerford shooting incident, *Injury*, **19**, 313–317.

Crafton, J.W. 2004. Bunter toolmarks, insignificant or significant? *AFTE Journal*, **36** (1) 39–46.

Di Maio, Vincent J.M. 1985. *Gunshot Wounds. Practical Aspects of Firearms, Ballistics and Forensic Techniques*, New York: Elsevier.

Downs, J.C., Nichols, C.A., Scala-Barnett, D.S. and Lifschultze, B.D. 1994. Handling and interpretation of crossbow injuries, *Journal of Forensic Sciences*, **39** (2), 428–445.

Eckert, W.G. and James, S.H. 1989. *Interpretation of Bloodstain Evidence at Crime Scenes*, New York: Elsevier.

Haag, L.C. 2004. Sequence of shots through tempered glass, *AFTE Journal*, **36** (1) 54–59.

Hain, J.R. 1989. Fatal arrow wounds, *Journal of Forensic Sciences*, **34** (3), 691–693.

Hunt, A.C. and Kon, V.M. 1962. The patterns of injury from humane killers, *Medical Science. Law*, **2** (3), 197–214.

MacDonnell, H.L. and Bialousz, L.F. 1973. *Laboratory Manual on the Geometric Interpretation of Human Bloodstain Evidence*, New York: Painted Post Press.

MacDonnell, H.L. and Brooks, B. 1977. Detection and significance of blood in firearms, *Legal Medicine Annual*, New York: Appleton-Century-Crofts.

Miller, J. and Neel, M. 2004. Criteria for identification of toolmarks. Part III: Supporting the conclusion. *AFTE Journal*, **36** (1), 7–38.

Nichols, R.G. 2004. Firearm and tool mark identification: the scientific reliability of the AFTE theory of identification discussed within the framework of a study of ten consecutively manufactured extractors. *AFTE Journal*, **36** (1), 67–88.

Sellier, K.G. and Kneubuehl, B.P. 1994. *Wound Ballistics and the Scientific Back-Ground*, Amsterdam: Elsevier.

Warlow, T.A. 1998. Ballistics examination of British citizens from Waco siege. *Science & Justice*, **38** (4) 255–259.

Williams, J. (Warlow, T.A.) 1991. *The Modern Sherlock Holmes*, London: BBC World Services, Broadside.

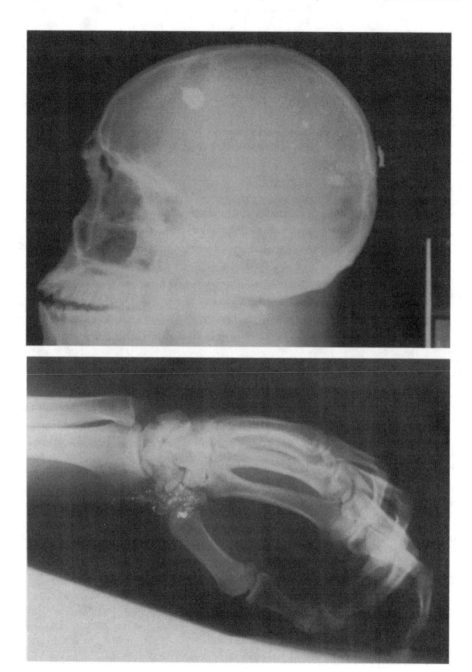

**Figure 8.28 and Figure 8.29**    This .38 in soft-lead round nose bullet has had parts of it shaved off during its penetration of the back of the skull of the victim limiting the bore features left upon it which would normally be used for comparison microscopy. Small lead fragments left by a second bullet inside the wound track in the hand indicate the use of a similar loading.

**Figure 8.30**   Scene reconstruction firing tests to bar wall of public house during the court recess described in Section 10.1. Defence expert holding 'over-limit' .22 in air rifle on the left and the author holding sound-moderated .22 in rim-fire rifle on the right, next to the damage to the bar wall produced during the firing tests.

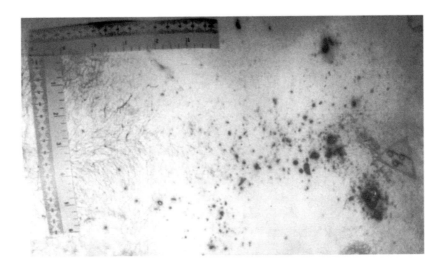

**Figure 8.31**   Multiple shallow punctuate injuries to chest of man shot by the police using 5.56 mm rifle and soft-point expanding bullet loading. The victim had raised his arm in front of his chest at the moment when the shot was fired. During its passage through the arm the relatively frangible high velocity bullet broke up prematurely into tiny fragments to inflict these clearly survivable punctuate injuries.

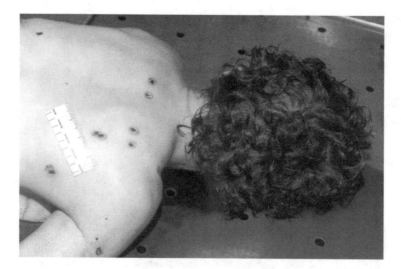

**Figure 8.32**    Multiple 9 mm pistol bullet entry holes in back of woman out on a picnic with her two young children in the Savernake Forest, approximately 7 miles west of Hungerford. The perpetrator of this offence then proceeded to the town of Hungerford, where he went on to commit the final massacre using the same Beretta 15-shot pistol and a Chinese self-loading variant of the Kalashnikov assault rifle. The use of these legally held high firepower weapons in these tragic offences caused the introduction of the Firearms (Amendment) Act 1988. The author attended the scene soon after the offences had been committed, and was able to examine the bodies of both the victims of the massacre and the perpetrator *in situ*.

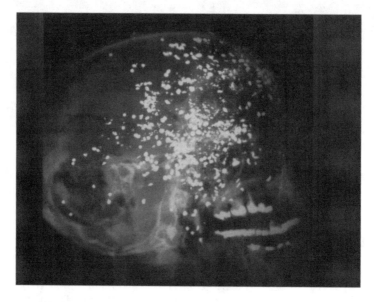

**Figure 8.33**    12-Bore charge of birdshot embedded in scalp tissue and inside head of deceased. Some of the pellets have broken into fragments during their impact with the skull.

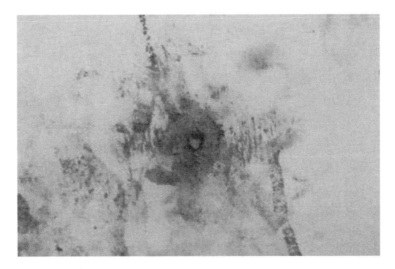

**Figure 8.34**   Shored entry wound from near-contact shot from 5.56 mm rifle. The bullet pierced an object held inside the clothing before it entered the chest. The outer clothing was blackened ripped and blackened on its inside by the discharge gases, but the skin in the wound margin was screened from such effects. The skin in the wound margin has slapped back violently against the object to produce the effects shown above.

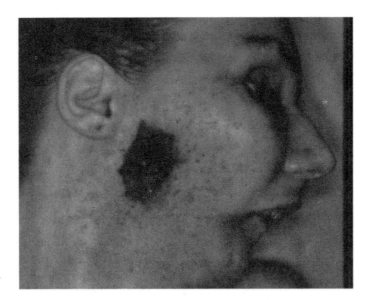

**Figure 8.35**   Close range injury from shotgun depicting open wad leaf injury and extensive punctuate injuries caused by powder tattooing about wound margin.

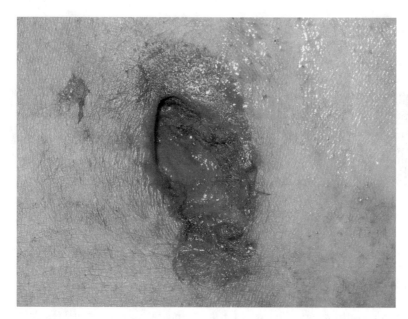

**Figure 8.36**    The back of a 2004 Gulf War victim of insurgents. The 7.62 × 39 mm lead core bullet has perforated his body armour to produce this 'shored entry' wound. Fragments of the bullet made it into his chest cavity.

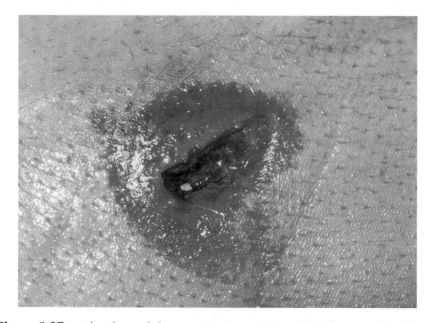

**Figure 8.37**    The chest of the same victim as Figure 8.36 shows a 'shored exit' wound produced by a second 7.62 × 39 mm bullet that entered so as to just miss the rear body armour panel, perforated the chest cavity, tumbling in the process, and exited from the front of the chest against the frontal body armour panel.

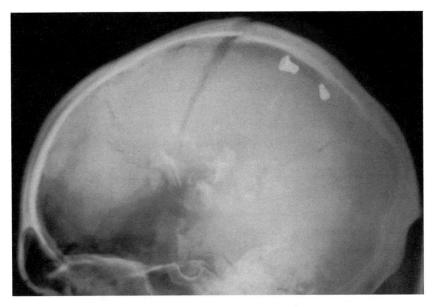

**Figure 8.38**    5.56 mm SS109 type bullet fragments inside the head of a soldier involved in a Gulf War range accident. The bullet first passed through the soldier's hand before entering the head, breaking up into fragments in the process. The steel penetrator core is present with other fragments inside the brain.

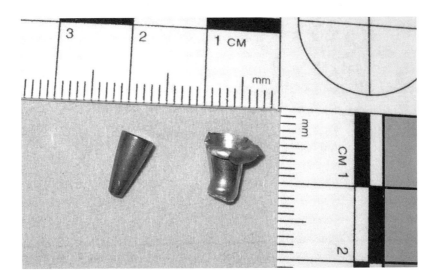

**Figure 8.39**    A fragment of copper jacket and the frontal steel penetrator core recovered during autopsy of the same victim as Figure 8.38.

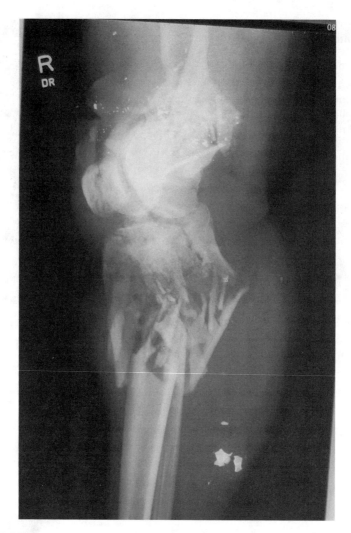

**Figure 8.40**    Massive damage to bones of leg of same victim as Figure 8.38 from several 7.62 ×39 mm lead core bullets, some of which have fragmented.

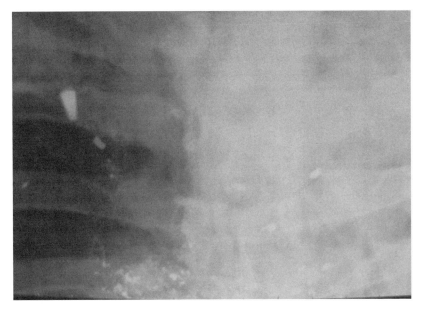

**Figure 8.41** X-ray image of the chest of a soldier killed by a 5.56 mm SS109 type bullet loading. This was a 2003 Gulf War incident involving a shot fired directly at an exposed area of the chest from close range. The missile has fragmented inside the chest cavity rather than perforating it. The characteristic shape of the steel penetrator core is evident alongside jacket and lead core fragments.

**Figure 8.42** A 7.62 × 51 mm tracer bullet recovered during autopsy of Gulf War victim from Figure 8.38 matched to test-fired bullet from tank chain gun.

# Examination of Exhibits at the Laboratory

# 9

A policy decision will in most instances be already in place regarding which scientist or department will be involved in the various aspects of the casework. This will result in the correct exhibits being transmitted to the appropriate parties. A decision was made some years ago within the Forensic Science Service for discharge residue work to be done in specialized departments of the London and Birmingham laboratories not involved with routine firearms casework. This was done both to ensure the department did sufficient work so as to allow it to gain the necessary level of expertise, and also to reduce the possibility of contamination taking place. The London laboratory uses adhesive stubs for collecting possible residues from suspects and their clothing, chiefly to search for primer-generated residues, while the Birmingham laboratory uses swabs for both organic propellant residues and inorganic primer residues. Hand and face swabs or adhesive stubs are therefore sent to this unit along with control samples of discharge material from inside any spent cartridge cases recovered and clothing or vacuum samples taken from the clothing of persons suspected of involvement in the shooting incident. The police scene of crime officers are in turn supplied with swabbing kits and a comprehensive advice leaflet on their use. In the same way blood samples from the body and the scene can be sent to the biologists at the local regional laboratory in the area in which the shooting has taken place. Before firearms and ammunition are forwarded to the central unit involved in this work all fingerprinting work must be completed as it is unrealistic for the scientist to examine a weapon properly if fingerprinting is to be requested afterwards. Fingerprinting work is done either by the police or by a special dedicated forensic team situated in a central location who are equipped with all the latest equipment. It is important to bear in mind however, that current fingerprinting techniques may require the immersion of the weapon in hot dye baths, and in some instances there may be a requirement to strip the weapon to check for fingerprints on internal component parts. Such treatments can change the mechanical state of the firearm or even cause the loss of other potential findings. Again a decision must be arrived by way of consensus to determine the order in which certain tests are done, so as to ensure the needs of all parties are met.

The forensic applications and sensitivity of deoxyribonucleic acid (DNA) analysis have advanced greatly over recent years. This is a constantly changing field of expertise where it seems that the impossible will be routine in six months time. The Forensic Science Service (FSS), with whom I was employed before my retirement, is an executive agency of the British Home Office. They currently hold, maintain and update the National DNA Database (NDNAD) consisting of over two million entries, using the Short Tandem Repeat (STR) loci to compare and update DNA samples from convicted criminals and criminal casework. They now offer the Second Generation Multiplex (SGM) capability which looks at seven areas (six plus a sex indicator area) to give a DNA profile with an average discrimination potential of one in fifty million, and at the date of writing this section, the SGMplus technique for profiling DNA samples on the NDNAD, which looks at eleven areas (ten plus a sex indicator area), that allows an average discriminatory power of one in a thousand million.

In addition, they have recently developed the most current sophisticated DNA profiling service to date, the Low Copy Number (DNA LCN). This technique allows DNA profiles to be obtained from samples containing very few cells, even if too small to be seen by the naked eye. This technique can be applied to target areas on items that may have been touched by an offender, so as to leave behind the residue from cells such as skin or sweat left in a fingerprint. Although this new technique is at present time consuming, it can be applied to both current and old cases of a serious nature that justify this additional effort, or those where other DNA techniques have failed. It is an extension of the FSS SGMplus profiling technique and is compatible with the NDNAD, copying ten informative DNA sites. It is much more sensitive than FSS SGMplus because a greater number of copies are generated from a smaller amount of starting material. Its average discriminating power is claimed to be one in one billion.

The dangers of contamination should be understood both by the police and the forensic scientist during the examination of the crime scene, the packaging and transportation of exhibits, and the bench-work where examinations will subsequently take place at the laboratory. The officer in charge of the case should impose priorities on how the scientific investigation should proceed. The scientist dealing with the firearms aspects of an investigation, either at the scene of the incident or back at the laboratory should bear all of these factors in mind to avoid the risk of contamination. In the same way, similar precautions should be maintained in preserving the value of finger-prints and gunshot residue swabs or clothing exhibits.

## 9.1   Initial Examination of Firearms

Before any firearm is placed in store after receipt or examined at the work-bench it must be routinely checked to ensure that it is not loaded by members of the firearms team or by properly trained staff. The most secure way of maintaining compliance with such a policy is to have the scientist initial and date a label attached to the weapon each time. Cartridges should not be chambered to check their fit, or worked through the action of a self-loading arm in any place other than the firing range. At all times safe working practices must be maintained, and weapons should be double checked for safety, preferably by another person, after range firing has taken place. A second person should always be on hand to assist in the event of an accident. This second person must always be positioned to the rear of the firer when-ever the weapon is loaded or fired. Failure to comply with these simple guidelines will eventually result in an incident.

During the initial part of the examination of the firearm it is important that materials of potential evidential value can be identified and appropriate action taken. For example, there may be an allegation that the barrel of the gun was used to break a window during the initial stages of the incident, or that the gun was used at some stage as a club to strike one of the victims. Evidence to support such effects can be discovered during the initial stages of the examination of the firearm under the stereo microscope. Glass frag-ments can be removed from the recesses of the barrel rib or other part of the weapon, and then submitted to the section of the laboratory specialising in the examination of glass. The refractive index of the glass fragments can then be determined along with its composition, using the electron microscope with microprobe analytical facility, and compared with control samples from the scene of the incident. In a similar way, bloodstains can be sampled for blood grouping or DNA analysis before other tests are carried out upon the weapon. Likewise, fibres can be recovered and sent for comparison along with control samples or tapings. In the case of a suspected suicide, or where there is an allegation that the barrel of the gun has been pushed into a person's mouth when threats have been made, then the muzzle end of the gun barrel should also be checked by the biologist. It is for these reasons that it is good policy for the scene of crime officers submitting the firearm in such instances for the last two inches of the barrel be protected by a plastic bag taped into place to protect it during fingerprinting treatments or during transfer. The weapon is then received in a fit condition for initial examination by the biologist who will carry out initial tests to determine the presence of saliva, followed by further tests to determine the presence of buccal cells. Any dark stains upon the firearm resembling bloodstaining should initially be checked using one of the presumptive tests for blood as a screening system. The Kassel Mayer test is frequently used for these purposes. This test involves a simple chemical reaction in which the haem part of the haemoglobin acts as a powerful oxidising agent. The three-part test kit consists of the following reagents:

1.  Absolute alcohol
2.  KM solution, made by boiling under reflux 100 ml solution contain-ing 2 g phenolphthalein, 20 g potassium hydroxide, and 10–30 g ground zinc metal, until colourless
3.  20 volume hydrogen peroxide

Gently rub the suspect stain with the folded corner of a small filter paper. Add one drop of alcohol to enhance sensitivity, followed by 1 to 2 drops of KM reagent. If no colour is produced at this stage, add several drops of peroxide. An immediate pink coloration indicates a positive reaction for blood. After this presumptive test additional tests are conducted to confirm that the stain is human blood, followed perhaps by blood grouping or DNA tests if these are considered to be necessary in the biology section.

The positioning of barrel selector switches, manual safety catches, and variable choke settings should be recorded, along with details of the make and model of the weapon and its serial number (if present). The next stage is that of removing any discharge residues left behind inside the bore. The recovery of these materials may well have been made at a previous stage prior to the fingerprinting work. A cleaning patch passed through the bore will allow these materials to be recovered. Although this will not allow you to determine exactly when the firearm was last fired, it will at least allow some proof of previous firing, and the residues may well contain unconsumed powder grains which can be compared with the propellant found in any ammunition recovered from a suspect person. Similarly, the presence of rust, dust, or dirty oil in the bore should also be noted, if present. The patch is then placed in a plastic envelope in the retained materials file along with glass fragments or other recovered materials of interest. A filter paper pressing of the muzzle end of the gun barrel subjected to the sodium rhodizonate test for lead, may well indicate if a sawn-off barrel of a shotgun has been fired since it was shortened. Conversely, the recovery of bright ferrous metal swarf (checked with a magnet) from the bore and the breech face will indicate that the shotgun has not been fired since its barrels were shortened. The absence or the presence and the nature of any corrosion present upon the cut face of a shortened barrel should also be recorded in your examination notes to provide some indication as to whether the barrel shortening is old or of relatively recent origin. The pitch of the blade used to shorten the barrel should also be recorded after measuring the saw marks under a stereo microscope set at a low magnification, and the presence of any transferred paint from the sawblade noted both on the muzzle and also upon the cut face of the stock, if similarly shortened.

Before any mechanical tests are carried out, it is important that test-firings should be obtained if there is a perceived need for subsequent comparison microscopy, as it is always possible for the gun to develop a serious fault or for the firing pin to fracture. It is usual for a primed cartridge case to be fired initially followed by at least three normal cartridges in these tests. Different types of primers can take up breech face marks to different degrees, thus reflecting both differences in breech pressures as well as differences in the deformability of the particular primer material. It may well be that the critical area exhibiting matchable breech face marks on the edge of the cartridge primer will only be reproduced on occasions, or by just one type of cartridge loading. Military primers in particular, are usually harder and more rigid in construction and hence less sensitive to light strikes or other effects than those used in most commercial loadings. It is important to bear in mind that different brands or batches of commercial ammunition can be assembled using primers of greatly different sensitivities. This can have a profound influence when testing home-made guns, converted blank firers, weapons which have been subjected to amateur repair or incidents of unexplained unintentional discharge. In these instances a gun may well not be capable of being fired with ammunition selected for the initial tests due to the effects of light or off-set firing pin strikes; tests using another brand of ammunition employing more sensitive primers may present no problems in these respects. In addition, other tests conducted to check if the weapon is prone to discharge by means other than by using the normal firing techniques, may well come out with very different answers with a change of test ammunition. It is a fact of life that some primers require a substantial central blow producing a significant indentation to cause them to fire, while some brands or lots can give rise to the occasional discharge with extremely light strikes likely to cause only a trivial deformation of the primer. Where this is likely to be an issue additional tests should be conducted with any live ammunition relating to the incident, or if there is none available, with laboratory stock ammunition similar to that used in the incident.

I recall dealing with two incidents involving the accidental discharge of police-issue Czech manufactured CZ-75, 9mm self-loading pistols, both involving holstered weapons. One officer was seated reading a newspaper with his pistol held in his shoulder holster; the weapon discharged when he lifted his arms to turn over a page. In another incident the pistol of a second officer discharged as he holstered it. This model of pistol is designed to allow double-action operation, and as it has an inertial firing pin it was considered to be safe for them to carry it with the hammer fully-down on a loaded chamber. An initial rapid shot could then be achieved by simply applying a long and relatively heavy pull to its trigger, as they did previously with their service issue .38 in Smith & Wesson revolvers. Initially I found no mechanical fault with either pistol, and suggested that the officers had been less than truthful in their accounts of the incidents, as it is always possible for a person to fumble when de-cocking the hammer of a pistol. In this design the hammer will fall only as far as a deeply cut safety bent (notch) where sear engagement will arrest its movement at a point a short distance away from its firing pin, so long as the trigger is not pulled back during the operation. In turn, the fully de-cocked hammer can also be pulled back a short distance to engage the sear in this safety bent. Pulling back the hammer a very short distance, and then releasing it just before it engages this safety bent, will cause the hammer to strike the firing pin with very little force so as to produce a barely audible 'tick'. I found that when actuated in these circumstances with various brands of laboratory stock ammunition at hand in the firing range, only a slight mark was produced on the primer, insufficient to cause its discharge. However, subsequent tests under the same circumstances, using primed cartridge cases produced by pulling the bullets from the police issue ammunition, caused the primer to fire. It was clear that this particular brand and batch of ammunition had very soft and sensitive primers. I was able to repeat such discharges with both police pistols and a further CZ-75 pistol and its Swiss manufactured counterpart from the laboratory reference collection, though this seemed remarkable, bearing in mind the seemingly trivial impact force imparted to the firing pin under these circumstances. Some time after the UK importers of Czech firearms and ammunition were made aware of these problems, the CZ-75 design was modified with the addition of a firing pin block safety.

Where appropriate, different bullet types should also be used in tests, especially if this involves plain lead and jacketed bullet loadings. Jacketed ammunition is far less deformable than plain lead loadings and can therefore take up rifling marks rather differently. Some lots of old wartime Service ammunition can often be found to be loaded with jacketed bullets of lesser diameter than their modern commercial counterparts, and as a consequence will pick up bore characteristics rather differently. For obvious reasons, ammunition recovered from the suspect or similar to that used in the incident should also be included in the test-firings. In the case of sawn-off shotguns it is now usual to collect some fired plastic cartridge wads for microscopy. In this instance, a particular brand should be chosen which has a long smooth bearing surface in its construction as such a choice will be better at picking up any markings imparted by the rough end of the shortened barrel.

The barrel length, the overall length, and the distance between the muzzle end of the barrel and each trigger should also be recorded along with the weight of the firearm. The experienced examiner will of course tailor his tests and recordings to suit the perceived needs of each particular case and examination. External markings should be noted, as well as details of any proof markings. In the US and some other countries there is no legal requirement for proof, and this is also true for most military arms, although some manufacturers will impose their own unrecognised test-marks. However, most developed countries have mandatory proof regulations which also involve the proof testing of legally imported and marketed firearms. In recent years, the International Proof Commission (CIP) regulations also call for a proof marking to be imposed upon all ammunition cartons, to show that the particular batch of ammunition has been found to generate acceptable pressure levels. Details contained in the proof marks will allow you to date the original testing of the gun, or at least place its testing within a particular period. In addition, some Proof Houses place an obvious datestamp upon the gun or a code marking to indicate the year of test. Knowledge of such code markings is particularly useful, especially if the serial numbers have been deleted. Weapons manufactured during World War II in Germany and countries under German occupation are also marked with a set of code letters or numbers denoting the ordnance plant; similar code markings are contained in the headstamps of cartridges manufactured in this period. In many instances the use of these codes persisted when these same countries became part of the Communist Bloc. A useful listing of these codes is contained in Appendix 2.

## 9.2   Trigger Pulls and Mechanical Tests

It is an extremely rare event for an accused person in a trial of murder or attempted murder, to admit to loading the gun, pointing it at the victim and then deliberating pulling the trigger. Guns are said to have become loaded and caused to fire by all manner of other ingenious forces or acts of mechanical caprice. The minimum trigger pull values will always feature in the subsequent trial, as will the effectiveness, or otherwise, of external and internal safety devices.

The trigger pull on a firearm is frequently checked by most gunsmiths with a simple spring gauge similar to that used by anglers to check the weight of a fish. Although this is a simple and convenient device, it does, however, lead to variable values. The deadweight system is the most accurate and one which will tend to yield repeatable values when conducted by different members of staff. In this system a scalepan is attached to a rod ending in a smooth L-shaped bar, which in turn is rested upon the trigger. The bar can be placed on the centre of the trigger and the weapon lifted directly upwards, with its barrel vertical, to record mean values likely to be encountered in general use. During this operation additional weights can be added to the pan between each lift until the weapon is dry-fired onto a suitable snap-cap. The snap-cap is a dummy cartridge fitted with a resilient spring-loaded false primer. Its use is recommended in all off-range testing of guns to avoid the possibility of firing pin breakage, which can occur when the firing pin comes to an abrupt stop at the end of its movement, without the usual cushioning effect afforded by the deformation of the soft primer material of the cartridge. The laboratory I have worked in has, however, always reported the minimum trigger pull values for firearms in its statements. These values are achieved when the bar is positioned towards the tip of the trigger to provide maximum mechanical advantage and to alter the inclination of the weapon during the lifting process to achieve the most advantageous angle. One will find that with English-style double-barrelled shotguns, the minimum pull on the rear trigger is achieved when the direction of pull is at a distinctly upward angle to the axis of the barrels. Provided that the gun is lifted smoothly and slowly between each test, it should be possible to repeat test results within an agreement of 1 oz (28 g). It is usual to record the distance through which the trigger is pulled to effect firing as well, and to note if the pull is applied in the form of a single or double stage. Electronic trigger pull gauges of varying sophistication are now available and capable of giving good service. These devices can also be used for measuring the force required to release a safety catch or similar fixture.

A search of the literature, reference to manufacturers' published data and experience in the testing of weapons using this technique, will allow you to form an opinion as to what constitutes a normal trigger pull. Over many years firearm manufacturers have arrived at a compromise between a trigger pull which is not so heavy as to unduly interfere with the normal aiming and firing processes and one which at the same time is not so light as to lend itself towards accidental discharge during normal conditions of handling and use. In a sporting shotgun this will be realised with a trigger pull range of between 3.5 and 5 lb (1.6 to 2.3 kg). The single-action pulls on most revolvers, pistols and sporting rifles will generally range between 3 and 4 lb (1.4 to 1.8 kg), with those on target weapons, especially .22 in rim-fire, being set close to 2 lb (1 kg). Trigger pulls on air weapons can range between 3 and 7 lb (1.4 to 3.2 kg), although the more expensive target weapons with adjustable trigger pulls can sometimes be set appreciably lower than this. Rifles or pistols fitted with 'set triggers' can usually be adjusted to very fine levels for special purposes and at the same time still retain their conventional trigger pull when this device is not operated. It is usual, when writing a statement upon a firearm, to state the minimum trigger pulls and then to compare or contrast these values with those which would normally be appropriate for the particular weapon type. The presence and the condition of any trigger adjusting screw should also be noted. The trigger pulls on firearms intended for military service use are generally higher than those encountered on commercial arms. Trigger pull values of 6 to 8 lb (2.7 to 3.6 kg) are not unusual; these higher settings reflect the often difficult circumstances in which soldiers have to operate. Double-action pulls tend to be heavier again and involve a considerable increase in the length of the trigger movement. In previous years a typical double-action pull would measure 12 to 13 lb (5.5 to 6 kg). Modern double-action pulls tend to be rather lighter. Measurements of a range of Smith and Wesson revolvers I made a few years ago came up with values of between 6 lb, 14 oz and 10 lb, 1 oz, with an average setting of 9 lb (4.1 kg).

The next things to check are the effectiveness and movement of manual and automatic safety catches. A safety catch should move between two positive detents after the application of a perceptible degree of force. If free to move too easily they can be caused to move inadvertently during normal use or handling. In some instances where the catch does not move into positive detent, it is possible to fire the gun when the catch is at some intermediate setting. This can happen with automatic safety catches of the type fitted to English-pattern guns which set whenever the breech is opened; in some circumstances it is possible to open the breech using an incomplete movement of the opening lever on the top of the action, which in turn can cause only a partial movement of the safety catch towards its proper setting. On some weapons one can pull the trigger hard when the safety catch is applied, and then cause the gun to fire merely by subsequently releasing the safety catch. On some lever-cocking air rifles the automatic safety catch is situated close to where one would grip the wrist of the rifle during the cocking operation; inadvertent pressure from part of the hand can then prevent this safety device being automatically set. The forces required to move safety catches or fire selector switches on automatic arms are conveniently measured using a small electronic strain gauge.

One must always consider that most safety catches merely bolt the movement of the triggers when applied. The dislodging of the sear from its bent, whether by the methods described above, or by jarring action will still cause the weapon to fire, unless there is some other form of intercepting mechanism, blocking the movement of the striker or firing pin, or the fitting of a second intercepting sear, which prevents firing in circumstances other than when the trigger is pressed. It may be necessary to partially dismantle the gun, or take X-ray photographs of it in operation, to confirm the nature of any internal faults. However, before stripping a gun one must always bear in mind that its subsequent condition can be altered, thus preventing a particular effect being witnessed by a second person or independent forensic examiner.

As mentioned above, with some firearms it is possible to cause their discharge without pressing the trigger if the sear is caused to come out of bent. The most common way in which this happens is if the weapon is subjected to some sharp impact or jarring force, which the Defence might suggest was caused in a fall or a scuffle. It is important when doing jarring tests upon a weapon that you do not get carried away, since if sufficient force is eventually applied, breakage will occur. Simple drop tests from sensible heights can be conducted using a hard, thin rubber mat placed upon the floor to provide the correct level of firm cushioning effect. Initial bumping tests will involve the gun being dropped butt first onto the mat from measured heights. Additional tests should be conducted to meet the needs perceived by reading witness statements; these could involve drop tests to the muzzle end or lateral shocks. Blows applied to the back of a hammer or cocking piece should involve the use of a small rawhide mallet or soft piece of wood. This test is usually conducted in the firing range with a primed cartridge case in the chamber of the gun. If the rebound safety stop for the hammer is worn or defective, a pin mark will be imparted to the primer which might be sufficient to cause the cartridge to fire. Again, you must not overdo these tests as too much force can damage the firing mechanism or cause alteration to the trigger pull. In such tests, do bear in mind that primers can vary in sensitivity from one make or batch to another, with military primers being the least sensitive to 'light strike' conditions. If sufficient live cartridges are submitted with the weapon in question, then do additional tests with these if there is any sign of primer indentation. Similar tests can also be conducted using primed cartridge cases to check if the gun can be caused to fire by abrupt closure of the action. On old hammer guns there is always the possibility that the rebound safety has become worn or defective. In normal circumstances the hammer should only strike the firing pin if the trigger has been pulled; otherwise the sear engages in a deeply cut bent (notch) in the hammer, thus arresting its forward movement. On defective weapons the hammer, when allowed to slip from a position just short of the full-cock position, will strike the firing pin with sufficient force to cause discharge or a light strike. Tests conducted as before and considering primer sensitivity must in these circumstances be conducted. In addition, it is essential to note the profile and condition of the checkering upon the hammer spur as this also can exert an influence upon the purchase (effective hold or grasp) of the thumb upon it, and hence the likelihood of an accidental discharge taking place due to a wet thumb slipping off the hammer when attempting to make the weapon safe.

## 9.3  Firing Range Tests

Before test-firing any weapon with full-power ammunition it is wise to check that the weapon is mechanically sound (Figure 9.1 through Figure 9.3). If there are any doubts as to the strength of the barrel or the integrity of its

**Figure 9.1**  Zinc alloy blank revolvers which had their blockages drilled out to allow their use with bulleted ammunition are often capable of surviving many firings; the one shown is an exception. A remote firing device should always be used when it is necessary to test fire such weapons.

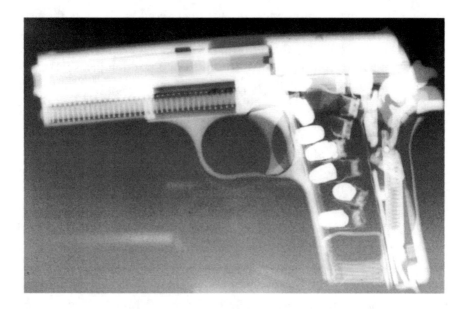

**Figure 9.2** X-ray plate of seized-up fire damaged pistol reveals that the cartridges inside its magazine have been caused to explode by the heat. The picture confirms that it is now safe to attempt to free the pistol and attempt its dismantling.

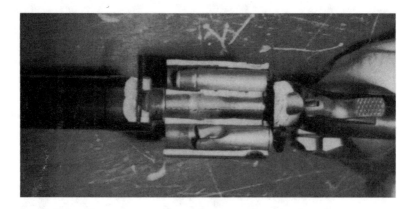

**Figure 9.3** On rare occasions even new guns can blow up when using factory ammunition. In this laboratory firing range incident the top strap and half of the cylinder of the revolver were left embedded in the ceiling. Always wear safety glasses as well as earmuffs. Whenever practicable, make use of a remote firing device.

locking system then initial tests should only involve primed cartridge cases. The next stage would be to use the lowest pressure cartridge loading available, which in shotguns will be those containing the lightest shot charges. Mechanically unsound guns should then be treated with due care on the firing range using only a single cartridge loading each time to minimise risk, and using the remote firing fixture if thought appropriate. The timing of revolver cylinders should also be checked, as this will have an effect upon the markings which will be imparted upon the bullets, and may also affect the double-action trigger pull on certain chambers. This latter effect could be significant if discharge effects left upon the weapon indicate that the fatal shooting involved the chamber subject to such a mechanical defect.

Over the years I have established a personal safety rule which involves only firing reloaded ammunition which I have assembled myself or which has been assembled by a person I consider to be competent for the task. It is not sensible to put your own safety at risk by firing a cartridge of uncertain ballistic characteristics unless you personally know and trust the person who assembled it. Factory loaded ammunition can occasionally generate unsafe pressure levels which can burst a gun, but this is a relatively rare occurrence. Such incidents are likely to be far more common with those people who are prepared to mix alcohol with a reloading session, or watch television when reloading ammunition. By all means dismantle sample cartridges in a case to check their loading, but conduct all of your firing tests with factory ammunition unless there is an absolute need for tests with the reloaded crime cartridges where use of the remote firing rig should be mandatory. Any well-equipped ballistics laboratory will have a reloading press and a comprehensive set of dies to allow the assembly of reloaded cartridges if there is a perceived need to conduct tests with such non-standard loadings. I am not trying to decry the relatively common practice of reloading, as almost all of my private shooting over the years with metallic ammunition has been conducted with reloaded ammunition of my own making, but it is important to recognise the inherent risks in using ammunition of unknown loading. In addition, it is not uncommon for the amateur reloader to have difficulties, especially with military cartridge brass, with achieving the correct primer seating. An incorrectly primed cartridge which has the primer sitting out proud from its pocket can be responsible for causing accidental discharge when forcibly put into battery by the closure action of a pistol slide or a turning rifle bolt.

Whilst on the subject of safe working practice, be certain as to the cartridge chambering of the weapon you are about to test. Some weapons are quite capable of chambering unsuitable cartridges which can produce dangerous pressure levels if fired in them. A good example is the .30 in (7.63 mm) Mauser 1896 pistol, which will chamber and fire a 9 mm Luger cartridge. Heavy magnum loadings should not be fired in a lightweight shotgun designed for use with light game loadings, and great care should be taken before steel shot loadings are used in a shotgun. The firing of old black powder guns, especially those fitted with Damascus barrels, should only be contemplated if there is a real requirement to conduct such tests, and again consideration should be given to the use of the remote firing facility. I have dealt with a great many shooting cases over the years which have involved the use of rickety old hammer shotguns using modern smokeless cartridges. I have never yet had one blow up on me during my tests, or blow up when used by the accused in a murder or wounding, but I am still aware of the real risks involved.

On the firing range it is usual safe practice never to allow another person to advance beyond the firing line when a weapon is loaded. Bearing in mind that firearms can occasionally malfunction, and badly timed revolvers can spit out pieces of lead or bullet jacket material from the sides of the cylinder gap, it is even better to position observers or assistants to the rear during firing. Safety glasses giving good lateral protection to the eyes should always be worn in conjunction with a correctly fitting pair of ear muffs of known performance rating. When firing in indoor ranges the noise of discharge is reflected back and forth off the walls, floor and other fittings, thus prolonging the acoustic signal of discharge. This prolongation of the audible signal greatly increases its ability to cause damage to hearing. To avoid the risk of noise-induced hearing loss, especially when tests are being conducted with sawn-off shotguns, magnum revolvers or high-power rifles, it is good policy to wear earplugs in conjunction with the muffs, as the safety glasses can reduce to some degree the effective sealing of the soft pads of the ear muffs. Use only good quality muffs, preferably ones of known high attenuation. Check the condition of the soft seals for compliance and fit, replacing the seals or discarding the muffs as seems appropriate. When using the remote firing facility, or at any other time when appropriate, additional protection from mishap should be sought behind a large clear polycarbonate ballistic screen mounted on castors.

The human ear is capable of perceiving sounds in the 20 Hz to 20 kHz band and is particularly sensitive in the 1–4 kHz region. As one grows older, and as a result of previous exposure to loud sounds, the perception in the upper frequencies tends to diminish. Sound intensity is measured as sound pressure level (SPL) using a logarithmic decibel scale. It is usual to express noise exposure measurements as dB(A), a scale weighted towards higher frequency sounds to which the human ear is more sensitive. Exposure to continuous sound levels of 85 dB(A) or higher over an 8 hour period can lead to permanent hearing loss. When considering noise levels it is important to bear in mind that the use of the logarithmic scale causes an increase of 3 dB(A) to represent a doubling of the sound intensity. It follows that 4 hours exposure to 88 dB(A) sound can inflict as much damage as exposure to 8 hours of noise at 85 dB(A). Gunshot noises are extremely brief but very energetic. A single gunshot producing a signal of between 140 to 170 dB(A), can inflict the same level of hearing loss as would be produced by exposure to 90 dB(A) noise for 40 hours. Noise-induced hearing loss is caused by injury to, or degeneration of the sensory or hair cells of the ear. The use of earplugs or muffs will attenuate the amount of noise entering the ear. A typical Noise Reduction Ratio (NRR) for disposable ear plugs would be in the region of 19 dB(A), although ear plugs can work loose over a period due to movements of the jaw. Good quality muffs can offer a greater level of protection, provided that their seals are operating effectively. Shooting glasses can sometimes reduce the effectiveness of the seals. Good quality muffs used in conjunction with disposable earplugs provide the best protection. The lining of the walls and other reflective surfaces of the firing range with sound attenuating materials or acoustic panels will greatly reduce the reverberation life of a gunshot signal and hence its ability to induce hearing loss. The measurement of the peak sound levels of the brief impulse signals normally produced by the discharge of firearms requires special equipment and specialized measurement techniques.

Bullets can be collected for microscopy by the use of a long wooden box, preferably lined with bullet resistant material, filled with cotton waste material separated at intervals with pieces of card. Avoid metal fitments or screws on the face fitted with the bullet entry port as the presence of such materials can have dangerous consequences if a misaligned shot is fired. However, the best way to get near perfect sample bullets is to use a water trap. These devices can be of vertical or horizontal design. The horizontal trap is the most convenient to use. As previously stated, the critical angle for the deflection off a still body of water is less than 7° so the degree of downward inclination for firing necessary on this type of entry port is relatively modest. Even so, the top of the tank should be provided with hinged polycarbonate covers which should be in position during firing, if only to reduce the effects of water splashing. Although all kinds of gadgets can be used to recover the bullets, the most simple and effective one is made of a rod, terminating in a small square end-plate covered with Blu-tack. A small electric pump and filter unit will help keep the water in the tank clear, as will the additional use of a fungicide and the occasional need to service clean the tank. High-velocity soft-point or hollow-point bullets can break up when subjected to such rapid deceleration, as will some modern military rifle bullets which are of composite design. In these instances, it is usual to use down-loaded reloaded cartridges assembled using a light charge of fast-burning powder such as Hercules 2400. The Lyman reloading manual will provide guidance for the assembly of safe low-velocity loadings of the type designed for cast lead bullets in rifles which will generally meet your requirements. One will sometimes hear people advise you simply to discard half of the original powder charge for these purposes. However, such practices are to be avoided as unusual and dangerous ballistic characteristics can be encountered, especially with powerful or magnum rifle loadings normally employing full cases of very slow burning powders.

One can usually estimate the approximate range of firing in cases involving shotguns or sawn-off guns from the examination of the body, the clothing or other damaged items from your previous experience. Bearing this in mind, one will then conduct firing tests at ranges likely to bracket the actual value by a sensible overlap. In this way the actual number of test firings can be reduced, which can be important if you have limited 'crime' or laboratory stock ammunition of the appropriate loading. The majority of unshortened double-barrelled guns will have quite different choke borings on their two barrels. On an English pattern side-by-side gun the left barrel will be bored with the greatest degree of choke. On over-and-under guns the top barrel will usually be bored with the heaviest choke. In this second type of weapon this is done to allow for an inherent design weakness by reducing the potentially damaging effects produced on firing as the choked barrel will tend to be fired the least, usually after an initial miss with the lower barrel. On side-by-side guns both barrels enjoy the same degree of retention against the standing breech as the axes of both barrels lie at the same short distance above the hinge-pin. On an over-and-under gun the axis of the top barrel is sufficiently out of alignment with the hinge to cause a significant difference in mechanical advantage, which on many guns eventually results in this barrel coming off-the-face if fired sufficiently often. However, it is noticeable in recent years as screw-in choke tubes have become more popular, that many of the owners are unaware of such factors and may choose to screw the choke tubes in reverse pattern, so it is wise to check the choke borings of each submission. This can be done with a proper gunsmith's barrel gauge, or with a button gauge, an extension rod and a micrometer. The choke is measured at its narrowest point near to the muzzle, whilst the nominal bore size is measured at a point approximately 9 in (230 mm) from the breech. The difference in measurements will indicate the approximate choke value as explained earlier.

For reasons of safety and convenience it is usual to load the gun with one cartridge at a time during the sequence of test fires, which for reasons previously stated, will involve the use of spare 'crime' cartridges or the closest type obtainable from the laboratory ammunition store. The laboratory stock should always be kept as extensive and up-to-date as possible and any deficiencies rectified at the earliest convenience. On each occasion the gun is fired at the witness target at a specific distance carefully measured from the screen to the muzzle end of the gun barrel. The alignment for this distance will be checked by an assistant or by a mechanical, optical or laser prompt device. Thick card of suitable size is used for most close-range tests as it is better able to withstand the close-range blast effects without ripping; where necessary the edges of the card can be reinforced with Sellotape. A long roll of white paper, approximately 12 ft (4 m) wide, hung from a roller near to the ceiling, is best used for tests on the indoor range up to its 20 to 50 m limit. This paper is the same as that used in some police firearms training facilities, where it is used for cinematic projection of crime scenarios which the trainee fires at, having correctly identified a stylised threat situation. One further advantage of using this system is that the section of the screen containing the pattern can be cut out with a sharp knife and then folded to a convenient size for subsequent examination at the bench along with the test cards. In many instances it is usual to retain some of these test patterns for future reference. They should always be marked with the case reference number, barrel fired, distance of firing and loading used and then dated and signed. Perfect uniform circular textbook patterns are rarely realised. Fliers, pellets straying outside the main pattern, will often be seen contained within a circle measuring twice that of the spread of the bulk of the pellets. With some cartridge brands and choke borings the patterns can be quite irregular, necessitating the firing of additional shots at the same ranges. The number of test firings, especially repeat tests at a given range, is a matter of discretion for the tester and will usually reflect the performance of the gun and cartridge in each instance. In some cases the weapon and cartridge combination will produce even and predictable results, thus allowing a very precise estimate of the range of firing in the incident; in other cases for the reasons stated the range estimation will be expressed within broader parameters. The effects produced by powder blackening, powdering, wad opening and fragmentation, explained in Chapter 7 will be used to supplement normal pellet spread effects at the closer ranges. Tests to determine the distance of firing in the vast majority of criminal casework will be accomplished at firing distances within no more than a few metres, although a longer firing range will give you the flexibility to deal with those cases involving more distant shootings, without the time-consuming problems and the restrictions imposed by light conditions or weather in going to an outdoor facility (Figure 9.4 through Figure 9.8).

It will be sometimes necessary to conduct accuracy tests with a firearm to check upon excuses offered by the accused to explain away a deliberate shooting injury. With rifles sighting faults will usually be attributable to

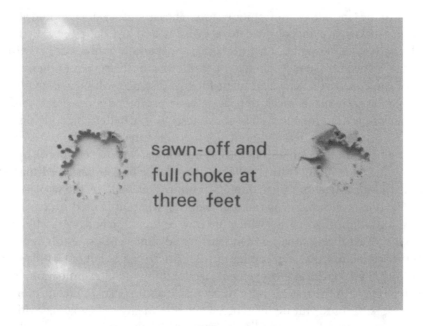

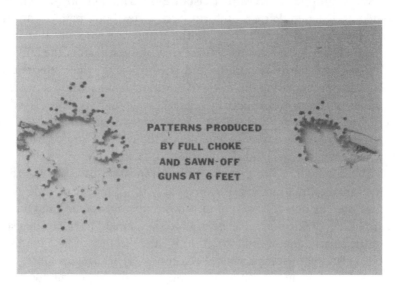

**Figure 9.4 and Figure 9.5**   At ranges of less than one metre there is very little difference between the spread of shot from a sawn-off shotgun and a conventional choke bored gun. Differences in pellet spread do however, become apparent beyond this range.

insecure mounting of the telescopic sight. In the case of air weapons, one may have to measure the velocity at a given range, or at least do penetration tests to confirm the ability of the weapon to inflict an injury of the type

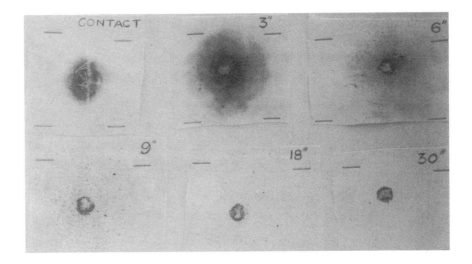

**Figure 9.6** A set of test patterns for a particular .45 in pistol and loading produced on test squares of white cloth mounted on heavy card. The contact shot shows typical stellate ripping of the material along with scorching and blackening. At greater distances the blackening and powdering intensities are lessened with increasing range of firing. Such test cards can be compared directly with clothing removed from the victim, along with additional tests, where necessary, using sodium rhodizonate reagent for discharge residues. Other testing techniques for propellant generated residues can also be utilised.

mentioned in the medical report at the alleged distance. In the majority of cases exterior ballistic checks can all be done in an indoor range offering shooting distances up to 20 or 50 m. Velocity tests at longer ranges can be estimated by a suitable exterior ballistics programme after inputting values obtained at two distances on the indoor range facility. Shot-pattern diameter can be similarly estimated by reference to a graph of the pattern spread rate at shorter distances. In some instances it will be necessary to conduct tests at extended ranges out of doors at a suitable range location, having set up suitable targets, patterning boards, or an outdoor chronograph unit.

Electronic chronographs are now widely available for use by reloaders which are priced within a relatively modest range. More sophisticated professional equipment is of course more expensive. A typical professional unit will employ at least two skygate units through which the missiles are fired. The lenses of the optical detectors at the bases of the skygates will scan a wide fan-shaped area of space above them which in turn is illuminated by an infrared-rich strip light source hung at a convenient height above the detector. The two detectors, which trigger the start and the stop units on the velocity computer are usually placed at least 1 m apart. The shadow of the nose or the base of the missile can be used to trigger the infrared detectors.

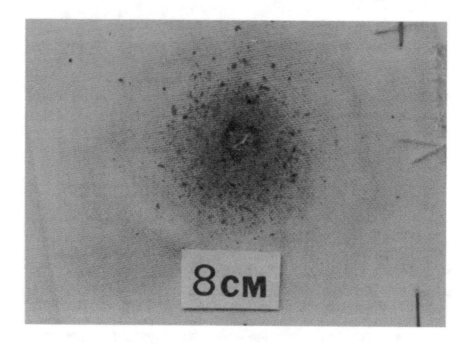

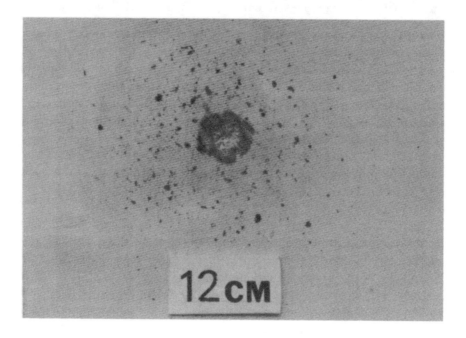

**Figure 9.7 and Figure 9.8**   Great differences are shown in the intensity of powdering and blackening on these witness cards, despite the small difference in firing range involved.

Secondary detectors can be set up to check each reading. The signals are then compared with a quartz chronograph so that the computer can then display and print out the velocity readings in units of choice. The standard deviation for a sequence of shots can also be included on the printout. Using the start unit alone, it is possible to determine the rate of fire of automatic weaponry, usually expressed in rounds per minute. Some detectors need to be adjusted or screened against the effects of blast and bright muzzle signature of certain magnum loadings. Flickering defective neon strip lights in the range can also cause problems, as will unburnt powder grains from previous firings left lying on top of the optical detector covers. At close distances unburnt powder grains from some magnum revolver loadings or from the firing of black powder charges can cause false triggering of the detectors, as some of the particles will be travelling in front of the bullet at these short distances due to the effects of muzzle blast. All expensive chronograph equipment mounted in unshielded positions in the firing range will eventually suffer bullet damage. It is best to have the detectors mounted inside pits set into the concrete floor, with the downrange overhead detector lights screened by ballistic sheeting. An additional chronograph channel can be used with a further set of detectors to provide downrange velocity values at a greater distance. This can be useful if it is necessary to do tests in this location. In addition, if the spacing is sufficiently large between the two units, then the difference in velocity readouts can be used for providing simple ballistic coefficient values for use in other external ballistics computations.

When conducting firing tests with pump-action or self-loading arms, it is often useful to measure the distance and pattern of ejected cartridge cases. This can be useful when attempting to interpret your findings at the scene of the incident, especially when attempting to reconstruct what has taken place and the likely sequence of movement of the firer. Do bear in mind however, that incidents in roadways in busy areas are not always subject to early containment. The tyres of passing vehicles can damage and fling spent cartridge cases to different locations, and on top of this they are able to roll for some distance on smooth or sloping surfaces. It has become fashionable for certain Hollywood actors to fire their pistols when held with a limp wrist and canted at rather ridiculous angles, presumably for added dramatic effect. Such antics, which only serve to make the handgun less effective, may be aped by some criminals. The direction in which the ejector port is facing will clearly affect the direction and pattern of cartridge case ejection, and this should be borne in mind.

Additional tests conducted on rarer occasions on the firing ranges, can include sound measurements using suitable equipment set at distances of interest, and high-speed photography showing the firing of weapons, the flights of missiles and cartridge wadding, and the interaction of the shot charge or the bullet with the target or some intermediate target such as glazing material. An intense pulse of light triggered by a microphone, piezo-electric sensor, or infrared detector can be used in otherwise dark conditions for single event photographs. High-speed video can also be a useful tool, especially considering its instant replay facility. The Hicam high-speed cine unit is expensive to run, especially if set at 16,000 frames/second with the exposure incorrectly set the first time around, and the processing is relatively slow.

High-speed cine X-ray is used by specialist laboratories conducting studies in wound ballistics. However, all of these techniques can on occasions provide useful additional information if you can afford the cost and the time involved in setting up test conditions.

It is sometimes necessary to conduct firing tests using a particular type of weapon or special loading upon tissue simulant, as described in Chapter 7. Swedish ballistic soap is very convenient and can provide information as to the relative nature of temporary cavity formation. The most realistic results are however obtained using 10% ballistic gelatine block as the preferred medium. When correctly prepared and calibrated as described in Chapter 7, this medium gives the best correlation with human tissue. The researcher Fackler has claimed that many erroneous results of some other researchers have been attributable to incorrectly prepared test blocks. He advises the following procedure for the preparation of 10% Type 250A Ordnance Gelatine, of the type supplied by Knox Gelatin Company:

1.  Always start with cold water (7–10°C).
2.  Add the gelatine powder to the water; never the reverse. 1 kg of powder to 9 litres of water for a 10% solution.
3.  Use only sufficient agitation to just wet all the particles and to avoid the entrapment of large amounts of air.
4.  Allow to hydrate by standing the mixture in a refrigerator for 2 h.
5.  Heat the container indirectly using a water bath or double cooker, stirring the mixture gently until all the gelatine is in solution and evenly dispersed. Do not heat above 40°C. Avoid rapid stirring so as not to entrap air in the mixture.
6.  Pour into moulds, set in a refrigerator or cold water bath set at 7–10°C until firmly set (overnight for best results).
7.  Remove blocks from the moulds and then store them in airtight plastic bags overnight in a refrigerator set at 4°C. Do not use the blocks until at least 36 h have elapsed from the time the gelatine mixture was first poured into the moulds.

General notes:

- Gelatine is insoluble in cold water.
- The concentration will affect block firmness.
- Maximum firmness will be assumed within 24–30 h of cooling.
- Test blocks may be reused by heating just to melting temperature and by then rechilling.
- Propionic acid (5 ml/litre) may be added if considered necessary to inhibit mould growth.
- Gelatine should be stored and calibrated at 4°C.
- The firmness of the block varies inversely with temperature to a marked degree. The temperature should be constant throughout the block, and there should be no variations in the temperatures of the blocks used in tests. Fackler conducts his tests within 30 minutes of the removal of the blocks from the refrigerator. In a 20°C range environment it takes 90 minutes to raise the temperature of the block 1° (measured 2 cm from the block surface).

## 9.4   Incomplete, Defective and Converted Arms

In some instances the recovered firearm suspected of being used in an incident will be received in a condition such that it cannot be test-fired to obtain cartridge cases or bullets for comparison purposes. Weapons can be partially dismantled and then thrown in a stretch of river, put on a fire, buried or simply broken by violent impact (one of the most common responses for an individual to take after reflecting upon his previous actions).

The firearm or its components can be cleaned up in an ultrasonic cleaning bath using a recommended cleansing liquid to free it of rust scale and silt (Figure 9.9). Afterwards it can be carefully dismantled to allow further cleaning and light lubrication prior to reassembly and testing. Where the bore has been subject to severe corrosion there will be little likelihood of obtaining satisfactory test bullets, as all of the fine detail will have changed. However, one can still make a note of the rifling form and dimensions. Sometimes one will be able to use a replacement barrel or other component from one of the weapons of similar manufacture in the laboratory reference collection to allow test cartridge cases to be obtained. In any event, it is amazing how often the breech face, ejector and firing pin features will still have retained enough of their original features for a positive association to be made. In those instances where it is simply not possible to fire the gun it is still possible to obtain comparison specimens by using a quick-setting flexible moulding material such as Silcoset. This casting material is made up from a two-part mix to produce a medium capable of taking up extremely fine surface details. Once it has set the moulding can be compared directly on the comparison microscope against the crime cartridge cases. The firing pin details can also be recorded simply by ensuring it is pushed forward during the casting process. This same material can be used in the muzzle end of the barrel to obtain a rifling cast to allow land and groove widths to be measured. Casts can also be made of drill impressions or other tooling marks where serial numbers have been obliterated or where home-made components are to be checked against machine tools.

Home-made guns are often encountered along with blank firing pistols or revolvers which have had their normal barrel blockages drilled out (Figure 9.5). Great care should always be exercised when it is necessary to test-fire such improvised weapons, and it is wise to use the lowest pressure cartridges first in your tests which should be conducted using the remote firing fixture. A great many of these adapted blank pistols and revolvers are made from zinc-base alloys such as Mazak which are considerably less strong than normal firearm steels (Figure 9.1). However, I have been surprised by the number of times such pot-metal guns have been able to survive the firing of factory cartridge loadings.

In Chapter 2, the status of firearms which had been subjected to an officially recognised deactivation process intended to allow their sale as non-firearms was mentioned. Although the deactivation processes were intended to defeat the skills of the average individual, it was recognised at the start that there would always be the odd dedicated individual possessing both machining and welding skills as well as access to the necessary equipment. I have seen a great many of these weapons which have been restored to a working condition coming into criminal hands. The increase in drug-related crime has raised the attractiveness of automatic fire weapons such as submachine guns and assault rifles, as well as self-loading pistols (Figure 9.9 and Figure 9.10).

Some of these reactivated arms are crudely restored, often using a replacement length of smooth-bore tubing of appropriate boring as a barrel. After rebuilding the bolt of a submachine gun with weld or braze, the crudest of protuberances will suffice in place of the fixed firing pin on a 'slam-fire' open-bolt submachine gun. Other individuals involved in volume reactivation use more sophisticated machining techniques which can only be differentiated from the originals by close inspection under the bench microscope. In these instances it is usual for the deactivated barrel to be replaced in whole or part by a machined length of suitably chambered rifled barrel blank. I was given the task of dealing with these matters by way of preparing an extended and more sophisticated set of deactivation standards to meet this challenge, especially in respect of portable automatic-fire weaponry. This resulted in the

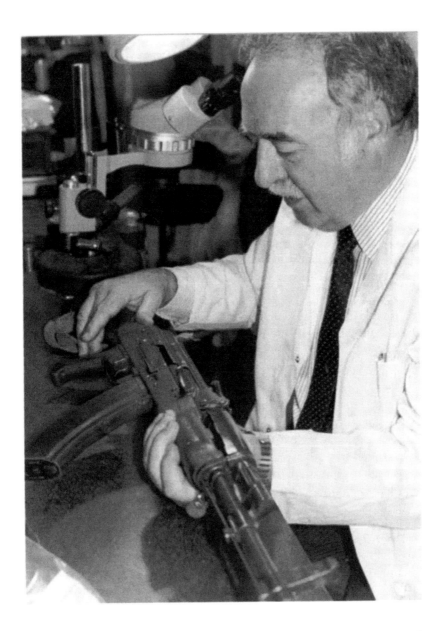

**Figure 9.9** Author at the laboratory workbench examining Kalashnikov assault rifle.

introduction of the new upgraded standards on 1 October 1995 and the release of a new manual containing approved deactivation specifications. One has to be aware however, that in view of the emergence of these hybrid

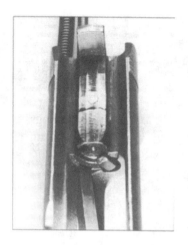

**Figure 9.10**  Deactivated firearms restored to a working condition for use in crime. Left: restored bolt of Czech Model 25 sub-machine gun. The deactivated area has been milled away, so as to allow the welding in place of a machined steel block which has a turned fixed firing pin. Excess material has then been removed by a milling process. Here the weld join is clearly visible. Right: view of underside and recoil face of a re-activated Colt .45 in self-loading pistol. A machined steel block drilled with a firing pin passage has been fitted as before. In this case the weld join can just be discerned.

weapons, which may contain a mixture of standard and non-standard components, that misleading cartridge case and bullet features can be present on items recovered from the scene of a shooting incident. In one example I dealt with recently a reactivated Tokarev T33 7.62 mm pistol had been fitted with a 9 mm barrel chambered for the Luger cartridge.

## 9.5   Recovery of Serial Marks

The majority of firearms are marked by their manufacturer with a serial number in at least one location. On some weapons the number may be repeated on all the major components, e.g., the frame, cylinder and the barrel of a revolver. In other instances one will find the last few digits of the main number repeated upon even relatively small components. These numbers can appear in obvious exposed areas of the exterior or in some cases in locations which can only be revealed by stripping the weapon. As it is common practice for criminals to obliterate the serial numbers on illegally owned firearms to make the tracing of the arms more difficult, it is a useful start if the forensic examiner learns where to look for them on a particular weapon, how many digits he should expect to find, and if the number is likely to include letters as well as digits. Knowing where to look for secondary numbers will often save a lot of time which might have been spent on acid etching. In the same way, the criminal will sometimes deface all external markings in his ignorance as to their relevance. Knowing where the true serial number should be located will save time otherwise wasted in etching less useful defaced areas, such as those originally containing proof markings.

Different techniques are used in an attempt to obliterate numbers, the most common being to file or grind off the offending mark. In other instances a line of holes may be left using a centre-punch or a drill. In extreme cases the area will be removed by using a milling process or fused by local welding. The experienced examiner will acquire the necessary skills in determining if chemical etching is likely to be productive or not. Time saved by deciding not to pursue a lost cause can be spent to better effect on other more productive examinations.

In many instances where a drill or punch has been used, it is amazing how often you are still able to discern the original number, or at least most of it, simply by examining the area under the low-powered stereo bench microscope and working out the most likely original numbers from those parts still remaining. On occasions, one will polish the defaced area flat with wet-and-dry abrasive paper to find the original number is visible under the correct lighting conditions without the need for chemical treatment. When flattening any area prior to etching it is important to degrease the area first with a suitable solvent before polishing with the coarsest grade of paper first, progressing to the finer grades towards the finish. In most instances the base material under consideration will be steel, although you will encounter the need to look at aluminium alloys, brass, and occasionally zinc base alloys such as Mazak. The appropriate chemical etching solution should be selected for each material. Some people heat iron, steel and aluminium articles up to 300°C then allow the article to cool down naturally before starting the etching process. It is claimed that this step helps develop the numbers more readily, although it is vital not to exceed the temperature stated. This equates to turning an exposed steel surface a very pale straw colour, a temperature which should induce a strong sensation of burning if momentarily touched with the tip of the finger. In some instances with very large objects, less likely to be found on most firearms, one can eliminate the polishing step. The etching can sometimes be a lengthy process, during which parts of the original number can appear (and disappear), so it is best to record all findings during the operation. At the end of the etching process the area of metal showing the revealed mark should be washed, dried and protected with a thin coating of Xam or similar material.

### 9.5.1   Iron and Steel

Fry's reagent is the one most used for firearm components. It consists of a mixture having the following:

> 80 ml of hydrochloric acid
> 60 ml of water
> 12.9 g of cupric chloride
> 50 ml of ethanol

The following procedure is then carried out:

1.  Apply reagent using a cotton swab to the area for 30–60 s.
2.  Dry the area with cotton wool and then apply 15% nitric acid for a similar period as in Step 1.
3.  Dry with cotton wool and then reapply the Fry's reagent as before. Repeat the procedure until the number is revealed. Wash the area, dry it and coat with a clear lacquer to preserve the revealed number.

### 9.5.2   Aluminium Alloys

Vinella's solution is an effective reagent for these materials, possibly also with the use of Hume-Rothery solution between each step in the case of alloys containing silicon, washing loose copper deposits away each time. Vinella's solution is made up as follows:

> 30 ml of glycerine
> 20 ml of hydrofluoric acid
> 10ml of nitric acid

Hume-Rothery solution is made up as follows:

> 200 gm of cupric chloride
> 5 ml of hydrochloric acid
> 1000 ml of water

### 9.5.3   Copper, Brass, German Silver and Other Copper Alloys

In this case best results are obtained when it is possible to immerse the article in a generous bath containing the following solution:

> 19 g of ferric chloride
> 6 ml of hydrochloric acid
> 100 ml of water

This particular process may take a long time to produce a satisfactory result (6 h to 3 days). An aqueous 20% ammonium persulphate solution can also be used for these materials, as can a 20% aqueous solution of nitric acid.

### 9.5.4   Stainless Steels

Griffin's Reagent can be used as an effective etching agent. Some formulations use ethanol as a substitute for methanol.

> 30g copper(II) chloride
> 30ml hydrochloric acid
> 30ml water
> 120ml methanol

### 9.5.5   Plastics

The increased use of plastics in the fabrication of firearms makes significant the use of thermal methods for the restoration of obliterated serial numbers. A visible light source, an infra-red light source, or a basic electrical heat gun normally used for stripping paint, can be employed to heat the obliterated region until the compressed character shapes in the plastic substrate swell up so as to raise themselves proud of their uncompressed surroundings.

## 9.6   Examination of Ammunition

This examination can take a number of different routes depending upon the particular objectives. Where the need is for classification only, then one will attempt to identify the make and calibre or gauge of the cartridge and then to check that it contains the essential components of a live cartridge. This later step will involve either dismantling the cartridge with an inertia bullet puller or a press-mounted collet puller, if the cartridge involved is of centre-fire design. Under no circumstances should these techniques be used with rim-fire ammunition. In the case of rim-fire ammunition, which will usually be .22 in calibre, it is a safer practice simply to test-fire it in a laboratory rifle, obtaining a chronograph reading of the velocity of the bullet at the same time, if thought necessary. Where it is deemed essential to dismantle a rim-fire cartridge, e.g., to obtain a sample of the propellant or to determine the bullet construction, the case should be firmly gripped with the gloved hand when wrapped in a piece of cloth and the bullet twisted and pulled out of the case with a pair of pliers. Safety glasses should always be worn when dismantling ammunition, and no attempt should be made to dismantle the more hazardous military loadings, such as those loaded with explosive projectiles.

The cartridge boxes containing ammunition should be examined, as there will often be a sticker identifying the retailer. In addition, some boxes will be marked either externally or upon the inside flap of the lid with a manufacturer's code mark which can be used to find out the date of their manufacture. When making notes on a cartridge or a spent cartridge case I always draw the headstamp and any other features of interest on top of a circular rubber stamp impressed upon the page of my notes. Where the identity of the manufacturer is not self-evident, reference should be made to suitable references concerning the identification of cartridge headstamps. In shotgun ammunition, the gauge will be marked upon the head, and this almost invariably will be in the English system. One will occasionally encounter some smaller gauge cartridges which will be given the metric designation, e.g., the rare 32 gauge 14 mm loading still loaded by some Continental cartridge manufacturers. Modern rim-fire cartridges will not be marked with their calibre; this is not a hardship as you will be involved with .22 in ammunition in most instances, or 9 mm garden shotgun cartridges on other occasions. Older larger rim-fire cartridges or modern diminutive loadings such as the 4 mm or the 5 mm can be researched if necessary in a suitable reference book.

Where you are attempting to identify an unknown bulleted cartridge not possessing a headstamp or marked with less informative details, the following procedure is adopted. Use a vernier dial gauge to measure the bullet diameter, the diameter of the case neck, shoulder, base, rim and the overall length of the cartridge case and the loaded cartridge. Compare these results with the literature. In most instances it will be listed in Barnes' *Cartridges of the World*, along with a full-size sketch or photograph. Metric calibres are generally the easiest due to the logical system used to describe them which refers to the calibre and the case length rather than the untidy mixed system used in the UK and US. For example, 7 × 57 mm refers to the 7 mm Mauser rifle loading which utilises a case 57 mm in length, or the .275 in as Rigby of London still refer to it. Reloaded cartridges should be self-evident due to the presence of die markings on the cartridge case, the use of cast lead bullets, incorrectly seated primers, ejector marks from previous firings, lack of case sealing lacquer, or residues from previous firing remaining inside the cartridge case. Your notes should record all such features as it may be possible to relate them to similar features found on ammunition in the possession of the suspect.

When one is examining recovered live ammunition of the type used in a serious incident, it will often be necessary to check the live cartridge for operational marks left upon it from having been loaded in the crime weapon (Figure 9.19). In such instances, the presence of extractor, ejector, chambering marks, light-firing pin or misfire marks, and other chambering or magazine-induced marks should be identified under the low-power stereo microscope, and their locations marked upon the headstamp sketch previously mentioned. Factory fresh unmarked cartridges from the store can then be worked through the action of the firearm to allow subsequent comparison microscopy to be carried out in respect of these features.

A record should be made of the bullet type and weight in your notes if there is a need to compare them with missiles recovered from the incident. Check to see if there are any telltale signs that the cartridge has been hand-reloaded. Is the bullet of factory swaged design, or is it of cast lead construction, if so, what kind of lubricant is present in its grease bands? Notes should include the type of jacket material, a simple check with a magnet will show you if it has a steel substrate, and you should note the number, nature, and dimensions of any cannelures, or at least check the missile directly against the crime exhibit. A sample of the propellant can be used to check against unburnt propellant found in the bore of the recovered weapon, on the clothing or embedded in the wound of the deceased person. As well as noting the size, colour and morphology of the power grains, a sample of the propellant can also be submitted to the section specialising in propellant and primer residue analysis. Useful information on analysing the newly introduced black powder propellants and their residues mentioned in Chapter 1, and the new lead/heavy metal-free primer formulations mentioned in Section 5.7, can be found in the two papers, 'Black powder substitutes: Their physical and chemical properties and performance' and 'Some basic analytical techniques for unfired primer compositions', by L.C. Haag noted in Further Reading at the end of this chapter.

Notes should also be made upon the dimensions and the type of wadding found in the dismantled shotgun cartridges (Figure 5.4 and Figure 5.8). The charge of shot should be weighed where this is relevant, and a representative sample of pellets should be individually weighed. Some people weigh 10 pellets and then record the average weight. I have found that the variation in the pellet weights contained in a particular cartridge loading together with details on the incidence of out-of-round pellets can furnish useful additional information. Pellets can also be sent for analysis to determine their antimony level if this is thought relevant.

## 9.7  Tear-Gas and Irritant Loadings

Cartridges or pressurized canisters designed to eject a rod of liquid agent, thought to contain loadings of tear-gas or irritant materials can be submitted for analysis to confirm their contents. In the case of ammunition, this will involve partially dismantling the cartridge to recover a portion of the chemical charge, which can then be packaged in a small vial ready for submission to the analytical section. The most common loadings consist of CN, CS, and Capsaicin all of which can be effectively identified using Gas Chromatography/Mass Spectrography (GC/MS). At one time CN was the most common loading to be found in tear-gas cartridges, which were often sealed with a red-coloured wad: muzzle-loaded CN capsules which were fired in these pistols when used in conjunction with a blank cartridge, were also similarly identified (Figure 9.11 and Figure 9.12). In most instances one could smell the characteristic locust blossom odour of CN leaking from the cartridge sealant. In recent years, German CN- and CS-loaded cartridges tend to employ a plastic seal which ruptures at a purpose-formed cross marked in its end. The split wad is retained in the cartridge, thus eliminating earlier problems of wadding or metal crimp material being discharged with potentially hazardous effects from the partially blocked barrels of these pistols. In modern CN loadings the plastic wad, particularly on 8 and 9 mm cartridges, tends to be mid-blue to lilac in colour. In recent years CS has become the predominant loading in 8 mm cartridges

**Figure 9.11** Tear-gas pistols, pens and propelling pencils along with CN and CS loaded munitions. Classified as 'prohibited weapons' in the UK along with stun guns and irritant spray devices. On free sale for self-defence purposes in some countries. Although intended for responsible self defence use such devices are frequently misused in criminal acts or by irresponsible or intoxicated persons causing disturbances in public places.

**Figure 9.12** CN, CS and Oleoresin Capsaicin irritant spray devices.

employing yellow-coloured closures. Most of the 8 mm blank cartridges in this calibre, which are usually of German or Italian Fiocchi loading, employ green or white closures. The Fiocchi 8 and 9 mm blank cartridge uses a hollow-ended plastic seal which is again intended to rupture upon firing.

Chloracetophenone (CN) tear-gas material, has a pleasant aromatic odour resembling locust or cherry blossom, and its crystals can vary in colouration due to the presence of impurities from white to brown. It is a very powerful lachrymator causing immediate weeping at very low concentrations, and also acts as an irritant to moist areas of the skin.

Orthochlorbenzalmalononitrile (CS) is a white crystalline material possessing a pungent pepper odour. This is a powerful irritant material which causes a burning sensation to the eyes, mouth and throat, tear flow, sneezing and skin irritation. It is more punishing than CN at higher concentrations where the full range of symptoms develop, inducing sinus and nasal drip, retching, vomiting, gripping chest pains, violent coughing and breathing difficulties which can induce panic in some persons. Police loadings frequently employ pyrotechnic burning mixtures to allow dissemination on smoke particles, or silica-based aerogel dispersion loadings on barricade penetrating missiles fired from shotguns or riot guns. This agent is frequently employed dissolved in a suitable carrier liquid in hand-held aerosol jetting canisters. Formulations in civilian loadings vary between 1 and 8% effective concentration. CS is the chosen agent for use by British police officers. It is issued in 37 mm pyrotechnic loadings, 12-bore barricade penetrating "Ferret" cartridges, and in small spray belt-mounted canisters.

Dibenz(b,f)-1,4-oxazepin (CR) a military agent may be encountered where theft of a spray device has been followed by its criminal misuse. It is a potent irritant to eyes and moist skin, causing a burning sensation and an inability to open the eyes. It also raises blood pressure, induces alarming variations in the heart rhythm, soreness to the throat, weeping and breathing difficulties. The victim will be in a state of distress or sometimes hysteria. The agent is however, said to be safer than CN.

One common property of the various tear gases is to cause pain to the eyes, induce copious weeping and restrict the ability of the victim to open the eyes (Figure 9.13). The additional individual properties add to the punishment suffered by the recipient, and hence to the level of incapacitation induced. The irritating properties depend on how the nerves in the mucous membrane and skin are affected, and are affected in turn by the ambient humidity and temperature. Most symptoms disappear after 15 to 30 minutes upon escape from exposure. The degree of sensitivity varies considerably between different individuals and is affected by their physical condition, emotional state and motivation. The expressions 'threshold concentration' (TC) and 'incapacitating/intolerable concentration' (IC) are used to express the general effectiveness of an agent. TC50 represents the concentration of the agent, in milligrams per cubic metre, necessary to induce a perceptible effect on 50% of recipients of the particular agent for one minute, whilst IC50 represents the concentration at which the effects would be intolerable to the same level of recipients after one minute (Table 9.1).

Capsaicin is the active ingredient extracted from African red peppers by refluxing them in boiling acetone. After evaporation the impure material is left in the form of an oleoresin capsicum. Often referred to as pepper spray, it is used with a carrier solvent in hand-held pressurised canisters where it is ejected as a jet into the face of the attacker (Figure 9.12). The agent produces burning and irritant effects similar in some respects to CS. Its effectiveness varies with the concentration of the active ingredient. Loadings can sometimes also incorporate a marker dye or CS agent. A newer variant of this

| Code - Name | CN | CS | CR |
|---|---|---|---|
| Chemical name | Chloroacetophenone | Ortho-chlorobenzylidene-malononitrile | Dibenz(b,f)-1,4-oxazepin |
| Chemical formula | 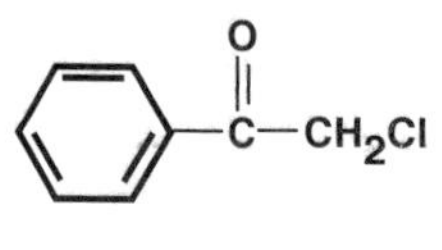 | 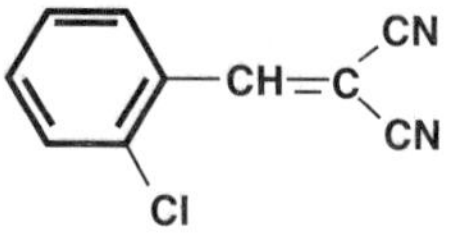 | 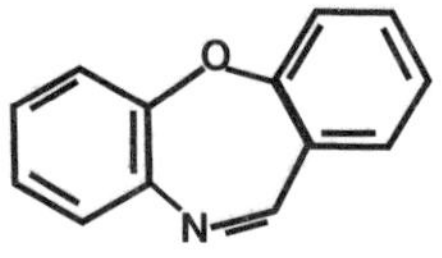 |

**Figure 9.13**   Chemical structures of irritant agents.

**Table 9.1 Threshold and Incapacitating Values for Irritant Agents**

|  | CN | CS | CR |
|---|---|---|---|
| $TC_{50}$ (eyes) | 0.3 | 0.004 | 0.004 |
| $TC_{50}$ (airways) | 0.4 | 0.023 | 0.002 |
| $IC_{50}$ | 20–50 | 3.6 | 0.7 |

agent based upon an acid higher in the chain is claimed by its suppliers to be even more effective.

## 9.8 Electric Shock Devices and Stun Guns

These non-lethal self-defence devices should not be confused with cattle prods which operate at much lower voltages and which are used as legitimate industrial tools to control the movement of livestock on farms or at abattoirs. Most stun guns are claimed to operate at peak voltage levels of between 50,000 and 200,000 V, although the effective current flow is extremely small. The electrical discharge is emitted in the form of a series of short pulses at a rate of approximately eight pulses per second. The electrical discharge is normally observed as blue sparks between the ends of the inner electrodes; at the same time a high-pitched crackling sound is emitted. Some devices use additional sound or light effects to startle or warn the would-be attacker. The devices can be categorised as follows:

1. Hand-held devices capable of being carried in a pocket or handbag, which are usually powered by one or two 9 V alkaline batteries. In use the two exposed electrodes at one end are placed against the body of the assailant to inflict a painful shock or to cause temporary incapacitation. These devices are intended to be used in self-defence as an alternative to a firearm, irritant spray device or tear-gas pistol.
2. Larger devices than (1), but disguised as umbrellas or walking sticks (Figure 9.14 and Figure 9.15).
3. A gun built into a hand-held torch which is designed to fire barbed darts towards the attacker. The darts stick into the chest of the target and are attached by thin wires approximately 15 ft (5 m) long leading back to the device. A switch on the torch allows a pulsed 50,000 V electric shock to be passed to the target. The most common form is the Taser device which is used by some US police forces when arresting violent or drug-affected persons. An "Air Taser" version is fitted

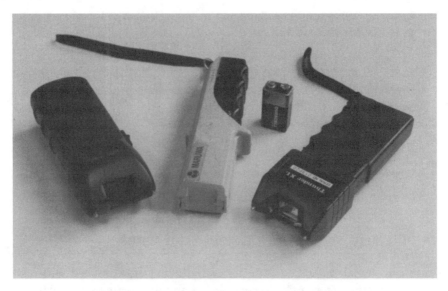

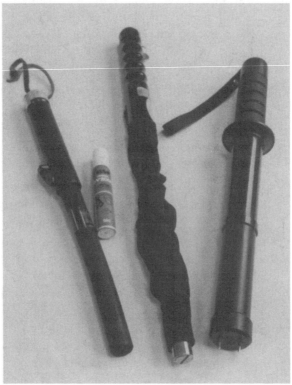

**Figure 9.14 and 9.15**   Electronic stun guns and batons (one of which is disguised as a telescopic umbrella).

with an extendable telescoping wand. Trials involving the Taser device are being undertaken by selected UK police forces at the time of writing this section (Figure 9.16).

4. Electric stun shields acquired by a few UK police forces to control or contain savage dogs.

The rate of discharge of the electrical pulses, their duration and output in terms of peak voltage and effective current can be measured in the laboratory using a circuit incorporating a potential divider hooked up to a storage oscilloscope (Figure 9.17). A plot of the pattern of discharge can then be made from the memory shown as an image upon the screen. The resistors used in the potential divider must be rated to a power sufficiently high so as not to overheat or burn out.

## 9.9   Recovered Cartridge Cases, Bullets, Pellets and Wadding

All of the features previously mentioned in respect of cartridge components should be recorded in your notes on these items. I always find it useful to include a sketch of the distorted bullet or bullet fragments and a recording of their weight, just in case these items get mixed up at a later stage (Figure 9.18). If there are a number of similar items in the exhibits I also mark the

**Figure 9.16**   Twin-barrelled unit containing barbed darts used in a combination torch weapon called the Taser. The 15 ft (5 m) long cables allow the passage of 50,000 V from the torch to the darts embedded in the target victim.

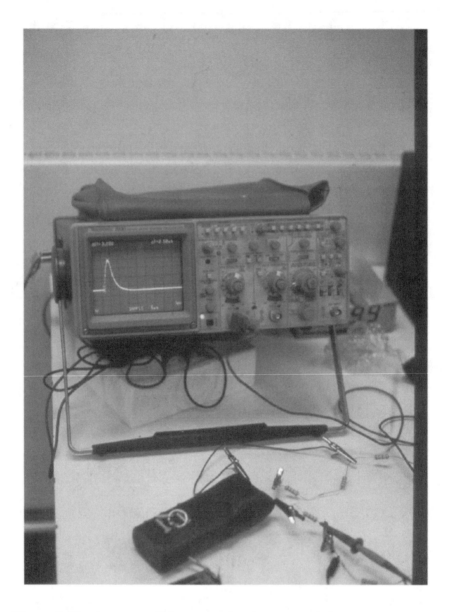

**Figure 9.17** Storage oscilloscope used in the testing of electronic stun weapons. Here the voltage output peak is shown on the screen.

base of the bullet or the side of the case with a fine scribe with an identifying mark for the same purposes. The cartridge case sketches will usually be shown with the headstamps similarly orientated (Figure 9.19). The position of the extractor, ejector or breech face markings will also be a quick prompt when going to the comparison microscope. The orientation of the headstamp in

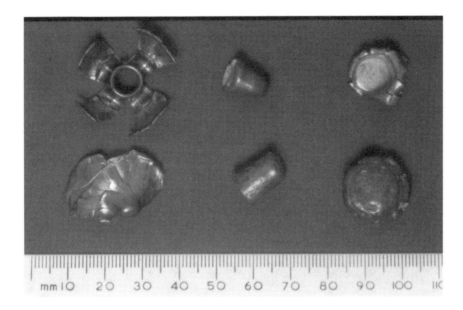

**Figure 9.18** In a perfect world the forensic scientist would always get perfect bullets from the crime scene or victim. In real life, badly damaged projectiles are often the case. However, careful examination will often reveal matchable areas of bore markings. The police scene of crime officer must however handle and package such items with great care before submitting them to the laboratory.

**Figure 9.19** Fired cartridge cases showing the locations of operational markings.

relation to the firing pin mark will usually provide definitive identification in your notes on spent rim-fire cartridge cases. Note whether the cartridge case is plain brass, nickel-plated brass, aluminium, lacquered or coated steel, and the type and nature of the priming. Similar notes should be made on the construction and the weight of the bullet, and if any core base marks are present.

In those instances where the crime weapon has not yet been recovered there will be a requirement to attempt to determine what type of weapon was used, what likely model and make of firearm was responsible, and if the same weapon has been used in other unsolved shooting incidents. Such notions are discounted by Burrard in his famous book, *The Identification of Firearms and Forensic Ballistics*, as follows.

> I can but repeat, therefore, that my own purely personal opinion is that it is a waste of time and effort to try to do much more than determine the general type of weapon used by examinations of either fired bullets, or cartridge cases, or both. And that the better plan is to examine any suspect weapon from time to time when "impossibles" and "possibles" can be ascertained quickly and with absolute certainty.

One has to remember that at the time of writing this statement Burrard was not in the business of attempting to operate a central ballistics service facility, which would overview submissions from many incidents. He would have been called out by the firm of defence solicitors involved on a job-by-job basis. There would be no need to even attempt to operate such a system in such circumstances. It is true to say that, in the absence of some special peculiarity, it is extremely difficult to be certain as to the type of weapon from bullet information alone. Data gleaned from cartridge cases can be very rewarding however, and if this is considered in conjunction with the rifling pattern then the chances of success can be quite high in many instances. When advising the police investigation team however, it is wise to attempt to indicate the degree of likelihood associated with your findings. In the worst situation this will unfortunately take the form...'The operational markings upon the bullet and cartridge case correspond to those which could have been imparted by a large number of different makes of self-loading pistols in this calibre'. In more favourable circumstances you will be able to be far more specific. I have worked for many years in a department which has achieved a very high rate of success in such matters. In any event, the intelligence you have generated will be incorporated into your Outstanding Crimes Files to be used to support the interrogation. This is one operation which Burrard would never have had to consider.

In order to do all of this it is necessary to carry out the examinations previously mentioned and then perform some additional measurements. The best, but the most abused system, is that developed by the FBI in the US. This system, which is referred to as The General Rifling Characteristics File (GRC), is available on application to the FBI. One can use this system by way of manually referring to the printout of the files, or by use of computer interrogation. The following steps are involved:

1. The cartridge type is identified and entered using the terminology acceptable to the program, e.g., 9 mm Luger, as indicated in the listing (Figure 9.20).
2. The likely firearm type is entered using a one or two letter code, e.g., PI for self-loading pistol.
3. The rifling pattern is entered, first by the direction of twist, followed by the number of grooves, e.g., R and 06 for six groove right-hand twist rifling (Figure 9.21).
4. The land and the groove width impressions are then entered after measuring them on a suitable instrument. The land width impression is the measurement in thousandths of an inch starting from the bottom left edge of the impression and then measuring to the bottom right-hand edge of the impression. The high and low values are entered thus — 072–076. If the bullet is damaged and you are only able to do limited measurements, you can enter a suitable range which brackets your best readings. The groove width, which of course appears in reverse as a raised section on the bullet, is measured between the two land impressions, measured from the bottom right-hand edge of the left-land impression to the bottom left-hand edge of the adjacent land impression. The range, or the estimated range by calculation if difficulties are encountered with this measurement, is entered as before in units of one thousandths of an inch, e.g., 104–110.
5. The shape of the firing pin impression is then noted using the correct code letter, e.g., H represents a hemispherical pin impression. It is also possible in circular or rectangular pin impressions to enter the width of the pin mark in hundredths of an inch, this is often used in the case of rim-fire cases, but is barely necessary in the case of centre-fire exhibits, e.g., C13. Special codes are of considerable value in rim-fire exhibits which also indicate the direction of slant of commonly encountered rectangular pin impressions.
6. The locations of any extractor and ejector markings on the spent cartridge case are then entered (Figure 9.22). A set of numbers on a clockface are used here to indicate the relative locations. A nominal location of three o'clock is used for the extractor mark as this is the most commonly encountered orientation on the weapon, and at this stage it is not possible to be sure of the exact disposition of the extractor claw on the particular weapon. The ejector location will then be set at a clockwise rotation of the clockhand from this point, e.g., 3–7 would represent a commonly encountered entry. If there is obvious evidence of a cut-out in the chamber for the extractor the notation 3C-7 would be appropriate, although this is not an essential point. The clock points used, starting at 12 o'clock are -1,

**Figure 9.20** Examination of cartridge cases and bullets using the profile projector allows the majority of the information for the FBI program computer search for weapon type to be accurately recorded.

2, 3, 4, 6, 7, 9 and T Marks falling between the clock points are coded according to their nearest position; if in doubt use the next higher value.

**Figure 9.21** Periphery camera picture showing the entire rifling pattern of a 9 mm bullet fired from a Luger pistol. Rifling pattern here is six turns right-hand twist. Even on this picture the very real differences in striation pattern from one land impression to the next are clearly visible.

**Figure 9.22** The unusual location of the ejector impact mark at 2 o'clock near to the primer is characteristic in this instance of the use of a Polish Radom P35 9 mm self-loading pistol.

7. A code representing the breech face marks caused by the machining process used on the breech face are then encoded using three entries: P = parallel lines; C = circular lines; S = smooth. Where there is a mark left by a slot cut in the breech face showing up on the edge of the cartridge case, as in the case of the slot in the recoil face of a revolver for the hand (pawl), this can also be entered, e.g., P7. The location of the slot on the weapon will be the mirror image of that found on the cartridge; this second type of entry is rarely used.

The successful use of this system depends entirely upon the skill of the examiner in correctly identifying the locations of the marks and entering rifling dimensions which have been correctly measured. If in doubt in this second area, it is advisable to enter a wider range in the land and groove widths and chance pulling more entries from the system, rather than entering a very tight search range which just misses registering a hit by one thousandth of an inch if you have chosen to adopt a computer search instead of manual reference. Great care must be taken when measuring the rifling impressions left upon damaged bullets, or when trying to determine the correct extractor and ejector marks on ammunition which has previously been cycled through the action of a firearm prior to being fired, which has resulted from the firing of reloaded ammunition, or involves a weapon design leaving other marks on the cartridge case which the uninitiated might confuse with ejector marks, e.g., the mark left by a loaded chamber indicator pin (Figure 9.23).

The system will usually indicate a few hits for each interrogation. It is useful at this stage if representative samples of the indicated weapons can be taken from the laboratory reference collection of firearms, so that test-firings from these can then be directly compared with the crime exhibit. It is a considerable help in this respect if you in fact have such an extensive laboratory reference collection. You can then use other non-listed characteristics to whittle down the list of possibles. An example of supportive features would be the chamber-loading indicator pin mark with cut-out in the breech left by a Walther PPK pistol, the fluted chamber marks left by a Heckler and Koch firearm (Figure 9.24), polygonal rifling upon the bullet, the blade-like firing pin impression of the Glock pistol, or the pronounced semi-circular machining marks which appear on the recoil face of many Tokarev pistols. There will of course be many other characteristic features for other makes of weapon, which with experience the ballistic examiner will file in the prime computer situated between his ears, which will allow him to make many

**Figure 9.23** The marks left at the 12 o'clock positions on the cartridge cases indicate a selfloading pistol with a loaded chamber indicator pin. In this instance a Walther PPK.

**Figure 9.24** Distinctive chamber fluting marks left upon 9 mm cartridge cases fired in a weapon of Heckler and Koch manufacture. Such distinctive effects greatly support or shorten the computer search for weapon type.

provisional findings at the scenes of shooting incidents in the years to come. In this respect however, it is important to verify all such findings by proper search and examination back at the laboratory.

The FBI system described is a very powerful tool which can give correct results in most instances. However, it is only as good as the operator using it. If fed erroneous information, or if the correct terminology is not used during the computer interrogation, it will not work. In this latter respect it is an advantage, particularly if the system is used only occasionally, to use it on a manual basis. The value of using the secondary supportive check by way of comparison with the reference collection of firearms is enormous. In the case of the 9 mm Parabellum cartridge, additional supportive information can be found in *The Matrix* publication if you do not have access to a reference collection. It is also possible for you to build up your own database by noting the significant characteristics in a file on every new weapon that passes through your hands. On this direct low-cost basis, it is amazing how soon you will end up with a wealth of potentially useful information. The information concerning the likely weapon used in the shooting incident can then be used to screen the exhibits for comparison against cartridge cases and bullets contained in the laboratory Outstanding Crimes Files.

These same principles will hold true when examining cartridge cases, bullets or cartridge wadding at the scene of shooting incidents if you are able to recall the use of the same unusual calibre or loading in previous shooting incidents. Once again however, all provisional stated findings should be properly confirmed back at the laboratory. In such instances access to an extensive reference collection of ammunition is a boon. It is also good practice to make up databases and reference collections of propellants, wadding and missiles from dismantled ammunition for future reference. This is no great chore if samples are placed in the system as part of the normal working routine, and it is amazing how the systems grow, and in turn become increasingly more useful.

## 9.10 Examination of Bullet- or Pellet-Damaged Items

Information has already been provided in Chapters 7 and 8 covering the postmortem examination in respect of the examination of wound samples and damaged clothing. The enormous value of the simple sodium rhodizonate test for lead cannot be stressed too highly in all examinations. The presence of this element in quantity around the margin of a hole will help you confirm that the damage is firearm missile related and not some previous form of damage. At the same time it will allow you to determine direction of fire and differentiate between entry and exit holes. Always sketch the item in question in your notes together with dimensions and the location of the damage with respect to other prominent features. Examination for close-range firing effects, such as blackening or powdering should be routine. The intensity and the pattern of discharge products shown on the filter paper pressing after treatment with sodium rhodizonate, can also be used to help determine distance of firing by comparison with test-firings on pieces of card or a witness material similar to the damaged object, or in some instances such as clothing tests this can be done on a convenient part of the garment distant from the area of missile damage. Chemical detection tests for the presence of nitrites produced from the combustion products of smokeless nitro powders can also be used for range of fire estimation upon missile-damaged clothing. This method is particularly useful in instances where lead-free cartridge loadings have been used. Such loadings may well employ steel or other non-toxic shotgun pellets, bullets constructed from copper alloys or bullets completely encapsulated in thick electrodeposited copper coatings. The Griess Test or one of its modifications is appropriate here. This test procedure can be followed by the sodium rhodizonate test.

The first simplified Griess test procedure, described by Robert J. Shem in 2001, involves the use of Marshall's Reagent N-(1-napthyl)–ethylenediamine, which consists of 5 grams dissolved in one litre of methanol, a 5 grams per litre aqueous solution of sulphanilic acid and glacial acetic acid. These stock solutions can be stored separately in tightly sealed opaque bottles for several years without deteriorating. Seven parts of each of the first two reagents are then mixed with one part of glacial acetic acid in a 10×12 inch plastic photographic developing tray. Dip a 185 mm Whatman No. 2 filter paper disc into the solution so as to ensure its saturation. Remove the disc and allow excess reagent to drip back into the tray. Place the paper on top of the area of clothing to be examined, overlaying it with several sheets of dry filter paper or copying paper. Press down with a clothing iron or photographic press, pre-warmed to approximately 225°F/107°C, for 30 seconds. On separating the papers the test paper will reveal transferred nitrites from partially burned propellant as brown-red azo-dye spots. Colour photographs, including a scale, will allow the documentation of this test result and those of subsequent ranging tests obtained with the same ammunition and preferably the crime weapon. The heat will cause the test papers to dry quickly ready for the follow up sodium rhodizonate test. After lightly spaying with a saturated aqueous solution of sodium rhodizonate followed by 5% aqueous hydrochloric acid, lead-rich areas will be revealed as magenta coloured spots. This test result can also be photographed to produce a convenient and lasting record to be kept in your case notes. Any written identification on the test papers should first be done in pencil, as the methanol will cause ink to run. The location of pockets, buttonholes, seams and buttons can be outlined in pencil. If required, an intermediate spray should be applied before the hydrochloric acid, using an aqueous buffer solution of 19 g/l sodium bitartrate and 15 g/l tartaric acid, to differentiate between barium and lead. In some instances the Griess test paper should be allowed to sit overnight before the rhodizonate test is conducted, if little or no response is first observed. This delay will allow intensification of the reaction sites for visualisation of the azo-dye spots indicating the presence of nitrites. An FBI procedure using pre-treated desensitised photographic paper calls for completed test result to be lightly sprayed with 5% aqueous hydrochloric acid. This causes the red-coloured reaction sites to turn deep purple, thus enhancing the visual result. Whichever method is used, the photographic record of the crime garment test can be compared on a side-to-side basis with those results obtained by test-firing the firearm at samples of cloth at various measured distances, in order to determine the likely range of firing.

The various modified Griess test procedures were introduced at a time when Marshall's reagent was thought to be carcinogenic, although no evidence at this date has been found to support this presumption. The test can involve the use of desensitised glossy or matte black and white photographic paper or Whatman No. 2 filter paper. The test papers are then treated with a mixture of equal volumes of an aqueous 5 g/l solution of sulphanilic acid, and a solution of 2.8 g/l of alpha-naphthol in methanol. The papers are then allowed to dry on an uncontaminated surface. Photographic paper has the advantage that sheets can be treated and stored in advance for future tests. Place a sheet of the test paper on the clothing site to be examined. Spray the paper with an aqueous 15% solution of acetic acid until very damp. Overlay with several sheets of filter paper and press with a hot iron (on "cotton" setting), as before. Nitrite sites will be revealed by the formation of an orange coloured azo-dye. Once again, the same care must be taken in marking the test papers and photographing the results for subsequent storage.

Traces of copper left by jacketed bullets or shotgun pellets may be detected upon impact or ricochet sites on hard surfaces, or even upon the margins of holes in fabric produced by such missiles. Although SEM/EDX techniques are mentioned in Section 9.13, there are considerable advantages to be gained from the convenience of simple chemical tests similar to the sodium rhodizonate test for traces of lead, particularly when examining possible missile impact sites at the scene of an incident. A choice of two reagents for the detection of copper have been used for such purposes. Dithio-oxamide (Rubeanic Acid) and 2-nitroso-1-napthol. The latter reagent is considered to produce more observable colour changes in work conducted by L.C. Haag (see Further Reading). Suitably thick filter paper or waxy plastic-backed paper such as 'BenchKOTE' may be used to lift traces of copper from the site for testing. If the use of the sodium rhodizonate test is also contemplated, then it is best done after the copper lift if the user employs a lift moistened with acetic acid or tartaric acid, as such materials will tend to remove any traces of copper present.

The first method uses a reagent consisting of 0.2% dithio-oxamide in ethanol, and a moistening agent for the lifting paper of 40% ammonium hydroxide solution in water. It is important that the lift is applied with firm pressure for about half a minute, and that the paper is not allowed to slip out of place on the site of interest. The paper can also be marked with an indelible marker to identify it and to note the positions of adjacent points of interest. Subsequent application of the reagent will reveal traces of copper with an olive green colouration, that can sometimes be difficult to discern if obscured by background colours from any gunshot residues, earth or rust. The second method uses a reagent consisting of 0.2% 2-nitroso-1-napthol in ethanol, which signifies the presence of traces of copper by a pinkish red colouration. This reagent will also indicate the presence of iron with a dark green colouration. The same 40% ammonium hydroxide lifting solution used above may be employed with this method, although, at the discretion of the examiner a 100% ammonium hydroxide solution will tend to yield a greater colour response and more detail.

Induction coupled mass spectroscopy (ICPMS) is sometimes advocated for the determination of trace elements contained in lead alloy bullets, shot-gun pellets or bullet fragments. However, before making wild claims for the discriminating power of this tool, it must be borne in mind that batches of lead supplied to the cartridge companies can be used to manufacture vast numbers of bullets, and that sub-batches of the same stock material can be sent to different cartridge manufacturers. (See Thompson and Wyant "Lead is Lead" at chapter end.)

## 9.11 Comparison Microscopy

Proper preliminary examination of cartridge cases, bullets and wads should always be conducted, as previously explained, at the bench using the stereo microscope set at a relatively low magnification before you move on to the comparison microscope. The observations and the notes you have previously made will act as a primer for all that is to follow and will also help guard against missing some important feature. You can then look for the presence of similar features on your test-fired exhibits. It is always good practice once you have settled at the comparison microscope to check that you are able to match your tests against each other. In doing this you will gain confidence in determining which major features will then serve you as starting points, since the crime bullet in particular may be damaged to a degree where a large portion of the original bore features have been obliterated (Figure 9.18). If you have trouble matching your tests then you can assume that the examination against the crime exhibit will not be particularly easy, and you may consider obtaining further tests. If there are any marks present on your tests which you find difficulty in accounting for, then it is again good practice to look at the workings of the suspect weapon so that you can identify their source. An example that comes to mind is the mark left by some types of pump-action shotguns on cartridges which have previously been in the tubular magazine. This mark is imparted to the edge of the head of the cartridge case by the magazine cartridge stop when the recoil produced by firing causes the cartridge at the end of the tube to impact upon this part of the mechanism. In shootings where several shots have been fired you might find these marks on cartridge cases associated with firings after the initial discharge, but not on the case associated with the first discharge as this cartridge will not have been subjected to recoil effects in the magazine or may have been manually inserted into the chamber.

The headstamps in Figure 9.19 indicate that all of the fired cases have originated from British Service 9×19 millimetre ammunition manufactured at the Radway Green Ordnance Plant in the year 1961. The nature and the relative locations of the operational marks imposed upon them will have been used, along with information concerning the rifling patterns on any recovered bullets, to help identify the make and model of the pistol used in the incident. The basic similarities exhibited by the markings indicate the likely use of a single pistol in the shooting. These simple sketches also ensure that you will not mix up the three exhibits when placing them back in their original labelled exhibit bags. The inclination of the firing pin drag mark relative to the position of the extractor (indicated inside the underlying rim) is typical of a weapon utilising a Browning type locking breech, where the breech end of the barrel is caused to drop a short way downwards as its locking lugs become disengaged from the recesses machined in the top of the slide. Helped by the indicated locations of the various markings you can now fix the cases in the correct orientations on the microscope stages to compare, for example, the extractor marks on two of them.

Your notes on the bullets should record their weights and include a simple sketch of them if they exhibit impact damage or deformation. In the case of bullets basic information such as the direction of the rifling pattern and the number of land impressions should always be noted. This last point might seem to be a very basic one to some people, but it can save a lot of time wasted upon fruitless or misleading comparison microscopy. I can recall one particular murder case outside the UK where a colleague from my department found that the original examination work carried out in previous years had failed to note that the number of grooves on the crime bullet did not match that of the rifling pattern in the suspect rifle. Notes made concerning the style of the bullet and the locations and widths of lubrication bands and crimping grooves, may also allow you to determine the brand of ammunition used. The reloading of handgun ammunition is relatively common, so it is important to note the presence of sprue and mould marks left from the casting of homemade bullets, and the nature and colour of traces of bullet lubricants present inside lubrication grooves. Reloading bullets are also available from cartridge companies or bulletsmiths. A reference collection of such missiles can again be very helpful.

Your initial notes made upon cartridge cases should include a sketch showing the headstamp, the shape and relative position of the firing pin impression, and any other operational marks or signs of damage. Lacquer present inside the case mouth and the primer area usually indicates the use of factory-loaded ammunition. Resizing die marks upon the case walls, badly seated primers, and multiple operational markings usually indicates the use of reloaded ammunition.

In the case of exhibit cartridge cases thought to have been fired from a self-loading pistol, your preliminary examination notes should contain a sketch of the features shown upon them. In the example below on three crime scene cartridge cases I have chosen to put the headstamps in the same orientation, and have then gone on to indicate the observed locations of the extractor marks, the ejector marks, the attitude of the firing pin drag marks, and the location of parallel impressed machining marks from the breech face upon the soft material of the primer (Figure 9.25 and Figure 9.26).

When setting the main exhibits on the stages of the comparison microscope, I find it useful to follow a routine in which the crime exhibit is always positioned on the left-hand stage; the connotation sinister intrudes here I think. The test-fires will be placed on the right-hand stage. Since it is often

**Figure 9.25** View of matching breech face features on .357 in Magnum cartridge cases.

**Figure 9.26** Another view of matching breech face impressions on cartridge cases.

necessary to look at several tests before you find one which clearly shows the features of interest to best effect, the adherence to a routine system such as the one suggested helps prevent irritating mix-ups of exhibits, although as previously recommended each of them will bear an identifying mark. Manufacturers of the most respected microscopes will provide devices specifically designed to hold bullets and cartridge cases in place during their examination. These little devices usually come with a disproportionate price tag. Most working laboratories end up leaving most of these gadgets in the drawer and use the basic flat mounts with a wad of Blu-tack or a special pressure-sensitive wax adhesive to allow infinitely variable adjustment of the way in which the exhibit can be conveniently mounted.

Always start at the lowest magnification, which should be about ×10, or perhaps a little less. Over the years I have seen so many people go off course during an examination by simply deviating from this approach, they fight to find a non-existent match in some fine detail at high magnification, when the correct match-point and obvious features of reference are somewhere else. One particular land or groove on the crime and test bullets may well be different in width than the rest, or may contain an unusual gross feature or mark that you can use as a starting point when mounting the crime and the test bullets on the stages of the comparison microscope. Such marks can be due to an uneven rifling tool, impact damage to the crowned muzzle end of the barrel, a particular irregularity in the machining of the cone at the end of the cartridge chamber in the barrel, or in the case of a revolver due to the bullet clipping the side of the barrel throat, due to poor barrel-chamber alignment (poor cylinder timing). Features such as an offset firing pin impression, the location of an extractor or ejector mark and other features recorded earlier in your examination notes can all be used during the initial stages of comparison microscopy to assist you in the initial orientation of your crime and control cartridge cases on the microscope stages before attempting to find individual matching features. If such gross effects are not evident, it will then be necessary to conduct a systematic search, initially at relatively low magnification on the comparison microscope until similar features or corresponding sub-class features are found, after which the crime and test bullets can both be rotated in phase with each other to confirm the agreement against the remaining areas of rifling. Once satisfied that your bullets are truly in phase with each other then you can examine areas of matching fine detail at higher levels of magnification, usually 20×, 40× and higher to resolve fine detail, although there is a price to pay each time magnification is increased, and very high magnification using a conventional optical microscope will act against your endeavours as it shrinks the field of view and the depth of focus. This latter aspect is important, as many of the objects you will have to look at will have curved surfaces, such as a bullet or cartridge case, firing pin impression, or an extractor mark left inside the rim of a cartridge case. The movement of both stages will necessitate constant changes to the focus adjustment, especially in the case of damaged and distorted objects. Continual adjustments to the incidence of illumination will be required to best reveal features, and stage adjustments made to compensate for natural variations in the reproduction and pick-up of operational markings (Figure 9.27).

Obtaining control test-fire bullets and cartridge cases from a firearm for comparison against crime submitted items, or exhibits held in the laboratory outstanding crimes files, should always involve the firing of several different cartridge loadings. The nature of the marks picked up by ammunition components will often differ markedly from one type of loading to another. A jacketed bullet will behave differently from a plain lead bullet during its passage through the rifling (Figure 9.28). Differences in the pressures generated during firing, and the hardness of the cartridge primer will also induce differences in pick-up of individual marks. The resistance to impact of the primer cups used in military cartridge loadings are usually greater than those used in commercial loadings. Even when firing several shots using the same type of loading, differences will often be observed in how well these marks are picked up due to natural variations in the pressure levels generated by individual cartridges upon their discharge. Your choice of control ammunition should always include some of a similar type to that used in the crime, and here it is useful to include tests using any live incident-related ammunition submitted. The same approach should be adopted when selecting pellets for control firings from air weapons (Figure 9.29). It is also important that these control firings be obtained during the early stages of your examination of the firearm.

The systematic approach set out will also help protect the novice from the ever-present danger of false-matches and missing real ones. It is of course good policy in any organisation to have a routine quality assurance process operating, which in the case of microscopy will involve a second reporting officer confirming the 'match'. I always remember some years ago a relative newcomer called me to check his match which he asserted consisted of a very marked feature containing a shape like the merging of the letters N and P on the primer. In this case I was able to point out that the live Swedish Norma manufacture ammunition had primers marked with this particular trademark in every instance and that it was not therefore a breech-face generated marking. As chance would have it, the orientation of this product marking and the other features were the same on the test and crime exhibits. Less obvious false-matches can occur if you use crime ammunition for your tests which have similar marks on their heads from faulty manufacturing bunters or primer seating dies. Check your live ammunition first under the low-power

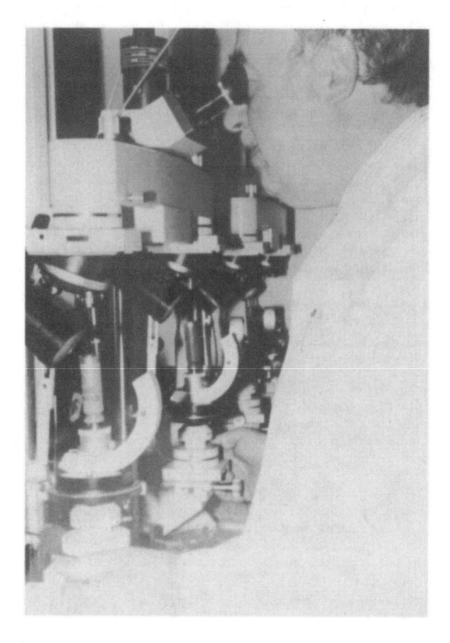

**Figure 9.27**   The author at the comparison microscope. This equipment consists of two microscopes joined together with an optical bridge so as to allow the simultaneous examination of 'crime' and 'test' exhibits. The stages allow freedom of movement and rotation of the items under examination along with a similar level of control over the illumination.

**Figure 9.28** View of matching rifling land impressions on a .38 in jacketed bullet. Once the initial match point has been found the bullets are then rotated to confirm matching points around the rest of the missile's rifled exterior.

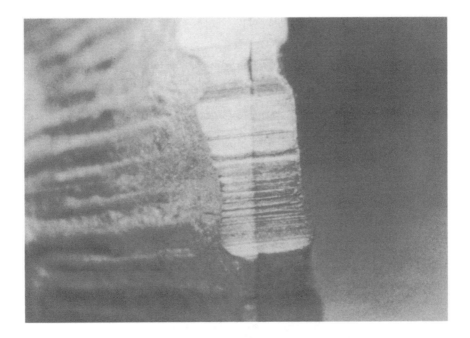

**Figure 9.29** Matching detail viewed by conventional comparison microscopy on the skirts of two waisted lead air rifle pellets.

stereo microscope before using it in your tests, especially when using some of the crime ammunition.

Examples of the types of markings which can be imparted by the mechanism or the rifling of a gun are provided in Chapter 5. Information is also provided concerning the possibility of finding reproducible markings on plastic shotgun cartridge wadding which has been fired from sawn-off guns (Figure 9.30). The examination of such wads is not easy, and it will often be necessary to recover a number of test wads to find one which has chanced to pick up these markings in the same manner as the crime wad. It is useful if you keep a stock of cartridges containing plastic wads which have a long bearing surface most likely to pick up the marks best from the rough features existing at the crudely sawn-off end of the barrel of the suspect weapon. In some instances the contrast can be increased if you briefly expose the wad to the smoke from a short length of burning magnesium ribbon, or simply apply an alcoholic suspension of colloidal graphite to the wad and then allow it to dry naturally.

Test-fired cartridge cases and bullets from submitted weapons will usually be checked against exhibits held in the laboratory Outstanding Crimes File, along with cartridge cases and bullets recovered from shooting incidents

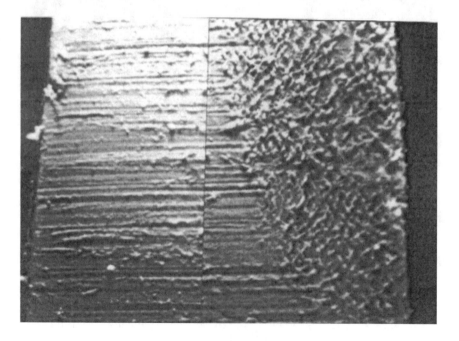

**Figure 9.30** Part of a matching pattern of marks left upon 12-bore plastic cartridge wadding when fired from a sawn-off shotgun with a rough muzzle end.

in which the weapon has not yet been recovered. The methods referred to in the examination of cartridge cases and bullets can allow you in some instances to narrow your search down to the most likely exhibits, to see if the same weapon has been used previously. Information of this nature represents a powerful source of intelligence for the various police forces, as these days a weapon can be used in incidents in other force areas. Electronic image storage is now possible for bullet and cartridge case exhibits. Automatic image storage and identification systems were introduced by Forensic Technology Inc. of Canada under the name Integrated Bullet Identification System (IBIS), along with the programme names Brasscatcher and Bulletproof. This became the system of choice for the Bureau of Alcohol Tobacco and Firearms (BATF). The Federal Bureau of Investigation (FBI) offered their own similar system called Drugfire. The name Drugfire was coined from the then dramatic increase in the use of 9 mm semi-automatic weaponry in drug-related crime in the US, and the perceived need for an automatic database. There was of course, some confusion and friction caused by two US federal agencies using different systems, which in turn affected the marketing of the two systems. There was also the real need for compatibility of data transfer between different police agencies.

In December of 1999 a memorandum of understanding was introduced between the two federal agencies that resulted in the setting up of a single federal ballistics imaging system combining the best features of the BATF IBIS system and the FBI Drugfire system. This became known as the National Integrated Ballistics Identification Network (NIBIN). Provisions of the agreement included the FBI being responsible for nationwide NIBIN communications, network and connectivity between system sites and the national network. The BATF became responsible for NIBIN hardware and software development, installations, training, security, maintenance, user protocols and support, and quality control. The joint integrated approach to ballistic imaging would thus benefit all federal, state and local law enforcing agencies by ending the competition between systems and providing law enforcement with enhanced crime fighting technology from both the FBI and the BATF. The BATF became responsible for replacing existing Drugfire systems, while the FBI continued to support any Drugfire systems not yet replaced during the transitional period, and for any NIBIN communications requirements. The system allows automatic searches to be made against stored images of cartridge cases and bullets held on record at individual sites or exchanged over the network. Hits are ranked in order of similarity, thus allowing manual microscopic examination of suitable candidate exhibits in order to confirm a match. In 2003, the Forensic Science Service acquired two IBIS stations, which were then installed at their London and Manchester firearms reporting laboratories. The London Metropolitan Police are in the process of acquiring their own Forensic Technology unit as part of the NFFID/ACPO initiative mentioned later in this section.

The Firearms Consultative Committee had recommended in their 10th and 11th annual reports that the information obtained from the examination of casework related firearms should be held on a computerised database. This information, along with any connections against exhibits held in the Out-standing Crimes Files System, and firearms licensing records, would then provide the police with a record of the criminal use of firearms and their possible provenance. Funding was provided through the Home Office to implement these recommendations, and in April 2003, the National Firearms Forensic Intelligence Database (NFFID) was launched using a matrix agreed between the Forensic Science Service (FSS) and the Association of Chief Police Officers (ACPO). This matrix uses a points system for guidance as to the nature of firearms to be submitted for inclusion on the NFFID. A score of 12 points or more denotes the suitability of a candidate firearm. The score includes points awarded in respect of the circumstances surrounding the recovery of the firearm, its condition, classification under existing firearms legislation, any unique features, whether it is disguised as another object, if it is a de-activated firearm restored to a working condition, aspects of interest for intelligence purposes, if it has been fitted with a silencer, if it has been used in crime and is the property of a holder of a firearms certificate, and if the Intelligence Bureau considers it to be of significant interest in respect of national or regional issues.

In February 2003, Forensic Technology Inc. announced the introduction of their Virtual Serial Number (VSN) system. They claim that it automates the process for capturing and storing digital images of the serial numbers of firearms and respective test-fired cartridge cases during their process of man-ufacture. It is further claimed that this new technology will allow police to identify a crime gun and begin to trace its history by simply examining a cartridge case at a crime scene. In the same way it is possible to obtain this same information from test-fired cartridge cases obtained from recovered weapons even if their serial numbers have been obliterated. Such methodol-ogy can only, of course, be conducted on cartridge cases related to new firearms produced by manufacturers participating in this system.

When considering the nature of marks that a firearm might impart to both bullet and cartridge case one need give consideration to aspects of their manufacture. In this respect the tools and the various mechanical processes involved during its fabrication are relevant. The glossary of the Association of Firearm and Tool Mark Examiners (AFTE) provides a large number of technical definitions that I have used as a guide in this section. The definition for a tool that might be used in such processes uses the expression An object used to gain mechanical advantage. Also thought of as the harder of two objects which when brought into contact with each other, result in the softer one being marked.

The cutting or impacting surfaces of tools will contain imperfections, and in turn a negative form of these imperfections will be transferred from them to the machined surface. The profile of the cutting face of the tool can change during use due to wear, thus changing the nature of the pattern of marks imparted by it. During the work process the cutting edge of the tool can heat up due to frictional forces, causing loss of temper and the need for re-sharpening or replacement. The break-up of chips of metal can create built up projections on its cutting edge, which in turn can become detached. High operating temperatures can weld chips to the tool's cutting edge. When subsequently broken off they can cause the forcible detachment of part of the tool's original cutting edge.

Striated tool-marks are contour variations, generally of a microscopic nature, imparted to an object by the application of a force where movement of the tool is directed approximately parallel to the plane being marked. The expressions friction, abrasion and scratch marks can also be applied here. These marks can exhibit both class and/or individual characteristics. They are observed under the microscope as a series of bright lines of the ridges interspaced by dark lines from the intervening troughs. The nature of the surface topography will dictate the width and the frequency of the striae. Very shallow scratch marks containing striae are referred to as 2D tool-marks, whilst those containing deeper impressions are referred to as 3D tool-marks. Impressed tool-marks, or impression marks, are produced when enough pressure is applied to a tool held perpendicular to the work surface so as to leave behind an impression. The observed class characteristics will suggest the nature of the tool used, whilst individual characteristics can be used to identify the particular tool involved in their production. These marks can contain Class and/or Individual Characteristics. Individual characteristicsare produced incidental to the manufacturing processes by the random nature of tool wear producing imperfections in its cutting surfaces, and by random imperfections caused by wear, damage and corrosion during the subsequent service life of the firearm. Due to their random, chance provenance, these imparted marks are unique. Sufficient agreement is reached if there is such a significant duplication of markings that they can be considered to be individual characteristics and that the likelihood that another gun could have made them is so remote that it can be discounted.

The majority of the striated tool marks left inside the completed rifled barrel are created during the drilling, reaming, rifling and finishing operations. Burrs are also left after the crowning of the barrel muzzle and the cutting of the chamber cone or throat. Bullets passing down the barrel during the firing process may not always bottom out into the grooves, especially when hard jacketed bullets are involved. Bore dimensions can vary within the limits of machining tolerances, and the jacketed bullets of some old military, e.g., 9 mm Parabellum ammunition can be relatively undersize. The fired bullets will therefore bear clear impressions of the rifling lands, and a lesser degree of marking from the bottoms of the grooves. Characteristic longitudinal tool marks will be left inside the bore where the rifling process involved the removal of metal, but the central land areas will have been little affected by the process, leaving behind a circular pattern of tool marks upon them from the initial drilling and reaming processes. Where swaging rifling techniques that do not involve metal removal are used, the drilling and reaming marks are flattened by the high pressures involved, leaving a very smooth interior finish containing concentric marks which impart individual characteristics upon fired bullets. Imperfections upon the profile of the rifling button or mandrel impart less obvious axial striae as they are moved along the inside of the bore. These latter features, along with imperfections produced during the crowning of the muzzle and the machining of the chamber cone and the leade will impart striations upon the bullet.

In a study of Heckler and Koch USP .40 in Smith & Wesson pistols described by Lardizabel in 1995, only poor quality markings were left upon test-fired cartridge cases. However, significantly corresponding and identifiable markings attributable to a tool-mark above the firing pin orifice in the breech face of two sequentially manufactured pistols, apparently made after the finishing process, persisted after over 250 test firings.

Marks found upon cartridge cases include firing pin impressions; scratches left as the cartridge slides across the lips of the magazine; impressed marks imparted by a loaded chamber indicator hole and pin set in the breech face; the ejector rod and the profile of its cut-out in the breech face; marks left by the ejected cartridge case striking the edge of the ejection port; the recoil induced mark left by the cartridge stop within the breech end of a tubular magazine; recoil impressed machining marks from the breech face; the circular marks produced by the rotation of a bolt; impressed marks left by striker housing plates set in the breech face, along with their fixing screws or the pin holes used to unscrew them; the slot cut in the recoil face of a revolver for its pawl; scratches on the case walls caused by imperfections in the edge of the chamber mouth or the cartridge elevator ramp; marks left upon the case wall from a chamber imperfection made during manufacture or as a result of a gas cut left by a previously fired ruptured cartridge case; erosion marks around the edge of the firing pin hole produced by pierced primers; damage to the recoil face caused by the careless use of a steel cleaning rod; impact marks on the cartridge head and mouth from the impact of the slide or bolt, characteristic marks in front of the rim of a cartridge from the extractor cut-out(s) in conventional single or double-barrelled shotguns;

marks left by the extractor inside the rim and upon the edge of the head of the cartridge case when it rides over it during the chambering action; firing pin drag marks caused when the breech mechanism unlocks so as to allow the breech end of the barrel to drop slightly and thus clear its locking rings in the slide. It should also be borne in mind that one can expect some of these marks will also be found upon live ammunition that has been loaded at some time into the suspect firearm.

Sometimes unexpected marks can be found. In one outstanding murder case dealt with by my laboratory, examination of rifling pattern, the shape and inclination of the striker impression, and the position of the extractor suggested the association of a .22 in Colt Woodsman self-loading pistol, using what was then an unusual new loading of Remington 'Yellow Jacket' hollow-point ammunition. The striker impression was different from that generally found upon Colt pistols of this model, although we did find it to exist in one of the duplicate Colt Woodsman pistols contained in our extensive reference collection. The ejector mark was however, something of a puzzle. A colleague visited the curator in charge of the arms collection at the Colt factory in the US, and was told that no Colt Woodsman had been produced with such a pattern of firing pin. However, after rummaging through their collection, one previously unknown example similar to the one in our laboratory collection was unearthed. The police force involved in the murder investigation sent in test-fired cartridge cases produced by their own firearms officer upon all of the .22 in Colt Woodsman pistols registered to people in their area. However, for some reason he chose to be guided by one owner that his pistol was in an unsafe condition for such test firing to be conducted, and it goes without saying that this same individual had been one of the very few shown in simultaneous police enquiries of firearm dealer records to have purchased 'Yellow Jacket' ammunition just prior to the murder. No connection was found between all of the test firings submitted and the murder exhibits. Some twelve years later the same individual was arrested on charges of kidnap and extortion. One of the officers recalled him being initially 'in the frame' for the earlier murder. His Colt Woodsman was recovered in a dismantled condition inside his garden greenhouse. It was so badly rusted that its bore, striker and extractor had been rendered useless for the production of meaningful test firings. However, its magazine was recovered in a better condition, and it was noted that its lips extended higher when inserted into its housing in this particular pistol frame than was normal for this model of pistol. Using the magazine in a suitably proportioned Colt Woodsman obtained from the duplicate stock of the reference collection, revealed that during the firing operation the spent cartridge case impacted with the top edge of one of the magazine lips, rather than the dedicated ejector rod. The marks left upon test fired cartridge cases contained sufficient matching details to the exhibits left over all of those years in the Outstanding Crimes File, thus enabling the successful prosecution of the pistol owner for the previous murder.

Severe rusting of a rifled bore due to the effects of poor storage and cleaning, especially after use with ammunition employing corrosive primers, can cause great changes to the bore characteristics of a firearm. In other circumstances involving the use of non-corrosive ammunition other researchers have been able to associate fired bullets with a particular firearm even after considerable use. A comparison of four thousand consecutively fired, steel jacketed bullets from the same gun barrel, conducted by Doelling in 2001, found it possible to associate bullets with each other, using the criteria set down in earlier work conducted by Biasotti and Murdock (1997), regarding the use of consecutive matching striae as a criteria for matching bullets:

1.  In the case of three-dimensional toolmarks at least two different groups of at least three consecutive matching striae should exist in the same relative position, or one group of six consecutive matching striae are in agreement in an evidence toolmark compared to the test toolmark.
2.  In the case of two-dimensional toolmarks there should be at least two groups of five consecutive matching striae appearing in the same relative position, or one group of eight consecutive matching striae are in agreement in the evidence toolmark.
3.  For the above criteria to apply, the possibility of subclass characteristics must be ruled out.

In studies conducted by Miller *et al.* published in 1998, the Ibis computer was used to compare approximately two million land impressions on bullets fired from different .38 Special revolvers in order to search for the best known non-match candidates to check the validity of the criteria expressed by Biasotti and Murdock in 1997. These studies confirmed the validity of the conservative numerical striated toolmark criteria set out above. None of the two-dimensional known non-matches exceeded the criteria, and all were well within the stated parameters. None of the three-dimensional known non-matches had more than one group of three, and no groups of over four matching striae. In a paper published in 2000 concerning single land impression produced by different firearms, inter-comparisons were made of 34,524 examples in .25 in Auto, 92,304 in .380 in Auto, and 102,276 in 9 mm Luger. He reported that no single group of consecutive striae exceeding 4× were found in the .25 in Auto and the .380 in auto land impressions, no single group exceeding 3× in the case of the 9mm land impressions, and no combination of groups exceeding 2×-3×-5× in all of the known non-match comparisons. The highest combination group seen in one land impression from known non-matches, regardless of calibre, of two or three-dimensional striae was 2× and 5×. He concluded that, 'striations viewed in consecutive groups and combinations of consecutive groups proposed by Biasotti and Murdock is a reliable criteria that excludes erroneous identification, especially in limited striae cases, as in this study, where agreement in single land impressions only was considered'. Two further papers by the same researcher using two and ten consecutively rifled barrels confirmed that although there was carry-over of sub-class characteristics, this did not prevent the striae on the bullets examined being correctly attributed with the respective barrels.

After you are satisfied with the match obtained you should seek the service of a colleague to re-examine the exhibits on the microscope in order to confirm that you have achieved this, as part of your quality assurance management, before he sets down his initials and note of agreement in the relevant section of your notes. The same principles apply to the examination of other marks noted on bullets, cartridge cases or plastic shotgun cartridge wads subject to examination. Tool marks and the other marks mentioned can thus be specifically associated with each other.

As explained in Chapter 3, challenging the validity of the results of firearms laboratory casework findings is not a new phenomenon, and the implications of the Daubert ruling will continue to set the stage for the future. The basic quality assurance guidance set out in the previous paragraph represents the minimum standard acceptable. The paper by Murdock and Grzybowski, Firearm and Toolmark Identification — Meeting the Daubert Challenge, published in 1998, and the paper published in 1995 by Peterson and Markham, Crime Laboratory Testing Results, 1978—1991, II: Resolving questions of common origin, both attempt to deal with the issue of known or potential error rate. When I worked in the British Home Office Forensic Science Service the peer checking of all significant casework findings mentioned above, represented only the first stage of our quality assurance procedures. The laboratory itself was inspected by an external outside scientific body, the National Physical Laboratory for recognition by the UKSAS quality accreditation system, as outlined in British Standard BS.5750 and ISO.9000/9001. Written standards for all casework procedures, as agreed by the Chief Scientist of the Service responsible for the quality management, were set down in prescribed form in the respective laboratory operational manuals. In addition to the above, all casework reporting officers took part in a series of trials to check the nature of their work, their adherence to the standards set out in the laboratory quality assurance manual and the validity of their findings. All draft statements and casework notes were subjected to additional peer review and then initialled as having been checked by the second officer involved. Internal trials were prepared and then issued to reporting officers on a regular basis as set out in the manual. In addition to the declared trials and those obtained from the American firearms proficiency testing service, blind trials were prepared by our research establishment and submitted to the laboratory by the police mixed in with normal criminal casework submissions. It was not possible to determine who would pick up the particular case, and the wording of the submission forms did not betray its actual nature, so to ensure that the scientist involved would deal with it as a real case, and report it accordingly. All of the results of these declared and blind trials were published and made available for scrutiny. In turn, a laboratory manager responsible for quality procedures would routinely check case-files taken at random from the archives, and would record his findings as indicated in the quality assurance manual. The entire system was subject to auditing on a regular basis by both quality assurance officers and then subject by the same UKSAS independent external scientific body to ensure that all procedures, involving casework methodology, the regular independent testing of scientific instruments, the integrity of casework files, the records of all blind and declared proficiency trials and the general administration of operational procedures were in keeping with the standards set down in the departmental operational procedure manuals and the quality assurance manual.

British Standard ISO 17025, now specifically interpreted by the International Laboratory Accreditation Co-operation for forensic science laboratories, applies to laboratories that carry out measurements, and stipulates the requirements necessary to meet and to demonstrate technical competence. It covers a wide range of technical and quality management issues that include, management and organisational structures, the quality manual used in the laboratory, test and calibration of instrumentation, along with issues relating to document issue, review, approval and amendment. It also addresses how the laboratories should co-operate with customers so as to ensure they possess the capabilities to meet their needs, and that they deal properly with any complaints.

In US laboratories, proficiency tests, the American Society of Crime Laboratory Directors Laboratory Accreditation Board (ASCLD/LAB) requirements, the AFTE guidelines and laboratory protocols may be used to help ensure that firearm and tool mark examinations are reliably conducted and yield valid conclusions.

## 9.12 The Electron Microscope

It is possible, but not generally convenient, to examine firearm related marks on bullets and cartridge cases on the electron microscope, and I am aware of at least one instrument purpose built for comparison microscopy.

Normally the target object must be mounted and scanned *in situ* without the advantage of rotation of the stage. For these reasons the object must be deliberately set to secure a view of the feature of interest. Several photographs can be taken of the scanned areas of the crime and test exhibits. One can then cut the photographs so as to allow the matching regions to be aligned or overlaid. Magnification levels far higher than those normally used on the conventional optical instrument can be used because of the almost unlimited depth of field possible using this type of equipment (Figure 9.31). The use of such equipment during normal casework will be rare, but if the equipment is on site at the laboratory its occasional use might prove productive.

If this instrument is fitted with a microprobe facility then it can also be used to good effect in the analysis of firearm missile related materials. In some instances X-ray fluorescence or some other technique may be the preferred method of analysis. However, there is one area in which the scanning electron microscope with energy dispersive X-ray analysis (SEM/EDX) stands alone and that is in respect of the analysis of firearms discharge residues.

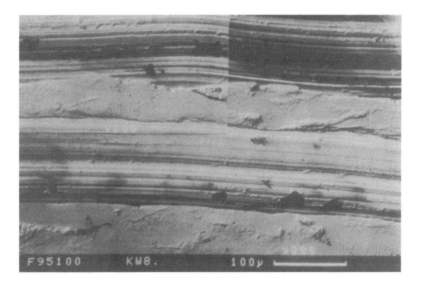

**Figure 9.31**  Scratch marks left by extractors, chamber mouths, magazines and edges of cartridge ejection ports are matched up in a similar manner. If high magnification is used on small scratches on curved surfaces, then reduced depth of focus can sometimes make things difficult. Here this problem is eliminated by the use of the electron microscope with its inherent great depth of focus, to match scratches on the exterior walls of two cartridge cases caused by the magazine lips.

## 9.13 Analysis of Firearms Discharge Residues

In Chapter 5, information is provided on the composition of propellants and primers. When a firearm is discharged the products of combustion of these materials, along with significant quantities of unburnt propellant, will be vented from the muzzle end of the barrel, the cylinder gap of a revolver, or from the breech of self-loading or pump-action arms during the ejection and reloading operations (Figure 9.32). There is a significant chance that some of this gas-borne material will be deposited on the hands, the face, the hair and the clothing of the firer. Some weapons will of course, by nature of their design or calibre, be more likely to deposit detectable quantities of these materials on the firer than others, and the level of deposition increases with the number of shots fired. High-speed cine or freeze-frame photography will reveal these effects. From the point of view of the analyst, there are two types of material of interest: propellant-generated organic residues and primer-generated inorganic residues.

Generally speaking, organic residues will be the easiest to detect and the ones most likely to be detected. The main constituents of modern smokeless powders are nitrocellulose in the case of single-base propellants, and nitrocellulose and nitroglycerine in the case of double-base propellants (Figure 9.33); 2,4-dinitrotoluene is another material frequently used in the formu-

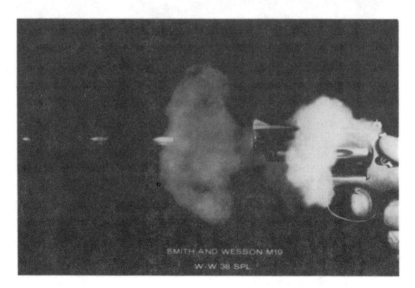

**Figure 9.32** High-speed triple flash photograph of revolver being fired clearly shows the venting of discharge gases from the area of the cylinder gap. Such an effect will increase the tendency for identifiable gunshot residues to be found upon hand and face swabs and upon the clothing of the firer. The opening of the breech as the slide or bolt of a self-loading or pump-action arm is moved to the rear, will have a similar effect.

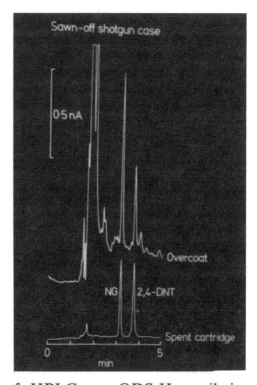

Results of HPLC on ODS-Hypersil in methanol aqueous phosphate (pH3), 100 : 89 v/v, with electrochemical detection at −1.0 V versus Ag/AgCl. The upper trace is from the overcoat of a man suspected of shooting another in a gang fight. The lower trace is from a spent shotgun cartridge left at the scene of the incident which contained nitroglycerin (NG) and 2,4-dinitrotoluene (2,4-DNT). Propellant residues have been detected on clothing a week or more after firing.

**Figure 9.33** High performance liquid chromatography recorder peaks for the organic constituents from the cartridge propellant found upon hand/face swabs or clothing of the firer. Nitrocellulose alone is not considered to be specific as its use is widespread in other industrial applications. The peaks here for nitroglycerine and 2, 4-dinitrotoluene are however indicative of the firing of a cartridge containing a double-base propellant.

lation of modern propellants. Unfortunately, nitrocellulose is a relatively common material frequently used in the formulation of lacquers and paints, and consequently cannot be considered on its own to be specific for gunshot residues.

The gunshot residue (GSR) particles range in size between 1 and 10 µm diameter. Their persistence on the hands of an individual during even normal activities is very limited; most will be cast off within 2 h and generally speaking a realistic time limit for their detection would be 4 h. However, these materials tend to cling to parts of the face, particularly, the hair. Residues have been detected on hair in casework 12 h after the shooting. Clothing worn by the firer is more likely again to reveal these materials, especially if the weave of the material is of a type likely to trap them. It is difficult to state the persistence of GSR on clothing, but successful detections can be made several days after the firing. If a fired pistol is placed in a pocket, then residues falling from its bore and its exterior could persist for a considerable period.

Non-woven cotton cloth swabs (Litex 10) prewetted with a mixture of isopropanol and water, are used in swabbing the hands, face and hair of the suspect. The swabs are centrifuged back at the laboratory and subjected to a cleanup process consisting of a solid-phase extraction with Chromosorb 104 prior to analysis using reversed phase High Performance Liquid Chromatography (HPLC) with electro-chemical reductive detector (EC). Peaks of interest are then injected for further study into a Gas Chromatograph (GC) which is equipped with a Thermal Energy Analyser (TEA). Any insoluble material is then passed on for inorganic analysis using SEM/EDX operated on an automatic search program. Clothing is vacuumed through a Gelman Acrodisc 1 µm, 2.5 cm diameter membrane filter. After steeping the filters in acetonitrile the solvent is recovered by centrifuging and cleaned up as before prior to analysis. Using these techniques nitroglycerine and 2,4-dinitrotoluene can be detected and confirmed on a regular basis at levels of a few nanograms.

Analysis for the inorganic primer-generated GSR material is conducted on the Electron Microscope with Energy Dispersive X-ray Spectrometry (SEM/EDX) (Figure 9.34 through Figure 9.36). If this is the only form of analysis for GSR under consideration then it is possible to use double-sided adhesive tape mounted upon plastic stubs for hand and face swabs as well as clothing lifts. Since this examination can be very time consuming, it is best to use an automated search program using the brighter image produced by back-scattered electrons from elements of high atomic number, at the same time limiting the search to particles above 1 µm in size which tend to contain a greater number of the elements of interest. In this way the system discriminates between particles which may be GSR and general debris and detritus (Figure 9.37). Full analysis is then conducted on particles of potential value. This automated process also records the location of these particles, thus allowing the analyst to give them personal individual consideration.

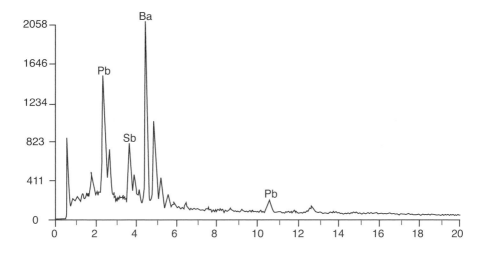

**Figure 9.34**   SEM/EDX printout of X-ray counts against X-ray energy in KeV.

**Figure 9.35**   Operator at the controls of a twin screen electron microscope fitted with energy dispersive X-ray analyser.

The chapter on internal ballistics provides comprehensive information on the elements under consideration and their source. When assessing what constitutes particles unique for GSR when only this inorganic technique is used, the following criteria have been established for the necessary combination of elements:

**Figure 9.36**   View of the X-ray emission from the electron microscope gun-shot residue target allows analyser to indicate peaks for characteristic primer generated elements such as lead, barium and antimony along with other elements.

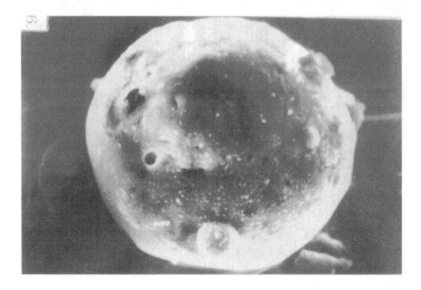

**Figure 9.37**   View of gunshot residue particle of approximately 5 μm in diameter as shown on the screen of the electron microscope.

1. Pb, Ba, Sb
2. Ba, Ca, Si
3. Ba, Al, no S
4. Pb, Ba, Ca, Si, Sn
5. Pb, Ba, Ca, Si
6. Ba, Sb, no S
7. Sb, Sn

Only composition No. 1 should be considered as unique for GSR. Compositions No. 2, 4 and 6 should also be considered as unique if the morphologies of the particles are consistent with GSR.

There is one further very important consideration to be given concerning the analysis and detection of GSR, and that is the risk of contamination. The swabbing kits must be made up under the most stringent manufacturing procedures. Police or scene of crime officers involved with firearm duties or who have handled firearms or firearm related materials at the scene of the shooting incident should not be involved with the swabbing of suspects. Laboratory staff involved in the analysis work should not be associated with shooting or other firearm related activities.

## 9.14 Laboratory Reference Collections

The importance of firearms laboratory reference collections and databases cannot be stressed too strongly. Over a period of time valuable collections of firearms, ammunition (both live and disassembled), spent shotgun cartridge cases showing operational markings left by repeating guns, shotgun cartridge wads, propellant powders, reloader bullets, air gun missiles, domestic and foreign shooting periodicals, trade brochures, technical books and test data can be compiled.

Government and Police laboratories are usually able to obtain firearms and ammunition surrendered by members of the public during official arms amnesties, and from exhibits associated with criminal casework that are subsequently subject to a court forfeiture order. This should be supplemented by an annual budgetary provision to purchase arms and ammunition of recent manufacture, so as to constantly update the systems.

The access to such databases can allow the forensic scientist to achieve breakthroughs during their casework activities. The collection will allow him to examine and test-fire weapons of the make suggested by the search methods explained in Section 9.9, usually resulting in eliminating some or all of the possible candidates bar one. Collection weapons will also show you where serial numbers are located, the number of digits and if they also contain letters as well as numbers. The locations of other markings can also be determined, as well as allowing the differentiation between partially obliterated serial numbers and misleading numbers associated with proof test marks. This is a valuable start if you are faced with the prospect of etching deleted serial numbers. It can even allow you to eliminate this task if study of the reference gun identifies the location of difficult to find serial numbers or part numbers repeated upon components otherwise out of sight. It is not unusual for a magazine to fall to the ground during the commission of an offence. Direct visual comparison against those fitted to laboratory reference firearms will identify the model of weapon involved.

A shotgun fore-end or a fragment of a pistol grip can also be left at the scene of an offence involving violent activity. Side-by-side comparison against reference collection arms will often allow you to identify the make and model of firearm used in the offence. In the same way, firearm components can be identified, or comparison made in the case of improvised guns, guns in poor mechanical condition, or those that have been subject to amateur repair or the fitting of improper or home-made components (Figure 9.10 and Figure 9.38). The comparison of handgun bullets recovered during the crime investigation, shotgun cartridge wadding, or unburnt particles of propellant recovered from the victim's clothing or the margin of a wound resulting from a close range

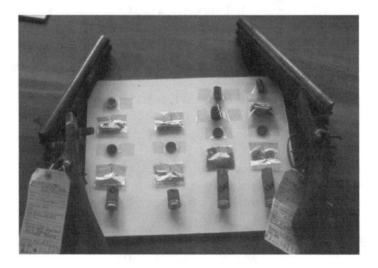

**Fig. 9.38** Two very old 12-bore hammer shotguns sawn-off for criminal use. Two of the modern nitro cartridges had been adapted by replacing their shot charges with improvised single slug missiles. Cartridge on extreme right was loaded with an 1866 pattern .577 in Snider bullet. The one to its left was loaded with a piece of copper water pipe filled with lead.

discharge, can often allow the scientist to determine the make and type of ammunition used in a shooting incident.

On a number of murder cases where the incident firearm was never recovered, I have been able to give evidence in court using an arm from the reference collection similar to the one determined to have been used in the offence by the techniques outlined above. It follows, of course, that the ability to do such things and the status of the discriminating potential of an operational laboratory in such matters is dependent upon the size and the scope of the laboratory databases at hand.

## Further Reading

Bailey, D.W. and Nie, D.A. 1978. *English Gunmakers,* London: Arms and Armour Press.

Barnes, F.C. 1989. *Cartridges of the World,* Northbrook IL: DBI Books.

Biasotti, A.A. 1981. Rifling methods — A review and assessment of the individual characteristics produced. *AFTE Journal,* **13** (3), 34–61.

Biasotti, A.A. and Murdock, J. 1997. *Firearms and Toolmark Identification, Modern Scientific Evidence—The Law and Science of Expert Testimony (Vol. 2).* St. Paul, MN: West Publishing.

Bonfanti, M.S. and De Kinder, J. 1999. The influence of the use of firearms on their characteristic marks. *AFTE Journal,* **31** (3), 318–323.

Bramley, R. 2003. Quality in the laboratory. *Science and Justice,* **3** (2).

Brundridge, D. 1998. The identification of consecutively rifled gun barrels. *AFTE Journal,* **30** (3), 438–444.

Burd, D. and Gilmore, A. 1968. Individual and class characteristics of tools. *Journal of Forensic Science,* **13** (3), 390–396.

Burrard, Major Sir G. 1934. *The Identification of Firearms and Forensic Ballistics,* London: Herbert Jenkins.

Byron, D. 1982. *The Official Guide to Gunmarks,* Orlando FL: The House of Collectables.

Carey, A.M. 1967. *English, Irish and Scottish Firearms Makers,* London: Arms and Armour Press.

Carroll, J. 2001. An evaluation of various Griess and modified Griess test protocols. *AFTE Journal,* **33** (1), 29–36.

Coffman, B.C. 2003. Computer numerical control (CNC) production tooling and repeatable characteristics on ten Remington 870 production run breech bolts. *AFTE Journal,* **35** (1), 49–54.

Collins, D.A. 1992. Gunshot Residues Detection Procedures in the Forensic Science Service (UK), presentation at the Forensic Science Symposium, Linköping, Sweden.

Collins, J.M. 1998. The language of toolmarks. *AFTE Journal*, **30** (1), 82.

Collins, M.J. 1999. Modern marking and serial numbering methods. *AFTE Journal*. **31** (3), 309–317.

Crudgington, I.M. and Baker, D.Y. 1989. *The British Shotgun Volumes I and II*, Southampton: Ashford.

Daubert V. Merrell Pharmaceuticals, Inc. 1135.CT. 2786 (1993).

DeFrance, C.S. and Van Arsdale, M.D. 2003. Validation study of electrochemical rifling. *AFTE Journal*, **35** (1), 35–37.

De Kinder, J. 2002. Ballistic fingerprinting databases. *Science and Justice*, **42** (4), 197–203.

Desjardins, G., Dion, J., Gravel, G., Gaulin, R. and Chaltchi, A. 2001. Determination of shot size in 12 gauge plastic wads. *AFTE Journal*, **33** (3), 267–268.

Desrochers, C., Desjardins, G., Deschenes, M., Chaltchi, A., Gaulin, R., Gravel, G., d'Auteuil, M. and Dion, J. 2000. Serial number restoration in plastic using a heat gun. *AFTE Journal*, **32**, (4), 367.

Dillon, J.H., Jr. 1990. A protocol for gunshot residue examinations in muzzle-to-target distance determinations, and the modified Griess test: a chemically specific chromophoric test for nitrite compounds in gunshot residues. *AFTE Journal*, **22** (3), 243–250 and 257–274.

Dodson, R.V. 1998. Bunter toolmarks — differences in production methods. *AFTE Journal*, **30** (2), 334–335.

Dodson, R.V. and Masson, J.J. 1997. Bunter marks, what do they mean? *AFTE Journal*, **29** (1).

Erlmeir, H.A. and Brandt, J.H. 1967. *Manual of Pistol and Revolver Cartridges*, Vols. 1 and 2, Schwend, Schwabisch Hall, W. Germany: Journal Verlag.

Fackler, M.L. and Malinowski, J.A. 1988. Ordnance gelatin for ballistic studies, *The American Journal of Forensic Medicine and Pathology*, **9** (3), 218–219.

Faigman, D.L., Kaye, D.H., Saks, M.J. and Sanders, J. 1997. *Modern Scientific Evidence, Vol. (I)- The Law and Science of Expert Testimony*, St. Paul, MN: West Publishing.

*FBI Gunshot Residue Manual*, 1981 Edition.

*FBI Gunpowder and Gunshot Residue Manual*, 1999 Edition.

Firearms Law. 1989. *Specifications for the Adaptation of Shot Gun Magazines and the Deactivation of Firearms* (Revised 1995). London: HMSO.

Gander, T.J. and Hogg, I.V. 1993. *Jane's Ammunition Handbook*, Coulsdon Surrey: Jane's Information Group.

*General Rifling Characteristics File*, Firearm and Toolmarks Unit, Washington, DC: FBI Laboratory.

Gibson, W.M. 1999. Serial number restoration in plastic. *AFTE Journal*, **31** (3), 378.

Grzybowski, R.A. and Murdock, J.E. 1998. Firearm and toolmark identification — meeting the Daubert challenge. *AFTE Journal*, **30** (1), 3–14.

Gunther, C.O. 1932. Markings on bullets and shells fired from small arms. *Mechanical Engineering*, **54**.

Gunther, C.O. 1932. Principles of firearms identification. *Army Ordnance*, **XII** (71 and 72).

Haag, L.C. 1997. 2-Nitroso-1-napthol vs. dithiooxamide in trace copper detection at bullet impact sites. *AFTE Journal*, **29** (2).

Haag, L. 2000. A rapid non-destructive method for analysing and comparing bullet lubricants. *AFTE Journal*, **32** (2), 143–153.

Haag, L.C. 2001. The sources of lead in gunshot residues. *AFTE Journal*, **33** (3), 212–218.

Haag, L.C. 2001. Black powder substitutes: their physical and chemical properties and performance. *AFTE Journal*, **33** (4).

Haag, L.C. 2001. Some basic analytical techniques for unfired primer compositions. *AFTE Journal*, **33** (4), 313–325.

Haag, L. and Haag, M. 2000. The Analysis and comparison of shotshell buffers. *AFTE Journal*, **32** (3), 326–331.

Hamby, J.E. and Thorpe, J.W. 1999. A historical perspective of firearms reference collections: their size, composition and uses (1). *AFTE Journal*, **31** (3) 277–284.

Harris, A. 1995. Analysis of primer residues from CCI lead free ammunition by scanning electron microscopy/energy dispersive X-ray. *Journal of Forensic Sciences*, **40** (1), 27–30.

Hassal, J.R. and Zaveri, K. 1988. *Acoustic Noise Management*, Denmark: Bruel & Kjaer.

Hogg, I.V. 1985. *Jane's Directory of Military Small Arms Ammunition*, London: Jane's Information Group.

James, R. 2000. Observations on fluted, annular-ringed and perforated chambers. *AFTE Journal*, **32** (4), 342–345.

Keeley, R.H. 1993. Size is no object, *Chemistry in Britain*, **29** (5), 412–414.

Kennington, R.H. 1992. *The Matrix; 9 mm Parabellum — An Empirical Study of Type Determination*, Miami: Metro-Dade Police. Library of Congress 92–097017.

King, R.M. 1992. The work of the explosives and gunshot residues unit of the Forensic Science Service (UK), *4th International Symposium on Analysis and Detection of Explosives*, Jerusalem, Israel.

Klees, G.S. 2002. The restoration of obliterated laser-etched firearm identifiers by conventional and alternative decryption methods. *AFTE Journal*, **34** (3), 264–267.

Krcma, V. 1971. *The Identification and Registration of Firearms*, Springfield IL: Charles C. Thomas.

Lardizabel. 1995. Case study of the Heckler and Koch USP. *AFTE Journal*, **27** (1).

Lloyd, J.B.F. 1986. Liquid chromatography of firearms propellants traces, *Journal of Energetic Materials*, **4**, 239–271.

Lloyd, J.B.F. 1987. Liquid chromatography with electrochemical detection of explosives and firearms propellant traces, *Analytical Proceedings of the Royal Society of Chemistry,* **24** (8), 239–240.

Lloyd, J.B.F. and King, R.M. 1990. One pot processing of swabs for organic explosives and firearms residue traces, *Journal of Forensic Sciences,* **35** (4), 956–959.

The London and Birmingham Gun Barrel Proof Houses. 1993. *Notes on the Proof of Shotguns and Other Small Arms,* London and Birmingham: The British Proof Authorities.

Lugs, J. 1973. *Firearms Past and Present Volumes I and II,* London: Grenville.

Mathews, J.H. 1962. *Firearms Identification, Volumes I-III,* Madison: University of Wisconsin Press.

Matty, W. 1984. Raven .25 automatic pistol breech face tool marks. *AFTE Journal,* **16** (3), 57.

Matty, W. and Johnson. 1984. A comparison of manufacturing marks on S&W firing pins. *AFTE Journal,* **16** (3).

Meng, H. and Caddy, B. 1995. Detection of ethyl cenralite in gunshot residues using HPLC with fluorescence detection, *Analyst,* **120** (6), 1759–1762.

Miller. J. 2000. Criteria for identification of toolmarks part II. Single land impression comparisons. *AFTE Journal,* **32** (2), 116–131.

Miller, J. 2000. An examination of two consecutively rifled barrels and a review of the literature. *AFTE Journal,* **32** (3), 259–270.

Miller, J. 2001. An examination of the application of the conservative criteria for identification of striated toolmarks using bullets from ten consecutively rifled barrels. *AFTE Journal,* **33** (2).

Miller, J. and McLean, M. 1998. Criteria for identification of toolmarks. *AFTE Journal,* **30** (1), 15–61.

Moltrecht, K.H. 1981. *Machine Shop Practice (Vol. 1 and 2).* New York: Industrial Press.

Moran, B. 2000. The application of numerical criteria for identification in casework involving magazine marks and land impressions. *AFTE Journal,* **32** (4), 326–331.

Murdock, J.E. 1981. A general discussion of gun barrel individuality and an empirical assessment of the individuality of consecutively button rifled .22 calibre rifle barrels. *AFTE Jounal,* **3** (3), 84.

Nennstiel, R. 1986. Computer supported method of firearm type determination, *AFTE Journal,* **18** (4), 4–32.

Nichols, R.G. 1997. Firearm and toolmark identification criteria—a review of the literature. *Journal of Forensic Science,* **42** (3), 466.

Nonte, G.C., Jr. 1973. *Firearms Encyclopedia,* London: Wolfe.

Ogihara, Y., Kubota, M., Sandama, M., Fukuda, K., Uchiyama, T. and Hamby, J. 1989. Comparison of 5000 consecutively fired bullets and cartridge cases from a 45 calibre M1911 A1 pistol. *AFTE Journal,* **21** (2).

Pawlas, K.R. 1970. *Pistols Digest Volumes 1–8,* Nÿrnberg: Pawlas.

Peterson, J.L. and Markham, P.N. 1995. Crime Laboratory Proficiency Testing Results, 1978–1991, Part 1 and 2. *Journal of Forensic Sciences,* **40** (6), 1009–1029.

Peterson, J.L. and Markham, P.N. 1995. Crime Laboratory Testing Results, 1978–1991, II: Resolving questions of common origin. *J.F.S.C.A.* **40** (6).

Powell, R.F. and Forrest, M.R. 1988. *Noise in the Military Environment,* London: Brassey Defence Publications.

Roberts, V. 1981. Restoration of serial numbers in plastic. *AFTE Journal,* **13** (4), 40.

Robinson, M.N., Brooks, C.B. and Renshaw, G.D. 1990. Electric shock devices and their effects on the human body, *Medical Science and the Law,* **30** (4), 285–300.

Rosati, C. 2000. The bunter controversy. *AFTE Journal,* **32** (2), 164–165.

Schrecker, P. 1984. The identification of cartridge case headstamps, *Crime Laboratory Digest,* **11** (3).

Shem, R.J. 2001. A simplified Griess and sodium rhodizonate test. *AFTE Journal,* **33** (1), 37–39.

Shoshoni, E., Nedivi, L. and Giverts, P. 2002. Ejector cut-out marks in shotguns and their comparison value. *AFTE Journal,* **34** (4), 391–393.

Song, J.F, Vorberger, T.V. 2000. Project Report (1998-99) of NIST Standard Bullets and Casings (National Institute of Standards and Technology, Gaithersburg, MD. *AFTE Journal,* **32** (4), 368–372.

Speers, S.J., Doolan, K., McQuillan, J. and Wallace, J.S. 1994. Evaluation and improved methods for the recovery and detection of organic and inorganic cartridge discharge residues, *Journal of Chromatography,* **674,** 319–27.

Steindler, R.A. 1985. *Steindlers New Firearms Dictionary,* Harrisburg PA: Stackpole.

Stevens K.D. and Gallant J.R. (2004) "Identification of Non-Toxic Shot". Paper presented at A.F.T.E. Seminar at Vancouver B.C. May 2004.

Swearengen, T.F. 1966. *Tear Gas Munitions,* Springfield IL: Charles C. Thomas.

Tam, C.K. 2001. Overview of manufacturing marks on centre-fire cartridges. *AFTE Journal,* **33** (2), 112–115.

Taroni, F.M.S.C., Champod, C. and Margot, P. 1996. Statistics: a future in toolmarks comparisons? *AFTE Journal,* **28** (4), 229.

Thompson, E. 1994. Phoenix Arms (Raven) breech face toolmarks. *AFTE Journal,* **26** (2).

Thompson, E. 1996. False breech face ID'S. *AFTE Journal,* **28** (2).

Thompson, E. and Wyant, R. 2002. Lead is lead. *AFTE Journal,* **34** (3), 314.

Thompson, E. and Wyant, R. 2002. 9mm Smith and Wesson ejectors. *AFTE Journal,* **34** (4), 406–407.

Thompson, E. and Wyant, R. 2002. Consecutively made cartridge cases. *AFTE Journal,* **34,** (4), 407–408.

Todd, R.H. and Allen, D.K. 1994. *Fundamental Principles of Manufacturing Processes.* New York: Industrial Press.

Todd, R.H. and Allen. D.K. 1994. *Manufacturing Process Reference Guide.* New York: Industrial Press.

Tomasetti, K.A. 2002. Analysis of the essential aspects of striated tool mark examinations and the methods for identification. *AFTE Journal,* **34** (1).

Tulleners, F. and Giusto, M. 1998. Striae reproducibility on sectional cuts of one Thompson Contender barrel. *AFTE Journal,* **30** (1), 62–81.

Uchiyama, Tsuneo. 1986. Similarity among breech face marks fired from guns with close serial numbers. *AFTE Journal,* **18** (3), 15–52.

Uchiyama, Tsueno. 1992. The probability of corresponding striae in toolmarks. *AFTE Journal,* **24** (3), 273–290.

Wagoner A. 1999. Griffin's reagent for serial number restoration in stainless steel. *AFTE Journal,* **31** (4), 497.

Wallace, J.S. and McKeown, W.J. 1993. Sampling procedures for firearms and/or explosives residues. *Journal of Forensic Sciences,* **33** (2), 107–116.

Warlow, T.A. 2000. The criminal re-activation of firearms. *Contact,* **28, 15–20.** Information Services, FSS Metropolitan Laboratory, London.

White, H.P. and Munhall, B.D. 1948. *Centrefire Metric Pistol and Revolver Cartridges,* Washington, DC: NRA Sportsmans Press.

White, H.P. and Munhall, B.D. 1950. *Centrefire American and British Pistol and Revolver Cartridges,* Washington, DC: NRA Sportsmans Press.

White, H.P., Munhall, B.D., Huntinton, R.T. and Dunn, D.R. 1977. *Cartridge Headstamp Guide,* Bel Air, MD.

Wilder, C.G. 1983. Handgun trigger pull. *The American Journal of Forensic Medicine and Pathology,* **4** (3), 207–208.

Winant, L. 1956. *Firearms Curiosa,* London: Arco.

Wirnsberger, G. and Steindler, R.A. 1975. *The Standard Directory of Proof Marks,* Paramus, NJ: John Olson (Jolex).

Wolten, G.M., Nesbitt, R.S., Calloway, A.R., Loper, G.L. and Jones, P.F. 1977. Final report on particle analysis for gunshot residue detection, ATR-77 (7915)—3, The Aerospace Corporation, El Segunde, CA.

**Figure 9.39** Just a few of the home-made guns (zip guns) received at the laboratory in casework submissions. The weapon shown at the top has been derived from an air weapon modified to allow the discharge of .22 in rim-fire ammunition.

**Figure 9.40** Even a relatively modest obstruction positioned inside the muzzle end of a shotgun barrel can result in this characteristic failure.

**Figure 9.41**   Seized-up pistol recovered from a pond in Bradford was treated in ultrasonic cleaner to remove rust and silt. Subsequent cartridge case test firings confirmed it to be the High-Standard .22 in pistol used in a series of post-office murders by a person christened by the press the 'Black Panther'. Characteristic marks left upon a cartridge case and bullet at an earlier killing in Accrington Lancashire, along with the shape and the pattern of checkering on a small piece of the grip-plate broken off when the postmaster's wife was clubbed about the head with the pistol, had already allowed the laboratory to identify the type and model of weapon used correctly. A microscopic link between cartridge cases and bullets was also established at a later shooting in Dudley, West Midlands and allowed this same person to be implicated in the kidnapping, and eventually killing, of Lesley Anne Downing, the daughter of a wealthy transport business owner. The pistol above has had its barrel modified to allow the fitting of a home-made silencer constructed from the body of a car grease gun.

**Figure 9.42** The top row shows three different unfired plastic cup wads. The wads shown on the right and left sides of the middle line have been fired from shotguns having conventional barrels. Their counterparts on the bottom line and the fired pair in the central column have all been fired from sawn-off shotguns. As can be seen, the unusually high gas pressures at the muzzle end of the short barrel involved have caused characteristic damage to the bases of the wads. Two bases have been blown completely back upon themselves, and in the centre bottom wad, the base has been ripped completely away. The types of wadding used in these particular tests happen to be of a type which do not tend to lose their cup leaves. Such findings at the post-mortem examination stage, along with observations made on cartridge cases and other recovered items, by the ballistics expert can often allow useful information to be imparted to the police concerning gauge of gun, brand of ammunition, cartridge loading and type of firearm used.

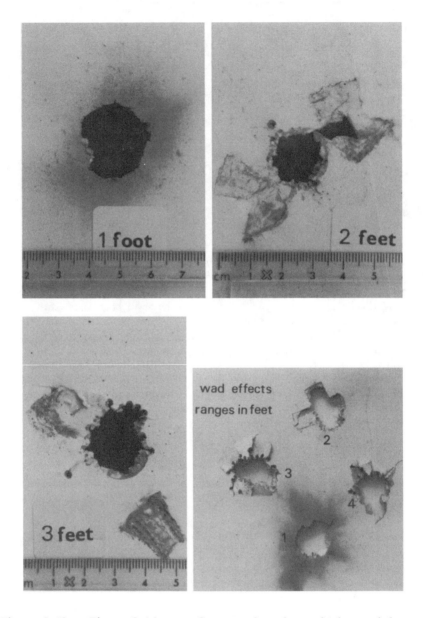

**Figure 9.43 to Figure 9.46**   Test firings such as these which reveal the performance of shotgun cartridge wadding must be conducted with loadings of the same type used in the offence as different results will be obtained using other loadings. Here the type of wadding used in the tests shown in Figure 9.3, Figure 9.8, and Figure 9.42 tend to shed their cup leaves in flight.

**Figure 9.47** Swiss-manufactured "Guardian Angel" self-defence device. This two-shot device uses the impulse generated by the discharge of a special blank cartridge to project the capsaicin-based agent through multi-holed nozzles as a dispersed pattern over an effective range of between 1.5 and 13 feet (0.5–4m).

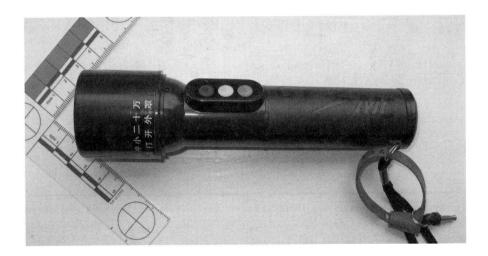

**Figure 9.48** Stun gun disguised as a working flashlight.

**Figure 9.49**   Stun gun disguised as a mobile telephone.

**Figure 9.50**   Walther CP99 carbon dioxide-powered repeating .177in/4.5 mm pistol.

# Presentation of Evidence to the Courts

# 10

All events are subject to individual perception or recollection. Misconceptions or untruths can often be intermingled with the truth when witnesses provide testimony in court. This will certainly be evident when giving consideration to written submissions and witness accounts of a criminal incident, if you are acting as expert witness for the prosecution or for the defence. Both sides can be expected to provide different interpretations of what took place as fact or reality, although in truth, the only inescapable 'fact' in this life is that at some point in the future we all die. When an expert witness is considering such matters he should adopt the underlying principles of a Bayesian approach.

The Reverent Thomas Bayes (1702–1761) was an English mathematician who produced a theorem expressing the probability of each of a number of mutually exclusive events, given some other event $E$, in terms of the probabilities of those events independently of $E$ and the probabilities of $E$ given each of those events in turn. Bayesianism is the advocacy or use of Bayesian methods. Concepts arising out of Bayes' work may be used in the calculations of probability, especially when designating methods of statistical inference in which use is made of prior information on the distribution of parameters.

When acting for the police and hence the prosecution, it is important to consider the merits of all submissions. Your findings at the scene of the incident, the post mortem (if appropriate), the examination of casework exhibits, and in particular the mechanical condition of the firearm involved, should all be used by you to see if any of the claims bear scrutiny before writing your witness statement. In turn, you will have to answer technical questions during your cross examination, and you will also have to give due consideration to the submissions made by your opposite number and any other expert witness providing pertinent evidence to the court. The jury will take account of all of this information before making their verdict.

In England and Wales the majority of minor criminal cases are heard at the Magistrates or the Youth Courts, where the accused will generally be represented by a solicitor. More serious cases, or those where a case is made for a trial by jury, are dealt with at the Crown Court. The 1971 Courts Act eventually abolished the old courts of assize and quarter sessions replacing them with the Crown Courts system we have today. The present system of the Supreme Court of Judicature consists of the Court of Appeal, the High Court and the Crown Court. Those towns where the Crown Court sits are classified as first-, second- or third-tier courts according to their business and the level of the presiding judge. The more serious criminal offences are dealt with at first-tier centres before High Court Judges. High Court Judges, Circuit Judges and Recorders sit at second-tier centres, while Circuit Judges and Recorders sit at third-tier centres. The seriousness of the case will generally be reflected by the seniority of the judge who will preside over it.

However, before a case can go to trial at the Crown Court it is necessary for it to pass Committal Stage at Magistrates Court level to determine whether there is sufficient evidence to form a *prima facie* or substantive case. Since the Criminal Justice Act 1967 the vast majority of Committal hearings are dealt with briefly by way of presentation of the necessary paperwork, which then allows the case to go into the Crown Court listing system; this is referred to as a Section 6(2) Committal where no witnesses are requested to attend. Under the terms of a Section 6(1) or old style committal some or all of the witnesses will have to attend to present their evidence, and in turn to be cross-examined by the Defence by way of challenge to the Prosecution case. In such instances the evidence and the responses of the witnesses are written down in the form of a deposition which each witness will be requested to sign. The Defence here will wish to present a submission of no case to answer, and the Magistrates will have to consider the evidence to ensure that the case presented against the accused is sufficient to warrant him being committed for trial. The Prosecution in turn will be allowed to reply to these submissions and it is again up to the court to decide if a *prima facie* case has been made against the defendant. In effect this latter procedure mimics the eventual trial, and in some respects can be regarded as a 'dry run', although it is always the hope of the Defence that the case will be thrown out at this stage.

In Scotland there are three levels of criminal court. The lowest level of court is the District Court; the middle tier is the Sheriff Court and the pinnacle of the hierarchy is the High Court of Judiciary. There are two types of criminal procedure — solemn and summary. In solemn procedure in both the High Court of Judiciary and the Sheriff Court, trial is before a judge sitting with a jury of 15 laymen. In summary procedure, which is used in less serious offences, the hearing can take place at either the Sheriff Court or at the District Court where the judge sits alone to decide questions both of law and of fact. The High Court of Judiciary sits in Edinburgh, Glasgow and other major towns and cities and has exclusive jurisdiction in certain serious crimes including murder, treason and rape. Prosecutions are conducted by the Lord Advocate, the Solicitor General for Scotland, or by Advocate's Depute, also known as Crown Counsel, of whom there are 13. The High Court of Judiciary also sits (in a court of at least three judges) as the Scottish Court of Criminal Appeal. In all other criminal courts the prosecutor is the Procurator Fiscal or, in busy areas, one of his Deputes. The 49 Sheriffs Courts deal with offences within the local areas of the six sheriffdoms. The bench of a District Court will usually be constituted by one or more lay justices of the peace; at present only Glasgow has stipendary magistrates.

## 10.1 The Prosecution Witness

In Scottish courts a rule which requires corroboration of evidence is strictly applied in criminal cases. In normal circumstances this will involve evidence from at least two witnesses, although under Section 26(7) of the Criminal Justice (Scotland) Act 1980 the evidence of one forensic pathologist or forensic scientist is sufficient to prove any fact contained in any report signed by him and another pathologist or forensic scientist provided that the Defence is forewarned of the intention to call only one such witness, and they do not object. In non-contentious cases this dispenses with the previous common law requirement that, for example, the cause of death in a homicide trial must be spoken to in oral testimony by both subscribers to a report.

When preparing a written statement for use in a criminal proceeding one must always bear in mind that every word will be subjected to close scrutiny, both by the Prosecution and the Defence. The substantive elements in your statement must be of a standard which will be proof against such scrutiny and be capable of withstanding the possible rigours of a robust cross-examination when you are in the witness box. In England and Wales if you are tendering evidence on behalf of the Prosecution you will have already signed a section at the top of the first page of your statement containing the following words:

> This statement (consisting of X pages each signed by me) is true to the best of my knowledge and belief and I make it knowing that, if it is tendered in evidence, I shall be liable to prosecution if I have wilfully stated in it anything which I know to be false or

do not believe to be true. (Criminal Justice Act 1967, s.9; M.C. Act 1980, s.102; M.C. Rules 1981, R.70)

Ideally you will have been working for an organisation operating an effective quality control system which ensures that all of the critical findings shown in your written examination notes will have been subject to peer checking, and that your written statement will have been checked on a similar basis to confirm compliance with your quality-assurance system. The presence of the initials of the checking officer and the date on which the checks were made throughout your notes and at the top of your draft statement best assures compliance with such a system and also visibly confirms that the work of the reporting officer is subject to such peer scrutiny.

If you are an independent forensic scientist operating as a one-man organisation, these active checks are not possible. The honest man playing the part of an expert witness will try to be as careful, impartial and as open-minded as he can be; those persons possessing less scruples will see this situation as an opportunity to gain a reputation for always coming up with 'the goods', whether they are working for the Prosecution or for the Defence. In most instances, the expert witness serving the Defence sets down his opinions in the form of a written report, rather than a statement. Such reports do not of course contain the oath section, and are written in a rather different style. In some instances these reports are written as if produced by an observer of the expert's actions: 'Bloggs examined the exhibits at the forensic laboratory and then made arrangements to visit the scene of the incident the next day, where he made the following observations...'.

Assuming that you have been called to give evidence, the following actions will take place at the Crown Court or its Scottish equivalent. After completion of the jury selection and swearing-in procedures, the judge will provide the jury with guidance as to the task they have to face and the responsibilities they hold. Both parties in the case will be represented by barristers, and in particularly serious or complicated cases, one or both sides may have two barristers, one serving as senior counsel, who in turn will be assisted by a less-experienced barrister acting as junior counsel. In addition, back-up will also be provided by a representative from the Crown Prosecution Service, who will manually produce notes of the evidence given by the various witnesses. It is not unusual for the Defence also to employ former CID police officers to provide additional assistance.

Prosecution Counsel will then make his opening speech for the Crown, in which he will briefly outline the nature of the alleged offence, indicating the nature and importance of the witnesses he will eventually call and the evidence he will present. In purely technical cases, and in certain other circumstances, agreement will be reached between the parties to allow the prosecution expert to sit in court throughout the trial prior to giving evidence. This concession will usually be demanded by the Defence in almost all circumstances for their own expert. In most instances the prosecution expert will have to wait outside the Court until he is called, although after giving evidence the Prosecution might wish him to remain in court, especially to advise the Prosecution during the period when it is the turn of the defence expert to give evidence. In trials of murder it is usual for the firearms expert to follow the pathologist in the listing of witnesses. Avoid contact with other persons at this stage unless you know them or they have been identified as officers in the case or members of the Crown Prosecution Service. Do not speak about the evidence you are scheduled to give, or which you have already given if a recess or lunch break is called during your period of examination. Do not speak to other persons about the evidence you have presented or questions you have been asked whilst you were being examined. If the presentation of your evidence is split by a lunch break it is probably best to take your lunch alone to avoid any accusations of passing likely questions or other information on to other witnesses due to go on after you.

After entering the witness box the witness will be sworn in. The manner in which this will be done will cater for the various religions. The way in which the oath is taken varies between different courts. In some the testament will be provided along with a card upon which the form of oath is printed. In other more formal settings, particularly in a court presided over by one of the older and most senior of judges, a witness will be obliged to repeat the oath, spoken in sections by an usher or other court official, in a solemn and near-ritualistic manner only after complete silence has been established in the court and the public gallery. In such circumstances it would be unwise for the expert to depart from the formal routine expected, possibly in a foolish attempt to convey to those present, his everyday understanding of court procedures.

Prosecution Counsel will then ask you to introduce yourself to the court, and to give brief details of your qualifications, experience, and current employer. Although you will be questioned during your period in the witness box by the various advocates, all of your responses should be directed towards the jury as these are the people chosen to consider your evidence; this will also hold true for some of your responses to questions posed by the Judge.

When giving evidence for the Prosecution it is always wise to avoid eye contact with the accused. Normally the accused will act impassively during the presentation of your evidence, particularly if he can see that it is impartial. This is not always the case however, and in some instances he might write notes upon your evidence, or in turn pass notes down to the Defence Counsel, or even send a message for him or his junior counsel to speak with him. Bear in mind that these persons can behave in an unbalanced manner if provoked, as in some instances this is the reason for their appearance in court. Refrain from looking in the direction of the accused when giving evidence since this can result in 'first to blink' eye contact which, as with dogs of unknown temperament, can result in conflict. Ignore any visible or audible threats made towards you as the accused is moved from the dock during periods of recess after the Judge has left the court. Do not get involved with or sit near to friends or members of the family of the accused during these breaks.

When giving your evidence always observe the Judge's actions, remembering to moderate the pace of your presentation whenever he decides to take a written note of your responses. Wait until you see his pen stop before you start a fresh sentence or attempt to cover a different point. Prosecution Counsel will then go through your 'evidence in chief', which in a murder trial will start with your visit to the scene of the shooting incident and the post-mortem examination, the confirmation of the receipt of exhibits at the laboratory, followed by your findings and conclusions; the way in which this will be done will generally follow the pattern of your written statement, concentrating of course on the most significant exhibits and findings.

There will be occasions when the Judge, or either of the two advocates, will request you to leave the witness box to demonstrate the operation of the firearm free from cramped restrictions. On a number of occasions I have been instructed to approach the jury to explain the operation of the weapon to each of the members in turn. This has included handing them the weapon and then talking them through the various operations. This type of demonstration can be particularly useful if the weapon exhibits mechanical faults which you have described in your previous evidence, as each of the jury members is then able to detect these significant features for themselves. Do bear in mind that any verbal instructions you give should be audible to all persons present in the court including the stenographer.

At all times when you are handling firearms in court your actions should reflect safe gun-handling principles. You should always prove the gun is safe by opening the breech each time it is passed to you after first pointing it in a safe direction, and avoid situations wherever possible which might involve the weapon being pointed towards any person. If it is really necessary to deviate from this last rule, then ask the Judge's permission first. The same is true if there is a requirement to use dummy rounds of ammunition to demonstrate some particular action.

In one high profile murder case I was involved in some years ago, the Defence had been spurred on by suggestions made by his own expert that the gun in court could be caused to fire if the breech was closed abruptly. Despite the Defence pursuing this point relentlessly I stood my ground as I had checked the weapon in this respect during my laboratory tests, something which his expert had not bothered to do. He finally declared that I could not prove this point, at least to his satisfaction in the courtroom, thus attempting to suggest to the jury that either I had been incompetent or perhaps less than truthful. It was by sheer chance that I happened to have a few primed shotgun cartridge cases in my briefcase that day, a residue from some previous investigation. I asked the Judge if I could use these in a courtroom demonstration to prove in front of the jury that this part of my evidence was beyond dispute, pointing out that although a sharp audible crack would be produced if one were caused to be fired, the lack of the normal charge of powder and shot would allow this to be conducted without attendant risk to persons in the court. The Judge rapidly agreed to this test, which I then conducted several times to a completely silent courtroom—people leaned forward with stifled breaths, perched on the very edges of their seats. In such conditions even the crack of a primer would have seemed like a thunder clap, followed by my immediate demise; the tests were, however, concluded without attendant incident. The jury box in this rather old courtroom was positioned immediately to my left. I recall taking the cartridge case from the gun, and then holding it, without looking at it first, so the nearest jury members could clearly see its head. I then remarked, to a great nodding of heads and audible agreement from members of the jury, that they should be able to see that the firing pin, initially projecting from the standing breech face, had merely marked the edge of the rim of the cartridge as I had predicted in my previous evidence. I then added that four of the live cartridges in the next exhibit in front of the Defence Counsel did in fact display markings from being loaded on some previous occasions in this weapon. This last remark had the desired effect in terminating the cross-examination. I do not advocate the adoption of such practices by others, as it is rather akin to calling a hand in a game of poker involving a stake the size of the rest of your career.

After the presentation of your evidence in chief it now becomes the turn of the Defence Counsel. This may involve a separate advocate for each person on trial to cross-examine the Prosecution witness. This will be in the form of a probing analysis of all the most critical points of your evidence, and in some instances seemingly trivial aspects of your previous evidence, often in the form of a prearranged plan after consultation with their own experts. It obviously serves the Defence case on the day if they can get you to change your evidence, suggest some previously undeclared uncertainty, or to generally discredit you in whatever manner as an expert witness. Each advocate will have developed his own personal menu of routines for dealing with expert witnesses, and will select the one which he has gauged from previous encounters with you, or from watching your presentation of evidence in chief, will be most likely to serve his needs best. In this choice he will clearly be motivated by the weight your evidence provides to the Prosecution case. Some specialise in bluster, bullying, insinuation and histrionics, and will use their chosen position in court nearest to the jury to maximum effect. I always feel most relaxed during these periods of cabaret, and conversely most on guard when being cross-examined by his polite, reasonable and softly-spoken counterpart, who might try to lead you on ever so gently by degrees to an exquisitely prepared trap. Certain basic rules must always be observed: if you do not know the answer to a particular question or feel that it is outside your field or personal experience, you should say so. Never agree with a proposition you do not understand in a silly attempt to appear more knowledgeable than you are or to get off the hook by way of an act of assent, as the next question will be your downfall. Similarly, do not attempt to change the nature of the contents of one of your answers in an attempt to tailor it to fit the propositions being strenuously put to you. Remember, a written transcript of all your previous evidence and responses will be at hand, and any inconsistencies will be immediately brought to the attention of the jury. You may have given evidence over a relatively long period, during which time the same topic may have been approached from various directions. In one case some years ago, I was in the witness box for four-and-a-half days, being questioned by five different advocates. In such circumstances you will be expected as an expert witness to be as consistent at the end of giving evidence as you were on day one.

It will then be the turn of the Prosecution to re-examine your evidence, and at the same time ask you to clarify or again to confirm important sections of the evidence previously given. In some cases this might also include asking a question that the Defence drew back from asking by way of enlargement during your cross-examination. It is usually at this stage that the Judge will ask questions of his own, although some judges will interpose at almost any point in the case. The type of questions asked will usually serve to clarify some technical point or part of your evidence which he feels was not adequately covered, or which he believes will assist the jury in their understanding of the technical content of your evidence. There will be occasions in which members of the jury will wish questions of their own to be put to you. This tends to take place more when one is dealing with technical issues rather than criminal offences. It is usual in these circumstances for the jury member to pass a note up to the Judge, who will then, after considering its contents, read it out to you. Always treat these questions with respect, even if they appear to be of a basic nature or show misconceptions. If this is the case try your best to reconstruct the issue in hand explaining each facet as clearly as possible, using simple terms and expressions in the process. Do not act in a way which will embarrass or alienate this person, as this will only set this juror against yourself and the evidence you have presented previously. If there is a need for the question to be clarified because of a possible misunderstanding or other doubt, then seek advice from the Judge. Once you have been formally released, it is best to leave the court directly unless Prosecution Counsel has asked you to stay behind. It is best not to stop to communicate or shake hands with the officers in the case, as this last impression upon the jury can be perceived as an indication of possible bias. If the officer in the case wishes to speak to you before your departure he will follow a short period afterwards, and you can chat or shake hands out of sight of the jury. It is not proper for the Prosecution's technical expert to be seen by the jury receiving thanks for his contribution by police officers. If, on the other hand, you have been asked by Counsel to remain in court, it is normal to take a seat on the bench behind him next to the Crown Prosecution representative. From then on you should avoid eye contact with the jury members and resist any compulsion to clear your throat or be involved in anything which may be regarded as body language or audible comment when the next witness, who might be the expert for the Defence, stands, regardless of the nature of the evidence being given. If the Defence expert is giving evidence, you should keep a written note of any contentious statements made during his presentation and produce a clear written list of topics which you feel should be raised or challenged when it is the turn of the Prosecution to cross-examine this witness. Focus on all the main points and resist contention for its own sake in the case of trivia.

Pass, or have any additional notes passed to counsel only when you think this is absolutely necessary, as it can be offputting if his presentation is needlessly disrupted. All notes should be concise and clearly written on white paper. Near the end of his cross-examination he may turn to ask you if there are any additional points which need to be raised. This provides you with the opportunity to fill in any gaps, but this must be done concisely and quietly. If a break is taken during the Defence expert's presentation, or before cross-examination, you will have plenty of time to talk counsel through the contentious parts of his evidence and to advise him on the best questions to ask, the responses he should receive and the nature of supplementary questions to fit each set of circumstances. If the expert has come up with some particularly bizarre scenario, which caused the accused to think the gun was unloaded, or which resulted in its discharge, it can be a useful exercise for counsel to request a reconstruction from the expert for the benefit of the court. This is another game of poker however, where you have to be sure of your facts, otherwise a plausible reconstruction will serve to strengthen his evidence.

The reconstruction might necessitate the court rising to attend a firing range or the scene to allow the members of the jury to have sight of effects you noted at the scene of the incident, or when it is necessary for you to conduct test-firing demonstrations. At one inquest in which I gave evidence, this necessitated the jury visiting the scene of a fatal incident, so as to enable them to observe damage I had referred to on the edges of a military firing range. I recall advising women members to wear appropriate closed shoes due to the large numbers of adders reported by the Range Warden to be residing in the heath they were to visit. I have also conducted firing tests with an old rifle with the court members present, at a shooting range situated close to the court, in a case where it was contested that its age and condition would surely cause it to blow up into pieces if fired with modern ammunition. On another occasion the judge suspended the hearing to allow firing tests to be carried out in the bar of a public house to resolve technical differences between the two experts. In this case my evidence was based upon witness statements only, describing how a man arguing with another fellow drinker claimed that he possessed an 'Armalite rifle'. This resulted in him returning from his parked car with a weapon corresponding in appearance with such a weapon, with which he then fired ten shots at the bar wall. The scenes of crime officers photographs of the damage, found concealed behind a gaming machine, taken after the incident was reported about a month later, showed damage to the thick plasterwork of the brick wall of the bar. I stated that the damage was in my opinion consistent with that which would have been produced by shots fired from a .22 inch rim-fire rifle or smooth-bore gun, and that it was likely to be one made by the Italian firm Armi Jager currently being marketed resembling a US M16 rifle. The landlord had described clearing up damaged plaster, pieces of lead and brass cartridge cases that he promptly put into the bin. The accused claimed that he had used a certain model of a .22 inch air rifle, resembling to some extent a military rifle, and which was fitted with a multi-shot pellet magazine for quick reloading. A well-known firearms expert and gun lobby activist supported the story of the defendant, and generally rubbished my findings, even though prosecution evidence had proved from a record of a credit card transaction that the defendant had purchased a suitable air rifle shortly after the police had questioned him about the incident. Although the pub had been closed and was in the process of changing hands, arrangements were made for us to conduct tests in the bar in the presence of the pub landlord and a police photographer, using a high-powered air rifle and a .22 inch rim-fire rifle. The out-going Irish pub landlord was more than delighted for us to shoot up the bar he was about to leave. The results of the firing tests were then photographed and the next day the defendant pleaded guilty to the offence, adding that he had in fact used a .22 inch rim-fire Armi Jager gun (Figure 8.30).

Presentation of evidence at a Coroner's Court inquest is conducted in a rather different manner. Here, the coroner will usually sit alone, or in other instances may choose to summon between 7 and 11 people to act as a jury if he perceives the need to do so. In addition, he may choose to open the hearing the day after the incident if it is one of particular concern to the public. In these situations you will be asked to present your interim findings and answer any of his questions before he suspends the hearing with the intention of reopening it at a future date. In any event, the way in which you can present evidence is less restrained than would be the case in the Crown Court.

You are much more likely to be asked questions by members of the jury, and even by members of the family of the deceased. They will do this directly towards you rather than by written note. Always bear in mind that these persons are likely to be in a distressed state, so it will be easy to upset them if you do not soften the presentation of certain parts of your evidence. The coroner will be in possession of your written statement and will thus understand your conduct. On the odd occasion a question from the wife or the mother of the deceased will constitute the worst question you could be asked. This will be the one they should have asked the pathologist who gave evidence before you and has now left the court: 'Did he die quickly and without pain?' This is an easy question to respond to if the person has placed a shotgun barrel inside their mouth before pressing the trigger. This will not, however, always be the reconstruction you have arrived at from visiting the scene and attending the post-mortem examination.

You can sometimes, however, be surprised by the conduct of members of the family of the deceased and other persons present at the inquest. I recall giving evidence in a case where a man had got into severe debt, lost his job, received demanding letters from his creditors, received notice to return his credit cards, drank too much at a public house in an attempt to drown his sorrows and was then stopped by the police and breathalysed on his way home. I described the details of how he had ritualistically shot his small children and his wife with a .38 in revolver as they lay in their beds, three times in the head and body along three separate, but in each case identical, lines of fire, before setting fire to the residence and then placing the muzzle of the revolver inside his own mouth to fire an upward shot into his brain. The totally impassive array of faces before me while I was giving this evidence made me feel that I must have been reading a copy of the weather forecast. It was at this point that the coroner asked me about the use of a second pistol in the incident which I had not bothered to refer to at this stage. I simply replied that he had used a .22 in pistol on the animals. The mundane atmosphere in the courtroom was suddenly replaced by agitated concern. I was then asked to give more details and some explanation as to the modes of use of the two different calibres. Somewhat surprised by this display of interest, I suggested that he had used the larger calibre weapon on human targets, and had then chosen to use the lighter calibre on the much smaller creatures, namely the four dogs and the three cats. This brought the house down. Next day the popular press titles read something like 'Man Slays Pets in Gun Horror.' The evidence I had given in respect of the shooting of the household pets and the possible reason for the particular choice of calibre was set out in considerable detail. Buried away elsewhere lay a brief reference to the demise of his wife and young children.

The Defence can appeal to the Crown Court against conviction by the Magistrate's Court or Youth Court; the appeal takes the form of a re-hearing of the evidence. The Defence can also appeal to the Court of Appeal against a Crown Court conviction; it is unusual for witnesses to have to give evidence in the Court of Appeal. However, in such an instance you will be asked questions by a judge and two magistrates if the hearing is being dealt with at a Crown Court, and by three High Court Judges, one of whom may be the Lord Chief Justice, at the Court of Appeal. Appeals on points of law are submitted directly from the Magistrates Court (or from the Crown Court when it has heard an appeal from the Magistrate's or Youth Court) by a procedure referred to as 'case stated', to the Divisional Court, Queens Bench Division of the High Court. Appeals here can be made both by the Defence and Prosecution. Appeal hearings here will be heard by at least two High Court Judges. Rulings produced at the Court of Appeal or the Divisional Court will be referred to in all subsequent cases dealing with similar matters. The final Court of Appeal for the Prosecution and Defence, but only in relation to issues of 'general public importance' is the House of Lords. At least three Lords of Appeal will be involved in this process.

You may at some time have to give evidence at other forms of court or disciplinary proceedings. Civil cases can be dealt with in a manner not too dissimilar to that of a Crown Court. Police disciplinary or military disciplinary or court martial hearings I have had to give evidence to on occasions were conducted in less than relaxed circumstances, in places well used to witnessing the ends of otherwise promising careers.

## 10.2 The Defence Expert

When acting as the expert witness for the Defence or involved in a case of civil action, the processes are somewhat different. In the first instance you will be briefed by the Defence solicitors and provided with a substantial amount of information. This will include copies of the statements made by the various experts acting for the Crown. After sifting through this information you can then decide on which of the exhibits you will in turn need to examine. In this respect you will be assisted by instructions from your solicitors to look for some particular defect in the weapon known by the defendant or to check out some course of events thought to have taken place.

You will then arrange through your solicitors for the chosen exhibits to be released for your examination. An officer involved in the case will be in charge of the security of the exhibits in all instances, and generally the examination will take place at the forensic science laboratory involved in the generation of the Prosecution evidence. This then allows you full access to all equipment and reference sources, as well as the opportunity, if you wish it, to discuss or resolve details with your opposite number. You will then be able to check relevant sections of his hand-written notes directly, as well as any charts produced during the chemical analysis of materials, and demand to see the reference sources used to substantiate any technical findings. In some instances you may choose to photocopy parts of the file to allow you to study them more closely at a later stage.

Your examination of the firearm has been made less of a burden for you as you can in effect use the other expert's statement and notes as you would use the services of one of your own assistants. This then allows you to concentrate on just those features you consider to be critical, bearing in mind the additional information already in your possession. All such features can be dealt with during your tests on the mechanical condition of the weapon and during periods of range test-firing. You may well find that the use of a digital camera capable of macro mode will assist you in recording your various findings. Although the original test-firings will be available when you move on to comparison microscopy of bullets, cartridge wads and cartridge cases, you are free to produce your own set of tests using ammunition contained in the casework exhibits or laboratory stock ammunition. If the laboratory has a suitable water tank to catch test bullets you will find this to be far better than any fibre-waste trap which you might normally have access to. The firing range at the Home Office or government laboratory should also have facilities for using much larger paper witness screens or cards for the patterning of shotguns than those which might be used on an improvised range.

If there is a need to examine damaged clothing or wound samples during your visit it will be necessary for you to comply with all biohazard safety regulations at the laboratory. In such instances it is always a wise move to arrange any wound specimens to be removed from the freezer when you first arrive at the laboratory, so that they will be suitably thawed out towards the end of your visit when this task is conducted. Although the police officer will have brought all the other exhibits to the laboratory from the Force exhibits store, it is usual for such perishable materials which involve potentially hazardous body fluids to be kept in the freezer at the forensic laboratory.

Where these samples have not been removed as part of the post-mortem examination, you can arrange to view the body, assuming that it has not been released for burial or cremation. In any event you should be able to obtain copies of the photographs taken by the police during the official examination along with a copy of the Pathologist's report. It may well be that the Defence has arranged for its own independent post-mortem examination, and if this is the case you can choose to assist the second pathologist directly.

If any significant differences exist between your findings and those of the Prosecution expert then from an official viewpoint it is considered best that these be discussed between the two experts and, hopefully resolved prior to the trial. The Prosecution expert can then put in an additional statement referring to the points in question, at the same time providing additional information and conclusions, as appropriate. However, in some instances you will have been instructed in advance by the Defence solicitors not to divulge any such information to the Prosecution expert without their express approval.

During the course of your investigations you might also have chosen to examine the scene of the incident; in most instances this will be arranged through the police. Failing this, it is always possible to request copies of the scene photographic record or have access to any video-recorded overview of the scene investigation. At the end of all of this, you will then be in a position to consider all aspects of the case and the contents of the various technical reports. One would hope that this will be done from a neutral and detached viewpoint to allow you to write a technically correct and balanced statement or report, which will bear the scrutiny of any cross-examination. If your findings are very different from those of the Prosecution expert, you should reconsider all of the aspects of your investigation which have led you to these conclusions, seeking peer advice if this is available to you.

During the trial the Defence expert will usually be allowed to sit in court throughout the period of testimony of other witnesses, which is in stark contrast to the experience of the Prosecution expert who will only rarely be allowed this privilege. Unlike him you will therefore know what has been said in court by other critical witnesses, including the Pathologist and the Prosecution firearms expert before it is your turn to go into the witness box. You will have been sitting immediately behind Defence Counsel, making notes and advising him on the contents of the evidence in chief given by the various witnesses. This task will be at its most critical stage when your opposite number is giving his evidence in chief. You will be expected to draw up a concisely worded list of any possibly contentious points he may have made, or any areas in which he has appeared to have changed the emphasis of his evidence away from that contained in his written statement. This list, together with any spoken advice sought from counsel will then be used in the cross-examination of this witness. It may be necessary during this process to pass further notes to counsel if you believe the questions have been answered incompletely or in error. Do bear in mind however, that such note passing is best done through the Defence solicitor sitting beside you, who will judge when best to pass this information on. Otherwise counsel will not relish the prospect of untimely intrusion into his presentation.

It will then be your turn to give evidence, if this is sought from your counsel. Bear in mind that at this stage your opposite number will be assisting Prosecution Counsel in a similar manner. If there are real differences in the expert evidence presented, you can be sure that it will be subjected to the closest possible degree of scrutiny to see if it is tenable. If any of your submissions are clearly shown when challenged to be unsound, then there is every likelihood that the jury will view the remainder of your evidence in a similar light.

## Further Reading

Field, D. 1991. *The Law of Evidence in Scotland,* Edinburgh: Green, Sweet & Maxwell.

Dracup, D.E.J. (former Chief Crown Prosecutor, SE Area Crown Prosecution Service). 1996. Private communication.

MacNiven, D. (Police Division, Scottish Office). 1996. Private communication.

Priston, A. 1985. A forensic scientist's guide to the English legal system. Parts 1 and 2. *Journal of the Forensic Science Society,* **25**, 269–279, 329–341.

Scottish Courts. Fact Sheet 9, The Scottish Office, October 1993.

Champod, C., Baldwin, D., Taroni, F. and Buckleton, J.S. 2003. Firearm and tool marks: the Bayesian approach. *AFTE Journal,* **35** (3).

# Proof Marks and the Proof of Firearms

11

The proof testing or reproof of a firearm involves the firing of cartridges containing a considerably greater charge than those intended for normal service use. The pressure and the stress to which the barrel and action are subjected are consequently higher and are intended to reveal any weakness. It is considered preferable, if such weaknesses do exist, that they are found at the Proof House rather than in the field where personal injury may be inflicted.

In the UK, the statutory proof testing of new firearms is compulsory before they can be offered for sale. The Gunmakers' Company of London was granted its Royal Charter in 1637 in an attempt to protect the public against the many unsound arms then being offered for sale. This practice was regarded both as a potential danger to the public and also something which indirectly brought discredit upon the reputable gunmakers. From 1670 the Gunmakers' Company was enabled to enforce proof in and around London, the original proof marks are still in use today. In 1813, the Birmingham Proof House was established for public security at the expense of the Birmingham Gun Trade by Act of Parliament. Marks previously used by the maker Ketland became the first proof marks of the new Proof House. Since 1813 it has been an offence to sell or offer for sale an unproved arm anywhere in the UK. The present law is to be found in Gun Barrel Proof Acts 1868, 1950 and 1978 and the various Rules of Proof, in particular those of 1925, 1954, 1986 and 1989 when the metric system of measurement was introduced.

Other countries around the world introduced similar procedures, although it is notable that the US did not follow suit by way of statute. In-house test marks will however be seen on many American arms, and the industry standards relating to firearm and ammunition manufacture generally adhered to as set down by the Sporting Arms and Ammunition Industries

369

(SAAMI) do offer some level of control. Recognised proof test marks became a symbol of quality, as did the tradenames of the better manufacturers. This lead to the use of false proof marks imposed upon shoddy firearms made outside the UK which were clearly meant to deceive would-be buyers. At about the same time a number of firearms were made engraved with deliberately misleading markings which at first sight might convey the impression that a particular revolver had been made by a reputable and well recognised manufacturer such as Colt or Smith and Wesson.

Today, the UK is a signatory member of the International Proof Commission (CIP) Secretariat at the Belgian Proof House, Liege, and recognises the proof marks of all other members of the CIP on a reciprocal basis. The Commission has worked for the standardisation of proof which also involves standardisation of pressure measurement, of chamber and bore sizes, and cartridge dimensions. The current membership includes Austria, Belgium, Chile, the Czech Republic, Finland, France, Germany, Hungary, Italy, Russia, Spain and the UK. A number of other countries are now close to the position where they also will become members. Details of most of the currently recognised proof markings are set down in the UK proof houses booklet *Notes on the Proof of Shotguns and Other Small Arms*. Additional markings are also used by some of the proof houses to indicate the date of proof. This can appear either as a simple date stamp or in the form of a codemark. Proof markings and these additional markings can be of considerable assistance to the forensic examiner.

The internationally accepted use of bore or gauge of a firearm, especially smooth-bored arms has already been described as the number of spherical lead balls which can be passed through the bore of a gun and which will collectively weigh 1 lb. Many old guns, and this will include rifled arms, will have their bore size marked somewhere upon the barrel. In large bore punt-guns a lettering system is used above 3-bore, with the exception of 1- and 2-bore. Table 11.1 will be of assistance to all of those people who wondered why a .44 in cap-and-ball revolver is sometimes referred to as a 54-bore, or a .577 in Snider rifle barrel is marked 25-bore. (All calibres are measured in inches.)

There is one major anomaly in the bore or gauge listing of firearms which is used by some continental firearm and ammunition manufacturers. Many European .410 in guns are marked 36-bore, and their cartridges sometimes listed as 12 mm or 36-bore, although the proof markings on the underside of the barrel will usually include the true bore size 10.4 mm. From the above table it is evident that 36-bore would in fact refer to a gun of .506 in bore size (approximately 13 mm), while the appropriate bore size would be 68-bore. The 32-bore, which at this date is still being manufactured in continental Europe together with some other odd gauges such as 24-bore and 14-bore, is often referred to under the cartridge size 14 mm.

**Table 11.1   Calibre vs. Bore Size in Inches**

| Bore | Calibre | Bore | Calibre | Bore | Calibre |
|------|---------|------|---------|------|---------|
| A | 2.000 | 11 | 0.751 | 34 | 0.515 |
| B | 1.938 | 12 | 0.729 | 35 | 0.510 |
| C | 1.875 | 13 | 0.710 | 36 | 0.506 |
| D | 1.813 | 14 | 0.693 | 37 | 0.501 |
| E | 1.750 | 15 | 0.677 | 38 | 0.497 |
| F | 1.688 | 16 | 0.662 | 39 | 0.492 |
| 1 | 1.669 | 17 | 0.649 | 40 | 0.488 |
| H | 1.625 | 18 | 0.637 | 41 | 0.484 |
| J | 1.563 | 19 | 0.626 | 42 | 0.480 |
| K | 1.500 | 20 | 0.615 | 43 | 0.476 |
| L | 1.438 | 21 | 0.605 | 44 | 0.473 |
| M | 1.375 | 22 | 0.596 | 45 | 0.469 |
| 2 | 1.325 | 23 | 0.587 | 46 | 0.466 |
| O | 1.313 | 24 | 0.579 | 47 | 0.463 |
| P | 1.250 | 25 | 0.571 | 48 | 0.459 |
| 3 | 1.157 | 26 | 0.563 | 49 | 0.456 |
| 4 | 1.052 | 27 | 0.556 | 50 | 0.453 |
| 5 | 0.976 | 28 | 0.550 | 51 | 0.450 |
| 6 | 0.919 | 29 | 0.543 | 52 | 0.447 |
| 7 | 0.873 | 30 | 0.537 | 53 | 0.444 |
| 8 | 0.835 | 31 | 0.531 | 54 | 0.442 |
| 9 | 0.803 | 32 | 0.526 | 55 | 0.439 |
| 10 | 0.775 | 33 | 0.520 | 56 | 0.436 |

continued...

The actual bore size of a shotgun will only rarely correspond to the theoretical value. This is particularly true for old Damascus barrelled guns where the manufacturing processes were somewhat hit-and-miss. In such instances the weapon would be chambered for the nearest appropriate cartridge. The proof houses allow limits for such variations in the actual bore dimensions and mark the guns accordingly.

Older guns which have become pitted, and as a consequence have been skimmed out in an attempt at rectification, can sometimes come out at a bore size lying very close to the top limit; subsequent wear can then leave the weapon 'out of proof'. On older guns the proof bore size in the case of a 12-bore gun is marked within the following three bands: 12/1, 12 and 13/1, which correspond to .74 in, .729 in and .719 in. The 1954 Rules of Proof provide this information in the form of the latter Imperial measurements only. The current 1989 rules use millimetre measurement within a similar band system set at one-tenth of a millimetre intervals (Table 11.2).

**Table 11.1   Calibre vs. Bore Size in Inches** (continued)

| Bore | Calibre | Bore | Calibre | Bore | Calibre |
|------|---------|------|---------|------|---------|
| 57 | 0.434 | 89 | 0.374 | 121 | 0.337 |
| 58 | 0.431 | 90 | 0.372 | 122 | 0.3365 |
| 59 | 0.429 | 91 | 0.371 | 123 | 0.336 |
| 60 | 0.426 | 92 | 0.370 | 124 | 0.335 |
| 61 | 0.424 | 93 | 0.368 | 125 | 0.334 |
| 62 | 0.422 | 94 | 0.367 | 126 | 0.333 |
| 63 | 0.419 | 95 | 0.366 | 127 | 0.332 |
| 64 | 0.417 | 96 | 0.364 | 128 | 0.331 |
| 65 | 0.415 | 97 | 0.363 | 129 | 0.330 |
| 66 | 0.413 | 98 | 0.362 | 130 | 0.3295 |
| 67 | 0.411 | 99 | 0.361 | 131 | 0.329 |
| 68 | 0.409 | 100 | 0.360 | 132 | 0.328 |
| 69 | 0.407 | 101 | 0.358 | 133 | 0.327 |
| 70 | 0.405 | 102 | 0.357 | 134 | 0.3265 |
| 71 | 0.403 | 103 | 0.356 | 135 | 0.326 |
| 72 | 0.401 | 104 | 0.355 | 136 | 0.325 |
| 73 | 0.399 | 105 | 0.354 | 137 | 0.324 |
| 74 | 0.398 | 106 | 0.353 | 138 | 0.323 |
| 75 | 0.396 | 107 | 0.352 | 139 | 0.322 |
| 76 | 0.394 | 108 | 0.350 | 140 | 0.3215 |
| 77 | 0.392 | 109 | 0.349 | 141 | 0.321 |
| 78 | 0.391 | 110 | 0.348 | 142 | 0.320 |
| 79 | 0.389 | 111 | 0.347 | 143 | 0.319 |
| 80 | 0.387 | 112 | 0.346 | 144 | 0.3185 |
| 81 | 0.386 | 113 | 0.345 | 145 | 0.318 |
| 82 | 0.384 | 114 | 0.344 | 146 | 0.317 |
| 83 | 0.383 | 115 | 0.343 | 147 | 0.316 |
| 84 | 0.381 | 116 | 0.342 | 148 | 0.3155 |
| 85 | 0.379 | 117 | 0.341 | 149 | 0.315 |
| 86 | 0.378 | 118 | 0.340 | 150 | 0.314 |
| 87 | 0.377 | 119 | 0.339 | | |
| 88 | 0.375 | 120 | 0.338 | | |

Under the current 1989 Rules of Proof which reflect CIP standards bore sizes are expressed in 1/10 mm steps within the approved range for the particular bore size (Table 11.3).

In recent years the London Gun Barrel Proof House has marked the year of testing as part of the proof markings, e.g., LP 92 (London Proof 1992). Over the years the Birmingham Gun Barrel Proof House has used a variety of code marks to indicate the date of proof. Between 1921 and 1942 this code mark consisted of crossed halberds with a letter contained

**Table 11.2 Acceptable Ranges of Actual Barrel Bore Diameters of Breechloading Smooth-Bore Guns with Respect to Cartridge Chambering**

| Nominal Size of Cartridge | Gauge as Marked | Diameter of Bore (In Inches) |
|---|---|---|
| | 5/2 | 1.026 |
| | 5/1 | 1.001 |
| **4** | 5 | 0.976 |
| | 6/2 | 0.957 |
| | **6/1** | **0.938** |
| | 6 | 0.919 |
| | 7/2 | 0.903 |
| | 7/1 | 0.888 |
| | 7 | 0.873 |
| | 8/2 | 0.860 |
| | 8/1 | 0.847 |
| **8** | **8** | **0.835** |
| | 9/2 | 0.824 |
| | 9/1 | 0.813 |
| | 9 | 0.803 |
| | 10/2 | 0.793 |
| | 10/1 | 0.784 |
| | **10** | **0.775** |
| | 11/1 | 0.763 |
| | 11 | 0.751 |
| | 12/1 | 0.740 |
| **12** | **12** | **0.729** |
| | 13/1 | 0.719 |
| | 13 | 0.710 |
| | 14/1 | 0.701 |
| **14** | **14** | **0.693** |
| | 15/1 | 0.685 |
| | 15 | 0.677 |
| | 16/1 | 0.669 |
| **16** | **16** | **0.662** |
| | 17/1 | 0.655 |
| | 17 | 0.649 |
| | 18 | 0.637 |
| | 19 | 0.626 |
| **20** | **20** | **0.615** |
| | 21 | 0.605 |
| | 22 | 0.596 |
| | 23 | 0.587 |
| | **24** | **0.579** |
| | 25 | 0.571 |
| | 26 | 0.563 |

continued...

**Table 11.2  Acceptable Ranges of Actual Barrel Bore Diameters of
Breechloading Smooth-Bore Guns with Respect to Cartridge Chambering**
(continued)

| Nominal Size of Cartridge | Gauge as Marked | Diameter of Bore (In Inches) |
|---|---|---|
| | 27 | 0.556 |
| | **28** | **0.550** |
| | 29 | 0.543 |
| | 30 | 0.537 |
| | 31 | 0.531 |
| | 32 | 0.526 |
| **32** | 33 | 0.520 |
| | 34 | 0.515 |
| | 35 | 0.510 |
| | 36 | 0.506 |
| | **37** | **0.501** |
| | 38 | 0.497 |
| .410 | 410 | 0.410–0.415 |
| **.360** | **360** | **0.360** |

*Note*: Figures in bold represent optimum values for the respective gauges.

**Table 11.3  CIP Specified Shotgun Bore Ranges for Designated Gauges**

| Gauge | Diameter in mm | Gauge | Diameter in mm |
|---|---|---|---|
| 4 | 23.3–24.0 | 20 | 15.6–16.2 |
| 8 | 20.4–21.1 | 24 | 14.7–15.2 |
| 10 | 19.3–20.0 | 28 | 13.8–14.3 |
| 12 | 18.2–18.9 | 32 | 12.7–13.2 |
| 14 | 17.2–17.7 | .410 | 10.2–10.7 |
| 16 | 16.8–17.3 | 9 mm | 8.5–9.0 |

in its upper quadrant indicating the year of proof, and an inspector's number in the lower quadrant (Table 11.4).

A second code series was used between 1950 and 1974 which again used crossed halberds. In this series the code letter was placed in the left-hand quadrant, along with a letter 'B' in the right quadrant, and with an inspector's number in the lower quadrant:

| | | | |
|---|---|---|---|
| AB—1950 | HB—1957 | PB—1964 | WB—1971 |
| BB—1951 | JB—1958 | QB—1965 | XB—1972 |
| BC or CB—1952 | KB—1959 | RB—1966 | YB—1973 |
| DB—1953 | LB—1960 | SB—1967 | ZB—1974 |
| EB—1954 | MB—1961 | TB—1968 | |
| FB—1955 | NB—1962 | UB—1969 | |
| GB—1956 | OB—1963 | VB—1970 | |

**Table 11.4   Date Code Marks Used by the Birmingham Proof
House from 1 July 1921**

| A | 1921–1922 | H | 1928–1929 | P | 1935–1936 |
|---|-----------|---|-----------|---|-----------|
| B | 1922–1923 | J | 1929–1930 | R | 1936–1937 |
| C | 1923–1924 | K | 1930–1931 | S | 1937–1938 |
| D | 1924–1925 | L | 1931–1932 | T | 1938–1939 |
| E | 1925–1926 | M | 1932–1933 | U | 1939–1940 |
| F | 1926–1927 | N | 1933–1934 | V | 1940–1941 |
| G | 1927–1928 | O | 1934–1935 | W | 1941–1942 |

Between 1975 and 1984 a circular field was used divided into three
sectors. For the first four years these sectors were marked out with an
upturned letter 'Y'. The left and right sectors were used as before with an
inspector's number placed in the lower sector:

| | |
|---|---|
| AB—1975 | FB—1980 |
| BB—1976 | GB—1981 |
| CB—1977 | HB—1982 |
| DB—1978 | JB—1983 |
| EB—1979 | KB—1984 |

In 1985 the code reverted once again to the crossed halberds format using
the left quadrant for the code letter, a constant letter 'C' in the right quadrant,
and an inspector's number in the lowest quadrant. For the period starting with
the year 1998, the sequence reverts to the letter 'A' in the left hand quadrant,
followed by the letter 'D' in the right hand quadrant. The left hand quadrant
code letters continue as before avoiding the use of the letters 'I' and 'Q':

| | | |
|---|---|---|
| LC—1985 | TC—1992 | AD – 1998 |
| MC—1986 | UC—1993 | BD – 1999 |
| NC—1987 | VC—1994 | CD – 2000 |
| OC—1988 | XC—1995 | DD – 2001 |
| PC—1989 | YC—1996 | Etc. |
| RC—1990 | ZC—1997 | |
| SC—1991 | | |

The Nottingham branch of the London Proof House followed a simple
date stamp similar to that of the main facility (e.g., NP/84 indicated the
identity of the proof house followed by the year 1984). However, a letter code
was then adopted:

1980s uses A0 to A9.
1990s uses B0 to B9.
2000s will use C0 to C9.
2010s will use D0 to D9.
2020s will use E0 to E9.
2030s will use F0 to F9.

Other marks will often be present on firearms, which in some instances will also constitute part of the original proof marks, the original military service markings, or previous proof marks or manufacturer's test marks, none of which will be recognised within the CIP system. As an example a sporting gun imported from Russia (before it became a member of the CIP) and put on sale within the UK will be inscribed with the original Russian Proof House markings as well as those imposed by the London or Birmingham Proof Houses shortly after arrival in this country. On some old and inexpensive guns of foreign manufacture, it is not unusual to find false or unofficial proof marks which will sometimes resemble those used in England or Belgium.

## 11.1 UK Proof Markings

The proof testing of firearms has been practised in England for a very long time, as has already been explained. The current Definitive Proof mark and the Inspection (View) mark used by the London Proof House are identical to those first used in 1637 and 1670, respectively. The pre-1904 equivalent markings of the Birmingham Proof House were first used in 1813.

### 11.1.1 Under 1989 Rules of Proof

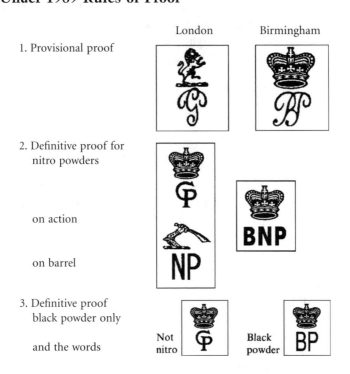

4. Ammunition inspection

5. Special definitive proof

6. Reproof

7. Reproof of shotgun when removable choke tubes fitted

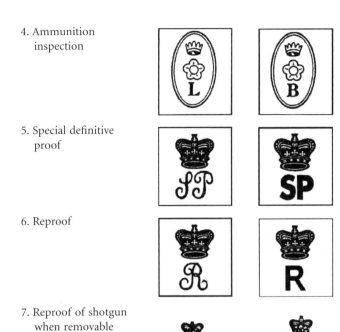

## 11.1.2 Under 1925 Rules of Proof

| | London | Birmingham |
|---|---|---|
| Definitive proof | | |
| View | | |
| Nitro | | |
| Military proof | | |

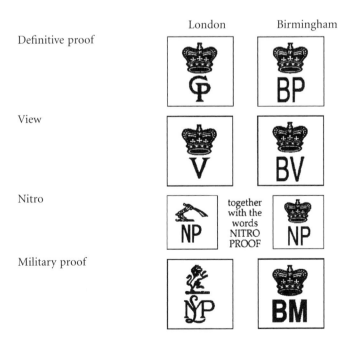

The encirclement of proof marks and the words 'Not English Make' indicated the proof of an arm of foreign manufacture.

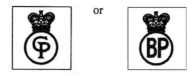

Additional marks were used to indicate nominal bore diameter (e.g., 12 or 13/1). Nominal gauge is indicated within a diamond, chamber length and maximum shot load. In the case of rifles, marks indicate the nominal calibre and case length and the maximum service load of powder and bullet. The 1986 Rules of Proof covered the transitional period from the Imperial to the Metric systems of measurement allowing the submitter the choice of measurement used. In metric measurement the minimum proof pressure would be stated in kilograms per square centimetre rather than tons per square inch. After 1989 the metric system was applied across the board with the minimum proof pressure being expressed in bars. The following examples represent the types of proof marks which would be impressed upon the flats of 12-bore shotgun barrels (Figure 11.1).

The CIP Cartridge control decision XV-7 introduced a system whereby all cartridges sold in CIP countries had to be tested to ensure that they complied with the agreed standards in respect of pressure, dimensions and performance. The cartridge boxes of such approved batches of ammunition are then stamped or printed with the CIP ammunition approval mark of the respective Proof House.

Under the UK 1989 Rules of Proof examples of commercial cartridges are tested to confirm their compliance with the agreed CIP standards. In this

| Rules of Proof | London | | | Birmingham | | | |
|---|---|---|---|---|---|---|---|
| 1925 | 12 | NP / ₲ | ⟨12/c⟩ Nitro proof 1⅛oz | 12/1  BV | BP  NP | ⟨12/c⟩ 2½" | Nitro proof 1⅛ |
| 1954 | ·729" | NP | ⟨12⟩ 2½" 3 Tons | ·729" | BNP | ⟨12⟩ 2½"-3 Ton per▫" | |
| 1989 | 18·3" | NP | ⟨12⟩ 65 mm 850 bar | 18·3 | BNP | 12-65  850 bar | |

**Figure 11.1**    Examples of marks impressed on shotgun flats of 12-bore guns by the London and Birmingham Proof Houses.

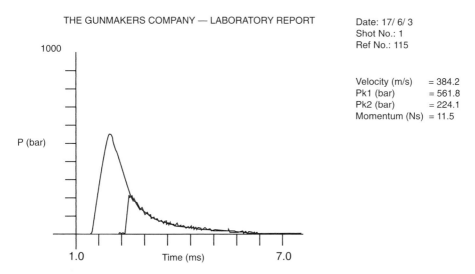

Figure 11.2    Cartridge proof test at the London Proof House.

example the testing of a batch of 12-bore cartridges involves the use of a special test gun fitted with piezo electric pressure sensors set at points 17 mm and 162 mm from its breech. This part of a laboratory test report, kindly provided by the London Proof House, shows the time–pressure curves generated during one of the test firings, along with the P1 and P2 pressure measurements and the momentum imparted to the gun. This is for a particular 12-bore cartridge of 67.5 mm case length, loaded with a charge of 30 grams of Number 6 size shot. The velocity of the shot charge is measured 2.5 metres from the muzzle. The initial testing of a shotgun chambered for use with such a loading would involve a proof cartridge generating a minimum of 850 Bar pressure. The peak service pressures allowed under CIP regulations, measured at P1 and P2, are 650 and 385 Bar, respectively (Figure 11.2).

### 11.1.3 Under Rules of Proof Prior to 1904

Marks used to indicate Proof and View by the Birmingham Proof House between 1813 and 1904. Unless associated with the wording 'Nitro proof' these indicate black powder proof only.

Birmingham
Company proof

View

Between 1887 and 1925 the following special definitive marks were used upon barrels proved once only. They may appear on single-barrel shotguns and on certain rifled arms.

London                    Birmingham

Between 1875 and 1887 the Birmingham Proof House used the marking *Not for ball* to indicate choke boring. The marking *Choke* was used during the same period to indicate recessed choke boring and for all significant chokes after this period up to 1954. Fractional bore size markings (e.g., 12/1 and 13/1) were in use between 1887 and 1954. The letters *CR* surmounted by a crown were used by Birmingham after 1984 to indicate reproof after fitting screw-in choke tubes, and the letters *BH* surmounted by a crown for industrial blank-operated tools.

Special Proof House Inspection Markings were introduced by the two proof houses to cater for changes introduced by the Firearms (Amendment) Act 1988 in respect of approved standards for the reduction of repeating shotgun magazines to two-shot capacity, and for arms de-activated to the standards accepted by the Secretary of State to allow their sale as non-firearms. These standards are set down in the Home Office publication *Firearms Law: Specifications for the Adaptation of Shot Gun Magazines and the Deactivation of Firearms*. The marks used by the two houses to indicate magazine alteration (MR), and de-activation (DA) also include the date of the inspection and issue of the appropriate inspection certificate. The Proof Houses may also use additional markings to indicate changes introduced by the 1995 Revision of the above standards:

London          Birmingham                      London          Birmingham
Proof House     Proof House                     Proof House     Proof House

  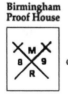  or      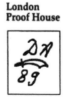    or

The figures '89' relate to the calendar year of 1989 and changes as appropriate.

In 1993 a CIP specification was introduced in response to concerns as to the use of steel shot loadings with traditional European shotguns, especially in respect of their use in old or lightweight game guns. This specification sets out the maximum sizes and hardness values for steel shot considered suitable, the number of proof rounds to be fired through each barrel, and the maximum permissible values for velocity and the breech pressure generated at 25 and 162 mm distances from the chamber. A special 'Steel Shot' CIP proof mark consisting of a 'fleur de lis' will be stamped upon each barrel. In the case of the UK the words 'steel shot' are added along with the higher proof pressure of 1370 Bar.

The following marks were used on British Military Service arms. These marks are not recognised under the Rules of Proof for the sale of weapons to the public.

(1) Engineer's stamp; (2) Percentage stamp; (3) Material stamp for batch of steel; (4) Crown Property; (5) Superseded by 4; (6) Proof stamp on assembled arms and spares; (7) Proof of bolts and breech blocks; (8) Property stamp; (9) Date stamp; (10) Cancellation stamp; (11) Enfield examiner's stamp; (12) Sale marks on wood and metal parts, respectively; (13) Sale of serviceable arms to public; (14) Serviceable arms with slight defect; (15) Mark used by travelling view for presence of wear in barrels; (16) Repair mark at Enfield; (17) Repair mark at Birmingham. Similar marks used at other locations as a letter under a star – 'O' Skinner & Woods; 'Q' Holland & Holland; 'U' Purdeys; 'Z' Westley Richards; 'V' Greeners; 'X' Cogswell & Harrison; 'R' Boss & Co; 'P' Parker Hale; (18) Components stored for emergency use only, also for rifle and machine gun barrels accepted with oversize bores; (19) Used for complete weapons as at 18; (20) Components which have passed hardness test; (21) Components and arms fit for drill purposes only; (22) Anything appertaining to Enfield; (23) Arms & components accepted for Royal Navy; (24) Arms fitted with Morris Tube .22″ barrel conversion unit; (25) Weapons fitted with aiming tube; (26) Serviceable part-worn items; (27) High velocity (sight on gun); (28) Barrels suitable for Mk VIII .303″ ammunition; (29) Vickers machine gun components for Air Ministry use; (30) Socket end of butt treated with paraffin wax prior to assembly; (31) Arm issued unproofed; (32) War Office approved .22″ arms; (33) School of Musketry; (34) 1914 Pattern rifles fitted with .22″ barrels; (35) Duplicate sealed pattern; (36) Small Arms Inspection Department property; (37) Martini rifles converted to .22″; (38) Condemned stamp; (39) Special sale mark of Oerlikon guns sold out of service; (40) Short butt on rifle; (41) Weedon mark used prior to issue of part-worn rifle; (42) Sale mark to Service Officers; (43) Sale of weapons for cadet use fitted with safe barrels to County Association; (44) As 41 but with unsafe barrels; (45) Sold for drill purposes but with safe and unsafe barrels, respectively; (46) Condemned by RAOC Workshop; (47) Draw lapped barrels; (48) Accepted for New Zealand Service; (49) Canada; (50) Australia; (51) Superseded by 50; (52)

Iraq; (53) Small components for Iraq Army; (54) South African Army; (55) Irish Free State; (56) Superseded by 55; (57) Mark used on silenced Welrod weapons—a star denotes proof, and a rectangle denotes functioning test.

## 11.2 Austrian Proof Marks

Proof Houses at Vienna and Ferlach were recognised in the UK prior to 1939, and again after 1956.

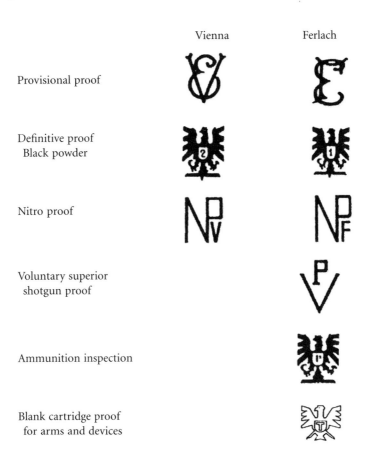

|  | Vienna | Ferlach |
|---|---|---|
| Provisional proof | | |
| Definitive proof Black powder | | |
| Nitro proof | | |
| Voluntary superior shotgun proof | | |
| Ammunition inspection | | |
| Blank cartridge proof for arms and devices | | |

Additional marks are used in conjunction with the above to indicate, e.g., quality of barrel steel, the gauge, the bore diameter or the calibre in millimetres and the case length.

## 11.3 Belgian Proof Marks

Marks used at the Liege Proof House since 1968.

(1) Muzzle
loading
Black powder

(2) View,
Black powder

(3) Definitive,
Black powder
Military
nitro

(4) Optional
provisional
proof

(5) Nitro proof

(6) Nitro
superior
proof

(7) Definitive
foreign arms

(8) Ammunition
control

Prior to 1968, the following marks were in use. Such marks may still be valid.

Provisional

Double
provisional

Triple
provisional

Former
definitive

Rifled
arms

View

Nitro
proof

Nitro
superior
proof

Ammunition
inspection

Additional marks are used to indicate bore diameter and chamber length in millimetres, and the weight of the barrel at proof. Some Belgian proof marks can be used to assist with the dating of arms using the information in Table 11.5 obtained from the Director of the Liege Proof House.

**Table 11.5  Significance and Periods of the Use of Marks by the Liege Proof House**

| Mark | Significance and Period of Use |
|---|---|
| (column symbol) | (1) Acceptance mark used from seventeenth century–18 May 1811. (2) Inspection mark used from 16 June 1853–today |
| **E LG** | Acceptance — 1810–1811 (?) |
| (E L G ★ in oval) | (1) Acceptance — 18 May 1811–14 September 1813 (2) Acceptance — 18 August 1818–11 July 1893 (3) Muzzle loaders — 11 July 1893–today |
| **32** | Gauge — 18 May 1811–6 March 1889 (?) |
| **13,2** | Calibre (mm) — 6 March 1889 (?)–today |
| **A E** | Guns made prior to 18 May 1811 (?) |
| (E L G ✱ in oval) | Acceptance — 14 September 1813–18 August 1818 (?) |
| (L.G. in oval) | Acceptance — 8 September 1846–11 July 1893 |
| **R** | Second testing of repaired guns — 8 September 1846–before 10 August 1923 |
| (crown) **N** | Countermark of controller — 30 December 1853 (?)–26 January 1877 |
| **ℰ𝓛** | Provisional proof — 21 December 1852–today |
| **ℒ** | Provisional admittance 7 July 1852–30 December 1853 |
| **★ Ä** | Countermark of controller 27 January 1877–today |
| (lion) **E C** | Smokeless proof with EC Schultze or other powders 2 March 1891–before 26 February 1968 |
| (lion) **SCH** | |
| **MAX** *2 gr 72 poudre 31 gr 50 plomb* | Charge of smokeless powder 30 October 1897–18 November 1903 |

**Table 11.5   Significance and Periods of the Use of Marks by the Liege Proof House** (continued)

| Mark | Significance and Period of Use |
|---|---|
| **P.V.** | Smokeless powder 4 October 1898–before 26 February 1968 |
| **1K355.5** | Barrel weight at nitro proof 11 June 1892–before 30 June 1924 |
| **1K355** | Barrel weight 30 June 1924–today |
| (crest E L G) | Acceptance 11 July 1893–before 26 February 1968 |
| **£ £** | Provisional black powder proof 30 January 1897–10 August 1923 |
| **NON POUR BALLE** | Choke bore 16 April 1878–30 January 1897 |
| **CHOKE** | Choke bore 30 January 1897–4 October 1898 |
| **CHOKE 17.0   16.3** | Bore and choke (mm) 4 October 1898–25 February 1910 |
| **CHOKE** $\dfrac{18.7}{18.0}$ | Choke bore measured at 22 cm from breech 25 February 1910–30 June 1924 |
| **CHOKE 17.0** | Choke bore measured at 22 cm from breech 30 June 1924–before 24 February 1968 |
| **CH. B. RAYE** | Rifled or part rifled choke bore 11 July 1893–30 June 1924; 26 February 1930–before 26 February 1968 |
| **CH RAYE** | … 30 June 1924–26 February 1930 |
| **NON RAYE 94** | Unrifled pistols, revolvers and carbines January 1894–end January 1984 |
| **NON RAYE** | … 30 January 1894–30 June 1924 |
| **EXPRESS NON RAYE** | Unrifled express carbines 30 January 1894–30 June 1924 |
| $\dfrac{70}{20.6}$ | Chamber length and bore (mm) 6 June 1892–30 June 1924 |
| (diamond 16 C) | Gauge 4 October 1898–30 June 1924 |
| **R** | Rifled arms 30 January 1894–before 26 February 1968 |

**Table 11.5  Significance and Periods of the Use of Marks by the Liege Proof House** (continued)

| Mark | Significance and Period of Use |
|---|---|
| **B. PLOMB** | .22 rifled arms best used with lead bullets 8 July 1910–today |
| **B. BLINDEE** | .22 rifled arms best used with jacketed bullets 8 July 1910–before 26 February 1968 |
| | Provisional proof for unfinished barrels 30 June 1924–before 26 February 1968 |
| | Double provisional proof for engraved arms 30 June 1924–before 26 February 1968 |
| | Triple provisional proof for engraved arms 30 June 1924–before 26 February 1968 |
| | Gauge and chamber length 30 June 1924–today |
| | Foreign arms 30 June 1924–today |
| | Acceptance 30 June 1924–today |
| | Arms for proof abroad 30 June 1924–before 26 February 1968 |
| | Smooth bore superior proof 26 February 1968–today |
| | Current powder acceptance 26 February 1968–today |
| | Proof for tempered components 26 February 1968–today |

## 11.4 Chilean Proof Marks

Marks used by the Santiago Proof House established in 1961.

One mark for all arms and          Ammunition inspection
blank operated devices

## 11.5 Czech Republic Proof Marks

Marks impressed by the Czech Proof House as of 1 January 1993 are shown below.

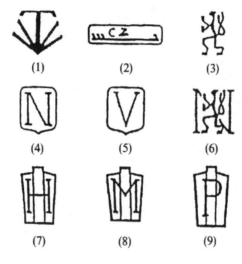

(1) Proof for alarm guns, blank operated tools and veterinary darting guns; (2) Small-calibre blank cartridge inspection; (3) Black powder proof of breech-loading arms; (4) Smokeless powder shotgun proof of breech-loading arms; (5) Superior shotgun proof; (6) Smokeless powder proof of breech-loading rifled arms; (7) Homologation of blank operated guns and devices; (8) Ammunition inspection; (9) Powder inspection.

   Additional marks may indicate chamber length, bore, choke and year of manufacture. During the period between 14 October 1963 and the above date, marks 3, 4 and 6 were accepted within the UK for all arms made in the former state of Czechoslovakia. After the break-up of Czechoslovakia, the Slovakian Republic adopted the same proof marks as the Czech Republic.

## 11.6 French Proof Marks

Proof was optional in France until July 1960. Other markings, not recognised, may be present from this period. Some earlier marks are however accepted; the Proof Masters will advise on these matters. The following marks are used by the St. Etienne Proof House:

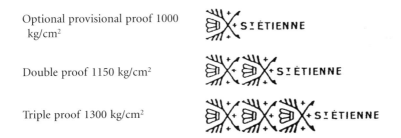

| | |
|---|---|
| Optional provisional proof 1000 kg/cm² | |
| Double proof 1150 kg/cm² | |
| Triple proof 1300 kg/cm² | |

### 11.6.1 Definitive Proof

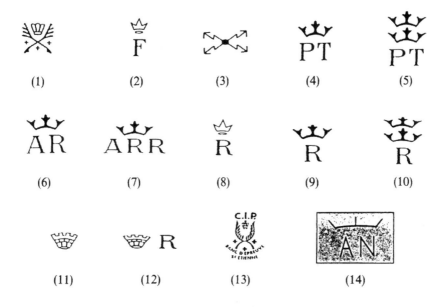

(1) Modal proof of devices classified as firearms; (2) Black powder proof; (3) Arms in finished state when proved; (4) Nitro proof of finished arms; (5) Superior nitro proof of finished arms; (6) Proof of long-barrelled rifled arms; (7) Re-proof of long-barrelled rifled arms; (8) Black powder re-proof of finished arms; (9) Nitro re-proof; (10) Superior nitro re-proof; (11) Proof

of short-barrelled arms; (12) Reproof of short-barrelled arms; (13) Ammunition inspection; (14) Mark used to indicate deactivated firearm.

Earlier markings used by the Paris Proof House are as follows:

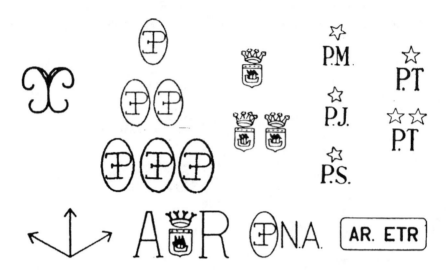

## 11.6.2 Proof Marks Imposed upon French Government Firearms

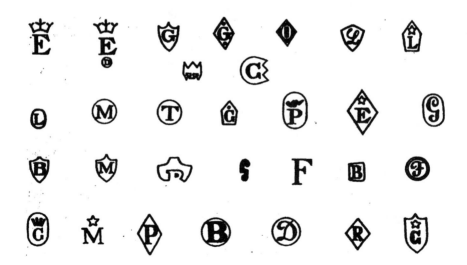

## 11.7 German Proof Marks

The following proof marks were valid on 1 January 1994 for the new Federal Republic of Germany:

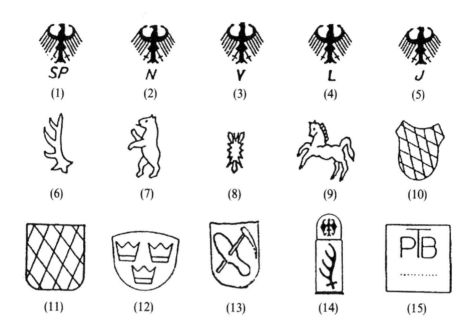

(1) Definitive black powder proof; (2) Definitive nitro proof; (3) Superior nitro proof; (4) Proof of firearm used to discharge a substance other than a solid projectile; (5) Reproof; (6) Ulm Proof House; (7) Berlin Proof House; (8) Kiel Proof House; (9) Hannover Proof House; (10) München Proof House; (11) Mellrichstadt Proof House; (12) Köln Proof House; (13) Suhl Proof House; (14) Ammunition inspection. Each proof house uses a stylised cartridge and eagle with its own distinctive proof mark, in this example that of Ulm; (15) Proof of blank-operated portable devices, starting pistols, etc.

The recognition of proof marks in the UK prior to 1939 was discontinued after the outbreak of World War II. Recognition was awarded again in the UK from 1 October 1984 for the following pre-war German proof markings:

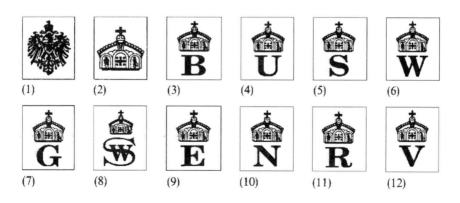

Muzzle-loading guns must bear 1, 1, 4 and 5 upon the barrel, and 1 and 4 on the breech, or 3 and 4 upon the breech and barrel. Breech-loading shotguns must have 1, 1, 4 and 5 upon the barrels; 1, 1, 4 and 6 if choke-bored. If rifled in the choked section of the bore then 1, 1, 4, 6 and 8 must be present; the action must be marked with 1 and 4.

Rifles must bear 1, 1, 4 and 7, together with 9 in express rifles. The breech or action should be marked with 1 and 4. Revolvers must bear marks 2 and 4 upon the barrel, cylinder, frame or body. Repeating pistols and Saloon pistols must bear the marks 2 and 4 upon the barrel and action.

Proved arms which have been subject to subsequent alteration must upon reproof be marked with 11 and 3 in addition to their original markings. Arms held in stock during the passing of the 1891 German Proof Act were exempted from the provisions of proof and received the mark 12 upon the barrel, breech or action.

The following marks used in Nazi Germany and the Sudetenland between 1940 and the end of the war in 1945 and also in Austria after the Anschluss (in this case with the addition of the mark of the Vienna, Ferlach or Weipert Proof House) have never been afforded recognition:

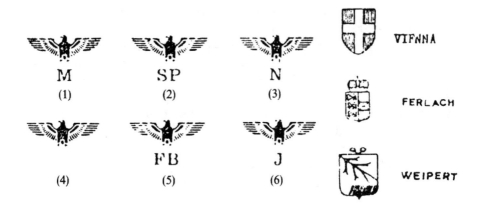

(1) Provisional mandatory black powder proof for shotguns; (2) Definitive black powder proof; (3) Definitive nitro proof, usually including the mark of the proof house and the year of proof; (4) Mark for Flobert guns; (5) Optional voluntary proof of weapon or component; (6) Re-proof of repaired arms.

The following marks have been recognised in the UK since September 1955. These include the proof house identifying marks, although the Kiel (Eckernforde) Proof House used an oakleaf prior to 1973:

(1)  (2)  (3)  (4)

(1) Provisional mark; (2) Voluntary proof of handguns; (3) Flobert rifles; (4) Kiel (Eckernforde).

After May 1973 the following markings were used:

(1)  (2)  (3)  (4)  (5)  (6)

(1) Nitro proof; (2) Superior or magnum proof; (3) Re-proof of repaired arm; (4) Black powder proof; (5) Firearms used to fire a substance other than a solid projectile; (6) The eagle surmounting the proof mark may appear in stylised form.

## 11.7.1 Marks of the Suhl Proof House

(1)  (2)  (3)  (4)

(1) Definitive proof; (2) Firearms used to fire a substance other than a solid projectile; (3) Superior or magnum proof; (4) Re-proof of repaired arms. In addition, the date of proof is marked, e.g., 5.81.

The German Proof House at Ulm has recently adopted a letter combination date code where the letters A to K correspond to the numbers 0 to 9, e.g., 1985=IF.

## 11.7.2 Early Proof and Other Marks Imposed upon German Military Firearms from the Period of the Franco-Prussian War

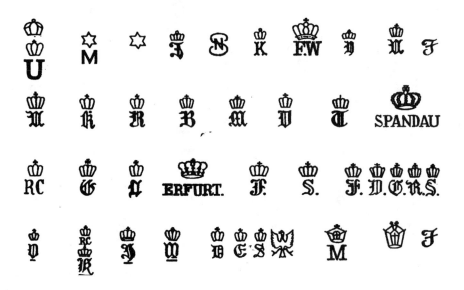

## 11.8 Finnish Proof Marks

On 27 June 1984 Finland became a signatory member of the CIP.

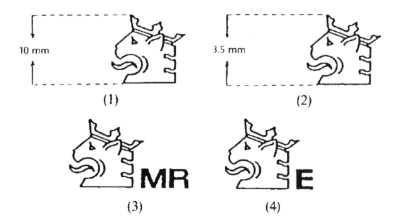

(1)          (2)

(3)          (4)

(1) Inspection mark for commercial ammunition; (2) Ordinary proof; (3) Black powder proof; (4) Magnum or superior proof. Various other marks were used by Finland prior to this date:

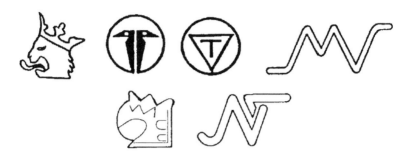

## 11.9 Hungarian Proof Marks

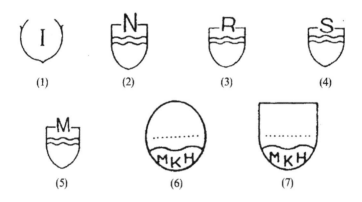

(1) Voluntary provisional proof; (2) Definitive proof of unfinished arms; (3) Reproof; (4) Superior or magnum proof; (5) Ammunition inspection; (6) Proof of starting pistols, gas pistols, alarm guns and gas compressed air guns or cartridge operated arms discharging missiles with kinetic energy up to 7.5 J; (7) Proof of blank operated tools and other devices.

## 11.10 Italian Proof Marks

The following marks are used by the Proof House at Gardone Val Trompia near to Brescia.

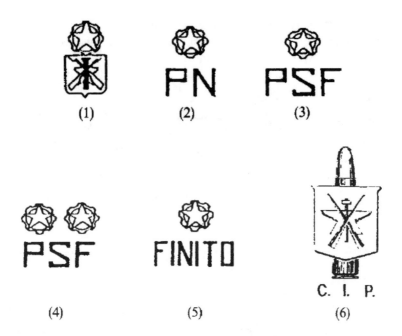

(1) Gardone V.T. Proof House mark; (2) Definitive black powder proof; (3) Definitive nitro proof; (4) Superior or magnum nitro proof; (5) Supplementary mark for arms proved in delivery condition; (6) Ammunition inspection. Additional markings may include the bore diameter in millimetres, the nominal gauge or calibre and the barrel weight in kilograms. A special code mark is used to indicate the year of proof, except for the period prior to 1954 when it was imparted in full Arabic numbers:

| | | | |
|---|---|---|---|
| X–1954 | XXII–1966 | AD–1978 | AZ–1990 |
| XI–1955 | XXIII–1967 | AE–1979 | BA–1991 |
| XII–1956 | XXIV–1968 | AF–1980 | BB–1992 |
| XIII–1957 | XXV–1969 | AH–1981 | BC–1993 |
| XIV–1958 | XXVI–1970 | AI–1982 | BD–1994 |
| XV–1959 | XX7–1971 | AL–1983 | BE–1995 |
| XVI–1960 | XX8–1972 | AM–1984 | BF–1996 |
| XVII–1961 | XX9–1973 | AN–1985 | BH–1997 |
| XVIII–1962 | XXX–1974 | AP–1986 | BI–1998 |
| XIX–1963 | AA–1975 | AS–1987 | BJ–1999 |
| XX–1964 | AB–1976 | AT–1988 | BK–2000 |
| XXI–1965 | AC–1977 | AU–1989 | |

...and so on, but omitting the letters G, O, V, Q and W.

The following marks were used previously in Italy at the various Proof Houses:

| Mark | Significance and period of use |
|------|-------------------------------|
| | **Optional Proof System of 1920** |
| | 1920-25 - Provisional proof of shotgun barrels in the rough at 14,700 psi. |
| PSF | 1920-25 – Second provisional and definitive smokeless powder proof of shotguns at 12,500 psi. |
| PN | 1920-25 – Second provisional and definitive smokeless proof of shotguns at 9,000 psi. |
| FINITO | 1920-25 - Supplementary definitive proof mark to completely finished arms. |
| | 1920-25 - Definitive proof of rifled arms at 30% over-pressure. |
| B.P.D. | 1920-21- Supplementary mark indicating proof of arms already manufactured before proof rules were passed. |
| | 1925-50 – Mark of Gardone Val Trompia Proof House. |
| | 1925-30 – Mark of Brescia Proof House. |
| | 1925-50 – Black powder proof at 15,600 psi of unjoined shotgun barrels. |
| | 1925-50 – Provisional black powder proof at 12,800 psi of joined shotgun barrels. |
| | 1925-50 – Definitive black powder proof at 8,800 psi of shotguns. Also used after 1929 for 30% over-pressure proof of black powder rifled arms. |
| PN | 1925-50 – Definitive smokeless powder proof of shotguns at 12,000 psi. Also used after 1929 for 30% over-pressure smokeless powder proof of rifled arms. |
| PSF | 1925-50 – Supplementary definitive proof mark used with the two previous marks and the following mark for blued and finished arms. |
| FINITO | 1925-29 – Definitive 30% over-pressure smokeless or black powder proof of rifled arms. |
| PD | 1925-29 Definitive 30% over-pressure smokeless or black powder proof of rifled arms. |
| | 1950 - Marks for Val Trompia and Brescia Proof Houses. |
| ☆ | 0.9 to 1.1 mm Full Choke restriction (Introduced in 1962 to indicate the degree of choke of smooth-bored guns). |
| ☆☆ | 0.7 to 0.8 mm Improved-Modified Choke restriction. |
| ☆☆☆ | 0.4 to 0.6 mm Modified or Half Choke restriction. |
| ☆☆☆☆ | 0.2 to 0.3 mm for Quarter or Improved Cylinder Choke. |
| CL | 0.1 mm or less for Cylinder Bore guns. |

## 11.11 Spanish Proof Marks

The following marks are used by the Proof House at Eibar:

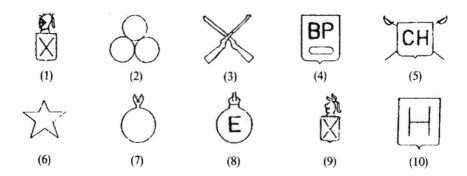

(1) Signifies arms proved at Eibar, used on action, frame or body; (2) Definitive black powder proof, used on the barrels and breech blocks of muzzle-loading smooth-bore guns; (3) Provisional black powder proof used on the barrels of breech-loading shotguns; (4) Obligatory nitro proof used on the barrel, action and frame of all breech-loading shotguns; (5) Supplementary nitro proof used on the barrel, action or frame of breech-loading shotguns; (6) Definitive proof mark used on the barrel, frame or body, bolt or slide, of saloon pistols and small-bore guns; (7) Definitive proof mark used on the barrel, frame or bolt of long-barrelled rifled arms; (8) Definitive proof mark used on foreign arms; (9) Ammunition inspection; (10) Proof of blank-operated tools and other devices.

The following unofficial proofmarks were used at Eibar until 1910:

Other marks signify chamber length in millimetres and gauge or bore diameter. Since 1927 all firearms tested at the Eibar Proof House in Spain (Banco Oficial de Pruebas) have a code mark to indicate the year of proof included in the proofmarks. In the Spanish alphabet the letter N is followed by a similar letter surmounted by the accent ~. At a later date this accented letter was discontinued (see next page).

| | | | | |
|---|---|---|---|---|
| A–1927 | N–1942 | C1–1957 | Q1–1972 | G2–1987 |
| B–1928 | Ñ–1943 | D1–1958 | R1–1973 | H2–1988 |
| C–1929 | O–1944 | E1–1959 | S1–1974 | I2–1989 |
| CH–1930 | P–1945 | F1–1960 | T1–1975 | J2–1990 |
| D–1931 | Q–1946 | G1–1961 | U1–1976 | K2–1991 |
| E–1932 | R–1947 | H1–1962 | V1–1977 | L2–1992 |
| F–1933 | S–1948 | I1–1963 | X1–1978 | M2–1993 |
| G–1934 | T–1949 | J1–1964 | Y1–1979 | N2–1994 |
| H–1935 | U–1950 | K1–1965 | Z1–1980 | O2–1995 |
| I–1936 | V–1951 | L1–1966 | A2–1981 | P2–1996 |
| J–1937 | X–1952 | M1–1967 | B2–1982 | Q2–1997 |
| K–1938 | Y–1953 | N1–1968 | C2–1983 | R2–1998 |
| L–1939 | Z–1954 | Ñ1–1969 | D2–1984 | S2–1999 |
| LL–1940 | A1–1955 | O1–1970 | E2–1985 | T2–2000 |
| M–1941 | B1–1956 | P1–1971 | F2–1986 | |

In 1910 the following marks were used at Eibar in conjunction with some of the above:

The following marks were used at Eibar between 18 July 1923 and 12 December 1925:

The following proof marks were used at Eibar and at Barcelona between 14 December 1929 and 9 July 1931:

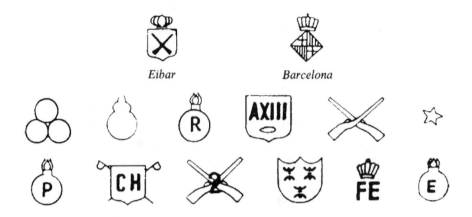

The following marks were in use at Eibar and at Barcelona after 9 July 1931. The Barcelona markings were discontinued in 1935.

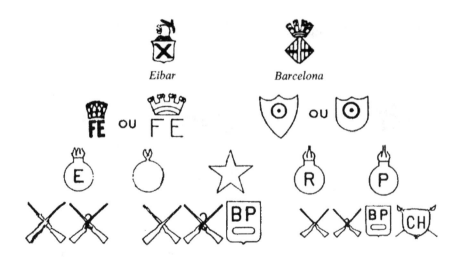

## 11.12 Yugoslav Proof Marks

The following marks have been used at the Proof House at Kragujevec. These were recognised by the CIP up to the break-up of the country on 30 September 1992.

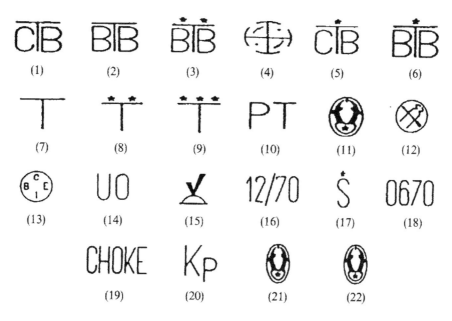

(1) Black powder proof of finished arms; (2) Nitro proof of finished arms; (3) Superior nitro proof of finished arms; (4) Arm in condition for sale; (5) Black powder re-proof; (6) Nitro re-proof; (7) Provisional proof of finished barrels; (8) Double provisional proof of finished barrels; (9) Triple provisional proof of finished barrels; (10) Voluntary provisional proof of roughly forged barrels; (11) Proof mark; (12) Mark used on action; (13) International mark for proof barrels; (14) Foreign arms; (15) Mark indicating satisfactory assembly of barrels; (16) Nominal calibre and chamber length; (17) Inspector's mark; (18) Month and year of proof; (19) Choke indication; (20) Weight of barrels; (21) Proof of blank-operated arms and devices; (22) Ammunition inspection.

## 11.13 The Russian Federation

The Russian Federation became a Signatory Member of the CIP in 1995. The following proof mark is now recognised:

Various other marks were used by the Proof Houses at Tula and Izhevsk in the past:

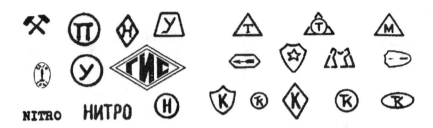

Marks used on Russian military firearms:

## 11.14 Choke Markings

Additional information, often positioned close to the proof marks, is provided by Italian and Japanese manufacturers and some others to signify the degree of choke boring on the original weapon:

| | | |
|---|---|---|
| Japan | * | = Full choke |
| | *_ | = Improved modified (3/4) choke |
| | ** | = Modified (1/2) choke |
| | **_ | = Improved cylinder (1/4) choke |
| | **$ | = Skeet choke |
| | *** | = Cylinder bore |
| Italy | * | = Full choke |
| | ** | = Improved modified choke |
| | *** | = Modified choke |
| | **** | = Improved cylinder |
| | CL | = Cylinder bore |

## 11.14.1 Denmark

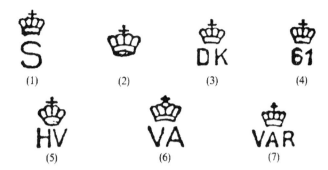

(1) Mark stamped upon some self-loading shotguns—discontinued 1908; (2) Barrel testing mark used up to 1933; (3) Barrel test mark used after 1933; (4) Mark used to indicate barrel testing and function check; (5) Firearm produced at the Royal Danish Armoury by Haerens Vaabenarsenal; (6) and (7) Firearm produced at the Royal Danish Arsenal by Vaabenarsenalet.

## 11.14.2 Austro-Hungarian Empire

The following marks were used at various stages of the disintegration of the AustroHungarian empire:

The following marks were used at Ferlach and Vienna between 1 September 1929 and 1940:

The following marks were used in Czechoslovakia between 1918 and 1931:

The following marks were used after 1932:

The Weipert Proof House closed in 1954 to be succeeded by that at Brno, which used a six-pointed star from 1952 to 1957.

The following marks were used in Hungary after 1929:

After the end of World War II, Austria became independent and used the following markings, which were accepted in the UK after January 1956. Markings previously used both by Austria and by Germany prior to 1939 were also recognised by the UK. The following Austrian markings were used after 1945:

Eastern Germany used the following markings after 1945:

## 11.14.3 India

### 11.14.3.1 Military Arms

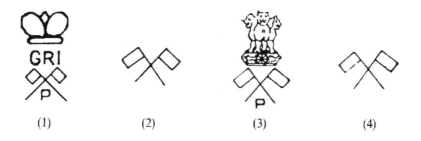

(1) Proof mark on barrel used between 1907/1908 and 1950; (2) Mark used on small components between the same period; (3) Barrel mark used after 1950; (4) Small components mark used during the same period.

### 11.14.3.2 Hunting Weapons
1953 to 1957—View, Definitive Proof and Choke Barrel:

Marks used after 1957:

### 11.14.4 Israel

Marks used at various times by Israel:

### 11.14.5 Australia

Proof marks used at the Lithgow Small Arms Factory, New South Wales:

## 11.15 Irish Proof Marks

A mark listed in the 1993 British proof booklet for use by the Proof House of the Republic of Ireland at the Institute for Industrial Research and Standards, Dublin, was awarded recognition in the UK on 9 June 1969. The Republic of Ireland is not a signatory member of the CIP. A single mark is used both for the provisional and definitive proof of shotguns:

Additional marks indicating gauge, chamber length, nominal bore diameter, the service pressure may also appear along with the last two digits of the year of proof. Since the introduction of this legislation in the Irish Republic, there has been no evidence of these marks actually being used.

## 11.16 Swedish Proof Marks

The following marks have been used by the Carl Gustafs Stads Gevarsfaktori, Eskilstuna:

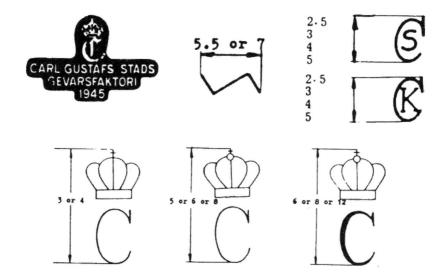

The following marks have been used on arms manufactured by Husqvarna Vapenfabriks AB:

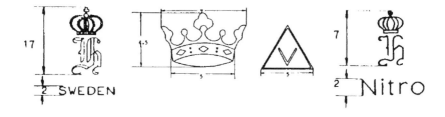

## 11.17 Swiss Proof Marks

Marks used by Swiss Chief Inspectors :

 Major Schmidt 1864–1874

 Major Werdmüller 1875–1879

 Major Vogelsang 1879–1912

 Major Mühlemann 1913–1941

 Captain Hauri 1942

 Mark of Chief Inspector used from 1943

 Mark used on model 1889 Schmidt–Rubin service rifle onwards

Markings which incorporate the Swiss cross may be found on military arms and also upon items made for export:

 Trademark of the Schweizerische Industrie-Gesellschaft Neuhausen, Switzerland.

## 11.18 American Proof Marks

There is no central proof house in the US and no laws to regulate the proof of firearms. Some makers do, however, proof test their own guns.

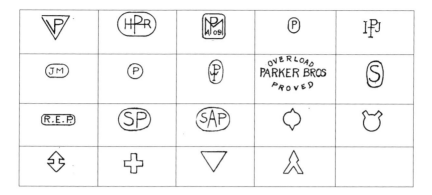

(1) Colt; (2) Harrington & Richardson; (3) Hunter Arms; (4 & 5) Iver Johnson; (6) Marlin; (7) Mossberg; (8) Winchester; (9) Parker Brothers; (10) R.F. Sedgeley; (11) Remington; (12 & 13) Savage; (14-19) Ithaca, Lefever and Western Gun.


## Further Reading

Firearms Law. 1989. Specifications for the Adaptation of Shot Gun Magazines and the Deactivation of Firearms (Revised 1995). London: HMSO.

Convention for the Reciprocal Recognition of Proof Marks of Small-Arms, Brussels, 1 July 1969. Treaty Series No. 84 (1980). Her Majesty's Stationery Office.

Goddard, C. 1946. Proof Tests and Proof Marks, Washington, DC: The Army Ordnance Association.

Notes on the Proof of Shotguns and Other Small Arms. 1993. The London and Birmingham Proof Houses.

Private correspondence, 1979, with M. Edmonds-Alt of the Liege Proof House.

Private communication, 1985, Landesgewerbeamt Baden-Württemberg, Beschussamt.

Private communication, 1994, with R. Martin, Nottingham Proof House.

Private correspondence, 1995, with M.M. Centi, CIP Bureau Permanent, Liege.

Private correspondence, 1995, with R. Hancox of the Birmingham Gun Barrel Proof House.

Private correspondence, 1995, with R. Pitcher and the Clerk for the London Proof House.

Wirnsberger, G. and Steindler, R.A. 1975. The Standard Directory of Proof Marks, Paramus NJ: Jolex.

# Appendix 1: Useful Data

## Legal Expressions

| | |
|---|---|
| Ab initio | From the beginning |
| Actus non facit reum nis mens sit rea | The act itself does not constitute guilt unless done with guilty intent |
| Actus reus | Guilty act |
| Ad hoc | For this purpose only |
| A fortiori | So much the more; with greater reason |
| Alitur | In other words |
| Amicus curiae | A friend of the court. Often Counsel who attends court to put a point of view which might otherwise be overlooked |
| Animus ferandi | Intent to steal |
| Ante | Before |
| Anti | Against |
| A priori | From cause to effect |
| Autrefois acquit | Previously acquitted |
| Autrefois convict | Previously convicted |
| Bona fide | In good faith |
| Bona vacantiag | Goods without an apparent owner and in which no one claims property except the Crown |
| Certeris paribus | Other things being equal |
| Certiorari | An order which issues from the High Court removing a cause from an inferior court to the High Court for retrial |
| Contra | Against |
| Corpus delicti | The substance of the offence |
| Custus morum | Guardian of morals |
| De facto | In fact; whether by right or not |
| Dejure | By right |
| De minimus non curat | The law does not concern itself with *les* trifles |
| Doli incapax | Incapable of committing crime |
| Durante minore aetate | During age of minority |

411

| | |
|---|---|
| Ejustem generis | Of the same kind |
| Et seq: et sequens | And the following |
| Ex cathedra | With authority |
| Exempli gratia (e.g.,) | For example |
| Ex gratia | As a favour |
| Ex hypothesi | Following from this assumption |
| Ex parte | On behalf of |
| Ex post facto | Retrospectively |
| Ferae naturae | Wild by nature (of animals) |
| Flagante delicto | In commission of the offence |
| Functus officio | A person whose duty has been discharged and whose authority is therefore at an end |
| Habeus corpus | Thou shalt have the body. A prerogative writ to a person detaining another in custody, and commanding that person to produce the other before the court |
| Ibrid (ibridem) | In the same place |
| Id est (i.e.) | That is |
| Ignorantia juris non excusat | Ignorance of the law is no excuse |
| In absentia | In the absence of |
| In camera | In court, the public is excluded |
| In extenso | In full |
| Infra | Below |
| In loco parentis | In the position of parent |
| In personam | An act proceeding or right done or directed against a specific person |
| In re | In the matter of |
| In rem | An act proceeding or right available against the world at large |
| Inter alia | Among other things |
| Inter partes | Between parties |
| Inter se | Between themselves |
| In toto | In entirety |
| Intra vires | Within the power (authority) of |
| Ipso facto | By the very fact itself |
| Ipso jure | By the law itself |
| Loco citato—loc-cit | In the place quoted |
| Locum tenens | Deputy |
| Mandamus | We command. An order of the High Court to compel performance of a public duty |
| Mens rea | Guilty mind |
| Mutatis mutandis | The necessary changes being made |
| Nemo dat quod non habet | No one can give what he does not possess |
| Nexus | Connection |
| Nisi | Unless. Also an order *nisi* is one which is not to take effect unless the person affected by it fails to show cause against it within a certain time |
| Nolle prosequi | To be unwilling by prosecution. An act of the Attorney General to stay proceedings upon an indictment for information pending in court |
| Non sequitur | It does not follow—in an argument |

| | |
|---|---|
| Nota bene (n.b.) | Note well |
| Obiter dictum (Obiter dicta) | A mere saying(s) 'by the way', a chance remark, which is not binding on future courts |
| Omnia praesumuntur rite esse acta | All acts are presumed to have been done rightly |
| Onus probandi | Burden of proving |
| Opre citato (*op. cit.*) | The work already cited |
| Particeps criminis | A person, taking part in a crime |
| Per | By |
| Per contra | On the other hand |
| Per curiam | By the court |
| Per incuriam | Without proper consideration of all relevant matters |
| Per pro | On behalf of |
| Per se | By itself |
| Post | After |
| Post factum | After the deed or act |
| Prima facie | At first sight |
| Pro rata | In proportion |
| Puisne | Junior; inferior |
| Qua | As; in the capacity of |
| Quare | Query |
| Quid pro quo | One thing in place of another |
| Ratio decidendi | The rule of law on which a decision is based |
| Reductio ad absurdum | Reduce to absurdity; pushing a principle to absurd lengths; reducing an argument to absurdity |
| Res gestae | The facts surrounding a transaction |
| Res ipsa loquitur | The facts speak for themselves |
| Res judicata | A point judicially settled by the High Court |
| Res judicata pro veritate accipitur | A thing judicially decided is accepted as true |
| Scienter | Knowledge |
| Sed quaere | But is it true? |
| Sic | Thus |
| Simpliciter | Absolutely; without qualification |
| Sine die | Without a day being fixed |
| Status quo ante | Current state of affairs; the same state as before |
| Sub judice | Under judicial consideration |
| Sub poena | Under penalty |
| Ultra vires | Beyond the power of. An act in excess of the authority conferred by law |
| Venire de nova | Order of the High Court for retrial |
| Vide | See |
| Viva voce | Orally |
| Viz (vide licet) | That is to say; in other words |

## Useful Conversion Factors

| Imperial | Metric | Reciprocal |
|---|---|---|
| 1 yard (yd) | 0.9144 m | 1.09361 |
| 1 foot (ft) | 30.48 cm | 0.0328084 |
| 1 inch (in) | 25.4 mm | 0.0393701 |
| 1 statute mile | 1.609344 km | 0.621371 |
| 1 square yard | 0.836127 m$^2$ | 1.19599 |
| 1 square foot | 0.092903 m$^2$ | 10.763915 |
| 1 square inch | 6.4516 cm$^2$ | 0.155000 |
| 1 cubic yard | 0.764555 m$^3$ | 1.30795 |
| 1 cubic foot | 0.0283168 m$^3$ | 35.3147 |
| 1cubic inch | 16.3871 cm$^3$ | 0.061024 |
| 1 Imperial gallon | 4.546092 l | 0.219969 |
| 1 US gallon | 3.7854131 l | 0.264172 |
| 1 pound (avdp) (lb) | 0.45359237 kg | 2.20462 |
| 1 ounce (avdp) (oz) | 28.3495 g | 0.0352740 |
| 1 ounce (troy) | 31.1035 g | 0.0321407 |
| 1 grain (gr) | 0.064798 91 g | 15.4324 |
| 1 ton (2240 lb) | 1.01605 tonne | 0.984207 |
| 1 ft/s | 0.03048 m/s | 3.28084 |
| 1 m/h | 1.609344 km/h | 0.621371 |
| 1 lb force | 4.4482216 N | 0.224809 |
| 1 ft.lb | 1.3558179 J | 0.737562 |
| 1 lb/in$^2$ | 0.068947 6 bar | 14.503774 |

1 lb (avdp-avoir dupois) = 7000 grain
1 lb (avdp) = 16 oz
1 oz (avdp) = 16 drachm (dram)
1 drachm (avdp) = 27.344 grain = 1.771845 2 g
1 Imperial ton = 20 hundredweight = 2240 lb
1 hundredweight = 8 stone = 112 lb
1 stone = 14 lb = 6.350 293 kg
1 slug = 32.1740 lb = 14.5939 kg
1 gallon = 8 pints = 4.54609 l
1 UK gallon = 1.20095 US gallon
1 US gallon = 0.83267 UK gallon
1 Kp force = 9.806650 N 1 Newton = 0.1019716 Kp
1 bar pressure = 100000 Pa
1 mile = 1760 yd = 8 furlong
1 furlong = 220 yd = 40 rod = 201.168 m
1 chain = 66 ft = 22 yd = 4 rod = 20.12 m
1 yd = 3 ft = 36 in = 9 hand
1 rod, perch or pole = 5 1/2 yd = 5.029 m
1 fathom = 6 ft = 1.8288 m
1 acre = 4840 yd$^2$ = 0.404 686 hectares
Temperature, °F = 5(t–32)/9°C
Temperature, °C = 9t/5+32°F
1 calorie = 4.1868 J
Velocity of sound in dry air at sea level at 0°C = 331.46 m/s
Velocity of sound in sea water at 20°C near to the surface = 1522.1 m/s

Acceleration due to Gravity—The standard value for the acceleration due to gravity is 9.80665 m/sec² (32.1740 ft/sec²) relative to the value for *g* of 9.81274 m/sec² measured at Potsdam.

Apothecary's Dram Weight = 60 Apothecary's grains = 3.542 g = approx. ¹/₈ oz.

Pound Troy = approx. 0.373 kg = 12 troy ounces.

Degrees Absolute (Kelvin or °K) = Degrees Celsius + 273.1°C.

## Approximate Densities of Some Pure Metals and Alloys

Here densities are expressed in grams weight per cubic centimetre. (1 in³ = 16.3871 cc: 1 ft³ = 0.0283168 m³): magnesium = 1.7, aluminium = 2.7, titanium = 4.5, iron = 7.9, nickel = 8.9, copper = 8.93, zinc = 7.1, molybdenum = 10.2, silver = 10.5, tin = 7.3, antimony = 6.7, tungsten = 19.3, platinum = 21.45, gold = 19.3, mercury = 13.55, lead = 11.3, bismuth = 9.8, uranium = 19.05, steel = 7.85, cupro-nickel = 8.88, brass = 8.6, tombac = 8.8.

## Cyrillic Alphabet

| Russian Letter | English Pronunciation | Russian Letter | English Pronunciation | Russian Letter | English Pronunciation |
|---|---|---|---|---|---|
| А а | A in car | Л л | L in lamp | Ц ц | Ts in sits |
| Б б | B in bit | М м | M in my | Ч ч | Ch in chip |
| В в | V in vine | Н н | N in not | Ш ш | Sh in shut |
| Г г | G in go | О о | O in hot | Щ щ | Shch |
| Д д | D in do | П п | P in pot | Ъ ъ | |
| Е е | Ye in yet | Р р | R as rr | Ы ы | I in ill |
| Ж ж | Zh in pleasure | С с | S in see | Ь ь | |
| З з | Z in zoo | Т т | T in tip | Э э | E in met |
| И и | Ee in see | У у | U as boot | Ю ю | U in duke |
| Й й | Y in boy | Ф ф | F in face | Я я | Ya in yard |
| К к | K in kitten | Х х | Kh as loch | | |

## Arabic Numbers

| 0 | 1 | 2 | 3 | 4 | 5 | 6 | 7 | 8 | 9 |
|---|---|---|---|---|---|---|---|---|---|
| ٠ | ١ | ٢ | ٣ | ٤ | ٥ | ٦ | ٧ | ٨ | ٩ |

# Appendix 2: German Ordnance Codes Used between 1938 and 1945

## Alphabetical Codes

| | |
|---|---|
| aa | Waffenfabrik Brünn AG, Prague |
| aac | Mannesman-Röhrenwerke, Komotau, Sudeten, Germany |
| aak | Waffenfabrik Brünn AG, Prague |
| aaj | Obenhütten, Vereinigte Oberschlesische Hüttenwerk AG |
| aak | Waffenwerke Brünn AG, Prague, Wrsoviace Plant, Czechoslovakia |
| aan | Mitteldeutsche Metallwarenfabrik, Erich Frank, Glauchau, Saxony |
| aar | Geba-Munitions-und Waffenfabrik, Breslau, Czechoslovakia |
| aaw | Metallwarenfabrik Gebr. Schmidt, Idar-Oberstein |
| aba | Unknown |
| abb | Friedrichsthaler Eisenwerk, Jennewein & Gapp, Friedrichsthal (Saar) |
| abc | Deutsche Metallwerke, Weinstraβe, Neustadt |
| abh | Koch & Söhne, Frankenthal-Plomersheim (Iron and metal products) |
| ac | Carl Walther, Zella-Mehlis, Thuringia |
| acu | Unknown |
| ad | Patronen-, Zündhütchen- und Metallwarenfabrik AG (formerly Sellier & Bellot), Schönebeck on the Elbe |
| adc | William Prym, Stollberg, Rheinland |
| aek | F. Dusek Waffenerzeugung, Oppeln near Nachod, Czechoslovakia |
| afb | Matabu, Werk Closs, Rauch and Schnitzler, Nürtingen |
| afu | August Winkhaus, Münster |
| ai | Unknown |
| aj | Unknown |
| ajf | Junker & Ruh AG, Karlsruhe, Baden |
| ajn | Union Sprengstoff- und Zündmittelwerke, Alt-Berum |

ak     Munitionsfabriken (formerly Sellier & Bellot, Prague), Vlasim, Czechoslovakia
akp    Deutsche Röhrenwerke, Poensgen Plant, Düsseldorf-Lierenfeld
akv    Unknown
al     Deutsche Leucht- u. Signalwerke, Dr. Feistel AG, Berlin-Charlottenburg
am     Otto Eberhardt, Patronenfabrik (Gustloff Co.), Hirtenberg, Austria
ama    Unknown
amh    Unknown
amj    Waggonfabrik L.Steinfurt, Königsberg
amn    Mauser-Werke KG, Neuwied Plant
amo    Mauser-Werke KG, Waldeck-Kassel Plant
amp    Dortmund Hoerder Hüttenverein, Dortmund
an     Beutemüller & Co., GmbH, Metalwarenfabrik (ammo), Bretten-Baden
and    Magdeburger Pumpenfabrik, Otterburg & Co., Magdeburg
anj    Kienzle-Uhrenfabrik, Komotau, Sudeten, Germany
anx    Königs-Laura-Hütte, Königshütte
anz    Maschinen- u. Armaturenfabrik, formerly L.Strube, division of Polte, Magdeburg-
       Buckau
ap     Gustloff-Werke, Wuppertal Plant, Ronsdorf
ape    Continental Caoutchouc Co., GmbH, Hannover
aqe    Deutsche Kabelwerke, Berlin
aqk    Unknown
aqt    Unknown
aqx    Rheinmetall-Borsig, Tegel Plant
ar     Mauser-Werke, Berlin-Borsigwalde
arb    Vereinigte Oberschlesige Hüttenwerke, Andreashütte
arl    Unknown
asb    Deutsche Waffen- u. Munitionsfabriken AG, Berlin-Borsigwalde
aso    Unknown
asr    HAK Hanseatisches-Kettenwerk GmbH, Hamburg-Langenhorn
asx    Hösch AG, Dortmund Plant
at     Klöckner-Werke, Div. Hasper Eisen- u. Stahlwerk
atb    Hydrometer AG, Breslau, Czechoslovakia
atl    Klöckner-Humbold-Deutz, Ulm
atr    Langbein-Pfannhauser-Werke AG, Leipzig
atw    Mannesman-Röhrenwerke AG, Wittenplant, Ruhr
aty    Maschinenfabrik für Massenverpackung, Lübeck-Schlutrup
au     Gute-Hoffnungshütte Oberhausen, Sterkrade Plant
auc    Mauser-Werke AG, Cologne-Ehrenfeld
aue    Metall u. Eisen GmbH, Nürnberg
auf    Metall-, Guss- und Presswerk, H.Dieh., Nürnberg
auj    Unknown
auu    Patronenhülsen- u. Metalwarenfabrik AG, Rokycany Plant, Pilsen, Czechoslovakia
aux    Polte-Werk, Magdeburg
auy    Polte-Werk, Grüneberg
auz    Polte-Werk, Arnstadt
av     Adam Gerhard, Motorenwerke, Oskau Friedrichsdorf, Sudeten, Germany

ave     Unknown
avk     Ruhrstahl AG, Brackwede-Bielefeld
avm     Rheinhütte GmbH (formerly Beck & Co.), Wiesbaden
avt     Silva-Metallwerke GmbH, div. of Polte, Genthin
avu     Unknown
awj     Unknown
awl     Union Gesellschaft f. Metallindustrie, Sils van de Loo & Co., Werl Plant, Fröndenberg,
         Ruhr
awt     Württembergische Metallwarenfabrik AG, Geislingen (Steig)
ax      Unknown
axq     Erfurter Laden Industrie, North Erfurt
axs     Berndorfer Metallwarenfabrik AG, Arthur Krupp, Berndorf, Austria
ay      Alois Pirkel, Elektrotechnische Fabrik
aye     Unknown
ayf     Waffenfabrik Erma, B.Geipel GmbH, Erfurt
ayg     Unknown
ayk     Unknown
aym     Unknown, located in Czechoslovakia
ayr     Unknown
az      VDM-Halbzeugwerke, Altena
azg     Siemens-Schukert-Werke AG, Berlin
azy     Maschinenfabrik Sangershausen
ba      Sundwiger Messingwerke, Iserlon, Westphalia
baz     Steyr-Daimler-Puch AG, Steyr, Austria
bb      A. Laue & Co., Berlin
be      Kupfer- u. Messingwerke KG, Becker & Co., Langenberg, Rheinland
bed     Wilhelm-Gustloff-Werke, Weimar
bch     Unknown
bck     Brüninghaus, Versmold
bcu     Gutehoffnungshütte, Oberhausen
bd      Metallwerke Lange AG, Bodenbach Plant, Sudeten, Germany
bda     Uhrenfabrik Villingen
bdq     Ehrhardt & Kirsten, Koffer- u. Lederwarenfabrik, Leipzig
bdr     Richard Ehrhardt, Lederwarenfabrik, Poeseneck, Thuringia
bdy     Pittner, Leipzig
be      Berndorfer Metallwarenfabrik, Arthur Krupp AG, Berndorf, Austria
bed     Gustloff-Werke, Weimar
beh     Ernst Leitz GmbH, Wetzlar
bej     Maschinenfabrik Wolf, Buckau
bek     Hensoldt-Werk für Optik und Mechanik, Herborn
bf      Deutsche Röhrenwerke AG, Mühlheim, Ruhr
bfn     New York-Hamburger Gummifabrik
bg      Enzesfelder Metallwerke, Vienna, Austria
bh      Brünner Waffenfabrik AG, Brünn, Czechoslovakia
bj      Niebecker & Schumacher, Iserlohn, Westphalia
bjm     Klöckner Werke, Deutz Plant

| | |
|---|---|
| bjv | Böhmisch-Mährische Kolben-Danek AG, Vysocan plant, Prague |
| bk | Metall-, Walz- u, Plattierwarenfabrik Hinrichs & Auffermann AG, Wuppertal |
| bkp | Gewehrfabrik Burgsmüller & Söhne GmbH, Kreiensen |
| bkq | Johannes Suremann GmbH, Röhrenfabrik, Arnsberg |
| bky | Böhmische Waffenfabrik AG, Prague, Ung.-Bro Plant Moravia, Czechoslovakia |
| bkz | Unknown |
| bl | Unknown |
| bla | e.g., Leuner GmbH, Bautzen |
| blc | Carl Zeiss, Military Division, Jena |
| bin | Unknown |
| blp | Burgsmüller & Sohn, Kreiensen |
| blr | Unknown |
| blu | Sprengstoffwerke, Blumenau near Felixdorf |
| blx | Unknown |
| bm | Unknown |
| bmb | Metallwarenfabrik Binder, Reichertshofen |
| bmd | Max G. Müller, Fabrik für Lederwaren & Heeresbedarf Nürnberg |
| bmf | Berndorfer Metallwarenfabrik, Berndorf, Austria |
| bmj | Hensoldt & Söhne, Mechanisch-Optische Werke AG, Wetzlar |
| bml | Unknown |
| bmu | Carl Kuntze, Sattlerwarenfabrik, Penig, Saxony |
| bmv | Rheinmetall-Borsig AG, Sömmerda Plant, Sömmerda |
| bmz | Minerva-Nähmaschinenfabrik AG, Boskowitz, Czechoslovakia |
| bn | Unknown |
| bnd | Maschinenfabrik Augsburg-Nürnberg, Nürnberg Plant, Nürnberg |
| bne | Metallwarenfabrik Odertal GmbH, Odertal |
| bnf | Polte, Contract Plant, Wolfenbüttel |
| bnz | Steyr-Daimler-Puch AG, Steyr, Austria |
| bo | Unknown |
| boa | Venditor, Troisdorf |
| bod | Venditor, Troisdorf |
| bot | Metallwerke Neheim |
| bp | Unknown |
| bpd | Optische Anstalt O. P. Görz, Vienna, Austria |
| bpr | Johannes Grossfuss, Metall-u. Locierwarenfabrik, Döbeln, Saxony |
| bpt | Unknown |
| bq | Unknown |
| bqo | Krupp-Gruson, Magdeburg-Buckau |
| bqs | Oderhütte Kürstin |
| bqt | Eugen Müller, Pyrotechnische Fabrik, Vienna, Austria |
| br | Mathias Bäuerle, Laufwerke GmbH, St. Georgen, Black Forest |
| brb | Unknown |
| brd | Hagenuk, Nurfeldt & Kuhnke GmbH, Kiel |
| brg | Unknown |
| bsv | Tönshoff, Horn in Lippe |
| bt | Unknown |

| | |
|---|---|
| bte | Unknown |
| btk | Aluminium-Werke Honsel, Werdohl |
| btn | Unknown |
| buc | Metallwerke Windelsbleiche near Bielefeld |
| buh | Röchling, Wetzlar |
| bv | Unknown |
| bvl | Theodor Bergmann & Co., Abteilung Automaten-& Metallwarenfabrikation, Hamburg-Altona |
| bvv | Unknown |
| bw | Unknown |
| bwc | Maschinenfabrik Brackwede |
| bwn | Krupp-Stahlwerk u. Maschinenfabrik, Essen |
| bwo | Rheinmetall-Borig AG, Düsseldorf |
| bwp | Berlin-Anhaltische-Maschinenbau, AG, Dessau |
| bwq | Unknown |
| bwr | Werk Lauchhammer |
| bwx | Ruhrstahl, Henrichshütte, Hattingen |
| bxb | Skoda-Werke, Pilsen, Czechoslovakia |
| bxe | Bochumer Verein |
| bxm | Vereinigte Zünder- u. Kabelwerke, Meissen |
| bxn | Unknown, Czechoslovakia |
| by | Unknown |
| bye | Brückenbauanstalt August Klonne AG, Dortmund |
| bye | Hanomag, Hannover |
| byf | Mauser-Werke, Oberndorf on the Neckar |
| byg | Johann Wyksen, Optische u. Feinmaschinen, Katowitz, Poland |
| bym | Genossenschafts-Maschinenhaus der Büchsenmacher, Ferlach, Austria |
| byq | Pohlmann & Co., Hammerwerke, Wetterburg, Hessen-Nassau |
| byr | Ruhrstahl, Witten-Annen |
| bys | Ruhrstahl, Witten |
| byw | Johann Schäfer, Stettiner Schraubenwerk, Stettin |
| bzt | Fritz Wolf, Gewehrfabrik, Zella-Mehlis, Thuringia |
| bzz | Unknown |
| ca | Vereinigte Deutsche Nickelwerke, Schwerte, Ruhr |
| cag | Swarowski, D., Glasfabrik u. Tyrolit, Wattens, Tyrol, Austria |
| cau | Unknown |
| cbl | VDM Halbwerkzeuge, Nürnberg Branch |
| cbr | Böhlerwerke, Böhler & Co., Waidhofen, Austria |
| cby | Schöller-Bleckmann, Ternitz, Niederdonau |
| ccb | Stahlwerke Brünninghaus AG, Westhofen, Westphalia |
| ccd | DEMAG, Wetter |
| ccx | Optische u. Feinmaschinenwerke, Hugo Meyer & Co., Görlitz |
| cdc | Kern, Klager & Co., Lederwaren, Berlin |
| cdg | Auwärter & Bubeck KG, Lederwarenfabrik, Stuttgart |
| cdo | Theodor Bergmann & Co., Waffen- u. Munitionsfabrik, Velten Plant, Velten on the Main |
| cdp | Theodor Bergmann & Co., Waffen- u. Munitionsfabrik, Bernau Plant, Berlin |

| | |
|---|---|
| cdv | Metallwarenfabrik Ludwig Maybaum, Sundern, Westphalia |
| ce | Sauer & Sohn, Waffenfabrik Suhl, Thuringia |
| cey | Karl Budischovsky & Söhne, Osterreichische Leder-industrie AG, Vienna |
| cf | Westfälische Anhaltische Sprengstoff AG, Oranienburg Plant e.g., FinowerIndustrie GmbH, Finow, Mark |
| cgn | Rohrbacher Lederfabrik, Josef Pöschels Söhne, Rohrbach |
| cgt | Unknown |
| ch | Fabrique Nationale d'Armes de Guerre, Herstal Liege, Belgium |
| chd | Deutsche Industrie-Werke AG, Berlin-Spandau |
| chh | DEW, Hannover Plant, Linden |
| cja | Unknown |
| cjg | Unknown |
| cjn | Uhrenfabrik, Gebr. Junghans, Schramberg, Black Forest |
| ck | Metallwerk Neumeyer, Munich |
| ckc | Deutsche Eisenwerke AG, Mühlheim, Ruhr |
| ckl | Eisen- u. Hüttenwerke, Thale, Harz |
| cko | Hüttenwerk, Eisengiesserei u. Maschinenfabrik, Michelstadt, Odenwald |
| cl | Metschke Karl, Auto- u. Maschinenreparatur, Berlin Plant |
| clg | Unknown |
| cma | Unknown |
| cmg | Metallwarenfabrik Halver, Peter W. Haurand GmbH, Halver, Westphalia |
| cms | Konrad Lindhorst, Berlin |
| cmw | Dr. Ing. Rudolf Hell, Berlin |
| cmz | Zünderwerke Ernst Brün, Krefeld, Linn |
| cnd | Krupp-National-Registrierkassen (cash registers) GmbH, Berlin Plant |
| cob | Netzschkauer Maschinenfabrik, Stark & Söhne, Netzschkau, Saxony |
| coe | Lübecker Maschinenbau-Gesellschaft |
| cof | Waffenfabrik Eickhorn, Solingen |
| con | Franz Stock, Maschinen- u. Werkzeugfabrik, Berlin |
| cos | Gebrüder Merz, Merz-Werke, Frankfurt, Main |
| cow | Wintershall AG, Spritzgusswerk, Berlin |
| cpj | Unknown |
| cpn | Werk Apolda |
| cpo | Rheinmetall-Borsig AG, Berlin-Marienfeld |
| cpp | Rheinmetall-Borsig AG, Breslau Plant |
| cpq | Rheinmetall-Borsig AG, Gubeb Plant |
| cq | Warz & Co., Zella-Mehlis, Thuringia |
| cdq | Unknown |
| cr | Unknown |
| crm | PhyWE, Göttingen |
| cro | R. Fuess, Optische Industrie, Berlin-Steglitz |
| crs | Paul Weyersberg & Co., Waffenfabrik, Solingen |
| crv | Fritz Werner, Plant II, Berlin |
| crw | Maschinenfabrik Hofmann GmbH, Breslau |
| csa | Skoda Werke |
| csq | Pollux, Ludwigshafen, Rhein |

| | |
|---|---|
| csx | Gothaer Metallwarenfabrik GmbH |
| cte | Klöckner Maschinenfabrik, Manstadt Division, Troisdorf |
| ctf | Eisenwerke Gaggenau GmbH, Gaggenau, Baden |
| ctg | Karlshütte Waldenburg, Altwasser, Silesia |
| ctn | Freidricks & Co., Hanseatische Werkstätten für Feinmechanik u. Optik |
| cts | Märkische Werke, H.Hillmans GmbH, drop forge plant, Halver |
| ctu | Unknown |
| cty | Unknown |
| cue | Röchling-Buderus-Stahlwerke, Finofurt Plant, Bradenburg |
| cuf | Röchling-Buderus-Stahlwerke, Melle Plant, Hannover |
| cuy | Unknown |
| cuz | Eisenwerk Maximilianhütte, Stamping Plant, Thuringia, Unterwellenborn |
| cva | Eisenwerke Maximilianhütte, Ironmongery Division, Fronberg |
| cvb | Otto Sindel, Lederwarenfabrik, Berlin |
| cvc | Zeschke Nachf. Gebr. L.Zeuschner, Koffer-und-Lederwarenfabrik, Müllrose near Frankfurt on the Oder |
| cvg | VDM, Frankfurt-Hedderheim |
| cvl | WKC Waffenfabrik, Solingen Wald |
| cvs | Paul Weyersberg & Co., Waffenfabrik, Solingen |
| cvv | Maschinenfabrik B. Holthaus, Dinklage (Vechte/Old) |
| cwb | Brandenburger Eisenwerke |
| cwg | Westfälisch-Anhaltische Sprengstoff AG, Coswig Plant |
| cww | Karl Weiss, Lederwarenfabrik, Braunschweig |
| cxa | Ruhrstahl AG, Stahlwerk Krieger, Düsseldorf-Oberhausen |
| cxb | Moll, Lederwarenfabrik, Goch, Rheinland |
| cxd | Maschinenfabrik Becker & Co., Magdeburg |
| cxe | Unknown |
| cxg | Metallwarenfabrik Spreewerk AG, Berlin-Spandau |
| cxh | Kienzle, Schwenningen on the Neckar |
| cxm | Gustav Genschow & Co., Berlin |
| cxn | Emil Busch AG, Optische Industrie, Rathenow |
| cxq | Spreewerke GmbH, Metallwarenfabrik, Berlin-Spandau |
| cxw | Unknown |
| cyd | Nottebohm, Lüdenscheid |
| cyh | Hüttenwerke Siegerland, Rolling Mills, Eichner |
| cyq | Metallwarenfabrik Spreewerk, Berlin-Spandau |
| cyw | Unknown |
| czf | Maschinenfabrik Steubing & Co., Berlin |
| czm | Gustav Genschow & Co., AG, Berlin |
| czn | Emil Busch AG, Optische Industrie, Rathenow |
| czo | Heereszeugamt, Geschoßwerkstatt, Königsberg |
| czq | Schichau-Elbing, Königsberg Division |
| czs | Brennabor Werke AG, Brandenburg |
| dah | Junkers, Dessau |
| dar | Metallindustrie Schönbeck AG, Schönbeck on the Elbe |
| daz | Maximilinahütte, Plant II, Unterwellenborn, Thuringia |

dbg      Dynamit AG, Düneberg Plant (formerly Alfred Nobel & Co.)
dbh      Mannesmann, Düsseldorf Plant, Rath
dbk      Unknown
dc       Unknown
dde      Robert Larsen, Fabrik für Leder u. Stoffwaren, Berlin
ddt      Unknown
ddx      Voigtländer u. Sohn AG, Braunschweig
de       Unknown
dea      Frankfurter Maschinenbau, Pokorny & Wittehind, Frankfurt
dec      Bleiwerk Goslar
dej      Unknown
dev      DEW, Remscheid Plant
dfb      Gustloff Co, Waffenfabrik, Suhl
dgb      Dynamit AG, Düneberg Plant (formerly A. Nobel & Co.)
dgl      Remo Gewehrfabrik Gebr. Rempt, Suhl
dgz      Böhler, Kapfenberg, Austria
dha      Krupp, Hannover Plant
dhn      Unknown
dhp      H.Burgsmüller, Gewehrfabrik, Kreiensen-Harz
djf      Draht-Bremer, Rostock, Mecklenburg
dkk      Friedrick Offermann & Söhne, Lederwarenfabrik, Bensberg
dla      Karl Earth, Militäreffekten-Fabrik, Waldbrohl, Rheinland
dld      Kromag, Hirtenberg, Austria
dlu      Ewald Lünenschloss, Militäreffekten-Fabrik, Solingen
dma      Heeresmunitionsanstalt u. Geschoβwerkstatt, Zeithain
dmk      Ilseder Hütte, Rolling Mill, Peiner
dmo      Auto-Union, Chemnitz, Czechoslovakia
dms      Unknown
dmy      Fritz Werner, Berlin-Marienfeld
dn       Vereinigte Deutsche Nickelwerke, Laband, Upper Silesia
dna      Unknown
dnb      Unknown
dnf      Rheinische-Westfälische Sprengstoff AG, Stadeln Plant near Nürnberg
dnh      Rheinische-Westfälische Sprengstoff AG, Durlach Plant Baden
dnv      Unknown
dnz      Schwarzwälder Apparatenbauanstalt, August Schwek & Söhne, Villingen, Black Forest
dom      Westfälische Metallindustrie, Lippstadt
dot      Waffenwerke Brünn, Brünn Plant, Czechoslovakia
dou      Waffenwerke Brünn, Bystrica, Czechoslovakia
dov      Waffenwerke Brünn, Vsetinplant, Czechoslovakia
dow      Waffenwerke Brünn, Prerauplant, Czechoslovakia
dox      Waffenwerke Brünn, Podbrezova Plant, Czechoslovakia
dpf      Unknown
dph      I.G. Farbenindustrie AG, Autogen Plant, Frankfurt
dpk      Hagenuk, Berlin-Tempelhof
dpl      Reno Gewehrfabrik, Gebr. Rempt, Suhl

dpm     Poldi-Hütte, Komotau, Sudeten, Germany
dps     Auto-Union, Mittweida, Saxony
dpu     Schlothauer GmbH, Metallwaren, Ruhla
dpv     Zeiss-Ikon, Dresden
dpw     Zeiss-Ikon, Görz plant, Berlin-Zehlendorf
dpx     Zeiss-Ikon, Stuttgart
drh     Unknown
drv     HASAG, Tschenstochau
drz     Unknown
dsb     Unknown
dsh     Ing. F. Janecek, Gewehrfabrik, Prague
dsj     WAMA Metallwerke, Oberlungwitz, Saxony
dsx     Röchling-Buderus, Wetzlar
dta     A.Waldhausen, Inh. M. Bruchmann, Sattler u. Kofferfabrik, Cologne
dtf     Unknown
dtu     G.J. Ensik & Co., Spezialfabrik für Militärausrüstung, Ohrdruf, Thuringia
dtv     C. Otto Gehrckens, Leder- u. Riemenwerke, Pinneberg
dun     Poldi Hütte, Kladno Plant, Czechoslovakia
dut     Unknown
duv     Berliner-Lübecker Maschinenfabrik, Lübeck Plant
dvc     Unknown
dvr     Johann Pröhlich, Lederwarenfabrik, Vienna
dvu     Schichau, Elbing
dvw     Unknown
dwc     Unknown
dwm     Deutsche Waffen- und Munitionswerke, Berlin-Borsigwalde
dxs     Thyssen, Duisburg-Hamborn
dye     Ed. Pitschmann, Pyrotechnik, Innsbruck, Austria
dym     Runge & Kaulfuss, Rathenow
dyq     DEW, Werdohl Plant
dza     Bleiwerke Dr. Schülcke, Hamburg
dzl     Optische Anstalt Oigee, Berlin
dzw     Metallwerke v. Galkowsky & Kielblock, Finow
eaf     Mechanoptik-Gesellschaft für Präzisionstechnik, Aude & Reipe, Babelsberg
eah     Brüninghaus, Werdohl
eak     Deutsche Werke Kiel
can     Eisen- u. Metallwerke, Lippstadt
eba     Scharfenberg & Teubert GmbH, Metallwarenfabrik, Breitungen
ebd     Unknown
ebf     Hüttenwerke Siergerland, Charlottenhütte Plant, Wiederschelden
ebk     Unknown
eca     Unknown
ecc     Oskar Lunig, Pyrotechnische Fabrik, Möhringen
ecd     Graf Lippold, Pyrotechnische Fabrik, Wuppertal-Elberfeld
ecv     Unknown
edg     J.A. Henckels, Zwillingserke, Solingen

| | |
|---|---|
| edk | Auto-Union, Zschoppau Plant, Saxony |
| edq | Deutsche Waffen- u. Munitionswerke AG, Lübeck-Schlutrup |
| edr | Unknown |
| eds | Zündapp, Nürnberg |
| edw | Unknown |
| edy | Unknown |
| edz | Unknown |
| eec | Unknown |
| eed | Gewehr- u. Fahrradteilfabrik H.Weirauch, Zella-Mehlis |
| eef | Unknown |
| eeg | Hermann Weirauch, Gewehr- u. Fahrradteilfabrik, Zella-Mehlis |
| eeh | Unknown |
| eej | Märkisches Walzwerk, Staußberg, District Potsdam |
| eek | Unknown |
| eel | Metallwarenfabrik Wissner, Brotterode Plant |
| eem | Selve-Kornbiegel, Dornheim AG, Munitionsfabrik, Sömmerda, Saxony |
| eeo | Deutsche Waffen- u. Munitionsfabriken AG, Posen Plant |
| eet | Unknown |
| ecu | Unknown |
| eev | Unknown |
| eey | Metallwarenfabrik Treuenbrietzen GmbH, Röderhof Plant |
| egy | Ing. Fr. August Pfeffer, Oberlind, Thuringia |
| eh | Unknown |
| eky | Volkswagenwerk, Wolfsburg |
| elg | WASAG, Elsnig Plant |
| emh | Unknown |
| emj | Adalbert Fischer, Berlin |
| emp | Dynamit AG (formerly A. Nobel & Co.), Empelde Plant |
| emq | Karl Zeiss, Jena |
| emu | Mathe Uhrenfabrik Schwenningen |
| enc | Unknown |
| enz | Enzesfelder Metallwerk, Enzesfeld Plant, Vienna |
| eom | H. Huck, Metallwarenfabrik, Nürnberg |
| eov | Unknown |
| eoz | Unknown |
| epf | Unknown |
| eqf | Karl Bocker, Lederwarenfabrik, Waldbrohl, Rheinlande |
| erg | A. Doppert, Treibriemenfabrik (driving belt mfr.), Kitzingen |
| erm | Unknown |
| erv | Unknown |
| eso | Optische Werke G.Rodenstock, Munich |
| etb | Steubing & Co., Graslitz, Sudeten, Germany |
| etl | Unknown |
| ety | Unknown |
| eue | Otto Reichel, Inh. Rudolf Fischer, Lederwarenfabrik, Lengfeld, Erzgebirge |
| eug | Optische Präzisionswerke GmbH, Warsaw, Poland |

| | |
|---|---|
| euh | Unknown |
| eun | Unknown |
| euo | Unknown |
| evv | Unknown |
| evz | Unknown |
| ews | Skodawerke, Königsgrätz Plant, Czechoslovakia |
| ewx | Franz u. Karl Vögels, Lederwarenfabrik, Cologne |
| exd | Auto-Union, Audi Plant |
| exp | Hans Kollmorgen, Optische Anstalt, Berlin |
| exq | Unknown |
| exs | Skodawerke, Königgrätz, Czechoslovakia |
| exw | Metallwerke Holleischen, Kreis Mies, Sudeten, Germany |
| exx | Unknown |
| eyd | Unknown |
| fa | Mansfeld AG, Hettstedt, Südharz |
| faa | Deutsche Waffen- u. Munitionsfabriken AG, Karlsruhe |
| fb | Mansfeld AG, Rothenburg Plant, Saale |
| fc | Mansfeld AG, Alstedt Plant, Thuringia |
| fck | Unknown |
| fco | Sendlinger Optische Glaswerke GmbH, Berlin-Zehlendorf |
| fcv | Unknown |
| fd | Stolberger Metallwerke AG (formerly Asaten, Lynen & Schleicher), Stolberg |
| fde | Dynamit AG (formerly A. Nobel & Co.), Förde Plant |
| fe | Unknown |
| fee | Augsburger Waagenfabrik, Ludwig Pfisterer, Augsburg |
| feh | Unknown |
| fer | Metallwerke Wandhofen, Schwerte, Westphalia |
| feu | Unknown |
| ffo | Unknown |
| fko | Unknown |
| fkx | Gustav Sudbrack, Lederwaren u. Gamaschenfabrik, Bielefeld |
| flp | Unknown |
| fnh | Böhmische Waffenfabrik, Strkonitz Plant, Prague |
| fnk | Unknown |
| fnq | Unknown |
| fpx | Schäffer & Budenberg, Magdeburg-Buckau |
| fqn | Vereinigte Leichtmetallwerke, Hannover-Linden |
| fra | Draht- und Metallwarenfabrik GmbH, Salzwedel |
| frp | Stahlwerke Harkot-Eicken, Hagen, Westphalia |
| fsx | Albin Scholle, Lederwarenfabrik, Zeitz |
| ftc | Frost & Jahnel, Breslau, Czechoslovakia |
| ftf | Unknown |
| fue | Skodawerke, Machine Shop, Dubnica Plant, Czechoslovakia |
| fuu | Strube GmbH, subsidiary of Polte, Magdeburg |
| fva | Draht- u. Metallwarenfabrik GmbH, Salzwedel |
| fwh | Norddreutsche Maschinenfabrik GmbH, Main Office, Berlin |

| | |
|---|---|
| fwr | Optische Ansalt Saalfeld GmbH, Saalfeld |
| fwz | Eisen- u. Emaillierwerke Wilhelmshütte (iron and enamel works), Sprottau-Wilhelmshütte |
| fxa | Eisenacher Karosseriewerke Assman GmbH, Eisenach (chassis plant) |
| fxo | C.G. Haenel, Waffen- u. Fahrradfabrik, Suhl |
| fxp | Hans Kollmorgen, Optische Anstalt, Berlin |
| fyd | Skodawerke, Adamsthal Plant |
| fze | Waffenfabrik Höller, Solingen |
| fzs | Waffenfabrik Heinrich Krieghoff, Suhl |
| ga | Hirsch, Kupfer- u. Messingwerk AG, Finow |
| gal | Unknown |
| gaq | Otto Stephan, Leder- u. Lederwarenfabrik, Mühlhausen |
| gau | Sudhaus & Söhne, Iserlohn |
| gb | Vereinigte N. Werke, Schwerte |
| gbc | Unknown |
| gbd | Unknown |
| gbv | Witte & Co, Velbert |
| gcd | Unknown |
| gcw | Göhring-Hebenstreit, Radebeul near Dresden |
| gcx | Karl Brettschneider, Mähr.-Schönberg |
| gey | Unknown |
| geu | Kuhbier & Co, Präzisionspreßstücke (precision stampings), Wipperfürth |
| gfg | Karl Hepting & Co, Leder- u. Gürtelfabrik, Stuttgart |
| ggb | I.G. Königshütte, OS |
| ggk | Unknown |
| ghf | Fritz Kiess & Co. GmbH, Waffenfabrik, Suhl |
| ghp | Ruf & Co, Optische Werke Kassel, Hessen-Nassau |
| ghx | Unknown |
| gil | Auto-Union, Spandau Plant |
| gjd | Unknown |
| gjh | Rudolf Conte, Nachf. Theodor Seibold, Fabrik für Lederwaren, Offenbach on the Main |
| gjk | Unknown |
| gk | Mansfeld AG, Hettstede, Südharz |
| gmo | Rahm & Kampmann, Lederwarenfabrik, Kaiserslautern Plant |
| gn | Aug. Wellner, Aue, Saxony |
| gon | Unknown |
| gpe | Unknown |
| gpt | Unknown |
| gqm | Unknown |
| grk | Unknown |
| grz | Gebr. Kruger, Lederwarenfabrik, Breslauy, Czechoslovakia |
| gsb | Rheinmetall-Borsig, Branch Office Liege, operated by Loewen (formerly S.A. des Ateliers de la Dyle) |
| gsc | S.A.Belge des Mecanique et de L'Armement, Monceau-sur-Sambre, Belgium |
| gtb | J.J. Eisfeld GmbH, Pulver- u. Pyrotechnische Fabriken, Güntersberge Plant |
| gug | Ungarische Optische Werke AG, Budapest, Hungary |

guj   Werner D. Kühn, Optische Industrie, Berlin-Steglitz
gum   Bergisch-Märkische Eisenwerke, Velbert, Rheinland
gut   Walter Schurmann & Co., Lederwarenfabrik, Bielefeld
guy   Werkzeugmaschinenfabrik Oelikon, Bührle & Co., Zurich, Switzerland
gvj   Ruhrstahl AG, Gelsenkirchen
gvm   Unknown
gxx   Unknown
gxy   Klinge, Lederwarenfabrik, Dresden-Lobtau
gyf   DEW, Bochum Plant
gyo   Hans Dinkelmaeyer, Lederwarenfabrik, Nürnberg
gyu   Unknown
gyx   Unknown
gyy   Unknown
gyz   Unknown
gzf   Westfälische Eisen- u. Blechwarenwerke, Siegen
ha    Treuenbritzen Metallwarenfabrik GmbH, Sebaldushof Plant
ham   Dynamit AG (formerly A. Nobel & Co.) Hamm plant
has   Pulverfabrik Hasloch, Hasloch on the Main
hbg   Alfred Schwarz AG, Metallwerk Frödenbrug on the Ruhr, Eisenach Plant
hbu   Heinrich List, Elektrotechnik u. Mechanik, Teltow & Steglitz
hck   Georg A. Lerch GmbH, Lederwaren u. Stanzwerk (leather goods and stamping),
      Mettman, Rheinland
hdk   Unknown
hdt   Märkischer Metallbau, Oranienburg
hdv   Optische Werke Osterrode GmbH, Osterrode, Harz
hen   Unknown
hew   Ing. F. Janecek, Waffenwerke, Prague
hft   Becker & Co. GmbH, Militär- u. Feuerwehrausrüstungen (military and firefighting
      equipment), Berlin
hgs   W. Gustav Burmeister, Pyrotechnische Fabrik u. Signalmittelwerk (firework and
      pyrotechnics), Hamburg
hgu   Unknown
hhc   Union Gesellschaft f. Metallindustrie, Sils van de Loo & Co., Frödenberg Plant
hhg   Rheinmetall-Borsig AG, Tegel Plant
hhj   Unknown
hhr   Unknown
hhu   Metallwarenfabrik Schmalkalden
hhv   Steyr-Daimler-Puch AG, Nibelungen Plant, St. Valentin, Austria
hhw   Metallwerke Silberhütte GmbH, Andreasberg, Harz
hhx   Unknown
hhy   Unknown
hhz   Röchlingwerke, Völklingen
hjg   Kimmach & Brunn, Fabrik für Heeresausrüstung, Kaiserslautern
hjh   Karl Ackva, Lederfabrik, Bad Breuznach
hkm   Karl Braun AG, Optische Industrié, Nürnberg
hla   Metallwarenfabrik Treuenbritzen GmbH, Sebaldushof Plant

| | |
|---|---|
| hlb | Metallwarenfabrik Treuenbrietzen GmbH, Selterhof Plant |
| hlc | Zieh- u. Stanzwerk (wire drawing and stamping), Schleusingen |
| hld | Metallwarenfabrik Treuenbrietzen GmbH, Belsig Plant |
| hle | Metallwarenfabrik Treuenbrietzen GmbH, Röderhof Plant |
| hlu | Unknown |
| hlv | Maury & Co., Lederwarenfabrik, Offenbach on the Main |
| hly | Unknown |
| hnx | Walter KG, Kiel, Kiel Plant and Tannenberg Plant |
| hre | Unknown |
| hrk | Unknown |
| hrl | Unknown |
| hrn | Preßwerk Metgethen, East Prussia |
| hta | Unknown |
| htg | Polte Armaturen- u. Maschinenfabriken AG, Duderstadt Plant, Westphalia |
| htl | Unknown |
| htq | Junghanswerke, Schwenningen Plant |
| hwd | Westfälische-Anhaltische Sprengstoff AG, Herrenwald Plant |
| i | Astra-Werke, Chemnitz |
| j | Unknown |
| ja | Schmöle, Menden |
| jan | Deutsche Versuchsanstalt für Luftfahrt, Berlin-Adlerhof |
| jba | A.Wunderlich Nachf., Fabrik für Heeresausrüstung (factory for military equipment), Berlin-Neukölln |
| jfp | Dr. Karl Leiss, Optische Mechanische Instrumente, Berlin-Steglitz |
| jfs | Junkers, Magdeburg Division |
| jhg | Gustav Genschow & Co., AG, Lederwarenfabriken, Alstadt-Hachenburg |
| jhv | Metallwaren, Waffen- und Maschinenfabrik AG, Budapest, Hungary |
| jkg | Königl. Ungar, Staatliche Eisen-, Stahl- u. Maschinenfabrik, Budapest |
| jkh | Karl Busse, Ausrüstungsgegenstände (equipment), Mainz |
| jlj | Heereszeugamt Ingolstadt |
| jln | Deutsche Lederwerkstätten GmbH, Pirmasens |
| jme | Armeemarinehaus Berlin, Berlin-Charlottenburg |
| jmh | Unknown |
| jnj | Hensoldt Werke für Optik u. Mechanik, Herborn, Dillkreis |
| jnk | Conti, Hannover |
| jnw | Eisenwerk Steele, Essen-Steele |
| joa | Dresdner Koffer- u. Taschenfabrik, Karl Heinichen, Dresden |
| jrr | Junghans, Renchen Plant, Baden |
| jrs | Junghans, Branch Office, Vienna |
| jry | Hermann Herold, Olberhain |
| jsd | Gustav Reinhard, Lederwarenfabrik, Berlin |
| jse | Metallwerke Zöblitz AG, Zöblitz |
| jtb | S.A.Tavaro, Ghent, Belgium |
| jtt | Unknown |
| jua | Danuvia Waffen- u. Munitionsfabriken AG, Budapest, Hungary |
| jut | Vereinigte Wiener Metallwerke, Vienna |

| | |
|---|---|
| jvb | Unknown |
| jvd | Unknown |
| jve | Optische Werke Ernst Ludwig, Weixdorf, Anhalt, Saxony |
| jvf | Wilhelm Brand, Treibriemenfabrik (Driving Belt Factory), Heidelberg |
| jwa | Moritz Stecher, Lederwrk, Freiburg |
| jwh | Manufacture d'Armes Chatellerault, Chatellerault, France |
| k | Fima Luch & Wagner, Suhl |
| ka | Gerhardi & Co., Lüdenscheid, Westphalia |
| kam | Hasag, Eisen- u. Metallwerke GmbH, Skarzysko Kamienna |
| kaw | Unknown |
| kbg | Erwin Backhaus, Remscheid |
| kce | Schneider & Co., Le Creuot, France |
| kdj | Unknown |
| keb | Manufacture d'Armes Nationale de Levallois, Paris |
| kfa | Staatliches Arsenal, Sarajevo, Yugoslavia |
| kfb | Unknown |
| kfg | Staatliches Arsenal, Sarejevo, Yugoslavia |
| kfk | Dansk Industrie Syndicat, Copenhagen, Denmark |
| kjj | Askania Werke AG, Berlin-Friedenau |
| kjl | Unknown |
| kkd | Wilhelm Stern, Lederwarenfabrik, Posen |
| kkn | Unknown |
| klb | J.F. Eisfeld GmbH, Kieselbach Plant |
| kle | Steyr-Daimler-Puch AG, Warsaw Plant, Poland |
| klg | Przemot, Präzisions Metallverarbeitung, Litzmannstadt |
| kls | Steyr-Daimler-Puch AG, Warsaw Plant, Poland |
| koz | Unknown |
| kgd | Junghans, Montagestelle, Exbrücke, Elsaβ |
| krd | Lignose Sprengstoffwerke GmbH, Kriewald |
| krg | Emil Busch AG, Optische Werke, Budapest |
| krj | Messerschmidt, Augsburg |
| krl | Dynamit AG (formerly A. Nobel & Co.), Krümmel Plant, Koblenz |
| krq | Emil Busch AG, Optische Werke, Rathenow, Brandenburg |
| kru | Lignose Sprengstoffwerke GmbH, Kruppsmühle Plant |
| kry | Lignose Sprengstoffwerke GmbH, Kruppsmühle Plant |
| ksb | Manufacture Nationale d'Armes de Levallois, Levallois, Paris |
| ksm | Junghans, Braunau Plant, Sudeten, Germany |
| ktz | Deutsche Sprengchemie, Klietz Plant |
| kum | J.F. Eisfeld, Pulver- u. Pyrotechnische Fabrik GmbH |
| kun | Lignose Sprengstoffwerk, Kunigunde Plant |
| kur | Steyr-Daimler-Puch AG, Warsaw Plant, Poland |
| kus | Unknown |
| kvu | Lignose Sprengstoffwerk GmbH, Kruppsmühle Plant |
| kwe | Gamma Feinmechanik u. Optik, Budapest |
| kwn | S.A. Fiat, Turin, Italy |

| | |
|---|---|
| kye | Intreprinderile Metalurgie, Pumitra Voina Societate, Anonima Romana, Fabrica de Armament, Brasov, Romania |
| kyn | Astra, Fabrica Romana de Vagone, Motoaene Armament si Munitione, Brasov, Romania |
| kyo | Intreprinderile Metalurgie, Pumitra Voina Aocietate, Anonima Romana, Fabrica de Armament, Brasov, Romania |
| kyp | Rumänisch-Deutsche Industrie u. Handels AG, Budapest |
| kza | Mauser-Werke, Karlsruhe |
| kzn | Kienzle, Dammerkirch Plant |
| kzu | Unknown |
| la | Dürener Metallwerke, Düren |
| lac | Zuchthaus (penitentiary) Coswig, Anhalt |
| lae | Heinrich Zeiss, Gastinger |
| lax | Lennewerk Altena |
| ldb | Deutsche Pyrotechnische Fabriken GmbH, Berlin Plant, Malchow |
| ldc | Deutsche Pyrotechnische Fabriken GmbH, Cleebronn Plant |
| ldn | Deutsche Pyrotechnische Fabriken GmbH, Neumarkt Plant, Oberpfalz |
| ldo | Unknown |
| lge | Kugelfabrik Schulte & Co, Tente, Rheinland |
| lgs | Unknown |
| ljp | Unknown |
| lke | Unknown |
| lkm | Munitionsfabriken (formerly Sellier & Bellot), Veitsberg Plant, Prague |
| lmg | Karl Zeiss, Jena |
| lpk | Unknown |
| ltm | Metallwarenfabrik Litzmannstadt |
| lwg | Optische Werke Osterrode GmbH, Freiheit near Osterrode |
| lww | Huet & Cie, Paris |
| lwx | O.P.L. Optique et Precision de Levallois, Levallois, Paris |
| lwy | Societe Optique et Mechanique de Haute Precision, Paris |
| lyf | Metallurgia Werke AG, Radomsko, Poland |
| lza | Mauser-Werke AG, Karlsruhe Plant |
| ma | Metallwerke Lange AG, Aue, Saxony |
| mdr | Vereinigte Leichtmetallwerke, Bonn |
| mhk | Metallwerke Schwarzwald AG, Villingen |
| mhv | Finow Kupfer- u. Messingwerke AG, Finow |
| mjr | Union Gesellschaft f. Metallindustrie, Sils van de Loo & Co, Thorn Plant |
| mkf | Trierer Walzwerk, Wuppertal-Langerfeld |
| ml | Unknown |
| mnf | VDM Heddernheim, Frankfurt on the Main |
| mng | VDM Heddernheim, Frankfurt on the Main |
| moc | Johan Springer's Erben, Gewehrfabrikanten, Vienna |
| mog | Deutsche Sprengchemie, Moschweig Plant |
| moo | Klöckner-Werke AG, Düsseldorf Plant |
| moz | Eisenwerk Gesellschaft Maximilianhütte, Maxhütte-Haidhof |
| mpp | Metallwerk K. Leibfried, Böblingen, Sindelfingen Plant |
| mpr | S.A. Hispano Suiza, Geneva, Switzerland |

| | |
|---|---|
| mpu | Unknown |
| mpv | Schmolz u. Bickenbach, Neuss Plant, Düsseldorf |
| mpy | Klöckner-Werke AG, Georgsmarienhütte, Osnabrück |
| mrb | Skodawerke, Prague Plant, Smichow |
| mrd | Hüttenwerke Siegerland, Wissen |
| mrf | Fr. Krupp, Berthawerk AG, Breslau |
| mws | Munitionswerke Schönebeck |
| myx | Rheinmetall-Borsig AG, Sömmerda Plant |
| na | Westfälische Kupfer- u. Messingwerke AG, Lüdenscheid, Westphalia |
| nas | Uhrenfabrik Junghans, Schramberg, Black Forest |
| nb | Waffenfabrik Kongsberg, Norway |
| nbe | Hasag, Eisen- u. Metallwerke GmbH, Tachenstocha Plant |
| nbh | Walther Steiner, Eisenkonstruktionen (iron construction), Suhl |
| nbr | Metallwarenfabrik Hubert Prünte, Neheim-Hüsten |
| ncr | Krupp-Germaniawerft, Kiel-Gaarden |
| ndn | Balkan Country under German Occupation |
| ndr | Krupp Essen |
| nea | Walther-Steiner, Eisenkonstruktionen, Suhl |
| nec | Waffenwerke Brünn AG, V Gurein Plant, Prague |
| ned | Krupp, Essen |
| nfw | Unknown |
| nfx | Rheinisch-Westfälische Munitionsfabriken GmbH, Plants in Warsaw and Prague |
| ngk | Dr. Grasse |
| njr | Rheinmetall-Borsig AG, Sömmerda Plant |
| nmn | Königs- u. Bismarckhütte AG, Walzwerk Bismarckhütte-OS (rolling mill) |
| nn | Unknown |
| nrh | Unknown |
| ntf | Unknown |
| nwk | Heinrich List, Rheinau, Elsaß |
| nxc | Unknown |
| nxr | Anschütz & Co., Kiel-Neumühlen |
| nyv | Rheinmetall-Borsig AG, Unterlass Plant |
| nyw | Gustloff-Werke, Otto Eberhard, Meinigen Plant |
| oa | Eduard Hück, Metallwalzwerk, Lüdenscheid |
| oao | Anschütz, Kiel-Neumühlen |
| obn | Hagenuk, Reichenbach Plant |
| ocw | Heinrich List, Berlin-Steglitz |
| odg | Deutsche Sprengchemie, Oderberg Plant |
| oes | Karl Kiehl, Peterswaldau |
| ols | Union Gesellschaft f. Metallindustrie, Sils van de Loo & Co., Auschwitz Plant |
| ona | Unknown |
| oss | Unknown |
| oxo | Teuto-Metallwerke GmbH, Osnabrück |
| oyd | Unknown |
| oyj | Atelier de Construction de Tarbes, France |
| p | Ruhrstahl, Brackwede |

| | |
|---|---|
| p | Polte Armaturen- u. Maschinenfabrik AG, Magdeburg, Saxony |
| pad | T. Bergmann & Co., Bernau Plant, Berlin |
| pcd | T. Bergmann & Co., Bernau Plant, Berlin |
| pjj | Haerens Ammunitionsarsenalet, Copenhagen, Denmark |
| pla | Unknown |
| pmf | Unknown |
| pmt | Unknown |
| pmu | Unknown |
| pvf | Optische Werke O. Reichert, Vienna |
| qa | William Prym, Stolberg, Rheinland |
| qlv | Unknown |
| qnv | Unknown |
| qrb | Pyrotechnische Fabrik, Bologna, Italy |
| qve | Karl Walther, Zella-Mehlis, Thuringia |
| r | Westfälische-Anhaltische Sprengstoff AG, Reinsdorf Plant |
| ra | Deutsche Messingwerke, C. Eveking AG, Berlin-Niederschönweide |
| rde | Unknown |
| rdf | Unknown |
| rfo | Unknown |
| rhs | Unknown |
| rin | Karl Zeiss, Jena |
| rrk | Unknown |
| rtl | Unknown |
| s | Dynamit AG (formerly A. Nobel & Co), Lumbrays plant |
| she | Unknown |
| skd | Selve-Kornbiegel-Dornheim AG, Suhl plant |
| suk | Unknown |
| sup | Unknown |
| svw | Mauser-Werke, Oberndorf on the Neckar |
| swp | Waffenwerke Brünn, AG, Brünn, Czechoslovakia |
| t | Dynamit AG, Troisdorf plant, |
| ta | Durener Metallwerke AG, Berlin-Borsigwalde |
| tjk | Unknown |
| tka | Unknown |
| tko | Unknown |
| tpk | Unknown |
| tpn | Unknown |
| tvw | Unknown |
| ua | Osnabruker Kupter-u. Drahtwerke AG, Osnabrück |
| unt | Unknown |
| uxa | Unknown |
| va | Kabel-u. Metallwerke Neumeyer AG, Nürnberg |
| vs | Unknown |
| vso | Unknown |
| vys | Unknown |
| vzg | Vereinigte Zünder-u. Kabelwerke AG, Meissen |

| | |
|---|---|
| w | Gesselschaft zur Verwertung Chem. Erzeugnisse, Wolfratshausen plant |
| wa | Hasag, Hugo Schneider AG, Lampenfabrik, Leipzig |
| wc | Hasag, Hugo Schneider AG, Meuselwitz plant, Thuringia |
| wd | Hasag, Hugo Schneider AG, Taucha plant |
| we | Hasag, Hugo Schneider AG, Langewiesen plant |
| wf | Hasag, Hugo Schneider AG, Kielce plant, Poland |
| wg | Hasag, Hugo Schneider AG, Altenburg plant |
| wh | Hasag, Hugo Schneider AG, Eisenach plant |
| wj | Hasag, Hugo Schneider AG, Oberweissbach plant |
| wk | Hasag, Hugo Schneider AG, Schlieben plant |
| wn | Hasag, Hugo Schneider AG, Dernabach plant, Thurignia |
| wtf | Unknown |
| x | Unknown |
| xa | Busch & Jäger, Lüdenscheider Metallwerke, Lüdenscheid |
| y | Jagdtpatronen, Zündhütchen-u. Metallwarenfabrik AG, Nagyteteny plant, Budapest |
| ya | Sächsische Metallwarenfabrik, August Wellner & Sohne, Aue, Saxony |
| zb | Kupferwerk Ilsenburg AG, Ilsenburg, Harz |

# Number Codes

| | |
|---|---|
| P25 | Unknown |
| 27 | B. Geipel GmbH, Waffenfabrik Erma, Erfurt |
| P28 | Waffen- u. Munitionsfabrik, Karlsruhe Plant |
| P34 | Unknown |
| 42 | Mauser-Werke, Oberndorf on the Neckar |
| R42 | Mauser-Werke, Oberndorf on the Neckar |
| S42 | Mauser-Werke, Oberndorf on the Neckar |
| S42G | Mauser-Werke, Oberndorf on the Neckar |
| S67 | H. Uttendorfer, Munitionsfabrik, Nürnberg |
| P69 | Selier & Bellot, Schönebeck on the Elbe |
| P94 | Kabel- & Metallwarenfabrik Nuemeyer AG, Nürnberg |
| B120 | Dynamit AG, Empelde Plant |
| 122 | Hugo Schmeisser |
| P131 | DWM-Werk, Borsigwalde |
| P132 | Unknown |
| P151 | Rheinisch-Westfälische Spiengstoffwerke, Nürnberg-Stadeln |
| P153 | Unknown |
| P154 | Polte, Lüneburg |
| P162 | Unknown |
| P163 | Unknown |
| P181 | Schneider AG, Altenburg |
| P186 | Unknown |
| P198 | Metallwarenfabrik Treuenbritzen, Belsig, Mark |
| P207 | Metallwarenfabrik Odertal GmbH, Odertal |
| P224 | Unknown |
| 237 | Mauser-Werke, Oberndorf on the Neckar |
| P249 | Finower Industrie GmbH, Finow |
| P265 | Unknown |
| P287 | Unknown |
| P315 | Marisches Walzwerk GmbH, Stramberg |
| P316 | Westfälische Metallindustrie, Lippstadt |
| P327 | Unknown |
| P334 | Mansfeld AG, Rothenburg, Saale |
| P340 | Metallwarenfabrik Silberhütte, St. Andreasberg |
| P345 | Unknown |
| P346 | H. Huck, Metallwarenfabrik, Nürnberg |
| P369 | Unknown |
| P370 | Unknown |
| P379 | Scharfenberg & Teubert, Breitungen |
| P382 | Unknown |

| | |
|---|---|
| P397 | Unknown |
| P398 | Unknown |
| P400 | Unknown |
| P405 | Dynamit AG, Durlach |
| P413 | Unknown |
| P414 | Unknown |
| P416 | Unknown |
| P417 | Unknown |
| P442 | Unknown |
| P457 | Unknown |
| 480 | Carl Walther, Zella-Mehlis |
| P490 | Unknown |
| P491 | Unknown |
| P635 | Munitionsfabrik Wöllerdorf, Vienna |
| 660 | Steyr-Daimler-Puch AG, Steyr, Austria |
| 925 | Mauser-Werke, Oberndorf on the Neckar |
| 945 | Waffenfabrik Brünn AG, Brno, Czechoslovakia |

# Index

## A